Lonely Planet Publications
Melbourne | Oakland | London

W9-BRX-886

Sandra Bao

# Buenos Aires

## The Top Five

### 1 Soccer
*Revere the idols of Argentina's most passionate sport (p136)*

### 2 Beef
*Devour meaty treats at an outdoor parilla (p91)*

### 3 Tango
*Witness amazing physical feats – and it's just a dance! (p129)*

### 4 Palermo Viejo
*Dine al fresco in the trendiest 'hood in town (p72)*

### 5 Recoleta Cemetery
*Admire the elaborate tombs of BA's rich and famous dead (p67)*

# Contents

**Published by Lonely Planet Publications Pty Ltd**
ABN 36 005 607 983

**Australia** Head Office, Locked Bag 1, Footscray,
Victoria 3011, ☎ 03 8379 8000, fax 03 8379 8111,
talk2us@lonelyplanet.com.au

**USA** 150 Linden St, Oakland, CA 94607,
☎ 510 893 8555, toll free 800 275 8555,
fax 510 893 8572, info@lonelyplanet.com

**UK** 72–82 Rosebery Ave, Clerkenwell, London,
EC1R 4RW, ☎ 020 7841 9000, fax 020 7841 9001,
go@lonelyplanet.co.uk

# The Authors

## SANDRA BAO

Sandra's relationship with Buenos Aires started when she was born there. After she turned nine her family left Argentina for the more lucrative shores of New York and California, and she spent much of her youth backpacking. Somewhere along the line Sandra picked up a psychology degree but after graduation realized she simply didn't like people's neuroses as much as traveling. 'Mi Buenos Aires Querido' has drawn her back many times over the years, and she is particularly fond of the gargantuan steaks, sugary *alfajores*, spontaneous street tango and her porteño godparents. Sandra would like to dedicate this book to Norberto Mallarini, her godfather, who passed away while this book was being edited. Norberto was a truly wonderful human being and always armed with a witty story, anecdote or joke. He will be sorely missed by his family and friends.

## CONTRIBUTING AUTHORS

### ASHLEY BALDWIN
Since graduating from University College London, Ashley Baldwin has divided her time between the UK and Buenos Aires, working as a journalist. She has written for various publications, including the *Buenos Aires Herald* and the UK's *Sunday Times*, on topics ranging from fashion to travel and culture. Ashley wrote the 'Fashion' boxed text in the City Life chapter and the 'Disabled Travelers' box in the Directory chapter.

### DERECK FOSTER
Born in Buenos Aires, Dereck Foster has written about food and wine for the *Buenos Aires Herald* for more than 30 years. He has written three books – *Food & Drink in Argentina, El Gaucho Gourmet* and *The Argentines: How They Live and Work* – and lectures frequently in both Spanish and English. Dereck wrote the 'Food' boxed text

in the City Life chapter, the 'Where's the Beef?' and 'Chef Thierry Pszonda' boxed texts in the Eating chapter, and the 'Argentine Wine' boxed text in the Drinking chapter.

### JOSH HINDEN
Living in Buenos Aires since 2003, Josh Hinden has DJ'd throughout Argentina while promoting his own BAbreaks events and handling international DJ bookings for breakbeat artists. Josh's first record was recently released – a track appropriately titled 'Buenos Aires' – under the name Majool. Josh wrote the Electronica in Buenos Aires boxed text in the Arts chapter.

### THOMAS KOHNSTAMM
A New York–based writer, Thomas Kohnstamm frequently covers South American politics, history and culture. He studied history and politics in Buenos Aires and taught in the Pampas, then watched Argentina's economic decline as an MA student in Latin American Studies at Stanford University. Thomas wrote the History chapter.

## PHOTOGRAPHER
### KRZYSZTOF DYDYNSKI
Born and raised in Warsaw, Krzysztof discovered a passion for Latin America, which took him to live in Colombia for nearly five years. In search of a new incarnation he made Australia his new home, but has regularly returned to South America ever since, writing and photographing for Lonely Planet. Buenos Aires is one of his great loves, and he has been back time and again, revisiting his old secret corners and looking for new inspirations.

# Introducing Buenos Aires

**Buenos Aires is absolutely buzzing with a new-found energy. The sudden crash of Argentina's peso in 2001 turned one of the most expensive cities in the world into one of the cheapest, and from a traveler's perspective this place feels like Prague –** *before* **it took off. Buenos Aires is getting hotter by the second and the secret's just coming out, so cash in your chips while you can: there's no better time to come visit this amazing metropolis.**

Buenos Aires (or BA) means something different to everyone you ask. It means watching the amazingly orchestrated kicks of a tango dancer's feet at a smoky *milonga* (tango dance hall). It means screaming and jumping up and down at a classic Boca/River match along with thousands of other impassioned *fútbol* fans. It means wolfing down tender, juicy steaks the size of your head for US$5, and ordering another bottle of that mesmerizing wine for US$10. It means wandering through the city's downtown under the grand facades of elaborate European buildings, while strolling past the locals' Anglo-Saxon faces – you'd think you were in the heart of London or Paris, not South America! It means stopping in at an old-time café and imagining what life was like 100 years ago, then popping back out into the mad rush of Av Florida and realizing you're very much in the 21st century. BA is a twist of modern infusion into old-world languor, thrown in and mixed wildly with Argentina's own effusive personality.

It's Saturday evening and dinner's at 10pm. Pick one of dozens of restaurants in Palermo Viejo and build up your energy for the long night to come. Check into a bar after dessert, then head out to the clubs at 2am – but no earlier! You'll be up all night dancing till the early morning light

## Lowdown

**Population** three million metropolitan; 12 million including suburbs

**Time zone** GMT minus three hours

**Three-star room** US$35

**Coffee** US$0.75

**Bus ticket** US$0.30

**Cheap soccer ticket** US$3.50

**Tango lesson** US$3

**Choripán (sausage sandwich)** US$0.50

**Essential accessory** cell phone, the snazzier the better

**No-no** your grungy backpacker's clothes. Go shopping!

## Essential Buenos Aires

- Cruising **Palermo Viejo** (p72) – cool retro stores, cutting-edge fashions and BA's best eateries
- Sunday brunch at **Olsen** (p109) – massively popular for a culture that doesn't really eat before noon
- **Museo Nacional de Bellas Artes** (p68) World-class art, including Impressionist masters, makes a fine stop
- **Feria de Mataderos** (p151) A wonderfully 'patriotic' way to spend a Sunday afternoon
- Boat ride in **Tigre** (p170) – the city is great, but sometimes you just need to get away and float down a peaceful river channel

and having the time of your life. And while BA's nightlife is world-class, your days will be memorable as well. Wake up Sunday and head to San Telmo, with its captivating Sunday antiques fair. Stroll around, then score a table at a sidewalk café and lazily watch the goings-on while sipping your *café cortado* (coffee with milk). Afterwards head uptown to Recoleta and its own large crafts market, and duck into the fantastic Recoleta cemetery for an afternoon of communing with the dead. You won't find these experiences anywhere else in the world, and they'll leave you quivering with a sense of wonder.

Culturally, Buenos Aires is exploding. Art exhibitions, theatrical productions, music concerts and fashion shows are being powered by an unending flow of creative energy and money that's recently infused the city, much of it a result of the fact that it's hard for natives to spend money *outside* the country now. New ideas are blossoming along the lines of 'what can we do here in Argentina *now*?'. After years of economic stagnation things are changing; there's hope in the air and fire in people's hearts – and a desire to improve the situation means many good things are yet to come.

And do consider these locals, or porteños – the hot-headed, opinionated and emotional folks that fill Buenos Aires with personality. Porteños have a reputation for being some of the most beautiful people on earth, and they've earned it. Coming mostly from Spanish or Italian rootstock has given them a generally dark European complexion; combine this with a keen eye to appearance, fine clothing and the highest rate of plastic surgery in the world and you'll come out with some pleasant-looking folks. And while you might encounter the occasional hard personality once in a while, most porteños are friendly and curious about the travelers visiting their fine city. Despite the gloomy undercurrent of a tragic economy, they'll keep on looking ahead and hoping for the best for their *querido* (beloved) Buenos Aires.

This elegant yet rough-edged city welcomes seasoned travelers looking for something different yet strangely familiar; it looks forward to meeting those offbeat adventurers keen to experience the unpredictable passions of a faraway destination slowly being discovered by more and more lucky souls.

# SANDRA'S TOP DAY

I start my Sunday morning with the *Buenos Aires Herald*, a *té negro* (black tea) and a couple of *medialunas* (croissants) at the local corner café. Head to San Telmo first, catch a free tango show at the antiques fair, then spend a while browsing through the stalls while watching the buskers. Walk over to the Reserva Ecológica Costanera Sur and rent a bike, then cruise the gravel paths while keeping a lookout for the ever-elusive nutria (aquatic rodent). Return to the center via Plaza de Mayo, taking in the impressive Casa Rosada while imagining Evita addressing her adoring crowds from a balcony. Veer west to the venerable Café Tortoni, where I meet my childhood buddy Claudina for lunch and keen porteño gossip. After kissing her goodbye, stroll up Av Florida, window-shopping all the way, until I reach the stunning Galerías Pacífico shopping mall. Pop inside for an emotional peep at the gorgeous ceiling murals (and take a bathroom break – they're downstairs). I keep heading north – perhaps quickly stopping by the gorgeous Museo de Arte Hispanoamericano – then straight up ritzy Av Alvear and into Recoleta, where I wander the crafts stalls before ducking into the cemetery for some quiet reflection. Backtrack to the Alvear Palace Hotel, where I have a late tea with my friends Bob and Flor. Perhaps I'll take in a movie at the modern cinemas in nearby Recoleta Village mall, then be ready for dinner with my crazy roommate Andrew at Bar Uriarte in Palermo Viejo.

# City Life

# City Life

## BUENOS AIRES TODAY

Maybe it's the beautiful, model-like women sauntering down hip Av Florida, or the handsome dark men power-suiting their way under the classic European buildings in the financial district. More likely you'll get it from the ubiquitous young couples stealing kisses on Plaza San Martín's grassy lawns, or strolling together on San Telmo's cobbled streets. And in the background there's the sultry tango halls and, deep in summer, the thick humidity that glistens on that cute guy giving you the long stare (whether you're gay or straight, male or female), that ever-so Latin American way of subtle flirting. Everyone knows everyone else is checking them out, and they also know they look good. You're in Buenos Aires now, and sensuality drips down every corner.

Sure, this is a bit of a stereotype, but these things have to come from somewhere. Porteños (BA locals) have mostly Italian and Spanish blood coursing through their hot veins, with strong emotions sustaining their personality, energies and hopes. And whether they're talking about *fútbol,* shopping or the current state of the economy (major citywide obsessions), you'll hear about it in spades and with accompanying hands madly gesturing in the air. Passions run wild and you won't find a porteño soul without an opinion on nearly everything.

On the surface, BA seems off-kilter with its image of both decline and prosperity. You'll hear no end of the economic crisis of late 2001 and how poor people have become, and witness cracking sidewalks and crumbling buildings even in the bustling heart of the city – yet in certain pockets a definite richness and rebirth have taken hold and not let go. The hundreds of millions of dollars sunk into Puerto Madero are most obviously spotlighted, and upscale restaurants in Palermo Viejo or even San Telmo now fill to capacity every weekend. Shopping streets are full of people making out with the goods, yet everyone complains about not being able to make ends meet. It's the rich-getting-richer-and-poor-getting-poorer-with-a-vanishing-middle-class phenomenon that's so prevalent in this

*Dog walkers (p66), Puerto Madero*

country, and unless you look beneath the surface you'll only be getting a facade of the truth. There's also a living-on-the-edge insecure mentality that's about needing to appear confident at all costs; being able to adapt to the current *what now?* tragic event without ruffling a feather. It's about feeling two meters tall one day when your country wins the gold in basketball at the Olympics but then crashing back down to a meter and a half when the IMF refuses Argentina another loan. The porteño psyche is as convoluted as it is open with feeling and pride, and comprehending the complete picture is not easy. With all they've had to deal with these past decades, what's the surprise?

Porteños make up the heart and soul of Buenos Aires, this city that they love so dearly and couldn't live without. And as a traveler you'll soon understand why it's such a great place. Sure, the architecture can be gorgeous and remind you of some far-off European city, but BA is also full of places to go and stuff to do, and it seems everyone's going everywhere and doing it. Whether it's dressing up for the theater, dancing tango at a smoky *milonga,* drinking at a trendy bar, partying with friends at the hottest rave or all of the above, these are social people who like to go out and stay out *late.* You'll soon learn not to call anyone on Sunday before noon – everyone's sleeping off the excesses of the night before.

Folks here may be down, but they're hardly out. Those lucky enough to have a bit of cash have taken to spending it here in Argentina rather than going off to Miami or anywhere else that's unaffordable for those with pesos. This internal windfall, along with renewed exports, an awakening manufacturing industry *and* a massive influx of foreign tourists, is starting to stimulate Argentina's economy – whether porteños are willing to admit it or not. And while not *everyone* is getting rich, there is still quite a lot of lemonade being made these days in Buenos Aires.

This city is rough, refined and being reborn all at once. The steaks are really that good, the night life is really that rockin', the economy is really that bad, the politicians are really that corrupt and life really does go on – even when everyone thinks they can't handle another pay cut or government robbery scandal. They'll grab a friend, head to an atmospheric café, perhaps do a little shopping, take in the latest theater production, go for a night out at the latest *electrónica* club and try to forget it all, bearing up as best they can for anyone who might be watching. Porteños are a resilient people and will survive this crisis as well as they've been surviving these up and down cycles for the last century – essentially all their lives. And they'll look their damn best doing it.

## Hot Conversation Topics

- Soccer and women – Who's winning and who's scoring?
- Shopping – Did you get that sweater at Laura Driz? It's *bárbaro!*
- Economy and politics – What's the government doing to screw us now?
- The *piqueteros* – Which vital street are they blocking today?
- Movies – Are you going to see Pablo Trapero's latest flick?
- Diego – Is he going to Cuba for rehab…*again*?
- The next rave – Where will it be and what will you be wearing?

# CITY CALENDAR

Most of Buenos Aires' traditional festivities are oriented towards its culture of horses, gauchos and tango, but recently many contemporary offerings focusing on the arts have cropped up. During much of the year you'll find these relatively new special events celebrating everything from fashion to dance to theater to wine to music of all kinds, though springtime sees the lion's share of these events.

The January and February summer months are unpleasantly hot and humid, and a time when the porteños who can afford it leave the city for the coasts. Consequently, some places, like museums and entertainment venues, close down in the capital for repairs or employee vacations. Still, there's always something happening somewhere, so check with the **Secretaría de Turismo de la Nación** ( ☎ 4312-2232) or free publications like *Ciudad Abierta* for current goings-on. See p191 for other special days that make good excuses for a celebration in this city.

# FEBRUARY

## CARNAVAL

Usually occurring in February, Buenos Aires' Carnaval is a newborn puppy compared to Rio's or Bahia's, but a long-running ban on tossing water balloons and confetti has recently been lifted in an attempt to liven things up a bit. Expect to be sprayed with canned foam while enjoying Brazilian-flavored *murga* groups (traditional Carnaval ensembles) dancing and drumming around Plaza de Mayo. If you want something with more oomph, head to Gualeguaychú in Entre Ríos province.

## CHINESE NEW YEAR

Yes, Buenos Aires has a Chinatown, but blink and you'll miss it. Check it out in Belgrano on Arribeños (p73); it's only about four blocks long and fairly tame as far as big-city Chinatowns go, but New Year's is a lively time and worth heading up here for a look-see (bring earplugs). Dates depend on the lunar calendar; upcoming dates are as follows: February 13, 2006; March 5, 2007; February 22, 2008.

# MARCH

## BUENOS AIRES TANGO

From late February to early March, this tango festival (www.tangodata.com.ar, in Spanish) is spread out all over the city – with dancers and musicians performing at various intimate venues – and offers a great way to see some of country's best *tanguistas* do their thing. Venues include the Academia Nacional del Tango (p130), the Centro Cultural San Martín (p189) and the Centro Cultural Recoleta (p189).

## EXPOSICIÓN DE CABALLOS CRIOLLOS

Horse lovers should not miss this specialty exposition that showcases the hardy Argentine-bred equines in their full glory. It takes place in late March at Palermo's Predio Ferial; for details contact the **Asociación Criadores de Caballos Criollos** (☎ 4961-2305; www.caballoscriollos.com, in Spanish; Larrea 670, 2nd fl).

# APRIL

## FERIA DEL LIBRO

Buenos Aires' annual book fair attracts more than a million book lovers for three weeks in April and May, featuring famous authors doing readings and signing books. Most exhibitors come from Latin America, but there are also displays from countries like England, China, France, Ukraine, Norway and Armenia. Look for it at the Predio Ferial in Palermo; for more info check www.el-libro.com.ar (in Spanish).

## FESTIVAL INTERNACIONAL DE CINE INDEPENDIENTE

This mid–late April's independent film festival highlights both national and international

## Argentine Jokes

Argentines are some of the proudest folks in South America, and are often made fun of for it. Want to make fun of an Argentine? It's easy. And don't feel too bad about it – they make fun of themselves all the time. Here are some classic jokes.

How does an Argentine commit suicide? He climbs to the top of his ego and jumps off.

How do you recognize an Argentine spy? From the sign on her back that says, 'I am the greatest spy in the world.'

How do you make a quick buck? Buy an Argentine for what he's worth and sell him for what he thinks he's worth.

An Argentine asks a Spaniard, 'Friend, do you know which country is closest to heaven?' 'Argentina, I suppose,' retorts the angry Spaniard. 'No, friend,' says the Argentine. 'It's Uruguay!' (Argentina's neighbor)

A man meets an Argentine on the street and asks him for a light. The Argentine starts patting his pants, chest and seat pockets. 'Sorry,' he says, 'I can't find my lighter – but man, do I have a great body!'

A psychologist calls her colleague at 2am. 'It's an emergency!' she says. 'At two in the morning? It better be good,' says the colleague. 'I have a unique client,' says the first. 'It's an inferiority complex!' 'An inferiority complex? But they're so common!' shouts the colleague. The psychologist responds, 'Yes, but…an Argentine?'

God is creating the different countries. He says to Gabriel, 'Here's a good one: lots of rich land, beautiful high mountains, great beaches, verdant forests and a wide variety of climates and animals. What do you think?' Gabriel replies, 'But that's so much to give to one place!' 'It's OK,' says God, 'I'll fill it with Argentines!'

## Top Five Quirky Events

- **Día de la Muerte de Carlos Gardel** (opposite) Understand why BA really loves this guy
- **Marcha del Orgullo Gay** (below) It may be regular fodder in San Francisco or Sydney, but here in BA it's downright different
- **La Rural** (opposite) Any time farm animals are spotlighted there's fun to be had
- **Campeonato Abierto Argentino de Pato** (p12) Tradition translated into strange sport, previously played with a dead duck
- **Día de la Tradición** (below) Gauchos riding horses, ladies dancing and great grilled food; what more is there to say?

independent films, with awards given out in separate categories; guest directors and actors are invited. Hundreds of films are screened in the city's cinemas, with a main venue being the Abasto shopping mall. Check www.bafilm fest.com for further details.

# MAY
## ARTE BA

This rapidly growing event in mid-May features exhibitions from hundreds of art galleries, dealers, institutions and organizations in Buenos Aires, with both national and international contemporary art on display. Conferences, presentations and discussions make the rounds; some 100,000 folks showed up in 2004. It takes place at Palermo's Predio Ferial; for more information check www.arteba.com.

# JUNE
## DÍA DE LA MUERTE DE CARLOS GARDEL

June 24 marks the anniversary of Gardel's death in a plane crash in Medellín, Colombia. Numerous tango events during the week conclude with a pilgrimage to the singer's tomb in the Cementerio de la Chacarita (see 'Glorious Death in Buenos Aires' on p68), where thousands of the singer's fans crowd the streets and leave him flowers. Gardel's birthday on December 11 sees similar festivities.

# JULY
## LA RURAL

Livestock lovers and seekers of the bizarre will go crazy at this event in July and August,

where prize cows, sheep, goats and horses are on display along with gaucho shows and agricultural machinery. It takes place at Palermo's Predio Ferial; for more information call ☎ 4324-4700 or sort through www.ruralarg .org.ar (in Spanish).

# AUGUST
## FASHION BA

Buenos Aires' fashion design scene has skyrocketed in the past three years, and these four days of clothing stalls and catwalk shows display the city's latest threads and their makers. It takes place at Palermo's Predio Ferial in late August or early September, with a fall collection showing in March. Plenty of models and other beautiful people of BA attend – bring out the voyeur in yourself.

# SEPTEMBER
## FERIA DE ANTICUARIOS

Those big on antiques shouldn't miss this extravaganza, which takes place from early to mid-September at the Palais de Glace (p69). The best antique pieces in Buenos Aires are exhibited and are up for sale, but don't expect any bargains; prices are in the thousands of US dollars. Check www.feriadeanticuarios.org (in Spanish) for details.

## VINOS Y BODEGAS

This festival is now in its fifth year of celebrating fine food and wine. Seventy of Argentina's best wineries pour some 700 sweet reds and whites to sommeliers, restaurateurs, journalists and the wine-loving public at large. About 15,000 show up for this event, which takes place in mid-September at Palermo's Predio Ferial. Most of the wines at this event are from Argentina's Mendoza region. Call ☎ 4382-2001 or email vinosybodegas@la-rural.com.ar for details.

## LA SEMANA DEL ARTE EN BUENOS AIRES

In mid-September five cultural centers, 25 museums and some 100 art galleries in Buenos Aires open their doors for a mega-event that highlights some of the best contemporary artists in the country. Media include everything from etchings to photographs to paintings, while conferences, concerts and cinema also come with the package. See www.lasemana delarte.com.ar (in Spanish).

# OCTOBER
## GUITARRAS DEL MUNDO
Guitars galore are played by dozens of Argentine and international musicians at the Centro Cultural San Martín, the Biblioteca Nacional and other venues around the city. Music genres run the gamut from tango to folk to jazz; look up www.festivaldeguitarras.com.ar (in Spanish) for specific schedules and dates.

# NOVEMBER
## MARATÓN DE BUENOS AIRES
In late October or early November, long-distance runners can go the whole 42km; last year's winners included Oscar Cortinez, with a time of 2:21:22, and Verónica Páez, with a time of 2:55:04. First-place prizes are US$1350, with a bonus of US$335 if you beat the Argentine record. There is a blind runners' category as well. Check www.maratondebuenosaires.com for entry details.

## MARCHA DEL ORGULLO GAY
Thousands of BA's gay, lesbian, transgender and more march from Plaza de Mayo to the Congreso on the first Saturday in November, and each year the colorful party gets bigger (the march was first held in 1992). Gay Pride Week follows later in November. For the full story, including exact dates and schedules, have a look at www.marchadelorgullo.org.ar (in Spanish) for exact dates and schedules.

## DÍA DE LA TRADICIÓN
This is the closest thing to traditional gaucho culture you'll probably witness, with folk music and dancing, traditional foods and feats of horsemanship taking the day. A great place to be during the mid-November festivities is San Antonio de Areco (p174), Argentina's ground zero for gauchos. If you can't get away, head to the Feria de Mataderos (p151), way west of center in the barrio of Mataderos.

# DECEMBER
## CAMPEONATO ABIERTO ARGENTINO DE POLO
Pretend to be aristocracy and come check out this championship, the culmination of the spring polo season – it's not your everyday thing. It takes place at Palermo's **Campo Argentino de Polo** (☎ 4774-4517). For exact dates and details, contact the **Asociación Argentina de Polo** (Map pp222-3; ☎ 5411-4777; www.aapolo.com; Hipólito Yrigoyen 636).

## CAMPEONATO ABIERTO ARGENTINO DE PATO
Steeped in gaucho culture, but still not quite the national sport of Argentina as it claims to be. A leather-covered ball (originally a dead duck) is the center of attention. Don't miss this spectacle; it's cool and quirky as hell. For details, contact the **Federación Argentina de Pato** (Map pp222-3; ☎ 4331-0222; www.fedpato.com.ar; Belgrano 530, 5th fl).

*Family feeding pigeons in the Plaza de Mayo (p51)*

**FESTIVAL BUENOS AIRES DANZA CONTEMPORÁNEA**

Every even-numbered year this two-week flurry showcases the contemporary dance scene. About 20 dance companies participate, including the Ballet Contemporáneo del Teatro San Martín. Performances, seminars and workshops take place in the city's cultural centers and theaters. For details check www .buenosairesdanza.com.ar (in Spanish).

# CULTURE

## IDENTITY

Ask any other Latin American what they think of their Argentine cousins and you're likely to get an unfavorable response. Argentines have a reputation for being spoiled, stuck-up, egotistical assholes who think they're better than anyone else, and who belong in Europe rather than at the tail end of a third-world continent like South America. It's no wonder nobody likes them and everyone makes fun of them – they're a great target. As the old saying goes, 'Argentines are Italians who speak Spanish, think that they're French and act as if they're English.' Cultural confusion, anybody?

Well, it wouldn't be a stereotype if it weren't a little bit true, but most Argentines simply don't fit this sniffy profile. Maybe it's because when folks think of Argentines, they think of porteños, that is, residents of Buenos Aires. While a huge number of people do live in the capital and its suburbs, a full two-thirds live in the rest of Argentina – where attitudes and egos are more modest. In fact, many folks outside the capital don't even *like* porteños. And, not all porteños are arrogant aristrocratic wanna-bes who go around disparaging everyone else and their mother. Quite a few, as you'll find out, can be very friendly, helpful and hospitable, and curious about where you come from and what you think. They're mostly great folks, really – just give them a chance.

Argentines are generally a gregarious bunch and, once you make contact, are likely to invite you out for drinks or a family *asado* (barbecue). They're also more physically demonstrative than you might be used to, always exchanging kisses on the cheek in greeting – even among men. If you are introduced by a friend to a person you've never met, you will be expected to kiss your new acquaintance on the cheek. In fact, if you hang out in Argentina long enough you may find yourself kissing complete strangers after a brief, serendipitous bonding experience. In formal situations, though, it is better if you just go with a handshake.

If you start chatting with the locals (many porteños can understand at least some English), be prepared to answer questions on topics like marriage and why you don't have any children yet, what life is like in your country of origin and what you make of Argentina's economy. Sports, especially soccer, is a good topic if you want to get porteños riled up; just ask your Argentine friend if he or she is for River or for Boca, and why. (River Plate and Boca Juniors are archenemies, which means their fans are too.)

It's not hard to see how Argentines got their reputation for being conceited. They live in a fabulous country, rich in scenery, culture and natural resources. Their capital, Buenos Aires, is a gorgeous city full of history and life. They have sultry tango, high

### The Color of Buenos Aires

Beginning in the mid-19th century, a trickle of European immigrants became a flood, as Italians, Basques, Welsh, English, Ukrainians and immigrants of other nationalities inundated Buenos Aires seeking a better life. Even Middle Eastern immigrants have carved out their niche – former president Carlos Menem is of Syrian ancestry.

Non-European immigrants have generally not been welcome in Argentina, and despite major upheavals in Asia over the past decade, only a relative handful of immigrants from that region have entered the country. Still, there is a conspicuous Japanese community in the suburb of Escobar and a small Chinatown in Belgrano, where many Chinese restaurants have opened in the past decade. Korean immigrants add some color to the neighborhoods of Once and Flores. Natives of other South American countries, such as Bolivia, Peru and Paraguay reside permanently in Buenos Aires, along with a small and barely visible population of urban Indians, most from the Andean Northwest and from Patagonia.

fashion and great soccer. Their women are beautiful and their steaks the best in the world. Why wouldn't they be proud of what they've created? Perhaps what some may see as a superior attitude is partly a veiled frustration for seeing their country – once one of the richest in the world – collapse over the decades into a corrupt entity now forced to ask for financial handouts. It's downright embarrassing, and if Argentines can maintain their proud spirit and polished self-importance in the face of this adversity, then let them – they deserve it.

## LIFESTYLE

In Buenos Aires, it's all about image. Despite the fact that a shocking 50% of the country's total population is now considered to be living in poverty (many in rural areas), Argentines are very conscious about their appearance and many will dress 'richer' than they really are, especially in big cities like Buenos Aires. This obsession with looks has given Argentina one of the highest rates of plastic surgery in the world, for both men and women, and helped to enforce their reputation as a nation of attractive people.

*Mate-drinker in action (see below)*

Many Argentines are as concerned about their mental health as their physical image and, if they can afford it, will go see a psychologist (that's 200 pesos a month for four sessions, or US$70, please!). Buenos Aires, in fact, has one of the highest concentrations of psychologists in the world; a section of Palermo is even nicknamed 'Villa Freud' because it harbors so many of these practitioners. Especially since devaluation and the neurosis it brought on, the porteño psyche desperately needs its shrinks – and there's little stigma attached to seeing these professionals.

### Mate & Its Ritual

Nothing captures the essence of *argentinidad* ('Argentinity') as well as the preparation and consumption of *mate*, perhaps the only cultural practice that truly transcends the barriers of ethnicity, class and occupation in Argentina. More than a simple drink like tea or coffee, *mate* is an elaborate ritual, shared among family, friends and coworkers. In many ways, sharing is the whole point.

Argentina is the world's largest producer and consumer of *yerba mate*, but it's also popular in parts of Chile, southern Brazil, Paraguay and especially Uruguay, which consumes twice as much of the stuff per capita as Argentina. In fact, many *mate*-drinking Uruguayans will not go anywhere without a thermos under the arm and a gourd clasped in the hand.

Preparing *mate* is a ritual in itself, and there is an informal etiquette for drinking it. The *cebador* (server) fills the gourd (which is also referred to as the *mate*) almost to the top with *yerba*, then pours very hot water into the vessel. It is then passed along to the group, beginning with the person on his or her left. Each participant drinks the gourd dry each time, before handing it back to the *cebador*, who fills it and gives it to the next person along in a clockwise direction. A *bombilla*, a silvery straw with built-in filter, makes drinking easier (and everyone shares it!).

An invitation to *mate* is a cultural treat, although it's definitely an acquired taste and you'll likely find it bitter and very hot at first. On the second or third round, both the heat and bitterness will diminish. And remember, don't hold the *mate* too long before passing it on — somebody else is waiting in line.

## Food  *Dereck Foster*

While home hospitality is not absent, porteños generally prefer meeting in a café or *confitería* (a more elaborate café), or sharing a meal in a restaurant.

Porteños love to eat out, and Buenos Aires has an immense number of sites that cater to all, from the street vendor peddling hot dogs *(panchos)* and peanut brittle *(garrapiñadas)* to elegant and costly restaurants, many of which rival standards in Europe or the US. From classic Spanish and Italian to exotic Asian to McDonalds, you'll find food to surprise you or soothe you with the familiar. A rough study revealed that the city offers more than 40 different types of restaurants.

The basic food of Buenos Aires is historically tied to the Spanish, who founded the city and kept it pretty much isolated from the world. However, French cuisine began to dominate elite cooking in the 1800s until the end of the century. The start of the 20th century saw an immense influx of Italians, and Italian influences quickly began to dominate the Spanish-French flavors and styles. Today the most dominant players in porteño cuisine are pasta and pizza – aside from beef, of course (see p91).

Lately, a type of cuisine has emerged which local food writers have taken to calling 'porteño cuisine'. This style is hard to categorize but possesses a definite character of its own. It is best described as food popular prior to about the 1930s, but which has largely fallen out of favor.

Prepared and served in simple style, eschewing shapes and colors in favor of hearty flavors and respectable portions, it comprises many ethnic and national touches, from German hambone with sauerkraut to Italian minestrone, and French coq au vin to the local *puchero* (a boiled meat and vegetable dish).

This style of cooking, found in many restaurants around town, may offer the most genuine flavor of Buenos Aires cuisine. See the Eating chapter (p88) for more.

### Top Five Food Books

- *How Argentina Cooks,* by Alberto Vazquez-Prego, has recipes in Spanish and English
- *Food and Drink in Argentina,* by Dereck Foster and Richard Tripp, is an English-language, full-color guide for visitors and expats
- *La Comida Criolla,* by Margarita Elichondo, is a brief history of food in Argentina, with recipes (in Spanish)
- *Gran Libro de la Cocina Argentina,* by JC Martelli, is a profusely illustrate, full-color recipe book in Spanish
- *El Gaucho Gourmet,* by Dereck Foster, offers a bilingual, brief history of eating in Argentina

To save on rent and also maintain family ties, many young Argentines live with their parents and even grandparents under one roof.

Families are generally pretty close, and Sundays (when many businesses close) are often reserved for the weekly *asado.* Guests are often invited, so if you get an offer don't miss it; not only are the grilled meats and side dishes usually delicious, but you'll get a good insight into Argentine relationships – and remember to give the *asador* (barbecue cook) a traditional hearty cheer!

Along with family, friends are also highly valued – being the social butterflies they are, Argentines love to go out to dinner or nightclubs in large groups. And it'll soon become apparent to you that this culture likes to stay out *late;* dinner is often at 9pm or later, and finishing dessert around midnight or 1am on a weekend night is not at all unusual.

Bars and discos often stay open till 7am or 8am – even though Argentines don't generally drink heavily, they *will* dance all night.

Something that surprises many travellers are those little cheek kisses that family and friends always give each other every time they meet, both coming and going. Even introduced strangers will get a kiss, and it doesn't matter if you're a man or woman. This is a bit counterintuitive, given the fact it's such a macho culture – women walking alone will often get verbal comments from passing males, and will always have doors held open for them or be allowed to board a bus first.

One last thing to keep an eye out for is the highly important culture of *mate* – you'll probably see Argentines sipping this bitter herb drink at home, work and play.

Consider yourself honored if you're invited to partake in a *mate*-drinking ritual (see opposite).

# Fashion  *Ashley Baldwin*

Notoriously well groomed, the average porteño has a sense of style probably best compared to that of the French. With very few exceptions, both Argentine men and women consider appearance to be of utmost importance, and like to appear well-put-together and fashionable, though without attracting unnecessary attention.

Local women of all ages reserve at least a couple of hours each week for the beauty salons, where a cut and blow-dry can cost as little as US$4; a manicure, US$2. Most main shopping streets have at least one salon. Appointments are rarely necessary for any salon, but Friday and Saturday evenings are usually busy.

As far as women's fashion is concerned, even casual wear is worn as provocatively as possible, with tight jeans and tops designed to accentuate the assets. Argentina is also an incredibly body-conscious nation. Being overweight is strongly frowned upon and women of all ages will spend hours in the gym, and even under the knife, to avoid piling on the pounds. As a result, Argentine women are comparatively smaller than other Latin Americans, and clothing sizes reflect this trend. Although larger sizes can be found in some stores, women who wear much over a US size 8 will find far less to choose from than thinner women.

For the latest Argentine fashion trends, a visit to the Las Canitas–based boutique Rapsodia (p150) is an absolute must. Here fashionistas can stock up on a creative blend of '70s-meets-modern bohemia, extremely popular among the city's bright young things. Rapsodia also makes some of the world's best-fitting and sexiest jeans with their unmistakable wing-logo gracing the back-pockets of the trendiest *argentinas*.

For something extra porteño, buy something from one of the local designers. Since 2001, hundreds of talented young designers have emerged from the woodwork in an attempt to scrape out a living during the economic crisis, and celebrities such as Britney Spears and Jessica Simpson have been spotted in their creations. Although some are now setting up small shops and boutiques of their own, many remain at stalls in the city's artisanal fairs. The feria at Plaza Serrano (p151) in Palermo Viejo remains the best showcase for hot new fashion talent, and you can pick up unusual clothes, jewelry and bags (most of which have been painstakingly handmade) for just a few pesos.

More conservative travelers, however, would be well advised to pay a visit to the city's numerous shopping malls for European designer labels such as Christian Dior, or the local and incredibly fresh designs of Laura Driz for a more sophisticated, typically Argentine look – all for a fraction of the price you'd pay in New York or Paris.

As far as men's fashion is concerned, the vast majority of males seem oblivious to any fashion movements that have taken place in recent years, rarely straying from their uniform of Ralph Lauren polo shirts, tight-fitting jeans and Maradona haircuts. In recent months, however, a surge in international youth culture and 'metrosexuality' has encouraged the younger generation to open their eyes to a veritable feast of hot, new trends.

Although the city's fashion scene still caters predominantly to women, several good men's stores can be found along Avenida Santa Fe and in the local shopping malls. Along Avenida Cordoba men can also pick up good-quality designer suits from either Christian Dior or Yves Saint Laurent (for example) for just a fraction of the price paid in Europe or the US. Twenty-something trendsetters should head straight to the boutiques around Plaza Serrano for the latest in local designer fashions.

Note that even in the city's hot and humid summer, people don't generally wear shorts unless they are exercising. Business attire is usually pretty formal, with plenty of dark suits, though it's not unusual to see men wearing ponytails and even earrings around the office.

*Boho designs at Gabriella Capucci (p148), Recoleta*

# RELIGION

Roman Catholicism remains the officially supported religion of Argentina, though the constitution was changed in 1994 to allow non-Catholics to serve as president. And while only a small percentage of Argentines attend mass regularly, you'll see many porteños exhibit signs of faith, such as crossing themselves when passing a church (whether they're walking, riding the bus or zipping along on motorbikes).

Argentina's national census doesn't track religious affiliation, so accurate figures are tough to come by, but it's estimated that Muslims and Jews each account for about 1% of the country's population. Buenos Aires' Jewish population numbers somewhere between 175,000 and 250,000, having undergone successive waves of emigration: under pro-Nazi Perón, during the Dirty War (when Jews were victimized in disproportionate numbers) and most recently with the economic troubles.

The country has its share of Jehovah's Witnesses, Mormons and Hare Krishnas. And, as in many other parts of Latin America, evangelical Protestantism is making inroads among traditionally Catholic Argentines – especially within the working class. In some parts of Buenos Aires, street preachers are a common sight, and many former cinemas and storefronts now serve as churches or centers for evangelical gatherings.

Spiritualism and veneration of the dead have remarkable importance in Argentina. Visitors to Recoleta and Chacarita cemeteries in Buenos Aires – vital places for comprehending Argentine religious culture – will see steady processions of pilgrims going to the resting places of icons like Juan and Eva Perón, psychic Madre María, and tango singer Carlos Gardel. Followers come to communicate and ask favors by laying their hands on the tombs and leaving arcane offerings (see p68).

# SPORTS

When it comes to sports, only one thing really matters to most porteños – soccer or *fútbol*, as it's known here. The sport is practically a national obsession for these folks. On popular game days, televisions in restaurants, bars, homes and hotels are tuned to the game channel, all eyes glued to the screen. Cheers erupt when goals are scored, and winning fans drive around the center's obelisk flying flags and honking horns. Going to a live match is an emotional spectacle every tourist should experience – human passion just doesn't get any higher than this. And Argentine soccer is certainly much more than the reputation of its most notorious figure, Diego Maradona, who now seems to spend most his time avoiding one drug scandal after another.

Surprisingly enough, other sports (and other sports stars) do exist in Buenos Aires. Basketball has gotten more popular, both as a spectator and participation sport, since Argentina won Olympic gold at the 2004 summer games. Horse racing attracts gamblers to Palermo's Hipódromo (racetrack), while polo and even *pato* (kind of rugby on horseback) have their own modest followings. Favorite activities include jogging, cycling, tennis and of course soccer; practically any grassy spot in the city can be quickly turned into a pitch, and on weekends you'll see soccer balls flying everywhere. For more detailed information on these sports and activities see p136.

# MEDIA
## Newspapers & Magazines

Argentina is South America's most literate country, supporting a wide spectrum of newspapers and magazines despite continuing economic crisis. For relevant newspaper websites see p189.

The capital is home to more than half a dozen nationwide dailies, several of them now online, and some with unambiguous political leanings. The centrist and somewhat tabloid-like *Clarín* has one of the largest circulations of any newspaper in the Spanish-speaking world, and publishes an excellent Sunday cultural section. *La Nación*, founded in 1870 by former president Bartolomé Mitre is another very popular and moderate paper revered by a more conservative readership. *La Prensa* is equally venerable, but much less influential.

The tabloid *Página 12* provides refreshing leftist perspectives, plenty of popular opinions and a good weekend pullout. *Ámbito Financiero,* the morning voice of the capital's financial community, also has an excellent entertainment and cultural section. *El Cronista* and *Buenos Aires Económico* are its rivals. All appear weekdays only.

The English-language daily *Buenos Aires Herald* covers Argentina and the world from an international perspective, emphasizing commerce and finance. It's a good resource for travelers and expatriates. *Argentinisches Tageblatt* is a German-language weekly that appears Saturdays. North American and European newspapers like the *New York Times, USA Today,* the *Guardian* and *Le Monde* are available at kiosks on Florida. Magazines like *Time, Newsweek* and the *Economist* are also fairly easy to obtain.

# Television

Privatization and the cable revolution have brought a wider variety of programming to the small screen, though prime time still seems overrun with reality shows, bimbo-led dance parties and *telenovelas* (soap operas). There are five regular channels:

**Canal 2** Also known as América TV (www.america2.com.ar, in Spanish); heavy on the sports, news and entertainment; check out Roberto Pettinato's personality show *Indomables*

**Canal 7** State-run channel and thus claims the lowest ratings; known for its general interest and cultural programming

**Canal 9** Smut at its best and expresses no shame in using sex to sell; imports trashy shows like *Top Model* and *Living with My Ex*

**Canal 11** (www.telefe.com.ar in Spanish) Also known as Telefé boasts Marcelo Tinelli's long-running *Videomatch,* along with popular transvestite Lisa Florencia de la Vega

**Canal 13** (www.canal13.com.ar in Spanish) Grupo Clarín's high-quality channel, offering the satire *Caiga quien caiga* along with the popular news show *Telenoche*

Eighty cable channels offer plenty of choice, including CNN, ESPN, BBC and a variety of European channels.

# Radio

Dozens of FM stations specialize in music, news and information for everyone. FM 92.7 has tango; FM 92.3 has Argentine folk; FM 97.4 has classical music; FM 95.9 has national/international rock and pop; FM 98.3 has Argentine rock and pop only; and FM 97.1 has BBC in English (from noon to 5pm). Radio 10 (AM 710) is something like the *National Enquirer* of radio stations, while La Colifata ('The Crazy One'; FM 100.1; www.la colifata.org, in Spanish) is a program that runs from 3pm to 7:30pm on Saturdays. It's operated by psychiatric patients from an asylum.

# LANGUAGE

Spanish, commonly referred to as *castellano,* is the official language of Argentina and is spoken throughout the country. The brand spoken in Buenos Aires has a strong Italian flavor to it, from the intonation to the amount and variety of gesticulation employed. (Among the many 'Argentine' jokes told elsewhere in the Spanish-speaking world, one of the kinder ones is 'If an Argentine falls overboard, how do you prevent him from drowning?... Just keep talking to

## Top Five Media Musts

- *La luna de Avellaneda* – Juan José Campanella directs this masterful movie about a social club and those who try to save it; you'll laugh and cry and laugh again
- *Clarín* – Buenos Aires' most popular catch-all newspaper; go for the *Buenos Aires Herald* if you don't read Spanish
- *Caiga quien caiga* – The TV show that poses the question 'What does it mean to be an Argentine?' Hidden cameras, satire and just what *do* foreigners think of Argentina?
- Mega 98.3 – Dial this radio station and get to know the best of 'Rock Nacional'. It's all they play.
- *Ficciones* – Argentine great Jorge Luis Borges, master of the fantastic, utterly messes with your mind in this collection of short stories. And you love it.

him.') Quite a few porteños study English, especially those in tourism and business, though you should never assume.

The practice is slipping these days, but some members of immigrant communities have retained their native language as a badge of identity. For example, literary giant Jorge Luis Borges, whose grandmother was English, learned to read in that language before Spanish. Though Argentina's largest historical immigrant group was Italian, the language is not as widely spoken (nor even understood) as some visitors from the Old Country expect it to be. Speakers of German are numerous enough to support their own weekly newspaper, *Argentinisches Tageblatt*.

For useful phrases in Argentine Spanish, see p198.

# ECONOMY & COSTS

Buenos Aires is Argentina's trade and financial center, and most of the country's imports and exports pass through the city's port. Industry – both processing of agricultural products and manufacturing – is mostly restricted to the surrounding suburbs. Tourism has been adding more dollars to the local economy since the 2002 peso devaluation, as foreign visitors come to the city in ever larger numbers, and porteños, scrambling to make ends meet, open hostels, rent out apartments, provide services and whatever else they can think of to bring in hard currency.

The Argentine economy is surging back from an excruciatingly difficult period. Following years of recession, rising unemployment and falling exports, it began to collapse in late 2001. When the government froze accounts to stop a run on banks (and the flow of billions of dollars out of the country), riots and enormous demonstrations broke out in Buenos Aires, leading to the resignation of President De la Rúa. A string of successors followed in rapid turn, during which time Argentina announced it would not honor US$80 billion worth of bonds it had issued, many of them to foreign investors and Argentine pension funds. In February 2002 the peso was unpegged from the dollar and allowed to float; by June it had fallen from 1:1 to 4:1. Later fluctuations eventually led it to settle around 3:1.

Just before the government floated the peso, it announced that citizens holding dollar accounts would see them converted into pesos at a rate of 1.4 pesos per dollar, which meant they eventually lost more than half their dollar value. Already high unemployment rates climbed even further, rising above 20%. GDP, which had shrunk by nearly 5% in 2001, plunged another 11% in 2002. To make things worse, inflation rose steeply in the same year. What remained of the middle class reeled and the country's nouveau poor suffered tremendously.

Things began to turn around in 2003 when the GDP, defying most projections, actually grew nearly 9% rather than shrinking, with the economy looking to do nearly as well in 2004. Exports rose by 14% in 2003 – fueled in part by the peso devaluation and increased sales of soy products to China – and Argentina's trade surplus for 2004 was projected to run in the billions of dollars. Unemployment, though still desperately high, dropped back into the teens (by most estimates).

In November of 2004, facing the prospect of the International Monetary Fund (IMF) refusing to extend any further loans to Argentina, economy minister Roberto Lavagna proposed a restructuring of Argentina's $100 billion in bond debt (the original $80 billion plus interest). Lavagna's plan would end up paying some bondholders as little as 30% of what they are owed. It remains to be seen how creditors and the IMF respond, and how the

## How Much?

Cup of coffee US$0.75

Glass of *chopp* (draft beer) US$2

An *empanada* (meat pie) US$0.50

Steak dinner US$5

Cheap hotel room US$15

Average taxi ride US$3

Liter of gasoline US$0.75

Movie ticket US$3

Cheapest opera ticket at the Teatro Colón US$2

Argentine economy continues to fare after waves of austerity measures and tweaking by the government. Some fear the country is becoming too dependent on one income source – soybeans – that is at the mercy of world markets and natural disasters. Other worries are the effects on industry and agriculture of the energy shortages that began to hit in 2004, and the possibility of the IMF effectively cutting off the country's line of credit.

At the time of writing, more than half of Argentina's population lives below the poverty line, many of them in dire circumstances. Crime rates have risen, as have the numbers of homeless, and the future is, as always, uncertain.

## COSTS

For the visitor with hard currency, Buenos Aires is a bargain. Good, cheap hotel rooms can be had for US$20 and great ones for US$50. Meals at fancy restaurants, including appetizer, main course and drinks, often come to less than US$15. Bus or Subte tickets are US$0.30 and most city taxi rides from US$3 to US$5. Entry to museums, theaters, nightclubs and special events is just a few bucks. You could spend US$60 per day and live like royalty. From your bank account's standpoint, this is an *excellent* time to be in Buenos Aires.

# GOVERNMENT & POLITICS

The politics of Buenos Aires is entangled with that of Argentina in general, because most national government institutions – not to mention the economic and financial sectors and a large percentage of the electorate – reside here.

The city of Buenos Aires (also known as the *Capital Federal*) was given the status of federal district (similar to that of Mexico City and Washington, DC) in 1880. Though at that point it began to function independently from the surrounding *province* of Buenos Aires (whose capital was moved to La Plata), the city's residents didn't have a lot of say in its administration; the president of the republic appointed the mayor.

Argentina's constitution was reformed in the 1990s, giving the Federal District the freedom to elect its mayor, and in 1996 Fernando de la Rúa of the Radical Party became Buenos Aires' first mayor elected by majority vote. De la Rúa went on to serve as Argentina's president until the economic crash of late 2001 drove him from office. The current mayor (at the time of writing) is Aníbal Ibarra, who won his second term in 2003 in a tight race against tycoon Mauricio Macri, owner of the Boca Juniors football club.

The reforms also gave Buenos Aires a 63-member Poder Legislativo (legislature), elected by proportional representation to four-year terms, with the possibility of reelection for an additional term. Half the seats are up for election every two years. After completing two consecutive terms, neither the mayor nor any legislator may run for the same office again until four years have elapsed.

At the national level, the Federal District chooses three senators to represent it in the national chamber of deputies, the same number that each of Argentina's 23 provinces is allowed.

# ENVIRONMENT

## THE LAND

At the continental edge of Argentina's fertile pampas heartland, Buenos Aires sits on an almost completely level plain of windborne loess and river-deposited sediments once covered by lush native grasses. The heart of the capital sprawls along the west bank of the Río de la Plata, which (despite every porteño's claim that it is the world's widest river) is more like a huge estuary. It ranges from 40km wide inland to over 200km at the mouth and discharges thick sediments along the coast and far out into the South Atlantic Ocean. Buenos Aires' highest elevation is only 25m, and much of the city is barely above sea level.

*Relaxing at the Reserva Ecológica Costanera Sur (p56)*

# GREEN BUENOS AIRES

You can jokingly refer to 'Buenos Aires' (literally, 'good airs') more accurately as 'Malos Aires' (bad airs). Indeed, air pollution can be astoundingly bad, and especially noticeable when you're walking down a street with a line of diesel buses roaring black clouds right into your path. The city's taxi fleet of over 40,000 vehicles doesn't help air quality either, nor do the hundreds of thousands of private vehicles clogging BA's streets every day. After all, this is not a city where emissions controls are taken seriously. Luckily enough for Buenos Aires, strong winds and rains frequently clear the air.

The center of Buenos Aires has hardly any rivers, which is fine enough since if they existed they'd probably be heavily polluted. La Boca's Riachuelo is the city's main waterway and so thick with pollutants that it looks viscous; cleanup has been promised but has ever so slowly progressed. Noise pollution is another big problem, with unmuffled vehicles making even more of a racket by liberal use of the horn.

From an ecological standpoint the biggest and brightest success story in the city is the Reserva Ecológica Costanera Sur (p56), strangely located east of downtown. This little marshy paradise was originally created from landfill as the base for a city expansion, but during economic and political stalls over the past two decades was taken over by indigenous marshy vegetation, migrating birds and aquatic rodents. Despite arson attempts, most likely by those with interests in developing the prime real estate, this green success story survives to give porteños an idea of what the Buenos Aires riverside used to be like hundreds of years ago.

Buenos Aires creates millions of tons of garbage annually, and feeble stabs at official

## Top Nature Breaks

- **Reserva Ecológica Costanera Sur** (p56) A bird-watcher's dream and just minutes from raging traffic
- **Plaza San Martín** (p63) It's not huge but the grassy hills are perfect for picnics and smooching lovers
- **Palermo's Parks** (p69) Acres and acres of grass and walking paths, with some thematic gardens adding interest
- **Parque Lezama** (p60) It's more of an urban green burp but it's San Telmo's best stab at open space
- **Tigre** (p170) Marshy tides and peaceful waterways go on and on, just an hour's drive north of center

## Buenos Aires' *Cartoneros*

You'll see them mostly at night, hunched over at the curb, picking through the garbage and pushing loaded-down carts. These are not the homeless, or the crazy, or the drug-addicted, or even the city's petty thieves. These are regular people, but some of Buenos Aires' poorest citizens – they're *cartoneros*, or cardboard collectors. Many of them used to have regular jobs as skilled laborers, but have been laid off since the crisis of 2001. With unemployment hovering at 25% and no social security to cover them, collecting recyclables is the only way they can now make a living.

It's estimated that up to 40,000 *cartoneros* rummage through Buenos Aires' trash heaps every night. Some are trucked into the city in special groups, but many commute into central Buenos Aires on *El Tren Blanco* (The White Train), a night train provided by the government and stripped of seats, heating and air-conditioning. It's a two-hour ride that leaves the shantytowns in the outskirts of BA after midnight, and returns again before dawn.

*Cartoneros* collect cardboard, paper, metal, plastic – anything they can sell by the kilo to recycling companies. They stake out their territory, perhaps about 15 city blocks, and are occasionally forced to pay police bribes. Many have been pricked by syringes or cut by broken glass. This isn't an easy job, but it's work – the average monthly take-home pay for a *cartonero* is from US$70 to US$100 per month. That's barely enough to pay for their food.

While some *cartoneros* work individually, others work for neighborhood cooperatives that pay them a regular wage and organize vaccinations. Some cooperatives even provide child care for parents who go off on their nightly rounds. In the poorest families, however, even the young children have to work all night long. And some *cartoneros* are in their 50s and 60s. Sorting through garbage has become a job that these desperate people are doing out of necessity.

It's not surprising that Argentina's crash has created this side-business in recyclables, and that those less fortunate had to use their creativity and ingenuity to organize for themselves what their government could not. The *cartoneros* are a reminder to us that there is another side to the glittering richness of Buenos Aires' center, and that there is another part of this city where the poor people live. It will be there for us to see on the streets, every night.

recycling had only partially reduced this quantity in the past. Most recycling is now done by *cartoneros*, garbage-pickers who've virtually created a new vocation brought about by necessity after Argentina's most recent economic crisis (see the boxed text on above).

# URBAN PLANNING & DEVELOPMENT

Buenos Aires' urban planning and development is not an issue that concerns most Argentine politicians, unless it's an election year. More often than not, promises made during campaigning go flying out the window following victory. It almost seems a fortunate thing that much of the city was constructed and developed in the late 1800s, when times were good and money flowed like wine; a time when Argentina was one of the richest countries in the world and heavy immigration brought skilled labor and organized ideas from old Europe. Even into the early 1900s, large parks and plazas were put into place and wide avenues constructed, along with the subway and train lines.

In the past few decades, however, economic times have gotten tougher, the population has risen and urban sprawl has seen the city's suburbs stretch for endless hundreds of kilometers; Buenos Aires has now become one of the most populated cities on the planet. Shantytowns or *villas miserias,* most of them located in barrios furthest from the center, hold the poorest of the city's inhabitants; some pop up even in the inner city, such as the sizeable shambles behind Retiro Bus Station. Puerto Madero (p55), however, is one relatively new development that has worked out well for Buenos Aires (even if it started out shakily) and now looks great to boot. Certain sections of the city that are often visited by tourists, such as San Telmo and Palermo Viejo, have also seen a gentrification process take place in the past few years. These days, however, money is too tight in Buenos Aires and, with regard to current construction, shortcuts too often take precedence over good planning and development.

# Arts

# Arts

The arts scene in Buenos Aires has traditionally been a lively one, and of late it's really been taking off. The current economic woes seem to be as big a stimulant to creativity as military rule in the 1970s and early 1980s was a drag on it. A refreshing, make-do approach is evident, particularly in cinema, theater and the visual arts. Gone is the booming '90s dominance of sniffy, pricey galleries, lavish cinematic productions, and overhyped plays. Filmmakers have been producing quality works on shoestring budgets, artists exhibit in funky storefront galleries or private homes and drama troupes perform in unconventional venues. Sprinkled over all this is are plentiful dashes of well-done graffiti – including some terrific stencils – much of it political, of course.

Although a lot of talented porteños (inhabitants of Buenos Aires) have fled the country in search of better employment prospects abroad, BA's arts scene has retained a cosmopolitan level of sophistication, and its practitioners remain plugged in to all the latest global developments. A new element in the mix is the ever-increasing number of foreigners coming to the city, attracted by a totally happening place that is now totally affordable for them thanks to favorable exchange rates.

## MUSIC & DANCE

Music and dance are well entwined in Buenos Aires, at least when it comes to the city's most famous export, the tango. The Buenos Aires opera performs in palatial Teatro Colón, one of the finest facilities of its kind in the world. The Colón, along with other venues like the Teatro Avenida, frequently hosts classical music, modern dance and ballet. And balletophiles will already know that BA is home to a superstar in the field.

### TANGO

The tango, both as music and dance, is without doubt the best-known manifestation of Argentine popular culture. Figures like the legendary Carlos Gardel, the late Julio Sosa and Astor Piazzola, and contemporaries like Susana Rinaldi, Eladia Blásquez, Adriana Varela and Osvaldo Pugliese have brought tango to the world. You'll find the music constantly on the radio (particularly on the 24-hour, all-tango station, FM Tango 92.7), it tops the bill at the capital's finest nightclubs and can often be heard in the streets.

For more on the history of tango, see the boxed text on p26-7; for classes, *milongas* (tango dance halls) and tango shows, see p130.

*Tango show at Bar Sur (p129), San Telmo*

### ROCK & POP

No one can deny that Argentine rock started in the late 1960s, with a trio of groups, Almendra (great melodies and lyrics), Manal (urban blues) and Los Gatos (pop), leading the pack. Evolution was slow however; the establishment originally resisted and the 1966 and 1976 military regimes didn't take a shine to the liberalism and freedom that rock represented. It didn't help that anarchy-loving, beat-music rocker Billy Bond induced destructive mayhem at a 1972 Luna Park concert, enforcing the theme of rock music as a social threat.

But underground groups and occasional concerts kept the genre alive, and after the Falklands War in 1982 (when English lyrics had not been allowed on the air) radio stations found *rock nacional* and helped the movement's momentum gain ground. Argentine rock was on its way up, and eventually produced national icons like Charly García (formerly a member of the pioneering group Sui Generis) and Fito Páez (socially conscious pop-hippie). Sensitive poet songwriter Alberto Luis Spinetta also had an early influence on the Argentine rock movement, later incorporating jazz into his LPs.

More recent popular Argentine groups playing *rock nacional* include the defunct Soda Stereo; hippyish Los Divididos (descendants of the famous group Sumo); Mendozan trio Los Enanitos Verdes; the wildly unconventional Babasónicos; cult-like Patricio Rey y sus Redonditos de Ricota; and Los Ratones Paranóicos, who in 1995 opened for the Rolling Stones' spectacularly successful five-night stand in Buenos Aires.

Los Fabulosos Cadillacs (winners of a Grammy in 1998 for best alternative Latin rock group) have popularized ska and reggae, along with groups like Los Auténticos Decadentes, Los Pericos and Los Cafres. Almafuerte, descended from the earlier Hermética, is Buenos Aires' leading (and surprisingly literate) heavy-metal band. The band Les Luthiers satirizes the middle class or military with irreverent songs played with unusual instruments, many of which the band built themselves. Another unusually colorful character is Sandro, a living Argentine clone of Elvis.

Singer Patricia Sosa owns a captivating voice and her closest counterpart in the English-speaking world would be Janis Joplin. The bands Dos Minutos and Expulsados emulate punk-rock legends the Ramones, who are popular in Argentina and have played in the capital several times.

Today some of Argentina's most cutting-edge bands include versatile Los Piojos (mixing rock, blues, ska, *murga* and *candombe*), wacky Bersuit Vergarabat (utilizing multigenre tunes with political, offensive and wave-making lyrics) and free-willed La Renga (blue-collar, no-nonsense and political). And don't miss the multicultural, alternative and eclectic Kevin Johansen: his *Sur o no sur* album is pure genius.

Keep an eye out as well for relatively new arrivals Gazpacho; their self-titled debut album reveals an amazingly polished young quartet performing in a range of rockin' pop styles.

# JAZZ & BLUES

Both these brands of music have substantial numbers of fans and performers among porteños, and you should have no trouble catching live shows at bars or cafés (see p124).

A fair number of Argentina's jazz greats have emigrated (Lalo Schifrin and Gato Barbieri among them). Among those who've stayed is guitarist Luis Salinas. Much of his music is mellow and melodic (along George Benson lines but a bit less poppy). Be sure to check out his jazz takes on such traditional Argentine forms as the *chacarera, chamamé* and – of course – tango.

Drummer Sebastián Peyceré has toured the country with Salinas, jammed at the Blue Note and played with the likes of Paquito D'Rivera, BB King and Stanley Jordan. He favors a funk-tinged fusion. BA's own version of the Sultans of Swing is the Caoba Jazz Band, who for years have been playing 1920s and '30s New Orleans–style jazz for the love of it (their trumpeter, Rolando Vismara, drives a taxi to get by).

The high degree of crossover between Buenos Aires' blues and rock scenes is illustrated by the path of guitar wizard Pappo. An elder statesman, Pappo was in the groundbreaking rock group Los Abuelos de la Nada and then became involved with the seminal blues/rock group Pappo's Blues, as well as Los Gatos and others. He recently reformed his '80s metal band, Riff. While living in London in the late '70s, Pappo gave up a chance to join the nascent Motörhead in order to tour with Peter Green, former Fleetwood Mac ace. Once he sets to wailing on his Gibson, you'll forget the fact that Pappo's voice and original lyrics aren't so hot. He plays hard-driving, full-tilt rockin' blues and is especially great when covering such American masters as Howlin' Wolf, BB King and Muddy Waters.

## The Tango

The air hangs heavy, smoky and dark. Streams of diffused light illuminate a large, open space. A lone woman, dressed in a slit skirt and high heels, sits with legs crossed at one of the small tables surrounding dance floor. Her eyes dart around the room, casually looking here and there, in search of the subtle signal. Her gaze sweeps over several tables and suddenly locks onto a stranger's eyes, and there it is: the *cabezazo*, a quick tilt of his head. She briefly considers the offer, then nods with a slight smile. His smile is broader, and he gets up to approach her table. As he nears she rises to meet him, and the new pair head out toward the dance floor, reaching it just as the sultry music begins to play.

The tango hasn't always been quite so mysterious, but it does have a long and somewhat complex history. Though the exact origins can't be pinpointed, the dance is thought to have started in Buenos Aires in the 1880s. Legions of European immigrants, mostly lower-class men, arrived in the great village of Buenos Aires to seek their fortune in the new country. They settled on the capital's *arrabales* (fringes), but missing their motherlands and the women they left behind, they sought out cafés and bordellos to ease the loneliness. Here, the men mingled and danced with waitresses and prostitutes. It was a strong blend of machismo, passion and longing, with an almost fighting edge to it.

Small musical ensembles were soon brought in to accompany early tangos, playing tunes influenced by Pampas *milonga* verse, Spanish and Italian melodies and African *candombe* drums. (The *bandoneón*, a type of small accordion, was brought into these sessions and has since become an inextricable part of the tango orchestra.) Here, the tango song was also born: it summarized the new urban experience for the immigrants and was permeated with nostalgia for a disappearing way of life. Themes ranged from profound feelings about changing neighborhoods to the figure of the mother, male friendship and betrayal by women. Sometimes, raunchy lyrics were added.

The perceived vulgarity of the dance was deeply frowned upon by the reigning porteño elites, but it did manage to influence some brash young members of the upper classes. These rebel jet setters took the new novelty to Paris and created a craze – a dance that became an acceptable outlet for human desires, expressed on the dance floors of elegant cabarets. The trend spread around Europe and even to the USA, and 1913 was considered by some 'the year of the tango.' When the evolved dance, now refined and famous, returned to Buenos Aires, it finally earned the respectability it deserved. The golden years of tango were just beginning.

### Gardel & the Tango

In June 1935, a Cuban woman committed suicide in Havana, and a woman in New York and another in Puerto Rico tried to poison themselves, all over the same man – whom none of them had ever met. The man was tango singer Carlos Gardel, El Zorzal Criollo, the songbird of Buenos Aires, and he had just died in a plane crash in Colombia.

Though born in France, Gardel was the epitome of the immigrant porteño. When he was three, his destitute single mother brought him to Buenos Aires. In his youth, he worked at a variety of menial jobs, but he also managed to entertain his neighbors with his rapturous singing. A performing career began after he befriended Uruguayan-born José Razzano, and the two of them sang together in a popular duo until Razzano lost his voice. From 1917 onward, Gardel performed solo.

Carlos Gardel played an enormous role in creating the tango *canción* (song). Almost single-handedly, he took the style out of Buenos Aires' tenements and brought it to Paris and New York. His crooning voice, suaveness and overall charisma made him an immediate success in Latin American countries. And the timing couldn't have been better, as

Guitarist/singer Miguel 'Botafogo' Vilanova is an alumnus of Pappo's Blues and an imposing figure in his own right. Memphis La Blusera have been around BA's blues scene a long time and still put on a good show; they've worked with North American legend Taj Mahal.

Two other bands among those worth checking out are La Mississippi and Las Blacanblus, a trio (formerly a quartet) of porteña singers and players who do humorous, nearly a cappella versions of blues standards.

# LATIN & ELECTRONICA

Buenos Aires' young clubbers have embraced the *música tropical* trend that's swept Latin America in recent years. Many a BA booty is shaken to the lively, Afro-Latin sounds of salsa, merengue and especially *cumbia*. Originating in Colombia, *cumbia* combines an infectious dance rhythm with lively melodies, often carried by brass or synthesized brass.

his star rose in tango's golden years of the 1920s and 1930s. Gardel became a recording star, but his later film career was tragically cut short by that fatal plane crash.

Every day a steady procession of pilgrims visits Carlos Gardel's sarcophagus in the Cementerio de la Chacarita in Buenos Aires, where a lit cigarette often smolders between the metal fingers of his life-size statue. The large, devoted community of his followers, known as *gardelianos*, cannot pass a day without listening to his songs or watching his films. Another measure of his ongoing influence is the common saying 'Gardel sings better every day.' Elvis should be so lucky.

## Tango at a Milonga Today

Tango is not an easy dance to describe, as it needs to be seen and experienced. Despite a long evolution from its origins, it's still a sensual and erotic dance. The upper bodies are held upright and close, with faces almost touching. The man's hand is pressed against the woman's back, guiding her, with their other hands held together and out. The lower body does most of the work. The woman swivels her hips, her legs alternating in short or wide sweeps and quick kicks, sometimes between the man's legs. The man guides, a complicated job since he must flow with the music, direct the woman, meld with her steps and avoid other dancers. He'll add his own fancy pivoting moves, and together the couple flows in communion with the music. Pauses and abrupt directional changes punctuate the dance. It's a serious business that takes a good amount of concentration, and while dancing the pair wear hard expressions. Smiling and chatting are reserved for between songs.

At a proper, established *milonga*, choosing an adequate partner involves many levels of hidden codes, rules and signals that dancers must follow. After all, no serious *milonguera* (female regular at a *milonga*; the male equivalent is *milonguero*) wants to be caught out dancing with someone stepping on her toes (and expensive tango heels). In fact, some men considering asking an unknown woman to dance will do so only after the second song, so as not to be stuck for the four tango songs that make a session. It's also considered polite to dance at least two songs with any partner, so if you are given a curt *gracias* after just one, consider that partner unavailable for the rest of the night.

Your position in the area surrounding the dance floor can be critical. At some of the older *milongas*, the more-established dancers have reserved tables. Ideally, you want to sit where you have easy access to the floor and to other dancers' line of sight. You may notice couples sitting farther back (they often dance just with each other), while singles sit right at the front. And if a man comes into the room with a woman at his side, she is considered 'his' for the night. For couples to dance with others, they either enter the room separately, or the man signals his intent by asking another woman to the floor. Then 'his' woman becomes open for asking.

The signal, or *cabezazo*, involves a quick tilt of the head, eye contact and uplifted eyebrows. This can happen from way across the room. The woman to whom the *cabezazo* is directed either nods 'Yes' and smiles or pretends not to have noticed (a rejection). If she says 'Yes', the man gets up and escorts her to floor. A hint: if you're at a *milonga* and don't want to dance with anyone, don't look around too much – you could be breaking some hearts.

So what is the appeal of the tango? Why is it that tango becomes so addictive, like an insidious drug? Experienced *milongueros* will tell you this: the adrenaline rush you get from an excellent performance is like a successful conquest. Some days it lifts you up to exhilarating heights and other days it can bring you crashing down. You fall for the passion and beauty of the tango's movements, trying to attain a physical perfection that can never be fully realized. The true *milonguero* simply attempts to make the journey as graceful and passionate as possible.

Dance music is big in BA, with DJs working the clubs well into the morning. A few major electronic names to look out for are Bad Boy Orange (big on drums and bass); Aldo Hayar (a true veteran); and local boy made international star, Hernán Cattaneo (you loved him at Burning Man, remember?). John Digweed has been known to DJ in BA on his way to laying down summer grooves in Punta del Este, the Uruguayan beach resort.

Not surprisingly, musicians have been sampling and remixing classic tango songs, adding dance beats, scratches and synth lines and committing other delightful heresies. Paris-based Gotan Project's album *La revancha del tango* throws into the mix samples from speeches by Che Guevara and Eva Perón and remixes of Gotan's mixes by the likes of Austrian beatmeister Peter Kruder.

The best of the genre's album output so far is *Bajofondo Tango Club*, by the group of the same name, though 'group' might be a bit of a misnomer. It's more of a collective effort spearheaded by Argentine producer Gustavo Santaolalla, whose other credits include producing albums by such artists as Café Tacuba and Los Divididos and scoring the films

## Electronica in Buenos Aires *Josh Hinden*

Buenos Aires might be known for its tango, but there is something else to keep you dancing until dawn. In recent years, the city has developed a wide variety of electronic music, thanks to loose laws and a late-night culture that generally looks to Europe for its trends.

Since 1990, the electronic music scene has evolved and grown to become a major force in the music world. Touting some of the world's best venues and biggest crowds, Buenos Aires is listed by many DJs as a favorite place to play. The websites mentioned in this section are generally in Spanish but are easy enough to navigate.

Some of those internationally acclaimed DJs include Argentina's own Hernán Cattaneo, who began his professional career in the early '90s playing commercial clubs of the time like El Cielo and Cinema. Several years later he secured a residency at **Clubland: Pachá** (p127; www.pacha-ba.com), where legend has it he was discovered and whisked off to international stardom by UK legend Paul Oakenfold. The success of Cattaneo and Clubland: Pachá marked the beginning of a new era, when electronica emerged into mainstream pop culture.

Nowadays, when the weather warms up in spring, enormous events with up to 50,000 people take place, such as **Creamfields** (www.creamfieldsba.com), the **South American Music Conference** (http://samc.net), **Southfest** (www.2netproducciones.com.ar) and **BUE** (www.festivalbue.com). In addition to these large commercial events, the club and underground scene is booming.

House music (referred to as 'punchi, punchi' because of the relentless kick drum) is no longer the only option. You'll find a variety of sounds, thanks to early diversification within Argentina's veteran underground DJ collective, DJ UNION, comprised of Carla Tintore, Dr Trincado and Diego Ro-k (www.djdiegoro-k.com). Notoriously wild underground parties like the Age of Communication and Ave Porco helped pave the way to a diverse underground tradition, which you can experience at **Cocoliche** (p126; www.cocolichesite.com).

Whether it's progressive house, breakbeat (www.babreaks.com), techno, IDM (http://zensible.com.ar), deep house, drum & bass (www.djorange.com, and http://buenosairesdnb.com) or even experimental *cumbia* (www.canalcumex.com), Buenos Aires has your electronica flavor.

Most porteños turn to websites such as www.buenosaliens.com to find out what's happening; www.whatsupbuenosaires.com caters more to tourists.

As the number of music venues grows, so does the number of aspiring DJs and music producers. The commercial success of electronica in Buenos Aires has now arguably surpassed the USA, where strict laws require bars to close early. And the increasing availability of technology to produce and play music, combined with the constant exposure to quality international artists, means BA electronica will likely become an even more serious player in the international music community in years to come.

Note: As this book went to press, the electronica scene was still in flux after the disastrous nightclub fire on December 31, 2004. Many clubs were forced to close down and go through rigorous inspections, and the long-term implications are yet to be seen.

*Amores perros* and *21 Grams*. Praised as more Argentine than Gotan Project (only one of whose core trio is Argentine) and more tango, the album's classic samples blend with subtle performances by current tango musicians (including a variety of *bandoneonistas* and some great vocals from Adriana Varela) within a hypnotic framework of lounge, house, trip-hop and other sounds assembled by the producers.

## FOLK MUSIC

The late Atahualpa Yupanqui was a giant of Argentine folk music, which takes much of its inspiration from the northwestern Andean region and countries to the north, especially Bolivia and Peru. Los Chalchaleros, a northern Argentine folk institution, have already celebrated their 50th anniversary.

Other contemporary performers include Mercedes Sosa of Tucumán (probably the best-known Argentine folk artist outside South America); Suna Rocha (also an actress) of Córdoba; Antonio Tarragó Ross; Víctor Heredia; León Gieco (modern enough to adopt and adapt a rap style at times); and the Conjunto Pro Música de Rosario.

Most of these folks live far from BA. Singer/songwriter/guitarist Horacio Guarany lives close by in Luján and gets into town more often. In 2004 his *Cantor De Cantores* was nominated for a Latin Grammy in the Best Folk Album category. For folk venues, see p124.

# BALLET & MODERN DANCE

How many cities can boast of packing stadiums with crowds for dance performances? We're not sure, but Buenos Aires is definitely one of them. The porteño love of things cultural takes some of the credit, but a larger part goes to BA's bad boy of ballet, Julio Bocca. And it's not just because he posed nude with his dance partner in *Playboy*. Born in 1967, Bocca started dancing at age four, and at 14 was soloing with the Teatro Colón's chamber ballet. In 1985, following stints with troupes in Caracas and Rio de Janeiro, he took the gold medal at Moscow's International Ballet Competition, and the next year was invited by Mikhail Baryshnikov to join the American Ballet Theatre as principal dancer.

In 1990 he formed his own troupe, Ballet Argentino, which has been wildly popular at home and very well received abroad, though their 2004 show featuring tango received mixed reviews in some circles. Catch him while you can: most dancers, even studs like Bocca, can't carry on into their 40s.

You can catch dance performances ranging from classical ballet to flamenco, Middle Eastern and all varieties of modern dance at venues such as the venerable Colón, Teatro Avenida and Teatro San Martín, which has its own ballet company.

# PAINTING

Argentina's latest economic crisis has been a mixed blessing for the visual artists of Buenos Aires. While the tough times have made it even harder to earn a living from art, they've also triggered a tidal wave of ideas and output, a wave that has largely swept aside the 'official arbiters' of public taste. At the same time artists have been banding together for mutual support, increasingly engaging one another and the public in dialogues (often of a political nature) that generate further ideas and projects.

The sense that 'we've all been through this together' has drawn public and artist closer, and helped break the tyranny of the toney gallery and conservative critics dictating what's acceptable. The alternative art scene in BA was going strong before the crash but has really taken off since, and you can find galleries, exhibits and art events in the most unlikely places these days. The influx of foreign visitors, eager to pick up quality works at bargain prices, has helped things along. The day may yet come when Buenos Aires' greatest innovators in painting no longer need to shop their works abroad (or die) to make it big.

As an example, porteño painter Guillermo Kuitca (b 1961), who lives and works in BA, did not exhibit in his home town from 1989 until 2003, when the city's new modern art museum put on a retrospective. Kuitca is internationally known for his imaginative techniques that include the use of digital technology to alter photographs, maps and other images and integrate them into larger-themed works.

One artist who gained fame at home and abroad in his lifetime is Antonio Berni (1905–81). Berni would sometimes visit shantytowns and collect materials to use in his works. Various versions of his theme *Juanito Laguna bañándose* (Juanito Laguna washing) – a protest against social and economic inequality – have been commanding prices in the hundreds of thousands of dollars at auction.

*Stencil graffiti, Microcentro (p51)*

Some works by dead artists you might want to check out are the restored ceiling murals of Antonio Berni, Lino Spilimbergo and others in the Galerías Pacífico shopping center in the Microcentro (p52). The late Benito Quinquela Martín, who put the working-class barrio of La Boca on the artistic map, painted brightly colored oils of life in the factories and on the waterfront. Xul Solar, a multitalented phenomenon who was a good friend of Jorge Luis Borges, painted busy, Klee-inspired dreamscapes. The former homes of both Quinquela (p63) and Solar (p69) are now museums displaying a lot of their work.

An interesting place to see works by living artists is the hotel Boquitas Pintadas (p161), which rotates the pieces in common areas and guest rooms every two months.

The economic and political chaos that began in late 2001 triggered a huge increase in graffiti in Buenos Aires. Though much of it consists of angry scrawls on targets of ire such as banks and government buildings, some of it is much more subtle and well crafted. Particularly appealing are the stenciled messages that show up on sidewalks, garbage cans, walls and elsewhere, many of them takeoffs on advertising slogans and logos. *Buenos Aires Trash,* a small book of photos by Pablo Fusco, captures many of the best stencils.

See p142 for art gallery listings.

# SCULPTURE

Given its European origins, official public art tends toward hero worship and the pompously monumental, expressed through equestrian statues of military figures like José de San Martín, Justo José de Urquiza and Julio Argentino Roca. Many have prominent positions in Buenos Aires' parks and plazas, especially in the neighborhood of Palermo. The median strips of Avenida 9 de Julio are another good – albeit busy – place to see some of the city's most prominent outdoor sculptures.

Much of León Ferrari's artwork deals with antireligious and anti-American political themes (he likes using cockroaches as symbols for the US). His most famous piece is *Western and Christian Civilization* (1964), which depicts Jesus Christ crucified on a fighter jet; his arms span the aircraft's wings as he holds a missile in each of his hands. The artist had to flee to Brazil during the military regime in 1976, but returned in 1991; despite his advanced age he still occasionally exhibits at the Centro Cultural Recoleta (p68) and other BA venues.

Another sculptor who has inspired political controversy is Alberto Heredia, whose pieces ridicule the solemnity of official public art. Heredia's powerful and controversial *El Caballero de la Máscara* depicts a 19th-century caudillo (strongman) as a headless horseman. During the military dictatorship of 1976–83, this sculpture could not be exhibited under its original title *El Montonero*, which authorities thought implied associations with guerrilla forces that had nothing to do with the artist's theme. Heredia also critiques general Argentine society and religion. Also overtly political is Juan Carlos Distéfano, who chose years of exile in Brazil while working on antigovernment themes. Distéfano used rich, textural surfaces of polyester, glass, fiber and resins to achieve colorful surfaces on his sometimes disturbing themes.

The late Rogelio Yrurtia's works deal sympathetically with the struggles and achievements of working people; see his masterpiece *Canto al Trabajo* on the Plazoleta Olazábal in San Telmo (p60). Many of Yrurtia's smaller pieces are displayed at his own museum in Belgrano (p74), along with other notable sculptors' artworks. For comic relief, the grotesque papier-mâché sculptures (made from trash and old books) of Yoël Novoa appeal to audiences of almost any age or political persuasion.

Strong women sculptors include Norma D'Ippolito, who has won over 20 artistic awards and works mostly with Carrara marble, creating contemporary designs that often incorporate the human figure. Her *Homage to Raoul Wallenberg* honors the Swedish diplomat who helped Jews in WWII; several copies are on display at different embassies in Buenos Aires. Lucia Pacenza is another prize-winning artist who also specializes in marble sculptures, and creates mostly outdoor urban pieces. She studied in Europe, Mexico and the US, and has art installations in countries as far away as Australia. Another renowned Argentine female sculptor is Claudia Aranovich, who converts diverse materials such as transparent resins, cast aluminum, glass and cement into organic shapes and natural portraits.

Around Buenos Aires, note the prominent and beautiful sculpture *Floralis Genérica* in Recoleta's Plaza Naciones Unidas (p66). This giant metal flower was created by architect Eduardo Catalano and actually closes up at night. Avid sculpture fans can also visit the **Museo de Esculturas Luis Perlotti** (Map p221; ☎ 4431-2825; Pujol 644) in the neighborhood of Caballito. It was closed at research time, but should have good things to offer when it's finally remodeled.

# ARCHITECTURE

Care for a colonial *cabildo*? Fancy some fine French folderol, or do you prefer a pink palace? Perhaps a plethora of houses painted in a pastiche of pastels? Or just a simple block of flats? Buenos Aires still holds examples of many of the architectural styles in vogue at one time or another throughout the life of the city. It has some amazing one-offs as

### Top Five Quirky Buildings
- Obelisco (p57)
- Confitería del Molino (p81)
- Palacio de las Aguas Corrientes (p58)
- Iglesia Ortodoxa Rusa (p60)
- Facultad de Ingeniería (p66)

well. You'll find old and new juxtaposed in sometimes jarring and often enchanting ways (occasionally in the same structure), though the new has been asserting itself more and more in recent years, and on a grander scale than ever before.

No trace remains of the modest one-storey adobe houses that sprang up along the mouth of the Riachuelo following the second founding of Buenos Aires in 1580. Many of them were occupied by traffickers of contraband, as the Spanish Crown forbade any direct export or import of goods from the settlement. The restrictions made the price of imported building materials prohibitively high, which kept things simple, architecturally speaking, since local materials left a lot to be desired.

The houses stayed simple and the streets remained unpaved as BA grew slowly until 1776, when the Bourbon Crown decreed the creation of the new Viceroyalty of the Río de la Plata, with Buenos Aires as capital. Now things started moving faster, and at the hub of the activity lay what is today known as the Plaza de Mayo. Back then it was the Plaza Mayor, or Main Plaza – the term applied to the main square in pretty much every colonial town.

*Facultad de Ingeniería (p60), Recoleta*

In the colonial scheme the street grid centered on the main plaza, which was surrounded by the town hall, cathedral and other important buildings. Arranged around the Plaza Mayor satellite-fashion were the various barrios, or neighborhoods, each with their own church, which usually shared its name with the barrio. Many towns in Latin America founded during the colonial period retain this layout at their centers.

Buenos Aires' **Cabildo** (town hall, though it no longer serves that function) is a fair example of colonial architecture, although its once plaza-spanning colonnades were severely clipped by the construction of Av de Mayo and the diagonals feeding into it. The last of the Cabildo's multiple remodels was a 1940s restoration to its original look, minus the colonnades. Most of the other survivors from the colonial era are churches. The Catedral Metropolitana, sharing Plaza de Mayo with the Cabildo, is not one of them. The present structure was begun in 1752 but not finished until 1852, by which time it had acquired its rather secular-looking (unless you're an ancient Greek) neoclassicist facade.

Many examples of postindependence architecture (that is, built after 1810) can be found in the barrio of San Telmo, one of the city's best walking areas. San Telmo also holds a wide variety of vernacular architecture, and is famous for its *casas chorizos* (sausage houses) – so called for their long, narrow shape (some have a 2m frontage on the street).

In the latter half of the 19th century, as Argentina's agricultural exports soared, a lot of money accumulated in Buenos Aires, both in private and government hands. All parties were interested in showing off their wealth by constructing elaborate mansions, public buildings and wide boulevards. This trend would continue intermittently into the 1940s, by which time the city would have a subway system with multiple lines.

Buildings in the first few decades of the boom were done mostly in Italianate style, but toward the end of the 19th century a French influence began to exert itself. Mansard roofs and other elements gave a Parisian look to parts of the city that remains to this day.

By the beginning of the 20th century, Art Nouveau was all the rage, and many delightful examples of the style remain. Some of them, like the former Confitería del Molino (p81) across from the Congreso, are not in such delightful condition, unfortunately.

Among the highlights of the building boom's first five decades is the presidential palace, known as the **Casa Rosada** (Pink House, officially Casa de Gobierno, p53), created in 1882 by joining a new wing to the existing post office. Others include the showpiece **Teatro Colón** (finished in 1907, p59) and the imposing **Palacio del Congreso** (completed in 1906, p58).

The 1920s saw the arrival of the skyscraper to BA, in the form of the 100m-high, 18-story Palacio Barolo. This fabled, rocket-styled building was the tallest in Argentina (and one of the tallest in South America) from its opening in 1923 until the completion of the 30-story Art Deco **Edificio Kavanagh** (p63) in 1936. The Kavanagh in turn, when finished, was the largest concrete building in the world, and remains an impressive piece of architecture.

Buenos Aires continued to grow upward and outward during Juan Perón's spell in power (1946–55). Though the economy flagged, anonymous apartment and office buildings rose in ever greater numbers. Bucking the trend were such oddball buildings as the Banco de Londres on Reconquista, designed in 1959 by Clorindo Testa, whose long architectural

## Abre La Boca

The brightly painted dwellings in the working-class barrio of La Boca are probably the most photographed architectural feature of Buenos Aires. Their history is nearly as colorful as their decoration. When Argentina's agricultural exports began to soar in the second half of the 19th century, the country attracted large waves of immigrants, many of whom hoped to farm the country's rich soil. Finding land to be unaffordable, the new arrivals, mostly from Italy and Spain, sought work in Buenos Aires. They poured into the south edge of town, settling in La Boca (named for its location at the mouth of the Riachuelo), and working as stevedores, building new port facilities, or in the slaughterhouses, meat-packing plants and other industries in the area.

Too poor to emulate the opulent doings of the established porteños, the *boquenses* (inhabitants of La Boca) crowded into simple houses with corrugated-metal exteriors. The story goes that they were too poor even to buy paint, and would thus hit the port to cadge what odd lots of leftover pigment they could from shipmasters and boat builders. The coat of many colors that resulted when the batches were applied was so pleasing to residents that it became a tradition, and the multichrome style brightens numerous La Boca dwellings to this day.

career in BA began in the late 1940s. The bank was finished by 1966, but Testa's Biblioteca Nacional (National Library, p191), which must've looked pretty groovy to him on the drawing board in 1962, was hideously dated by the time it opened (following many delays) in 1992. Its style is somewhere between late Offshore Oil Platform and early Death Star.

A heartening 'recycling' trend took off in Buenos Aires in the latter 20th century and continues today, helping to preserve the city's glorious old structures. Grand mansions have been remodeled (and sometimes augmented) to become luxury hotels, museums and cultural centers. Old markets have been restored to their original glory and then some, to live again as popular shopping malls, such as the Mercado de Abasto (p75) and Galerías Pacífico (p52).

At the same time, the first decade of the 21st century has seen an increasingly modern skyline develop in Buenos Aires. Soaring structures of glass and steel tower above earlier efforts. Many are innovative and quite striking, such as the Edificio Telefónica (originally named Edificio República) on Tucumán between Madero and Bouchard. It was designed by César Pelli, an Argentine native now living in the US, who also did Kuala Lumpur's Petronas Towers. The ultramodern building is super energy-efficient, and from some angles its shape evokes the hull of a ship. From others its concave and convex planes give the structure the look of a mirage or false front, something not all there.

One of the most ambitious architectural projects in BA today combines the repurposing of old structures and the construction of ultramodern ones. The ongoing renovation of Puerto Madero (p55) is turning dilapidated brick warehouses, silos and mills into smart shops, offices and restaurants, a luxury hotel and exclusive apartments.

# LITERATURE

All the greatest lights of Argentine literature called Buenos Aires home at one time or another, and all but one had been extinguished by the end of the 20th century. Many of their works are available in English.

The light that burned brightest was without doubt Jorge Luis Borges (1899–1986), one of the foremost writers of the 20th century. A prolific author and an insatiable reader, Borges possessed an intellect that seized on difficult questions and squeezed answers out of them. Though super-erudite in his writing, he was also such a jokester that it's a challenge to tell when he's being serious and when he's pulling your leg (though often it's a case of both at once). From early on one of his favorite forms was the scholarly analysis of nonexistent texts, and more than once he found himself in trouble for perpetrating literary hoaxes and forgeries. A few of these are contained in his *Universal History of Iniquity* (1935), a book that some point to as the origin of magic realism in Latin American literature.

Borges' dry, ironic wit is paired, in his later work, with a succinct, precise style that is a delight to read. His paradoxical *Ficciones* – part parable, part fantasy – blur the line between myth and truth, underscoring the concept that reality is only a matter of perception and the number of possible realities is infinite. Other themes that fascinated Borges were the nature of memory and dreams, and the relationship that exists between the reader, writer and the written piece. And, of course, labyrinths. *Collected Fictions* (1999) is a complete set of his stories, newly translated into English.

Though he received numerous honors in his lifetime – including the Cervantes Prize, the Legion of Honor and an OBE – Borges was never conferred the Nobel. He joked of this in typical fashion, 'Not granting me the Nobel Prize has become a Scandinavian tradition. Since I was born they have not been granting it to me.'

Julio Cortázar (1914–84) is, after Borges, probably the author best known to readers outside Argentina. He was born in Belgium of Argentine parents, moved to Buenos Aires at age four, and died in self-imposed exile in Paris at the age of 70. His stories frequently plunge their characters out of everyday life into surreally fantastic situations. One such story was adapted into the film *Blow-Up* by Italian director Michelangelo Antonioni. Cortázar's novel *Hopscotch* takes place simultaneously in Buenos Aires and Paris and requires the reader to first read the book straight through, then read it a second time, 'hopscotching' through the chapters in a prescribed but nonlinear pattern for a completely different take on the story.

The last surviving member of Borges' literary generation is Ernesto Sábato (b 1911), whose complex and uncompromising novels have been extremely influential on later Argentine literature. *The Tunnel* (1950) is Sábato's engrossing novella of a porteño painter so obsessed with his art that it distorts his relationship to everything and everyone else.

Adolfo Bioy Casares (1914–99) and Borges were close friends and sometime collaborators. Bioy's sci-fi novella *The Invention of Morel* (1940) not only gave Alain Resnais the plot for his classic New Wave film *Last Year at Marienbad*, it also introduced the idea of the holo-deck decades before *Star Trek* existed.

Manuel Puig's (1932–90) first love was cinema, and much of his writing consists solely of dialogue, used to marvelous effect. Being openly gay and critical of Perón did not help his job prospects in Argentina, and Puig spent many years outside the country. His novel *The Buenos Aires Affair* is a page-turner delving into the relationship between murderer and victim (and artist and critic), presented as a deconstructed crime thriller.

Federico Andahazi's first novel, *The Anatomist*, caused a stir when published in 1997. Its ticklish theme revolves around the 'discovery' of the clitoris by a 16th-century Venetian who is subsequently accused of heresy. Andahazi (b 1963) based his well-written book on historical fact, and manages to have some fun while still broaching serious subjects.

Anna Kazumi Stahl (b 1963) is an American who has been living in Buenos Aires since 1995. Her novel *Flores de un solo día* (2001), written in *rioplatense* (a variety of Spanish spoken in the Río de la Plata region), is the tale of an American girl who has lived in Buenos Aires from the age of eight with her Japanese mother, an enigmatic mute. It's received high praise from Argentine critics, and in 2003 was nominated for the prestigious Rómulo Gallegos Prize.

# FILM

Buenos Aires is at the center of the Argentine film industry, which is digging its way out of a period of terrible hardship. This began in the late 1990s when the government, facing a recession and mounting foreign debt, held back funds gained from entertainment taxes that by law should have subsidized film schools and the movie industry. With the economy melting down in late 2001 and the subsequent peso devaluation, things got even worse, as Argentine audiences dwindled and production costs shot up.

To add to the agony, all of this was taking place at a time when Argentine films were attracting increasing international attention, earning awards and screening at festivals in New York, Berlin, Rotterdam and elsewhere. For what it's worth, Juan José Campanella's *El hijo de la novia* (Son of the Bride) received an Oscar nomination for best foreign-language film in 2002.

The country continued to turn out new talent from its many film schools, including the Universidad del Cine de Buenos Aires. Some of these newcomers created enough buzz with their bare-bones productions to get future projects bankrolled by foreign sources. Others took lucrative employment abroad, while many others just got by as best they could.

## Top Five Buenos Aires Films

- *Nueve reinas* (2000), written and directed by Fabián Bielinsky, features David Mamet–like plot turns and great performances from Gastón Pauls and Ricardo Darín, as two con men chasing the big score
- Alejandro Agresti directed the semi-autobiographical *Valentin* (2002), a charming, poignant, almost-but-not-quite cloying tale of an eight-year-old boy being raised by his grandmother in 1960s Buenos Aires
- Adolfo Aristarain's *A Place in the World* (1992) is a rich coming-of-age story that untangles the relationships within a small community in central Argentina
- Héctor Olivera's *The Night of the Pencils* (1986) retells the notorious case of half a dozen La Plata high-school students who were abducted, tortured and killed by the military during the Dirty War (p44)
- Director Luis Puenzo's *The Official Story* (1985) deals with a delicate, controversial theme of the Dirty War – the adoption of the children of missing or murdered parents by those responsible for their disappearance or death. *Story* won an Oscar for best foreign-language film.

## New Faces, Old Places

Pablo Trapero is one of the foremost filmmakers in Argentine cinema today. Born in Ramos Mejía in 1971, he attended the Universidad del Cine de Buenos Aires, and in 1998 began shooting his first feature-length film, *Mundo grúa* (Crane World). It took more than a year to complete, with Trapero shooting largely on weekends and, at times, halting production entirely for lack of funds.

The film won awards at several international festivals, including Venice, Rotterdam and Buenos Aires. Shot in grainy black and white, it tells the story of Rulo, a middle-aged porteño keeping his head above water by working in construction. He is passed over for a crane-operator job because of his excess weight, and heads south for a position in Patagonia. In spite of the adversity he faces, Rulo maintains an almost heroic sanguinity.

Trapero's next feature film, *El bonaerense* – which like all his films was written, directed and produced by Trapero himself – hit the screen in 2002. It traces the downward moral slide of a naive locksmith from rural Buenos Aires province who joins the horrifically corrupt BA police department. Not meant as an exposé or a condemnation, the film shows the process through the protagonist's eyes, offering an explanation of how one can sink so far. *El bonaerense* played at Cannes in 2003, and in 2004 Trapero sat on the festival's short films jury.

Trapero's third feature, *Familia rodante* (Rolling Family), came out in 2004. It's an ensemble road movie that blends comedy with family drama as a large group pilots a decrepit motor home from Buenos Aires to tropical Misiones in northeast Argentina to attend a wedding. As with Trapero's other films, the cast consists mostly of non-actors, and includes Graciana Chironi, his real-life grandmother. Now in her 80s, she played the protagonist's mother in Trapero's first two features and an early short.

A ray of hope shone through in March 2004, when President Kirchner announced that the government would repay the three years of subsidies it had held back and would exempt moviemakers from paying duty on imported film stock.

The crisis that plunged an entire class of Argentina's citizens into poverty shows signs of easing. Its effects on the national psyche have been explored at great length by the country's filmmakers in a torrent of dramas and documentaries that rivals the amount of output on the Dirty War and its aftermath.

Other noteworthy films include Sandra Gugliotta's bust-out 2002 directorial debut *Un día de suerte* (A Lucky Day), which follows a young porteña fleeing dead-end, strife-torn Buenos Aires to Italy, reversing the route her grandfather took decades earlier. *Un oso rojo* (A Red Bear, 2002), directed by Israel Adrián Caetano, depicts a paroled murderer hoping to reconnect with a daughter who barely remembers him. Though marred by some ridiculous gunplay, the film depicts fascinating human interactions.

Another interesting Argentine-related film is *Evita* (1986), directed by Alan Parker. This flick outraged many Argentines, in part because Madonna played the title role. However, both she and Evita share similarities: both are/were smart, sexy women who rose from lower-class origins and became overglamorized by society.

# THEATER

Theater is *huge* in Buenos Aires. The city's venues number more than 100, and annual attendance is in the hundreds of thousands. While productions range from Spartan improvisational to musicals with lavish costuming and sets, the acting tends to be of a professional level across the board(s).

The city's vigorous theater community began in colonial times, a few years after BA became the viceregal capital in 1776, and continued in the 19th century with *sainete*, informal dramas focusing on immigrants and their dilemmas. Formally, theater really took off in the late 19th century through the artistic and financial efforts of the Podestá family and playwrights like Florencio Sánchez, Gregorio de Laferrere and Roberto Payró. These days, Argentina's most famous playwright is probably Juan Carlos Gené, a past director of the Teatro General San Martín.

Famous European writers like Federico García Lorca and Jean Cocteau have been involved in the Buenos Aires theater scene, and legendary Argentine performers include Luis Sandrini and Lola Membrives.

Unlike stage actors in some countries, those in Argentina seem to move seamlessly between stage, film and TV. Perhaps performers like Norma Leandro, Federico Luppi and Cecilia Roth feel less self-conscious about moving among the various media, since the Argentine public is smaller and work opportunities are fewer than in entertainment centers such as London, New York and Los Angeles.

Av Corrientes (between Avs 9 de Julio and Callao) is the traditional theater district of Buenos Aires – equivalent to New York's Broadway or London's West End – but theater companies and venues large and small are found throughout the city. Indeed, Av Corrientes has seen better days, and some theatergoers prefer to attend Off-Corrientes shows. The term has been around at least since 1982, the year Juan José Campanella wrote and produced the play of the same name. He's gone on to become a major figure in Argentine cinema. The term 'off-off Corrientes' has entered the lexicon as well, and don't be confused by the theater on Av Corrientes named Off Corrientes.

Companies can be very improvisational and unconventional. Some rent houses to stage performances, others act in plazas and parks, and one truly 'underground' company has performed in subway stations.

The theater season is liveliest in winter, from June through August, but performances are on tap year-round. Many of the most popular shows move to the provincial beach resort of Mar del Plata for the summer.

# History

# History

Ask anyone from Buenos Aires and they will tell you that the business, history and politics of the city are the business, history and politics of Argentina. As the capital of the country and the home of one-third of the national population, Buenos Aires is the epicenter of every major Argentine drama – from triumph to defeat and back.

## THE RECENT PAST

### THE RETURN TO DEMOCRACY

The recent history of the city starts with the end of the military dictatorship that ruled the country with an iron fist from 1976 to 1983. General Leopoldo Galtieri took the reins of the draconian military junta in 1981. Their power was unravelling: the economy was in recession, interest rates skyrocketed and protesters took to the streets of Buenos Aires. A year later, Galtieri tried to divert national attention by provoking the UK into a war over control of the Falkland Islands (known in Argentina as Las Islas Malvinas). The British had more resolve than the junta had imagined and Argentina was easily defeated. The greatest blow came when the British nuclear submarine *Conqueror* torpedoed the Argentine heavy cruiser *General Belgrano*, killing 323 men. Argentina still holds that the ship was returning to harbor.

Embarrassed and proven ineffectual, the military regime fell apart and a new civilian government under Raúl Alfonsín took control in 1983. Alfonsín enjoyed a small amount of success and was able to negotiate a few international loans, but he could not limit inflation or constrain public spending. By 1989, inflation was out of control and Alfonsín left office five months early, when Carlos Menem took power.

*Detail of the Torre de los Ingleses (p65), attacked during the Falklands War*

TIMELINE | **1536** | **1776**
--- | --- | ---
 | Pedro de Mendoza reaches the Río de la Plata and settles in; he is back in Spain within four years | Buenos Aires becomes capital of the new Spanish Viceroyalty of the Río de la Plata

## Three Turning Points

### European immigrants flood Buenos Aires (1869–95)

In the late 1860s, Buenos Aires was a reasonably sized port town of 90,000 people. Before the end of the century, massive European immigration boosted the population to over 670,000. The onslaught of Europeans not only swelled Buenos Aires into a major international capital, but gave the city its rich multicultural heritage, famous idiosyncrasies and sharp political differences, and jump-started the leftist labor movement.

### Eva Perón dies of cancer (July 26, 1952)

Evita played an essential PR role for her dictatorial husband. When she died at the age of 33, Juan Perón's tumultuous political decline began. His fall created a major vacuum that was filled by a succession of military juntas intent on imposing order. While Perón did mount a brief comeback in 1973 (and then promptly died in office), the military was again in control of the country by 1976. In an attempt to neutralize opposition to their rule, they carried out the Dirty War.

### Las Madres de la Plaza de Mayo march on the capital (1977)

On a Thursday in April, 14 mothers whose children disappeared in the Dirty War first marched in front of the presidential palace on the Plaza de Mayo. The continued to march every Thursday and became known as Las Madres de la Plaza de Mayo (the Mothers of the Plaza de Mayo). Las Madres were the first Argentines to openly protest the draco-nian junta and allege that atrocities were being committed, throwing open the gates for further protest. As civil unrest increased, the military government foolishly instigated the Falklands War in an attempt to rally the country round a nationalistic cause and, in so doing, brought about its own political demise.

# MENEM & THE BOOM YEARS

Under the guidance of his shrewd economy minister Domingo Cavallo, the consummately slick Carlos Menem introduced free-market reforms to stall Argentina's economic slide. Many of the state-run industries were privatized and, most importantly, the peso was fixed by law at an equal rate to the American dollar. Foreign investment poured into the country. Buenos Aires began to flourish again: buildings were restored and new businesses cropped up. The capital's Puerto Madero docks were redeveloped into an upscale leisure district, tourism increased and optimism was in the air. People in Buenos Aires bought new cars, talked on cell phones and took international vacations.

Although the economy seemed robust to the casual observer, by Menem's second term (1995–99) things were already amiss. The inflexibility imposed by the economic reforms made it difficult for the country to respond to foreign competition, and Mexico's 1995 currency collapse jolted a number of banks in Buenos Aires. Not only did Menem fail to reform public spending, but corruption was so widespread that it dominated daily newspaper headlines.

# THE ECONOMIC CRISIS

As an economic slowdown deepened into a recession, voters turned to the mayor of Buenos Aires, Fernando de la Rua, and elected him president in 1999. He was faced with the need to cut public spending and hike taxes during the recession.

The economy stagnated further, investors panicked, the bond market teetered on the brink of oblivion and the country seemed unable to service its increasingly heavy international debt. Cavallo was brought back in as the economy minister and in January 2001, rather than declaring a debt default, he sought over US$20 million more in loans from the IMF.

| May 25, 1810 | 1871 |
|---|---|
| Buenos Aires declares independence from Spain | A severe outbreak of yellow fever kills 10% of the city's population |

Argentina had been living on credit and it could no longer sustain its lifestyle. The facade of a successful economy had been ripped away, and the indebted, weak inner workings were exposed. As the storm clouds gathered, there was a run on the banks. Between July and November, Argentines withdrew around US$20 billion from the banks, hiding it under their mattresses or sending it abroad. In a last-ditch effort to keep money in the country, the government imposed a limit of US$1000 a month on bank withdrawals. Called the *corralito* (little corral), the strategy crushed many informal sectors of the economy that function on cash (taxis, food markets), and rioters and looters took to the streets. As the government tried to hoard the remaining hard currency, all bank savings were converted to pesos and any remaining trust in the government was broken. Pot-and-pan banging middle-class protesters joined the fray, and both Cavallo and, then, de la Rua resigned.

Two new presidents came and went in the same week and the world's greatest default on public debt was declared. The third presidential successor, former Buenos Aires province governor Eduardo Duhalde, was able to hold onto power. In order to have more flexibility, he dismantled the currency-board system that had pegged the peso to the American dollar for a decade. The peso devalued rapidly and people's savings were reduced to a fraction of their earlier value. In January 2002, the banks were only open for a total of six days and confidence in the government was nonexistent. The economy ceased to function: cash became scarce, imports stopped and demand for nonessential items flat-lined. More than half of the fiercely proud Argentine people found themselves below the national poverty line: the once comfortable middle class woke up in the lower classes, and the former lower classes were plunged into destitution. Businesspeople ate at soup kitchens and homelessness became rampant.

# KIRCHNER & THE PATH TO STABILITY

Duhalde, to his credit, was able to use his deep political party roots to keep the country together through to elections in April 2003. Numerous candidates entered the contest; the top two finishers were Menem (making a foray out of retirement for the campaign) and Néstor Kirchner, a little-known governor of the thinly populated Patagonian province of Santa Cruz. Menem bowed out of the runoff election and Kirchner became president.

Kirchner was the antidote to the slick and dishonest Buenos Aires establishment politicians. He was an outsider, with his entire career in the provinces and a personal air of sincerity and austerity. The people were looking for a fresh start and for someone to believe in – and they found that in Kirchner.

Since Kirchner arrived in Buenos Aires, he has defined himself as a hard-nosed fighter. Already refusing to negotiate with the holders of the US$100 billion of defaulted debt, he went a step further in September 2004, announcing that he was suspending Argentina's agreement with the IMF, to which it owes US$14.5 billion. He hopes to bully the fund into agreeing to better terms for the debt repayment. He is trying to stimulate internal consumption first and then deal with creditors when the country is on a stronger footing. So far it has worked, and by early 2005 the economy was registering an impressive 8% growth.

The president's belligerence aimed at outside forces (and deposed 'neoliberals' Cavallo and Menem) has helped to reintroduce a sense of trust and solidarity between the people and the government. According to the economy minister, Roberto Lavagna, investment, mainly by smaller firms, is back at the levels of the 1990s. Imports are up and the government actually has some cash to spare. While the growth is not expected to keep its current pace, the economy should continue to move in a positive direction. Confidence in Kirchner and the power structure in Buenos Aires will be essential for the long road ahead of the city and the country.

An interesting side effect of the collapse was a boom in international tourism, as foreigners enjoyed cosmopolitan Buenos Aires at bargain prices. Tourism injected money back into the economy and popularized Buenos Aires as a destination for years to come.

| 1892 | 1908 |
| --- | --- |
| Two-year-old Carlos Gardel and his mother arrive in Buenos Aires from France | Teatro Colón opens its doors |

# FROM THE BEGINNING

## THE SPANISH ARE COMING

Although the banks of the Río de la Plata (River Plate) had been populated for tens of thousands of years by nomadic hunter-gatherers, the first attempt at establishing a permanent settlement was made by Spanish aristocrat Pedro de Mendoza in 1536. His verbose name for the outpost, Puerto Nuestra Señora Santa María del Buen Aire (Port Our Lady Saint Mary of the Good Wind) was matched only by his extravagant expedition of 16 ships and nearly 1600 men – nearly three times the size of Hernán Cortés' forces that conquered the Aztecs. In spite of the resources and numbers, Mendoza did some fantastically poor planning and arrived too late in the season to plant crops. The Spanish soon found themselves short on food. When they tried to bully the local Querandí indigenous groups into feeding them, a bitter fight ensued. After four years of struggle, the Spanish were so short on supplies and food that some resorted to cannibalism and Mendoza fled back to Spain. A detachment of troops who were left behind retreated upriver to Asunción (now the capital of Paraguay).

Francisco Pizarro's conquest of the Inca empire in present-day Peru became the focus of the Spanish Crown and Buenos Aires was ignored for the next four decades. In 1580, Juan de Garay returned with an expedition from Asunción and attempted to rebuild Buenos Aires. The Spanish had improved their colonizing skills since Mendoza's ill-fated attempt and were also able to rely on backup from the cities of Asunción and Santa Fe.

Buenos Aires remained a backwater in comparison to Andean settlements such as Tucumán, Córdoba, Salta, La Rioja and Jujuy. Ranching was the core of the city's early economy. The development of mines in the Andes and the incessant warfare in the Spanish empire swelled the demand for both cattle and horses. Spain maintained harsh restrictions on trade out of Buenos Aires and the increasingly frustrated locals turned to smuggling contraband.

The city continued to flourish and the crown was eventually forced to relax its restrictions and try to co-opt the growing international trade in the region. In 1776, Madrid made Buenos Aires the capital of the new Viceroyalty of the Río de la Plata which included the world's largest silver mine in Potosí (in present-day Bolivia). For many of its residents, the new status as a capital was recognition that the adolescent city was outgrowing Spain's parental authority.

---

### Smuggling in Buenos Aires

It's not a coincidence that one of the most popular whiskeys served in Buenos Aires is called Old Smuggler. The city's history of trading in contraband goes all the way back to its founding. Some argue that the culture of corruption, so pervasive until the economic collapse of 2001, was tolerated because the historical role of smuggling in Buenos Aires led to a 'tradition' of rule-bending.

The Spanish empire kept tight regulations on its ports and only certain cities were allowed to trade goods with other countries. Buenos Aires was originally on the periphery of the empire, was hard to monitor and was therefore not allowed to buy from or sell to other Europeans. Located at the mouth of the Río de la Plata, the settlement was an ideal point of entry to the continent for traders. Buenos Aires merchants turned to smuggling everything from textiles and precious metals to weapons and slaves. Portuguese manufactured goods flooded the city and made their way inland to present-day Bolivia, Paraguay and even Peru.

Later, the British and high-seas pirates found a ready and willing trading partner in Buenos Aires (and also introduced a taste for fine whiskeys). An increasing amount of wealth passed through the city and much of the initial growth of Buenos Aires was fuelled by the trade in contraband. As smuggling was an open game, without favored imperial merchants, it offered a chance for upward social mobility and gave birth to a commercially oriented middle class in Buenos Aires.

Although smuggling has died down in recent years, it is never that far away. Buenos Aires is still an international money-laundering center and a growing transshipment point for cocaine en route to Europe and the USA.

---

| 1946 | 1976 |
|---|---|
| Juan Perón takes power and makes sweeping changes to the political structure | Military juntas take control of the country and carry out the Dirty War |

Although the new viceroyalty had internal squabbles over trade and control issues, when the British raided the city in 1806 the response was unified. Locals rallied against the invaders without Spanish help and chased them out of town. The British tried again the following year, and they were once again beaten back by the people of Buenos Aires. These two battles – now celebrated as La Reconquista (the Reconquest) and La Defensa (the Defense) – gave the city's inhabitants confidence and a new understanding of their ability to be self-reliant. It was just a matter of time until they broke with Spain.

## INDEPENDENCE

When Napoleon conquered Spain and put his brother on the throne in 1808, Buenos Aires became further estranged from Madrid and finally declared its independence on May 25, 1810. To commemorate the occasion, the city's main square was renamed the Plaza de 25 de Mayo.

Six years later, on July 9, 1816, outlying areas of the viceroyalty declared independence from Spain and founded the United Provinces of the River Plate. Almost immediately, a power struggle arose between Buenos Aires and the provincial strongmen: the Federalist landowners of interior provinces were concerned with preserving their autonomy, while the Unitarist businessmen of Buenos Aires tried to consolidate power in the city with an outward orientation toward overseas commerce and European ideas. Some of the interior provinces, unhappy with the strength of Buenos Aires, decided to go their own way, forming Paraguay in 1814, Bolivia in 1825 and Uruguay in 1828.

After more than a decade of violence and uncertainty, Federalist caudillo (strongman) Juan Manuel de Rosas took control of Buenos Aires, when he became governor of the province in 1829. Rosas' reign lasted 23 years, during which time Buenos Aires' influence increased dramatically. Although he swore that he was a Federalist, Rosas was a Federalist when it suited him and became more of a Unitarist once he controlled the city. He required that all international trade be funneled through Buenos Aires, rather than proceeding directly to the provinces, and set ominous political precedents, creating the *mazorca* (his ruthless political police) and institutionalizing torture.

## THE FLEETING GOLDEN AGE

Rosas' eventual overthrow came in 1852 at the hands of Justo José de Urquiza, a rival caudillo governor who tried to transfer power to his home province of Entre Rios. In protest, Buenos Aires briefly seceded from the union, but was reestablished as the capital when Bartolomé Mitre, the governor of Buenos Aires province and founder of *La Nación* newspaper, defeated Urquiza's forces in 1861. From there, Buenos Aires never looked back and became the undisputed power center of the country.

The city's economy boomed and immigrants poured in from Spain, Italy and Germany, followed by waves of immigrants from Croatia, Ireland, Poland and the Ukraine. Buenos Aires' population grew nearly seven-fold from 1869 to 1895. The new residents worked in the port, lived tightly in the tenement buildings and developed the famous tango in the streets and nightspots.

By Argentina's centennial in 1910, Buenos Aires was the biggest city in Latin America and the second largest in the Americas (after New York). With a population of over one million people, a subway was constructed and British companies built modern gas, electrical and sewer systems. Buenos Aires was at the height of a Golden Age, with bustling streets full of New World businesses, art, architecture, fashion and foods. By the beginning of WWI, Argentina was one of the world's 10 richest countries, ahead of France and Germany.

| 1982 | 1983 |
|---|---|
| The British win the Falklands War | The military regime collapses, bringing the Dirty War to an end; civilian government is restored |

Then the Argentine fortune started to change. Export prices dropped off, wages stagnated and workers became increasingly frustrated and militant. Tensions peaked in Buenos Aires in 1919, when the government (some say pressured by moneyed interests) mercilessly killed striking metalworkers in what has become known as Semana Trágica (Tragic Week). The Wall Street crash of 1929 dealt the final blow to the export markets and a few months later the military took over the country. The Golden Age became a distant memory. It was the first of many military coups that blemished the rest of the century and shackled the progress of the nation. Some scholars argue that the events that culminated in the 2001 economic collapse can be traced back to the military coup in 1930.

## THE AGE OF THE PERÓNS

During WWII, the rural poor migrated into Buenos Aires in search of work. The number of people living in Buenos Aires nearly tripled and soon the city held a third of the national population (similar to the percentage today). The growing strength of these urban working classes swept populist Lieutenant-General Juan Domingo Perón into the presidency in 1946. Perón had been stationed for a time in Italy and developed his own brand of watered-down Mussolini-style fascism. He quickly nationalized large industry, including the railways, and created Argentina's first welfare state. Borrowing from Fascist Italy and Germany, Perón carefully cultivated his iconic image and held massive popular rallies in the Plaza de 25 de Mayo.

Perón's glamorous mistress (and soon-to-be-wife) Eva Duarte, a onetime radio soap-opera star, became the consummate celebrity first lady and an icon who would eclipse Perón himself. Known as Evita, her powerful social-assistance foundation reached out to lower-class women through giveaways of such things as baby bottles and strollers, and the construction of schools and hospitals. The masses felt a certain empathy with Evita, as she was born into the working class. In 1952 she cemented her quasi-saintly legacy by dying of uterine cancer at age 33 at the peak of her popularity, just before things went sour.

After the death of his wife, Perón financed payouts to workers by simply printing new money, bungled the economy, censored the press and cracked down on political opposition. He was strikingly less popular without Evita by his side and was deposed by the military after only two terms in office. Perón lived in exile in Spain while a series of military coups ailed the nation. In 1973, Perón returned to Buenos Aires and was re-elected president, but died just two months later. His third wife, the hapless Isabelita, was left to rule in his place, but was replaced by a military junta in 1976.

Although the effects of Perón's personal political achievements are debatable, the Peronist party, based largely on his ideals, has endured – both Menem and Kirchner are Peronists (although their policies have little to do with anything espoused by Perón himself).

*Evita (above) impersonator, Recoleta*

| 1989 | 1992 & 1994 |
| --- | --- |
| Inflation reaches 197% per month; Carlos Menem institutes free-market reforms that trigger an economic boom | Bomb attacks at the Israeli embassy and at a Jewish community center in Buenos Aires kill over 100 |

## Taking It to the Streets

Just like the tango and *dulce de leche*, street protests are a well-known pastime of the people of Buenos Aires. Whether the city is booming or in the midst of a depression, unless there's martial law, someone is out on the street demonstrating against something. Plaza de Mayo has long been the focal point of protests.

The best-known voices of dissent are the famed Madres de la Plaza de Mayo (the Mothers of Plaza de Mayo). On April 30, 1977, 14 mothers whose children had disappeared in the Dirty War marched on the Plaza de Mayo. They demanded to know what had happened to their missing children. The military government dismissed them, saying that their children had simply moved abroad, but the women continued to march in their iconic white handkerchiefs every Thursday and their numbers grew steadily. They played an essential historical role as the first group to openly oppose the military junta and opened the doors for later protests. However, many of the mothers never got the answers they were looking for and still march every Thursday, to this day.

Even in 1996, when the economy was good and the country was under civilian control, a number of protests broke out against corruption and the reform of pensions. Senior citizens hurled eggs at government buildings and were chased by trucks mounted with water cannons. The protests after the economic collapse in 2001 were particularly large and vociferous. Thousands of people spontaneously gathered in public parks in Buenos Aires – not just in the poorer parts of the city, but in solidly middle-class areas too. Neighborhood groups developed plans for protests outside banks and government buildings. To the shouts of *'¡Qué se vayan todos!'* (get rid of all them all), the banging of pots and pans and sporadic street violence, the protesters took on the government, and both the economy minister and the president stepped down. Banks were vandalized and some of the politicians who hadn't fled the country were beaten in the streets of Buenos Aires. People felt betrayed by the government, and they made sure that this was known.

Government approval is currently high and protests are scarce, but it never stays that way for long.

# DIRTY TRICKS

The new and decidedly more evil military rulers instituted the Process of National Reorganisation, known as El Proceso, which involved harsh repression and eradication of civilian government. Ostensibly an effort to remake Argentina's political culture and modernize the economy, El Proceso was little more than a Cold War–era attempt to kill off or intimidate all leftist political opposition.

Based in Buenos Aires, a left-wing guerrilla group known as the Montoneros bombed foreign buildings, kidnapped executives for ransom and robbed banks to finance their armed struggle against the military government. The Montoneros were comprised mainly of educated, middle-class youths who were, in turn, hunted down by the military government in a campaign now known as La Guerra Sucia (the Dirty War). Somewhere between 10,000 and 30,000 civilians died; many of them simply 'disappeared' while walking down the street or sleeping in their beds. Most were tortured to death, or sedated and dropped from planes into the Río de la Plata. Anyone who seemed even sympathetic to the Montoneros could be whisked off the streets and detained, tortured or killed. A great number of the 'disappeared' are still unaccounted for today.

The military leaders did not have a particularly wide political view and let numerous aspects of the country's well-being slip into decay along with the entire national economy. When Ronald Reagan took power in the USA in 1981, he reversed Jimmy Carter's condemnation of the junta's human-rights abuses and even invited the generals to visit in Washington, DC. With a more positive relationship with the USA, they were able to solicit development loans from international lenders, but endemic corruption quickly drained the coffers into their Swiss bank accounts.

| 2001 | 2005 |
|---|---|
| Argentina commits the largest debt default in world history; the economy is ruined | Néstor Kirchner maneuvers the country to an unexpected economic rally with 8% growth |

# Neighborhoods

# Neighborhoods

Practically all the key attractions in Buenos Aires are located in just a handful of neighboring barrios in the eastern part of the city, either walking distance from each other or easily reached by public transportation. Most are placed on the maps in the back of this guidebook.

Most travelers visiting this city will either stay in or eventually visit the Microcentro, which teems with businesspeople in suits, some well-dressed shoppers and a few badly dressed tourists. Walking around, you'll see many wonderful old European buildings, along with some not-quite-so-charming modern constructions. Together, however, they complete Buenos Aires' unique style.

South of the downtown area, San Telmo is a big tourist draw. The buildings are lower and more colonial than in the city's center, and narrow cobblestone streets slow down traffic (a bit) while adding to the area's quaintness. Tango thrives here, and the Sunday antique fair always draws a bustling crowd. Farther south is blue-collar La Boca, BA's most visually colorful neighborhood, although only a few streets are of real interest to tourists.

Up north, Recoleta is another major tourist destination; its extensive Gothic cemetery is a must-see for any visitor, and on weekends the craft fair outside brims with activity. Recoleta is a great place to eyeball BA's upper classes, and harbors a wide range of ritzy cafés, restaurants and expensive boutiques.

Beyond Recoleta is Palermo, a refuge for the middle class, filled with extensive parklands and monumental statues. It features good places to stroll, and its sub-neighborhood of Palermo Viejo is home to some of the city's trendiest eateries and most fashionable boutiques. Belgrano is even farther north and offers glimpses into a higher-class, mostly residential neighborhood.

Over to the west, the more working-class barrios of Once and Caballito offer another glimpse into the porteño lifestyle, along with some color – the capital's main Jewish, Peruvian and Korean populations live here.

Note that on holidays, opening hours for the sights listed in this chapter tend to be similar to weekend hours.

*Hanging out at Mark's Deli & Coffee House (p109), Palermo Viejo*

# ITINERARIES

## One Day

Start early in San Telmo and have a peep at the cobbled streets and antique shops. If you luck out and it's Sunday you'll need to stay longer and browse the antiques market (p151) on Plaza Dorrego. Head up to Plaza de Mayo (p53), about 10 blocks to the north, and behold the Casa Rosada. Peek into the cathedral and Cabildo (town hall) – they shouldn't take long. If you need an atmospheric lunch break, head three blocks west to Café Tortoni (p118), then backtrack to pedestrian Av Florida and walk all the way up to Galerías Pacífico (p52). Look inside at the ceiling murals and do some shopping, if you haven't been doing so already on Av Florida. Veer to Plaza San Martín and along Santa Fe, cross Av 9 de Julio (a BA experience in itself) and work your way up north towards ritzy Av Alvear. Enjoy the rich mansions and upscale boutiques, and reach Plaza Intendente Alvear. If it's a weekend, stroll through the crafts market (p151), then enter the small city that is the Cementerio de la Recoleta (p67). You'll probably need another break, so drop into posh La Biela café (p120). If you like classical art, walk quickly to the Museo Nacional de Bellas Artes (p68), but hurry up – it closes at 7:30pm! Or if you like modern art, taxi into Palermo for Malba (p70). By now it's getting late, so taxi into Palermo Viejo and pick a restaurant...*any* restaurant (p72). And if you have the energy, think about taking in a tango show (p129) or perhaps the ballet or opera at the Teatro Colón (p59).

## Three Days

To your whirlwind day above, add a quick side trip to La Boca (p62). If you're a fan, be sure to take in a *fútbol* game at La Bombonera stadium – it's sports at its most passionate. In the Microcentro you can add some museums (p50) or take an extra stroll through Puerto Madero (p55), a good place to have lunch. If you like nature, sidestep Puerto Madero into the Reserva Ecológica Costanera Sur (p56). Get yourself over to Plaza del Congreso and check out the *palacio*, then walk four blocks north to bustling Av Corrientes, which is full of bookstores, cinemas and theaters. If you like to shop for bargains, go west to the barrio of Once and try to sort out the mayhem of merchants around the train station. Nearby, the Abasto mall (p152) is a gorgeous sight. Head north a bit to Palermo Viejo, where many new boutiques have sprouted up (along with the restaurants). If you like to shop they're worth a browse. If you don't like to shop, think about checking out Palermo's grassy gardens and relatively pleasant zoo (p70).

On your third day, an excursion to Tigre (p170) is in order. Take the Tren de la Costa route and enjoy the scenic, quiet train ride. The stations are all pleasant, and the San Isidro stop even comes with an outdoor shopping center. San Isidro (p171) itself is pleasant suburb for a walk. Back on the train, check out the Barrancas stop – if it's a weekend there's a cute antiques fair (p151). When you get to the end of the train line you'll have arrived in Tigre; go to the nearby Puerto de Frutos and stroll through housewares and fruit stalls; on weekends there's a crafts fair. Then walk about 15 minutes to the boat docks and take off on a two-hour ride through the delta. Afterwards head back to Buenos Aires and find yourself a steak restaurant.

## One Week

On your fourth day head out of town again; if you're *really* resourceful (and lucky with bus schedules) you could do a loop and see Luján (p172) and San Antonio de Areco (p174) in one day. Colonia (p175) is worth another day of your trip, and compact enough to see in a few hours. Several daily ferries right from downtown Buenos Aires make the journey in about 50 minutes.

Your last couple of days could be spent seeing more of BA's museums, taking a tango class or two (p130) or watching a show at a grand theater (p132). Spend your one Sunday (Saturday night in summer) at the jovial Feria de Mataderos (p151), but if you don't want to go that far out there are plenty of other fairs on Sunday, including San Telmo's (p151). Do some more shopping (p144) or just wander downtown and look around – the buildings are as gorgeous as the people. And make sure that at least one time during the week you stop in at an ice-cream shop (p94) – the confections are so delicious it could possibly be the highlight of your trip!

## Top Ten Buenos Aires

Ten things you shouldn't miss while in this great city.

- **Recoleta Cemetery** (p67) Rub shoulders with the rich and well-connected dead. Soaring angels and crosses decorate the grand old sarcophagi and line paths that go on and on. Look for Evita's grave – there's always a crowd leaving flowers there. Recoleta is a veritable city of the dead and well revered by porteños, who tend to celebrate famous figures' death anniversaries rather than their birthdays. Come on a sunny Saturday or Sunday, when the park outside bustles with a crafts fair and street performers. When you tire of walking, have a casual sit nearby at one of the elegant café patios for tea time and a snack.

- **Feria de San Telmo** (p151) A definite can't-miss Sunday activity is this lively antiques fair in Plaza Dorrego, the heart of tangoland San Telmo. Dozens of booths display old seltzer bottles, ceramics, keys, coins, jewelry, watches, pictures and many other antique knickknacks for your buying pleasure. In more open areas, tango dancers perform for a few coins, and nearby mimes and musicians ask for their share. Plenty of sidewalk cafés and restaurants provide nourishment, and fancy antique shops offer old collectibles, some in great condition (and very expensive). Charming cobbled streets and old colonial buildings complete the picture.

- **That Perfect Steak** (p91) Mmmm... slice into a thick, juicy strip of grilled *bife de lomo* (tenderloin) and savor that Pampas-grown beef flavor you can get only in Argentina. Buenos Aires is overflowing with *parrillas* (steak houses), that will cater to your tastes and serve up that perfect slab of meat. In many places, you can see the goods cooking, either at a grill or skewered in a circular *asado* (barbecue pit) next to the sidewalk window. Don't forget to ask for *chimichurri*, a spicy olive oil, garlic and parsley sauce that will tantalize your taste buds. (See the boxed text on p91 for more.)

- **Old-Fashioned Cafés** (p119) Tired of treading the streets of Buenos Aires? Need a break from the noise and frenetic pace of a big city? Have yourself an old-fashioned experience at one of the capital's many traditional cafés, some of which have been around for more than a century. Richly decorated with old wood details in spacious, high-ceilinged rooms, these cafés have harbored poets, politicians, activists, intellectuals – and countless stylish porteños needing a grand place in which to rest and sip their *café cortado* (coffee with milk). Many of these old-time places also serve meals, and a few even double as show venues for live music and tango. See p118 for a listing of the best.

- **A Tango Show, of Course!** (p129) No dance can compare with the tango – a sultry spectacle of sensual movement, choreographed like a water dance with only two characters: the slick, suited man and the arresting woman, who is traditionally dressed in a short skirt with high heels and fishnet stockings. Tango has been described as 'making love in a vertical position,' and watching a show you'll see why. The movements are made together, one affecting the other, the upper bodies maintaining their relatively stiff position while the legs circle and entwine one another. Buenos Aires has countless venues where you can enjoy this experience, from streets and restaurants to tango halls; and, if you can't resist and are tempted to go a step further, classes and *milongas* (dances) are widely available (see p130 for classes, and p26 for tango history).

- **A Walk Downtown** (p78) There's no better way to get to know Buenos Aires than to simply walk. Sure, traffic can be nightmarish, and you need to watch your step with the loose tiles and dog piles, but don't forget to look up.

# ORGANIZED TOURS

There are plenty of organized tours that help you take in Buenos Aires, from the large tourist-bus variety, to more intimate car trips, guided bike rides and straight-up walks. Backpacker-oriented travel agencies such as Say Hueque or Tangol (see p195) broker a wide variety of offerings, including the usual bus tour, boat rides in Tigre, Jewish sights, helicopter rides to night strolls. Pride Travel (p195) can help gay travelers with city tours, while the organization the **Gay Guide** (www.thegayguide.com.ar) offers neighborhood walks, guided nightlife

romps and even some fabulous shopping tours (US$55 for two).

The city of Buenos Aires organizes **free monthly tours** ( ☎ 4114-5791; equitur@buenos aires.gov.ar) with a historical slant; these follow the footsteps of Jorge Luis Borges, Federico García Lorca, Eva Perón and Carlos Gardel, utilizing both walking and bus rides to get from place to place. English guides may be available, so ask; reservations are crucial. They may also have regular city tours for free but contact them ahead of time for current schedules ( ☎ 4313-0187; www.bue .gov.ar). The free newsletter *Ciudad Abierta*

The older buildings that line many of the city's streets can be stunning, even if they could use more upkeep. Old Europe had a deep influence on the architecture of BA during the city's boom period in the mid- to late 1800s, and it shows. Stroll around, window-shop like the locals (especially on Av Santa Fe) and take in the super-busy Avs Florida and Lavalle pedestrianized streets to watch businessmen and fashion model wannabes go by in a blur. It's all part of the Buenos Aires experience.

- **The Shopping** Since Argentina's economic collapse in December 2001, Buenos Aires has become a shopper's paradise. Anything made in the country will be relatively affordable, and this will be the case with most things you find. Clothes are a good deal, and if you want something special head to Palermo Viejo, where a hot new crowd of young designers have opened up boutiques filled with cutting-edge fashions. Leather is also affordable, though in touristy shops you may find yourself bargaining for a good price (fine leather shops are a different animal altogether, so to speak – prices are generally firm). Antiques are less expensive than in most other Western countries, but you really should know what you're buying. For more see the shopping chapter on p142.

- **Palermo's Parks** Buenos Aires is a great city, but the center can be intense for small-town dwellers or country bumpkins. So, if you tire of the fumes and noise or just want some green space to relax in, head out to Palermo's open spaces for a more laid-back environment. There are several pretty gardens to take in, a decent zoo and many paths lined with benches; on weekends, some roads are closed off to traffic. Lovers come here to steal kisses, older folks feed pigeons or feral cats, and kids frolic everywhere. Cyclists can rent bikes to pedal around the lake or on the winding bike paths. And, of course, you can just stroll around and see how porteños take it easy; come here on a Sunday to witness sports and family activity at their peak.

- **Feria de Mataderos** Located way out in the Mataderos barrio, this market will take almost an hour to reach by bus – but it's worth it. Over 100 craft booths sell affordable handmade treasures like jewelry, *mate* gourds, horse-hoof ashtrays, leather and metalwork, ponchos, knives and musical instruments. There are pony rides for the kids, and the food is great – inexpensive, savory meats grilled right on the sidewalks, the smoke permeating the surrounding air, while homemade sweets like candied apples, *alfajores* (cookie sandwiches) and pastries tempt the buds. The best part, however, is the folk music, singing and dancing; the audience joins in, some wearing traditional costumes. It's a very patriotic scene, and if you're lucky you'll catch the impressive horse-riding exhibitions. See p151 for information on how to get there.

- **Well, this one's hard** To fun-loving partygoers, the best part of BA may be the raucous, stay-out-till-7am nightlife; to others, like opera or ballet buffs, the astounding Teatro Colón can't be missed; and hard-core *fútbol* fans will want to catch a classic Boca–River match. And that gourmand in all of us will appreciate the amazing variety of sweets to savor – ubiquitous pastries, *dulce de leche* (thick, spreadable caramel) and world-class ice cream. Perhaps Buenos Aires' real highlight is the Argentine people. Despite the hard facade you may encounter with some locals (a common trait in any big city during difficult times), many porteños do take an interest in travelers coming from Western countries. After all, they feel themselves a part of the First World, just stuck down south a bit. Connect with them in some way, even if you don't speak Spanish; after all, the best travel memories come from those serendipitous encounters with locals.

(available at the Secretaría de Turismo p195) often has information on all these tours on its back page.

## BIKE TOURS Map pp228-9

☎ 4311-5199; www.biketours.com.ar; Av Florida 868 14H

Those looking for an extra shot of activity in their tours should consider hopping on a bicycle. Nonstrenuous rides cover Retiro, Puerto Madero, the Reserva Ecológica and La Boca in four hours (US$25 per person). Another tour heads to Recoleta and Palermo (US$25 per person) while a

third goes to San Isidro and Tigre (US$30 per person). All prices include bike, helmet, water bottle, English-speaking guide and a souvenir. They also rent bikes for US$15 per 24 hours.

## BOB FRASSINETTI

☎ 15-4475-3983; bob@artdealer.com.ar

Friendly and bohemian Bob is an art dealer who also takes art-loving travelers on antique shopping trips to galleries, auctions and markets all around the city. Custom-made tours are also possible, and Bob can even pick you up at the airport; he speaks fluent English. Full-day tours start at US$40.

## Top Five Museums

- **Museo Nacional de Bellas Artes** (p68) Classic old maestros, both national and international, dominate – with the occasional modern exhibit thrown in
- **Museo de Arte Latinoamericano de Buenos Aires** (Malba; p70) Cutting edge all the way; the museum itself is as interesting as its presentations
- **Museo Nacional de Arte Decorativo** (p73) Gorgeous building with a rich couple's collection of decorative art – you *know* there's some good stuff here
- **Museo Municipal de Arte Hispanoamericano Isaac Fernández Blanco** (p65) Wonderfully peaceful grounds, a grand mansion and lush period items
- **Museo de Carlos Gardel** (p75) Argentina's shining star and spiritual figurehead, come down to earth with his own museum

### BUENOS AIRES VISIÓN Map pp222-4
☎ 4394-2986; www.buenosaires-vision.com.ar; 28th fl, Esmeralda 356

If you're looking to sightsee with up to 40 other *compañeros* from the vantage point of a large, comfortable bus, this tour's for you. Pick the half-day bus tours (US$7) that visit locations in the Microcentro, San Telmo, La Boca, Recoleta and Palermo. Or try a visit to Tigre and the Delta (US$14 to US$27), which includes train and boat rides. And don't forget the gaucho fiesta with dinner (US$34), which takes you out to an *estancia* (ranch) and includes a stop at the San Telmo Antiques Fair. Guides speak English, Spanish or Portuguese.

### CICERONES
☎ 4330-0880; www.cicerones.org.ar

This do-good, nonprofit agency offers free tours led completely by volunteers. A more personal cultural exchange is emphasized over straight sightseeing, and travelers are matched with friendly guides who speak their language. Groups are small – from two to six people – and the nontouristy walks take two to three hours. Donations are greatly appreciated.

### ETERNAUTAS
☎ 4384-7874, 15-4173-1078; www.eternautas.com in Spanish

More cerebral travelers will appreciate Eternautas' historian docents, who guide tours with themes such as Perón, Jewish history, and Argentine culture and economy. The costs of these tours depend on the number of people in the group, ranging from US$67 for two to US$107 for seven. General city tours are more affordable; the three-hour Imágenes de Buenos Aires minibus tour runs US$15 per person no matter how many are in the group, while guided weekend walks are just US$2 per person. All tours can be done in English, French and Italian, among other languages.

### URBAN BIKING
☎ 4855-5103; www.urbanbiking.com

Here's another bike-tour company that organizes rides to the north or south of the city, for US$24 including lunch. Three-hour night tours are also available (US$20), along with longer trips to Tigre (US$34) and La Plata (US$50). They also rent bikes for US$14 per day. Guides speak English, and tours include helmet, locks and child seats if necessary. Reservations are a must.

### WOW ARGENTINA Map p228-9
☎ 15-5603-2926; www.wowargentina .com.ar; Santa Fe 882 2F

Cintia Stella runs this travel agency with her husband Matías Mancuso, and either they or their guide will take you around Buenos Aires on a very personalized tour. In three to four hours you'll see BA's most important sights while getting a brief idea of the city's history and culture. An insight into the daily life of its citizens is also part of the deal, and you can customize the tour any way you want – see more churches or trace BA's Italian immigration patterns, for example. Tours for either one or two people cost US$95.

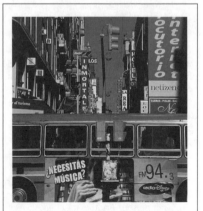

*A busy street in the Microcentro (p51)*

# MICROCENTRO & PLAZA DE MAYO

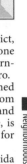

*Eating p89; Drinking p114 and p118; Shopping p143;
Sleeping p155*

Buenos Aires' Microcentro is where the big-city hustle begins, where you'll see endless lines of business suits and power skirts moving hastily along the narrow streets in the shadow of skyscrapers and old European buildings. It's home to the main banking district, nicknamed La City, and the historic **Plaza de Mayo** with its presidential Casa Rosada. If anyone has any business to do in Buenos Aires – even if it's just to complain about how the government should be thrown out – there's a good chance they'll do it here in the Microcentro.

Pedestrian Av Florida is in some ways the main artery of this region, always jammed during the day with businesspeople, shoppers and tourists seeking vehicle-free access from north to south without the ubiquitous bus fumes and honking taxis. Buskers, beggars and street vendors thrive here as well, adding color and noise. Its sister street, Av Lavalle, is also pedestrianized and runs perpendicular to Av Florida, providing east–west access for a few blocks.

The recent renovation of buildings, such as beautiful Galerías Pacífico, near Avs Florida and Córdoba, has added elegance to the area.

Farther south is Buenos Aires' busy financial district, where during work hours fashionably dressed businessfolk hurry around talking on their cell phones. For the traveler there are several museums to investigate, along with architectural styles that will have you wondering exactly what continent you're on.

After that comes Plaza de Mayo, often filled with people resting on benches, eating a snack or taking photos of the surrounding impressive buildings. This plaza is also the preferred target of many civil protests – most of which are peaceful – and marring the views are unsightly barricades meant to discourage large numbers of *piqueteros* (picketers) from congregating.

Adjoining the eastern edge of Plaza de Mayo and the Microcentro is Buenos Aires' newest barrio, **Puerto Madero**, a renovated waterfront area that stretches south toward San Telmo. A years-long project is turning formerly abandoned brick warehouses into upscale restaurants, offices and loft apartments, making the area one of the trendiest places to eat in the city.

## Orientation

The Microcentro is at the heart of Buenos Aires; the nearby Obelisco (p57) is often used as the zero point for measuring distances from the city center. Avs Florida and Lavalle are the main avenues for pedestrian traffic, while Avs Corrientes, Perón, de Mayo and Belgrano are thoroughfares for vehicles; over to the east, Av Leandro N Alem is a large and fast artery connecting the north of the city to the south. All north–south street names change at Av Rivadavia.

### ASOCIACIÓN CRISTIANA FEMENINA DE BUENOS AIRES Map p222-3
☎ 4322-1550; Tucumán 846

This modest building is the *solar natal* (birthplace) of Argentina's literary great Jorge Luis Borges. He lived here to age three, but don't expect to see anything stunning; his original house was torn down long ago. Only Borges-ophiles will appreciate the free guided tours in Spanish, which take place at 3pm on Tuesdays (call ahead to confirm).

## Transportation

**Bus** Bus No 24 to Congreso; No 29 to San Telmo; Nos 29, 64, 86 and 152 to La Boca; No 64 to Recoleta; Nos 29, 59, 64 and 152 to Palermo's Plaza Italia; No 111 to Palermo Viejo

**Subte** Líneas A, B, D and E all run from the Microcentro out to the suburbs; Línea C runs from Retiro to Constitución via the western edge of the Microcentro

Neighborhoods – Microcentro & Plaza de Mayo

## CORREO CENTRAL

☎ 4316-3000; Av Sarmiento 151; ⏲ 8am-8pm Mon-Fri, 9am-1pm Sat

It took 20 years to complete the impressive Correo Central (main post office; 1928); the beautifully maintained Beaux Arts structure was originally modeled on New York City's main post office. The mansard roof was a later addition. Inside is a small post and telegraph museum, but hours are unpredictable.

## GALERÍAS PACÍFICO Map p222-3

☎ 5555-5110; Av Florida; ⏲ 10am-9pm Sun-Thu, 10am-12:30am Fri & Sat

Covering an entire city block this Parisian-style shopping center has fulfilled the commercial purpose that its designers envisioned when they built it in 1889, with the proposed name of the Bon Marché. The worldwide economic crisis of the 1890s necessitated the sale of part of the building, subdivided into quarters by two large perpendicular passageways, to the Ferrocarril del Pacífico for its administrative offices. The railroad subsequently acquired the rest of the building, which became state property after Juan Perón's nationalization of the railroads.

In 1945, the completion of vaulted ceilings above those passageways and a central cupola at their junction made space for a dozen panels, covering 450 sq meters, by muralists Antonio Berni, Juan Carlos Castagnino, Manuel Colmeiro, Lino Spilimbergo and Demetrio Urruchúa. All were adherents of the *nuevo realismo* (new realism) school, heirs of an earlier social-activist tendency in Argentine art. For many years, the building went semiabandoned, but a joint Argentine-Mexican team repaired and restored the murals in 1992.

The beautiful structure is now a central meeting place, sporting upscale stores and a large food court. Tourist-oriented tango shows take place here at 8pm on weekends and the excellent Centro Cultural Borges takes up the 3rd floor. Guided tours are on tap twice a day.

## IGLESIA SANTA CATALINA

☎ 4326-6190; Plaza San Martín 705; ⏲ guided tours 3pm Fri

Santa Catalina was founded in 1745, when it became Buenos Aires' first convent. In 1806 British troops first invaded the city, and in July 1807 they took shelter in the convent. The soldiers holed up here for two days, and despite damaging the property did not hurt the nuns. Today Santa Catalina is a church, and a peek inside reveals beautiful gilded works and a baroque altarpiece created by Isidro Lorea, a Spanish carver.

## MUSEO DE LA POLICÍA FEDERAL

Map pp222-4

☎ 4394-6857; 7th fl, Plaza San Martín 353; admission free, children under 15 not permitted; ⏲ 1-6pm Tue-Fri

Across from the Museo Mitre, this museum is in the heart of the financial district. On display are a whole slew of uniforms and medals, all proudly presented. There's also the skeleton of a police dog who died on duty, plus 'illegal activities' exhibits (cockfighting and gambling displays) and grisly forensic photos, with dummies of murder victims. Bring your barf bag.

## MUSEO HISTÓRICO DR ARTURO JÁURETCHE Map pp222-4

☎ 331-6600; Av Sarmiento 362; admission free; ⏲ 10am-6pm Mon-Fri, tours by appointment

Spread out on different mezzanines, this museum actually makes sense of Argentina's chaotic economic history. It's in the heart of the financial district and includes good, well-lit displays on the country's early economic regions, the financing of political independence and the establishment of public credit. There are also exhibits on paper money and counterfeiting, which have probably been scrupulously studied by BA's current producers of phony banknotes. Examples of old currency, such as the million-peso bill from 1981, give an idea of the hyperinflation porteños had to live with not too long ago. One display offers tips on distinguishing between real and fake bills.

## MUSEO MITRE Map pp222-4

☎ 4394-8240; Plaza San Martín 336; admission free; ⏲ 1-6pm Mon-Fri

This museum is located in the colonial house where Bartolomé Mitre, Argentina's first legitimate president elected under the constitution of 1853, resided with his family. Two courtyards, salons, an office, a billiards room and Mitre's old bedroom are part of the sprawling complex. Mitre's term ran from 1862 to 1868, and he spent much of it leading the country's armies against Paraguay. After leaving office he founded the influential daily *La Nación*, still a porteño institution. The museum provides a good look into 19th-century upper-class life. Take a glance at the **library** ( ⏲ 12:30-6pm Mon-Fri), which holds more than 80,000 volumes. There are guided tours in Spanish on Thursday at 2pm; an expansion is planned for the 2nd floor.

# PLAZA DE MAYO

Where Diagonal Roque Sáenz Peña meets Av Rivadavia you'll find the historic Plaza de Mayo, ground zero for many of the city's most vehement protests. When Juan de Garay refounded Buenos Aires in 1580 (about 1km to 1½ km north of Pedro de Mendoza's presumed 1536 encampment near present-day Parque Lezama), he laid out the large Plaza del Fuerte (Fortress Plaza) in accordance with Spanish law. Later called the Plaza del Mercado (Market Plaza), then the Plaza de la Victoria, after victories over British invaders in 1806 and 1807, the plaza acquired its present and final name of Plaza de Mayo after the date Buenos Aires declared independence from Spain, May 25, 1810.

Today, the grassy plaza attracts camera-toting tourists (as well as the occasional camera thief) along with activists. And, on Thursdays at 3:30pm, the Madres de la Plaza de Mayo still march around the plaza in their unrelenting campaign for a full account of Dirty War atrocities during the military dictatorship of 1976–83.

In the center of the plaza is the **Pirámide de Mayo**, a small obelisk built to mark the first anniversary of BA's independence from Spain. Looming on the north side of the plaza is the headquarters of **Banco de la Nación** (1939), the work of famed architect Alejandro Bustillo. Most other public buildings in this area belong to the late 19th century, when the Av de Mayo first connected the Casa Rosada with the Plaza del Congreso, obliterating most of the historic and dignified Cabildo in the process.

## Keeping Your Mayos & Peñas Straight

Some first-time (or maybe second-time) visitors may get confused with certain similar-sounding street and attraction names. Keep them straight:

- **Plaza de Mayo** (left) BA's most important plaza
- **Av de Mayo** Large avenue that goes east–west from Plaza del Congreso to Plaza de Mayo
- **25 de Mayo** Street that goes north–south from Retiro to Plaza de Mayo (Mayo is not short for mayonnaise; it's Spanish for the month of May.)
- **Diagonal Roque Sáenz Peña** Diagonal street that stretches from Plaza de Mayo to the Obelisco
- **Luis Sáenz Peña** Street that goes from Plaza del Congreso through Constitución
- **Rodriguez Peña** Street that goes from Recoleta to Plaza del Congreso

## BASÍLICA DE SANTO DOMINGO
Map pp222-4

Farther south, at Defensa and Belgrano, the 18th-century Basílica de Santo Domingo prominently marks the approach into San Telmo. This Dominican church (also known as the Basílica de Nuestra Señora del Rosario) has a long and colorful history. On its left tower you'll see the replicated scars of shrapnel launched against the British troops who holed up here during the invasion of 1806. The **Museo de la Basílica del Rosario** (☎ 4331-1668; US$0.75; ☯ by appointment only) displays the flags that were captured from the British. Secularized during the presidency of Bernardino Rivadavia (1826–27), the building became a natural history museum, its original single tower serving as an astronomical observatory, until Governor Juan Manuel de Rosas restored it to the Dominican order. The building was gutted by fire during the 1955 Revolución Libertadora, which sent Juan Perón into exile.

## CASA ROSADA  Map pp222-4

Taking up the whole east side of the Plaza de Mayo is the unmistakeable pink facade of the **Casa Rosada** (Pink House), the presidential palace that was begun during the presidency of Domingo F Sarmiento. It now occupies a site where colonial riverbank fortifications once stood; today, after repeated landfills, it stands more than 1km inland. The offices of top dog Néstor Kirchner are here, but the presidential residence is in the calm suburbs of Olivos, north of the center.

The side of the palace that faces Plaza de Mayo is the back of the building. It's from these balconies that Juan and Eva Perón, General Leopoldo Galtieri, Raúl Alfonsín and other politicians have sermoned throngs of impassioned Argentines when they felt it necessary to demonstrate public support. Madonna also crooned from here for her movie *Evita* (though many Argentines resented her being cast in the role of such a revered figure).

The salmon pink color of the Casa Rosada, which positively glows at sunset, is thought to come from President Sarmiento's attempt at making peace during his 1868–74 term (by blending the red of the Federalists with the white of the Unitarists). Another theory, however, is that the color comes from painting

53

the palace with bovine blood, which was a common practice back in the late 19th century. During the Menem years another coat was painted on the front of the building, but funds ran out and today it remains a two-toned symbol of Argentina's volatile economy.

Underneath the Casa Rosada, excavations have unearthed remains of the Fuerte Viejo, a ruin dating from the 18th century. You can see the basement arcades, along with a few seemingly incongruous horse carriages, at the **Museo de la Casa Rosada** ( ☎ 4344-3802; Hipólito Yrigoyen 219; admission free; ⏰ 10am-6pm Mon-Fri, 2-6pm Sun, tours 3pm & 4:30pm Sun). This modest museum also displays Perón memorabilia and presidential canes, along with a chronology of Argentine presidents that stops at 1973 – perhaps because events since then are too contemporarily painful. You'll need photo ID to get past the guards and metal detector.

Off-limits during the military dictatorship of 1976–83, the Casa Rosada is now reasonably accessible to the public. Free guided tours take place at 4pm Monday to Friday (tours in English are only given Friday at 4pm). Make reservations at the museum earlier that day or show up at least one hour in advance; in either case bring photo ID.

In 1955, naval aircraft strafed the Casa Rosada and other nearby buildings during the Revolución Libertadora, which toppled Juan Perón's regime. On the north side of the appropriately bureaucratic **Ministerio de Economía**, an inconspicuous **plaque** commemorates the attacks (look for the bullet holes to the left of the doors). The inscription translates as, 'The scars on this marble were the harvest of confrontation and intolerance. Their imprint on our memory will help the nation achieve a future of greatness.'

Towering above the Casa Rosada, just south of Parque Colón on Av Colón, is the army headquarters at the **Edificio Libertador**, the real locus of Argentine political power for many decades. It was built by military engineers inspired by the Beaux Arts Correo Central. A twin building planned for the navy never got off the ground.

## CATEDRAL METROPOLITANA
Map pp222-4
☎ 4331-2845; Plaza de Mayo; admission free;
⏰ 8am-7pm Mon-Fri, 9am-7:30pm Sat & Sun

This solemn cathedral was built on the site of the original colonial church and not finished until 1827. It's a significant religious and architectural landmark, and carved above its triangular facade and neoclassical columns are bas-reliefs of Jacob and Joseph. The spacious interior is equally impressive, with Baroque details and an elegant rococo altar.

More importantly, however, the cathedral is a national historical site that contains the tomb of General José de San Martín, Argentina's most revered hero. In the chaos following independence, San Martín chose exile in France, never returning alive to Argentina (although in 1829 a boat on which he traveled sighted Buenos Aires on its way to Montevideo). Outside the cathedral you'll see a flame keeping his spirit alive.

In 1878, under President Nicolás Avellaneda, artisans began two years of work on the tomb, which was designed and executed by French sculptor Albert-Ernest Carrier-Belleuse. In 1998 the Dirección Nacional de Arquitectura spent approximately US$100,000 to rehabilitate the humidity-damaged tomb.

Tours of the church are at 11:30am Monday to Friday; tours of the crypt are at 1:15pm Monday to Friday, and tours of both are given at 4pm daily. All tours are in Spanish. Occasional free choir concerts are also on the docket.

## MANZANA DE LAS LUCES Map pp222-4

The Manzana de las Luces (Block of Enlightenment) includes the city's oldest church, the Jesuit **Iglesia San Ignacio**. In colonial times, this block was Buenos Aires' center of learning and, to some degree, it still symbolizes high culture in the capital. The first to occupy the Manzana de las Luces were the Jesuits, and on the north side of the block remain two of the five original buildings of the Jesuit **Procuraduría**. Dating from 1730, these buildings include defensive tunnels discovered in 1912. Since independence in 1810, this site has been occupied by the Universidad de Buenos Aires. (Note the designation 'Universidad' on the facade, which extended across the entire block until remodeling in 1894.)

After a demolition in 1904, there remains only a single original cloister of the Iglesia San Ignacio. It shares a wall with the **Colegio Nacional de Buenos Aires** (1908), where generations of the Argentine elite have sent their children to receive secondary schooling.

Tours in Spanish (US$1; 3pm on weekdays; 3pm, 4:30pm and 6pm on weekends) provide the only regular public access to the block's interior, where there is a small theater reconstruction of Buenos Aires' first legislature, the Sala de Representantes. Buy tickets at the **Comisión Nacional de la Manzana de las Luces** ( ☎ 4331-9534; Perú 272). Workshops, cinema, theater and even a small market take place on the premises.

## MUSEO DE LA CIUDAD Map pp222-4

☎ 4331-9855; Adolfo Alsina 412; locals/foreigners US$0.35/1, free Wed; ⏰ 11am-7pm Mon-Fri, 3-7pm Sat & Sun

Wander among the permanent and temporary exhibitions on porteño life and history, including historical photographs, old furniture and toys, and a research library. Salvaged doors, building motifs and ancient hardware are also on display, especially downstairs and next door at the museum's annex. Nearby, at the corner of Alsina and Defensa, is the **Farmacia de la Estrella**, a functioning homeopathic pharmacy with gorgeous woodwork and elaborate late-19th-century ceiling murals depicting health-oriented themes.

## MUSEO DEL CABILDO Map pp222-4

☎ 4342-6729; Bolívar 65; US$0.35, free Fri; ⏰ 10:30am-5pm Tue-Fri, 11:30am-6pm Sun & holiday, tours in Spanish 4pm

Modern construction (including the building of Av de Mayo) has twice truncated the mid-18th-century Cabildo (town council; 1765), but still standing is a representative sample of the *recova* (colonnade) that once ran across the Plaza de Mayo. The two-story building, now a museum, is more intriguing than the scanty exhibits it holds, which include mementos of the early 19th-century British invasions, some modern paintings in colonial- and early independence-era styles and temporary exhibits. The interior patio is home to a small crafts fair on Thursday and Friday from 11am to 6pm.

## MUSEO ETNOGRÁFICO JUAN B AMBROSETTI Map pp222-4

☎ 4331-7788; Moreno 350; US$0.35; ⏰ 3-7pm Wed-Sun

This small but attractive anthropological museum was created by Juan B Ambrosetti not only as an institute for research and university training, but as an educational center for the public. On display are archaeological and anthropological collections from the Andean Northwest and Patagonia, with a sample of materials from elsewhere in South America. Beautiful indigenous artifacts, including intricate jewelry and Mapuche ponchos are presented, while an African and Asian room showcases some priceless pieces. Guided tours are given on weekends from 3pm to 5pm.

# PUERTO MADERO

The newest and least conventional of the capital's 48 official barrios is Puerto Madero, located east of the Microcentro and Plaza de Mayo. It's a wonderful place to stroll, boasting cobbled paths and a long line of attractive brick warehouses that have been converted into ritzy new lofts, business offices and upscale restaurants (big target destinations for power lunches). There's an unusual museum in the form of the **Museo Fragata Sarmiento** (p56), a former naval ship that mostly served as a training ground for Argentina's navy. It floats in one of Puerto Madero's four *diques* (dikes), which are lined up end to end and stretch from Retiro to San Telmo. Another museum nearby is the **Museo de la Inmigración** (p56), which details the experiences of Argentina's early European immigrants.

Unique structures have also found a home in this neighborhood; check out the attention-grabbing **Opera Bay** building at the north end of Dique 4; it was modeled after Sydney's Opera House and now holds a trendy nightclub (p127). And spanning Dique 3 is the distinctive **Puente de la Mujer**, a beautifully modern bridge that resembles a sharp fishhook or even a harp, but is supposed to represent a couple dancing the tango. Designed by Spaniard Santiago Calatrava and mostly built in Spain, this 160m-long pedestrian span cost US$6 million and rotates 90° to allow water traffic to pass (when it's functioning, that is).

*Opera Bay (p127), Puerto Madero*

The city's waterfront has been the object of controversy since the mid-19th century, when competing commercial interests began to fight over the location of a modernized port for Argentina's burgeoning international commerce. Two ideas came to light. One was to widen and deepen the channel of the Riachuelo to port facilities at La Boca, which indeed happened as planned. The other was proposed by Eduardo Madero, a wealthy exporter with strong political ties and solid financial backing. Madero proposed transforming the city's mudflats into a series of modern basins and harbors consistent with the aspirations and ambitions of a cosmopolitan elite. This also occurred, but not quite as he had planned.

By the time of its final completion in 1898 (four years after Madero's death), Puerto Madero had exceeded its budget and Madero himself had come under scrutiny. Suspicions arose from Madero's attempts to buy up all the landfill in the area and from his links to politicians who had acquired nearby lands likely to increase in value. And the practical side of the scheme didn't go so well either. By 1910, the amount of cargo was already too great for the new port, and poor access to the rail terminus at Plaza Once made things even worse. New facilities in a rejuvenated La Boca partly assuaged these problems, but congressional actions failed to solve the major issues until the 1926 completion of Retiro's Puerto Nuevo.

Today you'll find some of the most expensive real estate in Buenos Aires in Puerto Madero, and many of the buildings envisioned by planners are still works in progress. On the east side of the dikes, a slew of five-star hotels like the Hilton, the Four Seasons and – the newest and fanciest of the lot – the Philip Starck–designed **Faena Hotel & Universe** (p156) have already planted roots and invested millions. There are future plans to construct more high-rises and apartment buildings, and the **Museo Fortabat** – a museum designed by Rafael Viñoly and housing the collection of rich Argentine socialite Amalia Fortabat – is due to open soon (look for the works of Frida Kahlo and Jorge de la Vega inside). Ask at the Puerto Madero **tourist office** (p195) for the latest.

On the easternmost side of Puerto Madero – with the muddy waters of the Río de la Plata lapping at its sides – is the **Reserva Ecológica Costanera Sur** (below), a large marshy space full of reedy lagoons, wildlife and peaceful gravel paths. Come here when the air, noise and concrete of downtown Buenos Aires become too much to bear, and you need to see green. The reserve is a sharp contrast to the upscale lofts, restaurants and hotels nearby, and thankfully it's available to everyone for no cost at all.

## MUSEO DE LA INMIGRACIÓN

Map pp228-9

☎ 4317-0285; Av Antártida Argentina 1355; admission free; ◷ 10am-5pm Mon-Fri, 11am-6pm Sat & Sun
Housed in the historic Hotel de Inmigrantes, this museum tells the story of the thousands of European immigrants who began arriving in Buenos Aires in the late 1880s. Old photos, videos and memorabilia show how the settlers were treated, as well as the progress of their new lives.

## MUSEO FRAGATA SARMIENTO

Map pp222-4

☎ 4334-9386; Dique 3; US$0.75; ◷ 9am-6pm
Over 23,000 Argentine naval cadets and officers have trained aboard this 85m sailing vessel, which traveled around the world 40 times between 1899 and 1938. Built in Birkenhead, England, in 1897 at a cost of £125,000, this impeccably maintained ship never participated in combat. On board are detailed records of its lengthy voyages, a gallery of its

commanding officers, a poster for a 1945 film based on its history, plenty of nautical items including old uniforms, and even the stuffed remains of Lampazo (the ship's pet dog) in a serene pose. Peek into the ship's holds, galley and engine room and note the hooks where sleeping hammocks were strung up.

US president Theodore Roosevelt was a distinguished guest on board, but perhaps the greatest test of the ship's seaworthiness was the visit of Roosevelt's successor, William Howard Taft, who weighed more than 140kg and, no doubt, came to dine on board.

## RESERVA ECOLÓGICA COSTANERA SUR Map pp220-1

☎ 4315-1320; Av Tristán Achával Rodríguez 1550; ◷ 8am-7pm Nov-Mar, 8am-6pm Apr-Oct
During the military Proceso of 1976–83, access to the Buenos Aires waterfront was limited, as the area was diked and filled with sediments dredged from the Río de la Plata. While plans for a new satellite city across from the port

stalled, trees, grasses, birds and rodents took advantage and colonized this low-lying, 350-hectare area that so mimics the ecology of the Delta del Paraná.

In 1986, the area was declared an ecological reserve. Mysterious arson fires, thought to have been started by those with financial interests in the prime real estate, have occasionally been set. But permanent scars haven't remained – this beautifully lush marshy land survives hardily, and the reserve has become a popular site for weekend outings and hikes. It has also become something of a cruising area for the capital's gay residents, though on sunny weekends you'll generally see picnickers, cyclists and families out for a stroll. Bird-watchers will adore the 200-plus bird species that pause to rest here, and a few lucky folks might spot a river turtle or nutria (aquatic rodent).

# CONGRESO & AVENIDA CORRIENTES

*Eating p92; Drinking p119; Shopping p144; Sleeping p159*

Congreso is an interesting neighborhood mix of old-time cinemas, theaters and bustling commerce tinged with a hard-core political flavor. The buildings still hold a European aura, but there's more grittiness here than in the Microcentro – it's more local-city feel and worn-out atmosphere – and it lacks the well-dressed crowds. It's also a great place to wander around and explore.

Separating Congreso from the Microcentro is Av 9 de Julio, 'the widest street in the world!' as proud porteños love to boast. This may be true, as it's 16 lanes at its widest; nearby side streets Cerrito and Pellegrini make it look even broader. Fortunately traffic islands provide raised breaks for the thousands of pedestrians who cross this monstrosity every day, but it's still an intimidating walk (and can't be done in one green light without running – try it!). At Avs 9 de Julio and Corrientes lies the city's famous **Obelisco**, which soars above the oval Plaza de la República. Dedicated in 1936, on the 400th anniversary of the first Spanish settlement on the Río de la Plata, the stately Obelisco symbolizes Buenos Aires much as the Eiffel Tower represents Paris or the Washington Monument does Washington, DC. Following major soccer victories, boisterous fans circle this landmark in jubilant, honking celebration.

Just a couple of blocks to the northwest of the Obelisco is Plaza Lavalle and the austere neoclassical **Escuela Presidente Roca** (1902). Across the way lies the French-style **Palacio de Justicia** (1904; Talcahuano 550), and its Tribunales (federal courts). The landmark **Teatro Colón** also stands nearby and adds its own elegance to the area. At the northeast end of Plaza Lavalle, Jewish symbols adorn the facade of the **Templo de la Congregación Israelita**, Argentina's largest synagogue. Concrete sidewalk planters, constructed after recent attacks against Jewish targets, discourage potential car bombs, and police stand guard nearby. The **Museo Judío Dr Salvador Kibrick** ( ☎ 4372-2474, Libertad 769; US$2, bring ID; 4-6:30pm Tue & Thu) is alongside the synagogue and contains many items and exhibits related to Jewish history.

Six blocks west of Plaza Lavalle is the **Palacio de las Aguas Corrientes**, a wonderful Scandinavian-designed building covered in English bricks and enameled tiles. If you like unusual buildings it's worth a look; time your visit to catch the bizarre little museum inside.

Finally, head around seven blocks south of Plaza Lavalle to the **Palacio del Congreso**, together with its plaza and obligatory monument. This site is another locus for the nation's *piqueteros* and their many grievances. On the edge of the plaza is the funky **Museo Histórico de la Dirección Impositiva**.

## Orientation

Congreso lies west of Av 9 de Julio and is a short walk from the Microcentro. Av Corrientes is a major thoroughfare and the city's old theater district. Av Callao runs north to south and is also a big street; it crosses right in front of the Palacio del Congreso. All north–south street names change at Av Rivadavia.

## MUSEO Y ARCHIVO HISTÓRICO DE LA DIRECCIÓN GENERAL IMPOSITIVA
Map pp226-7

☎ 4384-0282, 5th fl, Av de Mayo 1317; admission free; ⏰ 11am-5pm Mon-Fri

This strangely located museum deals with the history of taxation (or perhaps more accurately, tax evasion), an always-interesting theme in Argentina. You'll find false tax certificates and one of the world's first photocopy machines which dates from the 1970s. The museum is in the former (decaying) Hotel Majestic, a landmark in its own right. Hours can be sporadic.

## PALACIO DE LAS AGUAS CORRIENTES
Map pp226-7

cnr Avs Córdoba & Riobamba

Swedish engineer Karl Nyströmer and Norwegian architect Olaf Boye helped create this stunning and eclectic waterworks building. Popularly known as Obras Sanitarias, it dates from 1894 and occupies an entire city block. Topped by French-style mansard roofs, the building's facade consists of 170,000 glazed tiles and 130,000 enameled bricks from England.

On the building's 1st floor is the small but interesting **Museo del Patrimonio Aguas Argentinas** ( ☎ 6319-1104; museo_patrimonio@aguasarg entinas.com.ar; admission free; ⏰ 9am-1pm Mon-Fri). The collection of pretty tiles, faucets, handles, ceramic pipe joints from England and even old toilets and bidets is well lit and

## Transportation

**Bus** Bus No 150 from Retiro; or take the No 24 from the Microcentro
**Subte** Líneas A and B from the Microcentro

displayed. Guided visits in Spanish are given on Mondays, Wednesdays and Fridays at 11am; you'll need to show photo ID. Enter on the Riobamba side of the building.

## PLAZA DEL CONGRESO Map pp226-7

Down in the Congreso area, at the west end of Av de Mayo, is the Plaza del Congreso, often full of cooing pigeons and the families feeding them. The **Monumento a los Dos Congresos** honors the congresses of 1810 in Buenos Aires and 1816 in Tucumán, both of which led to Argentine independence. The enormous granite steps symbolize the high Andes, and the fountain at its base represents the Atlantic Ocean.

Across Av Callao from the plaza is the colossal green-domed **Palacio del Congreso**. Costing more than twice its original budget, the Congreso set a precedent for contemporary Argentine public works projects. Modeled on the Capitol in Washington, DC, and topped by an 85m dome, the palace was completed in 1906. It faces the Plaza del Congreso.

Free guided tours of the **Senado** (Senate; ☎ 4010-3000 extension 3885) are available

*Palacio del Congreso (above), Congreso*

on weekdays at 11am (in English, Spanish and French), 4pm (in English) and 5pm & 6pm (in Spanish); go to the entrance at Hipólito Irigoyen 1849.

### TEATRO COLÓN Map pp226-7
☎ 4378-7132 for tours, 4378-7344 for shows; www.teatrocolon.org.ar in Spanish; Libertad 621; tours US$2.50; ☽ tours in English 11am, 1pm & 3pm

Buenos Aires' major landmark and source of pride is the gorgeous and imposing seven-story Teatro Colón, a world-class facility for opera, ballet and classical music. The Colón is the city's main performing-arts venue and the only facility of its kind in the country. It was the southern hemisphere's largest theater until the Sydney Opera House was built in 1973. It occupies an entire city block, seats 2500 spectators and provides standing room for another 500. Opening night was in 1908 with a presentation of Verdi's *Aïda*, and visitors have been wowed ever since. Even through times of economic hardship, the elaborate

Colón remains a high national priority; a major facelift is planned for the years ahead. Presidential command performances sometimes occur on the winter patriotic holidays of May 25 and July 9.

Excellent guided visits provide a very worthwhile, behind-the-scenes peek into the workings of the Colón. Tours are available in many languages (call ahead), but only Spanish and English tours have regular schedules. On these tours, visitors see the theater from the basement workshops (which employ over 400 skilled carpenters, sculptors, wig makers, costume designers and other *técnicos*) to the rehearsal rooms and the stage and seating areas. Note especially the *maquetas* (scale models) used by the sculptors to help prepare the massive stage sets. The enormous pillars, statues and other props consist of painted lightweight Styrofoam. The main entrance is on Libertad, opposite Plaza Lavalle, but tours enter from the Viamonte side. It's a good idea to reserve one day in advance.

# SAN TELMO

*Eating p93; Drinking p114; Shopping p144; Sleeping p161*

Full of charm and personality, San Telmo is one of Buenos Aires' most attractive and historically rich barrios. Despite the fact that it's only a quick walk south of Plaza de Mayo, the area remains mostly as it was 100 years ago. Narrow cobbled streets and low-story colonial housing retain an old-time feel, though the tourist dollar is bringing about a few changes. The *municipalidad* continues to spruce up the area bounded

by Defensa and Av Independencia, Paseo Colón and Av San Juan. Improvements have included widening sidewalks for cafés and street fairs, planting trees, installing traditional street lamps and repairing the cobbled roadways. The idea is to encourage tourist activities beyond the usual Sunday visit to Plaza Dorrego or night-time excursion to the barrio's tango bars, and it seems to be working. Some porteños think San Telmo might become the next Palermo Viejo (p72).

Historically, San Telmo is famous for the violent street fighting that took place when British troops, at war with Spain, invaded the city in 1806 and occupied it until the following year, when covert porteño resistance became open counterattack. British forces advanced up narrow Defensa, but the impromptu militia drove the British back to their ships; women and slaves helped by pouring cauldrons of boiling oil and water from the rooftops and firing cannons from the balconies of the house at **Defensa 372**, which is now the Museo Nacional del Grabado. Victory gave porteños confidence in their ability to stand apart from Spain, even though the city's independence had to wait another three years.

After a yellow-fever epidemic hit the once-fashionable San Telmo area in the late 19th century, the porteño elite evacuated to higher ground west and north of the present-day Microcentro (such as Recoleta). As European immigrants began to

### Transportation

**Bus** Bus No 29 goes down Bolívar from the Microcentro; Nos 64, 86 and 152 take Av Paseo Colón instead, on the eastern edge of San Telmo

**Subte** Línea C goes down the western edge of San Telmo

pour into the city, many older mansions in San Telmo became *conventillos* (tenements) to house poor families. One such *conventillo* was the **Pasaje de la Defensa** (Defensa 1179), originally built for the Ezeiza family in 1880; it later housed 32 families. These days, it's a charmingly worn building with antique shops clustered around atmospheric leafy patios. Other *conventillos* have more recently attracted artists, bohemians and expatriates looking for large spaces at low rents.

The heart of San Telmo is **Plaza Dorrego** (Defensa & Humberto Primo), which hosts its famous and extremely popular Sunday flea market, the **Feria de San Telmo** (p151). Side streets are closed to traffic, and the plaza itself is filled with dozens of booths selling antiques and old collectibles. Street performers, ranging from a one-woman band and metallic human statues to professional tango performers, entertain the crowds. The market has gotten so well attended that it now stretches down Defensa all the way to **Parque Lezama**, which has its own weekend crafts fair/flea market – though it's much less crowded than Dorrego's. Across Av Brasil from the park is the striking late-19th-century Russian Orthodox church **Iglesia Ortodoxa Rusa**, the work of architect Alejandro Christopherson and built from materials shipped over from St Petersburg. It was inaugurated in 1904 and sports blue Muscovite domes that are wonderfully onion-shaped.

To the north, on the more industrial Av Paseo Colón, the oval **Plazoleta Olazábal** features Rogelio Yrurtia's masterful sculpture *Canto al Trabajo* (moved here from its original site on Plaza Dorrego). Across the *plazoleta*, the neoclassical and seriously ugly **Facultad de Ingeniería** of the Universidad de Buenos Aires (originally built for the Fundación Eva Perón) is an oddball landmark once described by Gerald Durrell as 'a cross between the Parthenon and the Reichstag.' One block southwest, a different sort of architectural oddity is the brick **Iglesia Dinamarquesa** (Carlos Calvo 257), a neo-Gothic Lutheran church dating from 1930 and designed using blueprints from Danish architects Rönnow and Bisgaard. Two blocks to the west, the **Mercado San Telmo** (1897) is mostly an antique market harboring a mishmash of knickknacks, collectibles and rubbish. A small section is still a fruit and vegetable market, and the whole thing takes up the interior of a city block, though you wouldn't be able to tell just by looking at the modest sidewalk entrances.

The neocolonial and Baroque **Iglesia Nuestra Señora de Belén** (Humberto Primo 340) was a Jesuit school until 1767, when the Bethlemite order took it over. The complete construction of the building spanned the 1730s to early 1900s and involved at least five architects.

## Orientation

San Telmo is barely south of the center (but that's enough to make it officially blue-collar in Buenos Aires). The two main veins in this barrio are Balcarce and Defensa; they're where you'll find most things of interest to tourists. To the east of Balcarce the streets become industrial and deserted at night, and, along with the more southern edges toward La Boca, should probably be avoided. During the day they're fine, however, and way over to the east is one end of Puerto Madero – an upscale area that's easily walkable from San Telmo.

*Yrurtia's* Canto al Trabajo *(above)*

## MUSEO DE ARTE MODERNO Map p225

☎ 4361-1121; Av San Juan 350; locals/foreigners US$0.35/1, free Wed; ☾ 10am-8pm Tue-Fri, 11am-8pm Sat & Sun

Housed in a recycled tobacco warehouse, the Museo de Arte Moderno is a roomy, brightly lit and simple space exhibiting the works of contemporary Argentine artists, as well as special rotating exhibitions and video events. Only hard-core modern art lovers need visit.

## MUSEO DEL CINE PABLO DUCRÓS HICKEN Map p225

☎ 4361-2462; Defensa 1220; locals/foreigners US$0.35/1, free Wed; ☾ 11am-7pm Tue-Fri, 11:30am-6:30pm Sat & Sun

Hardly worth the price of admission, this scanty cinema museum displays a few old movie photos and posters, along with some cinematic memorabilia. It does screen the occasional Argentine film in its small video room, however. A research library on the premises contains a collection of 12,000 *sucesos argentinos* (newsreels) and 8000 Argentine movies.

## MUSEO DEL TRAJE Map p225

☎ 4343-8427; Chile 832; admission free; ☾ 3-7pm Tue-Sat)

Near the Microcentro border, this small clothing museum is always changing its wardrobe. You can hit upon civilian and military clothing from colonial times to the present, '60s vintage hippie wear (sorry – dressing rooms not available), or early 1900s party and Sunday-drive dresses. If you're lucky, accessories such as hair combs, top hats, antique eyeglasses and elegant canes might be on display. Come by and see what hot fashions the dummies are wearing when you're in town.

## MUSEO HISTÓRICO NACIONAL Map p225

☎ 4307-1182; Defensa 1600; US$0.75; ☾ 11am-5pm Tue-Fri, 11am-7pm Sun

Located at the supposed site of Pedro de Mendoza's original foundation of the city in 1536 is this sizable national historical museum. Inside, a panorama of display rooms full of artifacts, paintings, weapons and period furniture relives the Argentine experience, from its shaky beginnings and independence to the present. The Sala de la Conquista has pictures depicting the Spanish domination of wealthy, civilized Peru and Columbus' triumphant return to Spain, which contrast sharply with paintings of the Mendoza expedition's struggle on the shores of the Río de la Plata.

## Top Five Quirky Museums

- **Museo del Patrimonio Aguas Argentinas** (p58) Tiny but unusual collection of fancy plumbing, toilets and bidets; inside the waterworks building, which definitely is worth a close-up look also
- **Museo Evita** (p72) Museum of Argentina's number-one diva, with well-displayed memorabilia that includes the fashions she wore during important functions and even her perfumes
- **Museo de la Pasión Boquense** (p63) Best for soccer fans, with lots of video screens showing off past goals for the Boca Juniors and a Diego tribute; tours of La Bombonera stadium are available
- **Museo de la Policía Federal** (p52) Typical police paraphernalia, like old uniforms, weapons, a stuffed police dog, cockfighting panorama and, best of all, forensic photos
- **Museo del Traje** (left) Clothing is the theme here, but you don't know what you'll get – exhibits are ever changing, and we've witnessed everything from military and vintage to formal dress

The museum has portraits of major figures of the independence and republican periods, such as Simón Bolívar and his ally and rival José de San Martín, the latter shown both in his youth and in disillusioned old age (San Martín's bedroom has also been reconstructed here). Juan Manuel de Rosas and his bitter but eloquent enemy Domingo Sarmiento are represented as well, the latter with his trademark perpetual scowl.

In addition, there are portrayals of the British invasions of 1806 and 1807, along with period knickknacks from late-19th-century porteño life. A small indigenous collection and Jesuit artifacts are also showcased. Tours in Spanish are given on Sundays at 2pm; opening times may vary throughout the year, so call ahead.

## MUSEO PENITENCIARIO Map p225

☎ 4362-0099; Humberto Primo 378; US$0.35; ☾ 2-5pm Tue & Fri, noon-7pm Sat & Sun

Dating from 1760, this building was a convent and later a women's prison before it became a penal museum. The most thought-provoking exhibits are a photograph of the famous anarchist Simón Radowitzky's release from prison in Ushuaia, in Tierra del Fuego, and a wooden desk carved by inmates at Ushuaia for president Roberto M Ortiz. Reconstructed old jail cells give an idea of the prisoners' conditions. Opening hours can be erratic.

# LA BOCA

*Eating p94*

Eating p94

Blue-collar and raffish to the core, La Boca is very much a locals' neighborhood – and whether it likes it or not, is often portrayed as a symbol of Buenos Aires. In the mid-19th century, La Boca became home to Spanish and Italian immigrants who settled along the Riachuelo – the sinuous river that divides the city from the surrounding province of Buenos Aires. Many of them came during the booming 1880s and ended up working in the numerous meat-packing plants and warehouses here, processing and shipping out much of Argentina's vital beef. After sprucing up the barges, the port dwellers splashed leftover paint on the corrugated-metal siding of their own houses – unwittingly giving La Boca what would become one of its main claims to fame. And while much of the barrio's color comes from its bright buildings, some of it is also in the river itself: industrial wastes and petroleum have taken their toll over the years, and today the abandoned port's waters are trapped under a thick layer of rainbow sludge. Rusting hulks of sunken ships can also be seen offshore, keeping La Boca's history very much in the present.

**La Boca Warning**

La Boca is not the kind of neighborhood for casual strolls – it can be downright rough in spots. Don't stray from the riverside walk or the tourist sections of El Caminito, Del Valle Iberlucea and Magallanes, especially if you're alone or toting expensive cameras. There's nothing you'd really want to see outside these areas anyway.

**El Caminito** is the barrio's most famous street and the target tourist destination here. Named after a tango song, this short alleyway offers a colorful panorama that has sprung a million photographs. Busloads of camera-laden tourists often crowd the lively surrounding streets, especially on weekends, when a small crafts fair sets up near the river. Buskers and tango dancers perform for spare change, and you can get your photo taken with them or behind fun cardboard cut-outs. Nearby, the **Museo de Bellas Artes de La Boca** displays a permanent collection of the late local painter Benito Quinquela Martín, along with other Argentine artists. Over by the river, a pedestrian walkway gives you a close-up sniff of the Riachuelo.

The symbol of the community's solidarity is the Boca Juniors soccer team, the former club of disgraced superstar Diego Maradona. The team plays at **La Bombonera** stadium, which is just four blocks inland and contains a museum detailing the team's successes, among other things.

On the way into La Boca, note the **Casa Amarilla**, which is found in the 400s along Av Almirante Brown. This is a replica of the country house belonging to Almirante Brown, the Irish founder of the Argentine navy. Three blocks farther on (look to your left at the kink in the road), you'll notice the curious Gothic structure called **Torre Fantasma** (Ghost Tower). As you reach the Riachuelo, you can alight from the bus and walk the last few hundred meters. Get a good look at the **Puente Nicolás Avellaneda**, which spans the Riachuelo, linking La Boca to the industrial suburb of Avellaneda; before the bridge's completion in 1940, floods had washed away several others. From here follow the riverside walkway all the way to El Caminito.

## Orientation

La Boca sits at the southern end of downtown, just south of San Telmo. The main avenue, Av Almirante Brown, runs down the middle of the neighborhood and to the river, where it turns west onto Av Don Pedro de Mendoza and passes by El Caminito. All buses stop here and then head back. La Bombonera stadium is four blocks north of the river, up Del Valle Iberlucea.

### FUNDACIÓN PROA

☎ 4303-0909; www.proa.org; Av Don Pedro de Mendoza 1929; US$1; 🕑 11am-7pm Tue-Sun
High ceilings, clean white walls and just four large halls do well in displaying all the changing exhibits that pass through this elegant art foundation. Only the most cutting-edge national and international artists are invited to show here. Stunning contemporary installations in woven textiles and nontraditional media like butcher paper help stir the BA art scene; video rooms have modern offerings as well. The rooftop terrace is open for drinks and snacks, and boasts a expansive view of the Riachuelo. Guided tours are available in English or Spanish, so call ahead.

## MUSEO DE BELLAS ARTES DE LA BOCA

☎ 4301-1080; Av Don Pedro de Mendoza 1835; US$0.35; ⏰ 10am-5:30pm Tue-Fri, 11am-6pm Sat & Sun

Once the home and studio of Benito Quinquela Martín (1890–1977), La Boca's fine-arts museum exhibits his works and those of more contemporary Argentine artists. Most exhibits change monthly but always offer good and well-displayed collections in spacious halls.

In keeping with the museum's maritime theme is the small but excellent permanent collection of painted wood bowsprits, which are the poles projecting forward at the front of ships. There are also outdoor sculptures on the rooftop terrace, which has awesome views of the port. The top floor displays Martín's surrealist paintings, whose broad, rough brushstrokes and dark yet bright colors use the port, silhouettes of laboring men, smokestacks and water reflections as recurring themes.

The museum is marked 'Museo Quinquela Martín' and it may close in January for maintenance, so call ahead.

## MUSEO DE LA PASIÓN BOQUENSE

☎ 4362-1100; www.museoboquense.com; Brandsen 805; with/without ISIC card US$2/$3; ⏰ 10am-7pm, to 8pm in summer

High-tech and spiffy, this funky *fútbol* museum chronicles the rough-and-tumble neighborhood, La Bombonera stadium, some soccer

## Transportation

**Bus** Bus Nos 29, 64, 86 and 152 from the center all end up at El Caminito

idols' histories, past highlights on many TV videos, the championships, the trophies and, of course, the gooooals. There's a 360° theater in a giant soccer-ball auditorium, an old jersey collection and a fully stocked gift shop. Stadium tours are available for US$3; a museum ticket with a stadium tour is US$4.50. The museum is right under the stadium, a couple blocks from the tourist part of El Caminito.

## MUSEO HISTÓRICO DE CERA

☎ 4301-1497; www.museodecera.com.ar in Spanish; Del Valle Iberlucea 1261; locals/foreigners US$1.25/2; ⏰ 10am-6pm Mon-Fri, 11am-8pm Sat & Sun

Wax reconstructions of historical figureheads (literally) and dioramas of scenes in Argentine history are the specialty of this small and very tacky private institution. Among the historical Argentine personages depicted are Juan de Solís, Guillermo Brown, Mendoza, Garay and Rosas. Indigenous leaders such as Calfucurá, Catriel and Namuncurá are also immortalized. Stuffed snakes, along with creepy and gross wax limbs depicting bite wounds, are barely worth the price of admission.

# RETIRO

*Eating p95; Drinking p120 and p115; Shopping p145; Sleeping p162*

Well located and exclusive, Retiro is one of the ritziest neighborhoods in Buenos Aires – but it hasn't always been this way. The area was the site of a monastery during the 17th century, and later became the country retreat *(retiro)* of Agustín de Robles, a Spanish governor. Since then, Retiro's current **Plaza San Martín** – which sits on a bluff – has played

host to a slave market, military fort and even a bullring. Things are much quieter and more exclusive these days.

French landscape architect Carlos Thays designed the foresty Plaza San Martín, whose prominent monument is the obligatory equestrian statue of José de San Martín. Important visiting dignitaries often come to honor the country's liberator by leaving wreaths at its base. On the downhill side of the park you'll see the **Monumento a los Caídos de Malvinas**, a memorial to the young men who died in the Falklands War.

Surrounding the plaza are several landmark public buildings, such as the **Palacio San Martín**, an art nouveau mansion originally built for the elite Anchorena family but later became the headquarters of the Foreign Ministry; today it's used for official purposes. The impressive **Círculo Militar** (Palacio Paz; ☎ 4311-1071 for tours; www.circulomilitar.org in Spanish), built in 1909 for *La Prensa* founder Jose C Paz, was the largest private residence in Argentina at 12,000 sq meters. Now military property, it houses the **Museo de Armas** (Weapons Museum; p64).

*Edificio Kavanagh (right)*

On an odd triangular block at the corner of Avs Florida and Santa Fe, the neo-Gothic **Palacio Haedo** (Av Santa Fe 690) was the mansion of the Haedo family at the turn of the 19th century, but now houses the country's national park service. Nearby is a private apartment building, which author **Jorge Luis Borges' last residence** (Maipú 994); look for a plaque on the wall. One landmark you can't miss is the 120m **Edificio Kavanagh** (1935; Av Florida 1035), an Art Deco monstrosity that at the time of its construction was the tallest concrete structure in the world. Close by is the **Basílica de Santísimo Sacramento** (1916; Plaza San Martín 1039), a French-style church built by the Anchorena family.

The 76m **Torre de los Ingleses**, across Av del Libertador from Plaza San Martín, was a donation by the city's British community in 1916. During the Falklands War of 1982, the tower was the target of bombs; since then, the name of the plaza in which it stands has changed from Plaza Británica to **Plaza Fuerza Aérea Argentina** (Argentine Air Force Plaza). Opposite the plaza is the **Estación Retiro** (Retiro train station), built in 1915 when the British controlled the country's railroads. While much of Retiro is a chic, upper-class area, the part beyond the Retiro bus station has long been a shantytown and not a place in which to go exploring.

Toward Retiro's north is the luxurious **Museo de Arte Hispanoamericano Isaac Fernández Blanco** (opposite), whose leafy garden makes a welcome break from the bustle of Retiro. And on the other side of Av 9 de Julio is the remarkable **Teatro Cervantes** (opposite), which boasts Spanish architecture and a small theatrical museum. Across the street is Plaza Lavalle and other sights; see the Congreso neighborhood (p57) for details.

## Orientation

Retiro is just north of the Microcentro and east of Recoleta; most of the area is compact and easily seen on foot. Major transport hubs include the train and bus stations, and important thoroughfares are Avs del Libertador, Santa Fe and Córdoba.

### PALACIO SAN MARTÍN Map pp228-9
☎ 4819-8092; Arenales 761; ☺ tours 11am Thu, 3pm, 4pm & 5pm Fri
Built in 1912 for the powerful Anchorena family, this impressive mansion is actually three independent buildings around a stone courtyard. It was designed by architect Alejandro

Christophersen and sports marble staircases, grandiose dining rooms and a garden containing a chunk of the Berlin Wall. A small but good museum displays pre-Columbian artifacts from the northwest, along with some paintings by Latin American artists.

### MUSEO DE ARMAS Map pp228-9
☎ 4311-1071; Av Santa Fe 702; US$0.75; ☺ noon-7pm Mon-Fri
Unless you've spent time in the armed forces or George W Bush's imagination, you'll never have seen so many weapons of mass destruction. This maze-like museum exhibits a frighteningly large but excellent collection of bazookas, grenade

launchers, cannons, machine guns, muskets, pistols, armor, lances and swords; even the gas mask for a combat horse is on display. The evolution of rifles and handguns is especially thoroughly documented, and there's a small but impressive Japanese weapons room. The whole collection is very extensive, impressive, clean and well labeled, and may make you feel like blowing something up. Call for guided visits.

## MUSEO MUNICIPAL DE ARTE HISPANOAMERICANO ISAAC FERNÁNDEZ BLANCO Map pp228-9

☎ 4327-0228; Suipacha 1422; locals/foreigners US$0.35/1; ☼ 2-7pm Tue-Sun

Dating from 1921, this museum is in an old mansion of the neocolonial Peruvian style that developed as a reaction against French influences in turn-of-the-19th-century Argentine architecture. Its exceptional collection of colonial art includes silverwork from Alto Perú (present-day Bolivia), oils with religious themes, Jesuit statuary, costumes, furniture, colonial silverware and antiques. There's little effort to place items in any historical context, but everything is in great condition and well lit, and the curved ceiling on the 1st floor is beautifully painted. The museum sits in attractively landscaped grounds that offer sanctuary from the bustling city.

Also known as the Palacio Noel, after the designing architect, the museum building and its collections suffered damage (since repaired) from the 1992 bombing of the Israeli embassy, which at the time was located at Arroyo and Suipacha. The space where the embassy was located has since become a small park.

## MUSEO NACIONAL DEL TEATRO

Map pp228-9

☎ 4815-8883 ext 156; Av Córdoba 1099; admission free; ☼ 10am-6pm Mon-Fri

Inside the Teatro Cervantes (enter via the corner door) is the tiny Museo Nacional del Teatro (National Theater Museum). Exhibits trace Argentine theater from its colonial beginnings. They stress the 19th-century contributions of the Podestá family, Italian immigrants who popularized the *gauchesca* drama *Juan Moreira*. Items include a gaucho suit worn by Gardel in his Hollywood film *El día que me quieras* and the *bandoneón* belonging to Paquita Bernarda, the first Argentine woman to play the accordionlike instrument (she died of tuberculosis in 1925 at the age of 25). There is also a photo gallery of famous Argentine stage actors.

## TEATRO NACIONAL CERVANTES

Map pp228-9

☎ 4816-4224; www.teatrocervantes.gov.ar in Spanish; Libertad 815; tours in Spanish 2pm Fri

Six blocks southwest of Plaza San Martín, you can't help but notice the lavishly ornamented Cervantes theater. This landmark building dates from 1921 and was built with private funds but acquired by the state after it went broke in 1926. Its facade was designed as a replica of Spain's Universidad de Alcalá de Henares. The building underwent remodeling after a fire in 1961.

From the grand tiled lobby to the main theater, with its plush red-velvet chairs, you'll smell the long history of this place. Some of it might be musty, however; the Cervantes is definitely showing its age, with worn carpeting and rough edges that cry out for a remodel. Enjoy the elegance – however faded – with a tour (call for current schedules).

## TORRE DE LOS INGLESES Map pp228-9

☎ 4311-0186; Plaza Fuerza Aérea Argentina; ☼ noon-7pm Thu-Sun (for elevator)

Standing prominently across from Plaza San Martín, this 76m-high miniversion of London's Big Ben was a donation from the city's British community in 1916. During the Falklands War of 1982, the tower was the target of bombs, and the government officially renamed it Torre Monumental – but the name never really stuck. The plaza in which it stands used to be called Plaza Británica, but is now the **Plaza Fuerza Aérea Argentina** (Argentine Air Force Plaza). Free elevator rides to the top of the tower are possible but opening days are limited.

*Detail of Teatro Nacional Cervantes (above)*

# RECOLETA & BARRIO NORTE

*Eating p97; Drinking p116 and p120; Shopping p147;*
*Sleeping p164*

Buenos Aires' wealthiest citizens live and breathe in Recoleta, the city's most exclusive neighborhood. This fashionable barrio was, interestingly enough, built as a result of sickness. Many upper-class porteños in the 1870s originally lived in southerly San Telmo, but during the yellow-fever epidemic they relocated as far away as they could, which was across town to Recoleta and Barrio Norte. Today you can best see much of the wealth of this sumptuous quarter on **Av Alvear**, where many of the old mansions (and newer boutiques) are located.

Full of lush parks, grand monuments, French architecture and wide avenues, Recoleta is best known for its cemetery, the **Cementerio de la Recoleta**. This must-see attraction is an astonishing necropolis where, in death as in life, generations of the Argentine elite repose in ornate splendor (p68). Alongside the cemetery, the **Iglesia de Nuestra Señora del Pilar** (1732) is a Baroque colonial church and national historical monument; next door is the **Centro Cultural Recoleta** (p68), one of the city's best cultural centers. Just in front, the **Plaza Intendente Alvear** holds the city's most popular crafts fair (p151), which is livelier on weekends. And across the way in RM Ortiz is Restaurant Row, Recoleta's culinary tourist trap – although a few places are worth a sit-down (p88).

Recoleta has some worthy museums, including the fabulous **Museo Nacional de Bellas Artes** (p68), full of national and international masterpieces; and the **Museo Xul Solar** (p69), honoring the Argentine surrealist painter. Notable buildings in this barrio are the beautiful French-styled **Palais de Glace** (p69) and the decrepit neo-Gothic **Facultad de Ingeniería** (Engineering School; cnr General Las Heras & Azcuénaga), which was designed by Uruguayan architect Arturo Prins and never quite completed. Thankfully they balance out eyesores like the unusual and unattractive **Biblioteca Nacional**.

A beautiful and interesting sculptural piece to the north is **Floralis Genérica**, located smack in the center of Plaza Naciones Unidas (just behind the Museo Nacional de Bellas Artes). It was designed and funded entirely by architect Eduardo Catalano, and finished in 2002. The giant aluminum and steel petals are 20m high and actually close up from dusk until dawn, glowing with red lights at night.

## Orientation

Recoleta sits elegantly between Retiro and Palermo. Most attractions are concentrated around the cemetery, and you can easily walk here from the center. Main thoroughfares include Avs Las Heras, Santa Fe, Callao and del Libertador. Barrio Norte is not an official neighborhood but rather a largely residential southern extension of Recoleta.

Neighborhoods – Recoleta & Barrio Norte

---

### Walking the Dog

Buenos Aires supports a legion of *paseaperros,* or professional dog walkers, who can be seen with up to 20 canines on leashes. They'll stroll through areas like Recoleta, Palermo's parks and even downtown with a variety of dogs ranging from scruffy mongrels to expensive purebreds, each of their tails happily a-waggin'.

*Paseaperros* are employed by busy apartment dwellers who either can't or won't take the time to exercise their animals properly – and are willing to pay about US$30 per month for this unique walking service. Since most *paseaperros* don't pay taxes, they can really 'clean up' in the city – figuratively speaking.

Every day, thousands of canines deposit tons (almost literally) of excrement in the streets and parks of the capital. You'll be aware of this fact soon after stepping into the streets of Buenos Aires. Cleaning up after one's pooch is already a city requirement, but enforcement is nil, so be very careful where you tread – you'll see dog piles of all textures and sizes lining almost every sidewalk. (One to especially step clear of is the author-named *dulce de leche* variety.) Remember to look down from the elegant buildings once in a while.

Still and all, the capital's leashed packs are a remarkably orderly and always entertaining sight, and make great snapshots to bring back home.

## BIBLIOTECA NACIONAL Map pp230-1

☎ 4808-6088; www.bibnal.edu.ar; Agüero 2502;
🕙 9am-9pm Mon-Fri, noon-7pm Sat & Sun, tours in Spanish 3pm Mon-Sat

After two decades of construction problems and delays, the national library finally moved into this rather ugly, mushroom-shaped behemoth in 1992; the plaster and floor tiles, however, are already cracking. Prominent Argentine and Latin American literary figures, such as Ernesto Sábato, often lecture here. Other literary events, concerts and cinema also take place here. From up above, you can see panoramic views of the capital.

Whenever they can get away with it, skateboarders and cyclists use the terrace's pyramid-shaped feature as a freestyle ramp; at least this brings the kids *close* to the library. Check out the south side of the terrace, where a smaller lecture building sits about 10 feet away; freestyle cyclists have jumped the chasm between the two buildings to land on the lower roof, and you may still be able to see the landing tread marks on the smaller building's roof.

## CEMENTERIO DE LA RECOLETA

Map pp230-1
☎ 4803-1594; admission free; 🕙 7am-6pm

This is arguably Buenos Aires' number-one attraction, and a must on every tourist's list. You can walk for hours in this city of the dead, wandering among the feral cats, impressive statues and marble sarcophagi. Peek into the crypts and check out the dusty coffins – most of which hold the remains of the city's most elite sector of society – and try to decipher the history of its inhabitants. Past presidents, military heroes, influential politicians and the just plain rich and famous have made it past the gates here – hunt down Evita's grave, as all visitors try to do. And bring your camera. Tours in English are possible, but you'll need to call ahead. For more information see the boxed text Glorious Death in Buenos Aires (p68).

---

### Transportation

**Bus** Bus Nos 59 and 64 go from the Microcentro up Av Las Heras
**Subte** Línea D covers the southern section of Recoleta

---

Neighborhoods – Recoleta & Barrio Norte

*Jardín Zoológico (p70), Palermo*

## CENTRO CULTURAL RECOLETA

Map p230-1

☎ 4803-1041; www.centroculturalrecoleta.org in Spanish; Junín 1930; donation US$0.35; ⏱ 2-9pm Tue-Fri, 10am-9pm Sat & Sun

Part of the original Franciscan convent, alongside its namesake church and cemetery, this renovated cultural center houses a variety of facilities, including museums, galleries, exhibition halls and a cinema. Its Museo Participativo de Ciencias (p71) is a children's hands-on science museum. There are frequent free outdoor films in summer, almost daily movies in the Microcine, and a good art bookshop inside.

## MUSEO NACIONAL DE BELLAS ARTES Map p230-1

☎ 4803-0802; www.aamnba.com.ar; Av del Libertador 1473; admission free; ⏱ 12:30-7:30pm Tue-Fri, 9:30am-7:30pm weekends & holidays, tours in Spanish Tue-Sun 5pm & 6pm

This former pumphouse for the city waterworks was designed by architect Julio Dormala and later modified by Alejandro Bustillo (famous for his alpine-style civic center in the northern

*Tomb, Cementerio de la Recoleta (p67)*

# Glorious Death in Buenos Aires

Only in Buenos Aires can the wealthy and powerful elite keep their status after death. When decades of dining on rich food and drink have taken their toll, Buenos Aires' finest move ceremoniously across the street to the Cementerio de la Recoleta, joining their ancestors in a place they have visited religiously all their lives.

Argentines are a strange bunch who tend to celebrate their most honored national figures not on the date of their birth, but on the date of their death. Nowhere is this obsession with mortality more evident than at Recoleta, where generations of the elite repose in the grandeur of ostentatious mausoleums. Real estate here is among Buenos Aires' priciest: there's a saying that goes 'It is cheaper to live extravagantly all your life than to be buried in Recoleta.'

It's not just being rich that gets you a prime resting spot here: your name matters. Those lucky few with surnames like Alvear, Anchorena, Mitre or Sarmiento are pretty much guaranteed lay-down. Evita's remains are here, but her lack of aristocracy and the fact that she dedicated her life not to BA's rich but rather to its poor infuriated the bigwigs. To find her, go up to the first major intersection from the entrance. Turn left, continue until a mausoleum blocks your way, go around it and turn right at the wide 'street.' After a few blocks you'll look to the left and probably see people at her site, along with bunches of flowers.

Juan Perón himself lies across town, in the much less exclusive graveyard of **Chacarita** (pp220–1), in a tomb marked under his father's name, Tomás Perón. The cemetery opened in the 1870s to accommodate the yellow-fever victims of San Telmo and La Boca. Although much more democratic and modest, Chacarita's most elaborate tombs match Recoleta's finest. One of the most visited belongs to Carlos Gardel, the famous tango singer. Plaques from around the world cover the base of his life-size statue, many thanking him for favors granted. Like Evita, Juan Perón and others, Gardel is a quasi saint toward whom countless Argentines feel an almost religious devotion. The anniversary of Gardel's death (June 26, 1935) sees thousands of pilgrims jamming the cemetery's streets.

Another spiritual personality in Chacarita is Madre María Salomé, a disciple of the famous healer Pancho Sierra. Every day, but especially on the second day of each month (she died on October 2, 1928), adherents of her cult leave floral tributes – white carnations are the favorite – and lay their hands on her sepulcher in spellbound supplication. Another crypt to look for is that of aviator Jorge Newbery. To visit Chacarita, take Línea B of the Subte to the end of the line at Federico Lacroze and cross the street.

Patagonian city of Bariloche). This national arts museum is the country's most important fine-arts museum and contains many works of international significance, including many on porteño themes by Benito Quinquela Martín and other Argentine artists of the 19th and 20th centuries. There are impressive works on the ground floor by European masters such as Renoir, Rodin, Monet, Toulouse-Lautrec, Gauguin, Rembrandt and Van Gogh. Other offerings include temporary exhibits, a cinema, concerts and classes. Reserve in advance for tours.

## MUSEO XUL SOLAR Map p230-1

☎ 4824-3302; www.xulsolar.org.ar in Spanish; Laprida 1212; US$1; ☷ noon-8pm Mon-Fri, 2-7pm Sat, tours in Spanish Tue-Thu 4:30pm, Sat 4pm, closed Jan

Xul Solar was a painter, inventor and poet, and a good friend of Jorge Luis Borges. This museum, which is located in his old mansion, showcases over 80 of his unique and colorful yet subdued paintings. Solar's Daliesque style includes fantastically themed, almost cartoonish figures placed in surreal cubist landscapes. It's great stuff, and bizarre enough to put him in a class by himself.

## PALAIS DE GLACE Map p230-1

☎ 4804-1163; Posadas 1725; US$0.75-3.50 depending on exhibition; ☷ 2-8pm Tue-Sun

Housed in an unusual circular building that was once an ice-skating rink and a tango hall (not necessarily at once though!), the spacious Palais de Glace now offers a variety of rotating cultural, artistic and historical exhibitions. The venue also hosts the occasional commercial event necessitated by financial considerations.

# PALERMO

*Eating p97; Drinking p117; Shopping p148; Sleeping p165*

Palermo is heaven on earth for Buenos Aires' middle class. Its large, grassy parks – regally punctuated with grand monuments – are popular destinations on weekends, when families fill the shady lanes, cycle the bike paths and paddle on the peaceful lakes. Many important museums and elegant embassies are also located here, mostly in the subneighborhood of **Palermo Chico** (also called Barrio Parque), a superelite area

OPlaza de Mayo

bordering Recoleta that is home to many of the city's rich and famous. Palermo offers some exceptional shopping opportunities, particularly in **Palermo Viejo** (p72), which has the most cutting-edge boutiques and restaurants in the city. And, while Palermo's day-life is great, the nights are even better – gourmets will love the endless selection of eateries to try out, while bars and nightclubs fill in the void between dusk and dawn.

Palermo's green spaces haven't always been for the masses. The area around **Parque 3 de Febrero** was originally the private retreat of 19th-century dictator Juan Manuel de Rosas' and became public parkland only after his fall from power – on February 3, 1852. Ironically for Rosas, the man who overthrew him – former ally Justo José de Urquiza – sits on his mount in a mammoth **equestrian monument** at the corner of Avs Sarmiento and Presidente Figueroa Alcorta. The park's more interesting destinations, however, include the **Jardín Japonés**; the **Jardín Zoológico**; the **Jardín Botánico Carlos Thays**; the **Planetario Galileo Galilei** (planetarium; see p71); the **Campo Argentino de Polo** (polo grounds); and the **Hipódromo Argentino** (racetrack). Just south of the zoo, and a major landmark in Palermo, is **Plaza Italia**, a half-moon shaped traffic island and important transport hub. Close by is the **Predio Ferial**, a large venue hosting anything from fashion shows to agriculture and farming expositions.

Another popular (but much smaller and more laid-back) neighborhood in Palermo is farther north in **Las Cañitas**, which occupies a six-block section close to the polo grounds. It's mostly a residential area on the border with Belgrano and named after the fields of sugar cane that used to grow here. The only sweets here now, however, are the luscious desserts at the dozens of ethnic restaurants on Av Báez, the main business street. It's only a few blocks long but densely packed with eateries, bars, cafés and even a club or two, and it positively buzzes at night. On some weekend nights a street market at Av Báez' southern end adds color and buying excitement. Southeast of Las Cañitas is the landmark **Centro Islámico Rey Fahd** (☎ 4899-0201; Av Bullrich 55; tours available), built with Saudi money on land donated by ex-president and current outlaw Carlos Menem.

Worth a note in passing is the site of **Ernesto 'Che' Guevara's former residence** (Aráoz 2180), the space where the famous revolutionary's house once stood – it's since been torn down. There's an apartment building now (dating from 1972) but hard-core Che fans might appreciate the neighborhood that the Guevaras moved into in 1948.

# Orientation

Palermo is one of Buenos Aires' largest barrios and lies northwest of Recoleta. It has various subneighborhoods, including Palermo Chico and Palermo Viejo (with the latter further subdivided into Palermo Hollywood and Palermo Soho). Main thoroughfares include Av Santa Fe, Av del Libertador and, at Palermo's southern edge, Av Córdoba.

## JARDÍN JAPONÉS Map pp232-3

☎ 4804-4922; www.jardinjapones.com; Parque 3 de Febrero, cnr Avs Casares & Berro; US$1.50; ☺ 10am-6pm

First opened in 1967 and then donated to the city of Buenos Aires in 1979 (on the centenary of the arrival of Argentina's first Japanese immigrants), Jardín Japonés is one of the capital's best-kept gardens – and makes a wonderfully peaceful rest stop. Inside you can enjoy a Japanese restaurant (great sushi) along with lovely ponds filled with koi and spanned by pretty arched bridges. The teahouse makes a good break, and bonsai trees are available for purchase. Japanese culture can be experienced through occasional exhibitions and workshops on ikebana, haiku, origami, *taiko* (Japanese drumming) and many other things; check their website for schedules.

## JARDÍN ZOOLÓGICO Map pp232-3

☎ 4806-7411; cnr Avs Las Heras & Sarmiento; US$2-3.50, under 13 free; ☺ 10am-6pm Tue-Sun, daily in summer; guided tours Sat 3pm

Set on 18 hectares in the middle of Palermo, Buenos Aires' Jardín Zoológico is a relatively decent zoo, with around 350 species represented. On sunny weekends it's packed with families enjoying the large green spaces, artificial lakes and, of course, the creatures themselves. Some of the buildings housing the animals are impressive; be sure to check out the elephant house. An aquarium, monkey island and large aviary are other highlights. Keep an eye on your young ones too, especially near the alligator pit and big cat enclosures; the fences are easy to breach.

The zoo is noted for successfully breeding condors and white tigers, and for having an educational farm and petting zoo for the kids. Waterfowl, Patagonian hares, nutria and feral housecats roam wild. The zoo may be shut in bad weather.

## Transportation

**Bus** Bus Nos 29, 59, 64 and 152 from the Microcentro to Plaza Italia; No 39 from Congreso to Palermo Viejo; No 111 from the Microcentro to Palermo Viejo
**Subte** Línea D is the fastest way to Palermo's Plaza Italia area

## MUSEO DE ARTE LATINOAMERICANO DE BUENOS AIRES (MALBA) Map pp232-3

☎ 4808-6500; www.malba.org.ar; Av Figueroa Alcorta 3415; admission US$2, students with ISIC card US$1; ☺ noon-8pm Thu-Mon, to 9pm Wed

Sparkling inside its glass and cement walls is this airy modern-art museum, one of BA's newest and finest. Created by art patron Eduardo Costantini, it contains the best work of classic and contemporary Latin American artists, such as Argentines Xul Solar, Emilio Pettoruti and Antonio Berni, Chilean Roberto Matto, Uruguayan Pedro Figari and Mexican duo Diego Rivera and Frida Kahlo. Temporary exhibits are shown in the basement and on the 2nd floor, there are occasional kids' programs and a cinema screens art-house films. A small bookstore, gift shop and fancy café complete the picture.

## MUSEO DE ARTES PLÁSTICAS EDUARDO SÍVORI Map pp232-3

☎ 4774-9452; www.museosivori.org.ar in Spanish; Av de la Infanta Isabel 555; locals/foreigners US$0.35/1; ☺ noon-8pm Tue-Fri, 10am-6pm weekends, open later in summer

Named for an Italo-Argentine painter who studied in Europe, this modern museum of Argentine art – in Palermo's Parque 3 de Febrero – has open spaces allowing frequent and diverse exhibitions. Sívori's Parisian works reflect European themes, but later works returned to Argentine motifs, mainly associated with rural life on the Pampas. There are also

# Buenos Aires for Kids

Travelers with children have a good range of choices when it comes to activities in Buenos Aires. On weekends Palermo's parks bustle with families taking walks, picnicking or playing sports. The shopping malls fill with strollers, while family-friendly places like zoos, museums and theme parks also make popular destinations for grown-ups trying to entertain the little ones. Porteños just adore children, and it shows.

Good green spots in the city include Palermo's **Parque 3 de Febrero**, where on weekends traffic isn't allowed on the lakeside ring road (and you can rent bikes). Boating is also possible, and there's a pretty rose garden. Other good stops for kids here include a **planetarium** (below), **zoo** (opposite) and **Japanese garden** (opposite). If you're downtown and need a nature break, think about the **Reserva Ecológica Costanera Sur** (p56), a large nature preserve with good bird-watching, pleasant gravel paths and no vehicular traffic.

Some shopping malls make safe destinations for families (especially on rainy days), and most come with playground, video arcade and cineplex. **Paseo Alcorta** (p150) is a particularly good choice, with plenty of mechanical rides next to the large food court. **Galerías Pacífico** (p52) has a kids' show at 5pm on Sunday. Finally, the **Mercado de Abasto** (p75) boasts a full-blown **Museo de los Niños** (Children's Museum) where kids enter a miniature city complete with post office, hospital, supermarket, TV station and even port.

If you're in San Telmo, check out the **Museo Argentino del Títere** (Puppet Museum; see below). Three small rooms display a fascinating collection of international and Argentine puppets, but it's the inexpensive shows that will amuse the little urchins. In Recoleta make sure to visit the **Museo Participativo de Ciencias** (below), in the Centro Cultural Recoleta. This is a young people's science museum with interactive displays that focus on fun learning – signs say '*prohibido no tocar*,' (not touching is forbidden). Christian parents might want to take the kids to **Tierra Santa** (p74), a religious theme park unlike anywhere else you've been.

A bit outside the center, in Caballito, is the good **Museo Argentino de Ciencias Naturales** (Natural Science Museum; p76). A myriad of rooms containing giant dinosaur bones, dainty seashells, scary insects and amusing stuffed animals and birds are all worth a peek; just beware the masses of chortling students who visit during school hours.

Heading to **Tigre** (p170), just north of the center, makes a great day excursion. Take the **Tren de la Costa** route; it ends at **Parque de la Costa** (p170), a typical amusement park with fun rides and activities. Boat trips and a fruit and housewares market are on tap nearby.

Outside the city is Buenos Aires' premier zoo, **Parque Temaikén** (below). Spaces here have been beautifully created and flow well with the tidy landscaping. Services include stroller rentals, gift stores and restaurants; plenty of benches help parents with needed breaks. Only the most charming animal species are on display (think meerkats, pygmy hippos and white tigers), roaming freely around spacious, clean and natural enclosures – there are no cages here. An excellent aquarium comes with touch pools, and plenty of interactive areas provide mental stimulation. Just outside Temaikén is a large playground run by Heladería Munchi. Both places make very popular destinations for porteño families on sunny weekends.

Another **zoo** outside the city is in Luján (p172), but it's not nearly as nice as Temaikén.

There are some hotels that make great choices for families. Try the **Hotel Lyon** (p159) or **Fiamingo Apart Hotel** (p159), both of which have large multibed apartments with fridge and/or microwaves for quick snacks. More upscale places with kitchenettes include **Suipacha y Arroyo Suites** (p163), **Art Suites** (p164) and **Aspen Suites** (p162).

A few restaurants cater specifically to families by stocking high chairs, fun food or even miniplaygrounds. Good places for child-friendly meals are **Garbis**, **TGI Fridays** and **Cumaná** (see p88 for these). And finally, many ice-cream shops serve those tasty treats that calm temper tantrums and provide a welcome break for adults too (p94).

For more particulars on traveling with children in BA, see p187.

**Planetario Galileo Galilei** (Map pp232–3; ☎ 4771-9393; www.planetario.gov.ar in Spanish; Av Sarmiento & Roldán; ☽ 2-8pm Sat & Sun) Astronomy shows at 6pm & 7:15pm Sat & Sun (US$1.50).

**Museo de los Niños** ( ☎ 4861-2325; www.museoabasto.org.ar in Spanish; Av Corrientes 3247; 2 adults & 1/2 children US$5/7; ☽ 1-8pm Tue-Sun)

**Museo Argentino del Títere** (Map p225; ☎ 4304-4376; www.museoargdeltitere.com.ar in Spanish; Piedras 905; admission free; ☽ 3-6pm Tue-Sun) Puppet shows on weekends and holidays at 4pm, daily in summer (US$0.75).

**Museo Participativo de Ciencias** ( ☎ 4807-3456; www.mpc.org.ar in Spanish; Junín 1930; US$2; ☽ 3:30-7:30pm in summer, 12:30-7:30pm Mon-Fri, 3:30-7:30pm Sat & Sun in winter). Call ahead as hours can vary depending on school schedules.

**Parque Temaikén** ( ☎ 03488-436-900; www.temaiken.com.ar in Spanish; Ruta Provincial 25, Escobar; adults/children under 10 US$5/3.50; ☽ 10am-7pm in summer, 10am-6pm Tue-Sun in winter, closed Easter, Christmas & New Year's Day) Taxis here cost US$20 and take 40 minutes, or take bus No 60 marked 'Escobar' from the center (US$0.50).

rotating collections by other well-known Argentine artists like Sixto Aurelio Salas, María Inés and Gerardo Ramos. Other offerings include a cinema, theater and concerts, while courses and workshops are also organized.

## MUSEO DE MOTIVOS ARGENTINOS JOSÉ HERNÁNDEZ Map pp232-3

☎ 4803-2384; www.museohernandez.org.ar; Av del Libertador 2373; locals/foreigners US$0.35/1, Sun free; 🕑 1am-7pm Wed-Sun, Spanish tours 4:30pm Sat & Sun

Half of this modest-sized museum has permanent exhibitions on Mapuche crafts, such as exquisitely detailed ponchos and indigenous items from a women's cooperative in Santiago del Estero. Incongruous, gaudy Carnaval costumes are also strangely on display. The other half of the museum showcases diverse changing exhibitions, ranging from gaucho accoutrements and modern toys to chess and photography.

## MUSEO EVITA Map pp232-3

☎ 4807-9433; Lafinur 2988; locals/foreigners US$0.75/1.75; 🕑 2-7:30pm Tue-Sun

Practically everybody who's anybody in Argentina has their own museum, and Eva Perón is no exception. The Museo Evita displays lots of videos of the Argentine heroine, along with plenty of historical photos, books, old posters, newspaper headlines and even papers with her fingerprints. Prize memorabilia is her wardrobe: dresses, shoes, handbags, hats and blouses lie proudly behind glass, forever pressed and pristine. Even Evita's old wallets and perfumes are exposed for everyone to see. Our personal favorite is a picture of her kicking a soccer ball.

## MUSEO NACIONAL DEL HOMBRE

Map pp232-3

☎ 4783-6554; 3 de Febrero 1370; US$0.35; 🕑 10am-7pm Mon-Fri

On the border with Belgrano, this small museum displays some good-quality crafts (such

## Hip Old Palermo

Palermo Viejo is probably the capital's most trendsetting spot, and you shouldn't miss a visit to this charming neighborhood. Roughly bounded by Avs Santa Fe, Scalabrini Ortiz, Córdoba and Dorrego (though everyone might tell you something different), Palermo Viejo is further divided into Palermo Hollywood and Palermo Soho. The former is north of the train tracks (or Av Juan B Justo) and was named for the TV and radio stations located there; the latter is south of the tracks and has a more bohemian feel. The atmosphere is, for the most part, low-key and pleasant, with two-story residential buildings, leafy sidewalks and the occasional cobbled street marking its general style.

Literary great Jorge Luis Borges' childhood home (JL Borges 2135) is only four blocks southwest of Plaza Italia. Look for the (private) brick house marked 'Serrano 2135'; a sign claims Borges lived here from 1901 to 1914. Six blocks farther southwest is one of the main centers of porteño nightlife and the heart of the barrio – lively and raucous Plaza Serrano. Visit on a Saturday night after midnight and you'll see groups of young hipsters hanging out on the benches and drinking from bottles of beer while merrymakers pack the surrounding restaurants' tables and cruising oglers back up the side streets with their cars.

Palermo Viejo has attracted dozens of ultramodern hip restaurants, most of which actually aren't parrillas – though there are plenty of these too. Porteños are a fickle lot and many eateries have come and gone over the last few years; even so, it's unlikely you'll get a bad meal anywhere. The best restaurants are packed all the time, and on weekends you may need a reservation at the hottest joints.

Ethnic themes are the idea here; anyone yearning for Japanese, Vietnamese, Brazilian, Polish, Middle Eastern, Greek or even Norwegian food can satisfy their craving. Modern international cuisine tops the list, however, and the quality is surprisingly high. You can order an appetizer, main dish, dessert and wine for less than US$15 (including tip) – and the food might just blow you away. But despite the innumerable culinary treats available here, Palermo Viejo offers more than just food. A whole slew of young fashion designers have opened up shop here since the devaluation of 2001 – not only have imports of good-quality clothing gone sky-high, but everyone's still looking for a decent job. Incredibly creative and well-made garments are available, and the prices are relatively affordable (see boxed text, p16). Many trendy houseware stores and small themed boutiques will also demand your wallet's attention.

It's worth noting that these restaurants and shops are, for the most part, spread out in all of Palermo Viejo, which takes up a huge area. This makes it fun to just walk around and discover someplace new. For a more defined approach, pick up one of the many available maps to help you find that perfect clothing store, shoe shop or Spanish café. And be aware that, at night, Godoy Cruz mutates into the capital's transvestite red-light district. This doesn't necessarily make it dangerous, and there's enough traffic (and even pedestrians) that it's not totally isolated, but it attracts iffy characters and you should be very careful here – try not to walk alone.

as textiles, pottery and baskets) from the indigenous peoples of the Argentine provinces. It's a bit out of the way and would probably please only hard-core, indigenous-crafts fans.

## MUSEO NACIONAL DE ARTE DECORATIVO Map pp232-3

☎ 4802-6606; Av del Libertador 1902; admission from US$0.75; ⏰ 2-7pm Tue-Sun

This museum is housed in the stunning Beaux Arts mansion called Palacio Errázuriz (1911), which features beautiful elements like Corinthian columns and a gorgeous marble staircase inspired by the palace of Versailles. It was once the residence of Chilean aristocrat Matías Errázuriz and his wife, Josefina de Alvear, and now displays some 4000 of their very posh belongings. Everything from Renaissance religious paintings and porcelain dishes to Italian sculptures and period furniture was owned by Errázuriz, and some artwork by El Greco and Rodin can also be seen. On the 1st floor is a smaller museum showcasing exquisite pieces of Asian art. There are also rotating exhibitions;

the entry price is determined by what there is to see.

There are guided tours in English, but call ahead as they are by appointment only.

## MUSEO CASA DE RICARDO ROJAS

Map pp230-1

☎ 4824-4039; Charcas 2837; admission by donation; ⏰ 10am-5:30pm Mon-Fri

Walk under the facade, modelled after the Casa de Independencia in Tucumán, and behold a quaint courtyard surrounded by European and Incan architectural motifs. Famous Argentine educator and writer Ricardo Rojas lived here from 1929 to 1957, and in his office wrote his renowned *El Santo de la Espada* (1933). Note the glass case displaying his original books; the library contains 20,000 volumes. An old dining room with period furniture also gives an idea of the past. The small theater holds Friday concerts and the occasional workshop; the donation entry includes a short tour in Spanish.

# BELGRANO

*Eating p111*

Bustling Av Cabildo, the racing heartbeat of Belgrano, is an overwhelming jumble of noise and neon. It's a two-way street of clothing, shoe and housewares shops that does its part in supporting porteños' mass consumerism. For a bit more peace and

## Transportation

**Bus** Bus Nos 29, 59, 64 and 152 all connect Belgrano to downtown
**Subte** Línea D is the fastest way to Belgrano; the Juramento stop leaves you a block from the plaza

quiet, head to the blocks on either side of the avenue, where Belgrano becomes a leafy barrio of museums, plazas, parks and good local eateries.

A block east of Av Cabildo, the barrio's plaza is the site of a modest but fun **Feria Plaza Belgrano** (p151). On a sunny weekend it's full of shoppers, families with strollers and a few buskers and tarot-card readers. Near the plaza stands the Italianate **Iglesia de la Inmaculada Concepción**, a church popularly known as La Redonda (the round one) because of its impressive dome.

Just a few steps from the plaza is the **Museo Histórico Sarmiento**, which honors one of the most forward-thinking Argentines in history. Also close by is the **Museo Enrique Larreta**, a beautiful house with beautiful period pieces and beautiful gardens. About five blocks north is yet another museum, the **Museo Casa de Yrurtia**, honoring the well-known Argentine sculptor.

Four blocks northeast of Plaza Belgrano, French landscape architect Carlos Thays took advantage of the contours of **Barrancas de Belgrano** to create an attractive, wooded public space on one of the few natural hillocks in the city. Retirees spend the afternoon at the chess tables beneath its *ombú* tree, while children skate around the band shell.

Across Juramento from the Barrancas, Belgrano's growing **Chinatown** fills the 2100 block of Arribeños, with more Chinese businesses spilling over into the side streets.

## Orientation

You'll probably head into Belgrano via Av Cabildo, either by bus or Subte (the Subte runs right under Av Cabildo). Plaza Belgrano is one block east of Cabildo at Juramento; most sights are around the plaza. Barrancas de Belgrano is the location of Belgrano's local bus and train stations and about four blocks from the plaza.

# Praying for Kitsch

Find yourself in Buenos Aires with some religious yearnings but are sick and tired of the same old Sunday sermons? **Tierra Santa** might be exactly what you need.

This religious theme park – 'the world's first,' according to the literature – is roughly based on Jerusalem and is just 10 minutes from BA's bustling center. Enter the park and head straight to Calvary, where plastic crosses support replicas of Jesus and two thieves being crucified above a group of wailing disciples and jeering Roman soldiers. The extravaganza begins with a laser show depicting the creation of the world, and continues as you follow a path into Bethlehem and a complete line of statuary depicting a manger scene (supposedly the 'world's largest'). From here it's a 30-second walk to witness the 40ft-tall animatronic Jesus rise from the Calvary mound, open his eyes and finally turn his palms toward the emotional devoted below. And if you missed the show, don't fret: another resurrection is just around the corner. Just ask an employee when the next one will be – they'll immediately look at their watches.

The park is not just for Christians, as it also has an ecumenical flavor. Once you descend from Calvary you enter a labyrinthine Old Testament world complete with Wailing Wall and praying plastic statues of Jewish devotees. Off the beaten Jerusalem path are also a synagogue and chapel – both containing more fake devoted engaged in solemn prayer – and of course the rendition of the Last Supper isn't to be missed.

*Reproduction minaret, Tierra Santa*

Tierra Santa is a magnificent blend of the tacky and religious rolled into one. Many devoted Argentines take it very seriously, and are visibly moved when the oversized Jesus gazes upon them. Regardless of religious affiliation, you will definitely want to spend an afternoon here nibbling on baklava at the Baghdad Café, conversing about religion with employees dolled up in Middle Eastern garb and just enjoying a spectacle you won't find anyplace else on earth – especially not in Jerusalem.

**Tierra Santa** ☎ 4784-9551; www.tierrasanta-bsas .com.ar in Spanish; Av Costanera R Obligado 5790; adults/ children 3-11 years US$3.50/1.50; ☺ 9am-9pm Fri, noon-11pm Sat, Sun & holidays Apr-Nov, 4pm-12.30am Fri-Sun Dec-Mar; bus Nos 28,33,37,42,45,107,160

## MUSEO CASA DE YRURTIA Map pp220-1
☎ 4781-0385; O'Higgins 2390; US$0.35; ☺ 1-7pm Tue-Fri, 3-7pm Sun, tours in Spanish 4pm Sun

Reclusive Rogelio Yrurtia (1879–1950), best known for his sculpture *Canto al Trabajo* on Plazoleta Olazábal in San Telmo, designed this neocolonial, Mudéjar-style residence with the expectation that it would one day house a museum. The building is full of Yrurtia's work – which focuses on human torsos – and works by his wife, painter Lía Correa Morales. There are also pieces by Yrurtia's teacher, Lucio Correa Morales, and by other sculptors and artists; some exhibitions change monthly. Especially noteworthy is Yrurtia's eclectic furniture collection, which includes pieces from Japan, the Middle East and India.

A small and attractive garden contains the larger-than-life-size *Boxers* (titled in English), first exhibited at the St Louis World's Fair of 1904. Yrurtia seems to have been ambivalent about fig leaves; only around half his figures sport them. There's some great furniture here too, as well as Picasso's *Rue Cortot, Paris.*

## MUSEO ENRIQUE LARRETA Map pp220-1
☎ 4784-4040; Juramento 2291; US$0.35, free Thu; ☺ 2-8pm Mon & Wed-Fri, 3-8pm Sat & Sun, tours in Spanish 4pm & 6pm Sun

Hispanophile novelist Enrique Larreta (1875–1961) resided in this elegant colonial-style house across from Plaza Belgrano, which now displays his private art collection to the public. It's a grand and spacious old building, and contains classic Spanish art, period furniture, tapestries, shields and armor, lithographs and religious items. The wood and tiled floors are beautiful and everything is richly lit. The magnificent gardens are free and open September through April, when open-air theater performances are given; access them via Vuelta de Obligado 2155.

## MUSEO HISTÓRICO SARMIENTO

Map pp220-1

☎ 4782-2354; www.museosarmiento.gov.ar in Spanish; Juramento 2180; US$0.35, free Thu; ☾ 2-7pm Tue-Fri, 3-7pm Sun, tours in Spanish 4pm Sun

Opposite Plaza Belgrano, this museum contains memorabilia of Domingo F Sarmiento, one of Argentina's most famous presidents, diplomats and educators. Despite his provincial origins and a perpetual scowl on his face, the classically educated Sarmiento was an eloquent writer. He analyzed 19th-century Argentina from a cosmopolitan, clearly Euro-centric point of view, most notably in his masterful polemic *Facundo*, or *Civilization and Barbarism*.

The building itself was briefly the site of the Congreso Nacional during the presidency of Nicolás Avellaneda (1874–80), when both chambers voted to federalize the city of Buenos Aires (inciting a brief civil war with the powerful Buenos Aires province). The once-deteriorating house has undergone restoration and now holds Sarmiento's desk, bed and other furnishings, along with old photos, antique knickknacks, some incredibly intricate hair combs and a library.

# ONCE & CABALLITO

You'd have a hard time finding more of a melting pot in Buenos Aires than the ethnically colorful neighborhood of Once, which holds sizable populations of Jews, Peruvians and Koreans. Its busy commercial heart is at Estación Once (Once train station), where an astounding concentration of inexpensive garment shops are located. Lively trade keeps the area bustling both day and night with the energy of immigrant commerce. There's an almost third-world feel to this neighborhood – a welcome change in Buenos Aires.

Near Estación Once is the **Mercado de Abasto**, one of the city's most attractive shopping malls, both inside and out. Carlos Gardel first sang in this neighborhood; look just outside the eastern side of the Abasto mall for a small statue of the singer. Also, a museum honoring Gardel has sprouted about four blocks northeast on Jean Jaurés.

West of Once is Caballito, a calm and pleasant neighborhood where locals go about their daily routines and tourists are nowhere to be seen. The large and circular Parque del Centenario holds the **Museo Argentino de Ciencias Naturales**, a good natural-science museum that's definitely worth a peek. Farther south of that is a storefront that holds the one-man show **Museo Ernesto Che Guevara** – it's hard to explain this one.

## Orientation

Once is west of Congreso and easily accessed by Subte. From Estación Once (the Subte stop here is called Plaza Miserere), the Abasto mall is four blocks north up Av Pueyrredón, then four blocks west on Av Corrientes. Gardel's museum is just a few blocks from the mall.

Caballito is west of Once; the closest Subte stop to Parque del Centenario is Ángel Gallardo, which is three blocks north of the park.

### MERCADO DE ABASTO Map pp230-1

☎ 4959-3400; www.altopalermo.com.ar; cnr Avs Corrientes & Anchorena; ☾ 10am-10pm

Farther west, in the Abasto district, the historic Mercado de Abasto (1895) has been recycled by US-Hungarian financier George Soros into one of the most beautiful shopping centers in the city. The building, once a large vegetable market, received an architectural prize in 1937 for its Av Corrientes facade; at night, the spotlighted and lofty arches are visible all the way from Av Pueyrredón. The small Abasto neighborhood was once home to tango legend Carlos Gardel, and on the gentrified pedestrianised street off Av Anchorena is a statue of the singer.

## Transportation

**Bus** Bus No 26 from the Microcentro to Once; bus No 105 from the Microcentro to Caballito

**Subte** Líneas A and B are the fastest way to Once & Caballito

### MUSEO CASA CARLOS GARDEL

Map pp232-3

☎ 4964-2071; Jean Jaurés 735; locals/foreigners US$0.35/1, free Wed; ☾ 11am-6pm Mon & Wed-Fri, 11am-7pm Sat & Sun

Small but noteworthy is this tribute to tango's most famous voice. Located in Gardel's house, the museum traces his partnership with José Razzano and displays old memorabilia. There isn't a whole lot to see, so only true fans or the curious should hike it over to this section of town; look for the colorfully painted buildings. Occasional tango-related activities are on the roster, so call ahead to find out what's up.

## MUSEO ARGENTINO DE CIENCIAS NATURALES Map pp220-1

☎ 4982-6595; Ángel Gallardo 470; US$0.75; ⊗ 2-7pm, tours in Spanish 2:30pm Sat & Sun

Way over to the west, the oval Parque del Centenario is a large open space containing this excellent natural-science museum. On display are collections of meteorites, rocks and minerals, seashells, insects and dinosaur replicas. Life-size models of a basking shark and ocean sunfish are impressive, as are the preserved remains of a giant squid. The taxidermy rooms are especially noteworthy and amusing. Bring the kids; they can mingle with the hundreds of schoolchildren who visit during school hours.

Nearby is the **Observatorio Astronómico** ( ☎ 4863-3366; Patricias Argentinas 550; adult/child US$1.50/0.75; ⊗ 9-10pm Fri & Sat). Call ahead, as times change depending on the season.

## MUSEO ERNESTO CHE GUEVARA
Map pp220-1

☎ 4903-3285; museocheguevara@yahoo.com.ar; Rojas 129; admission free; ⊗ 9am-7pm Mon-Fri

It's something of a mystery why Argentina has seemingly turned its back on Che Guevara, the famous guerrilla who played a key role in Cuba's 1959 revolution and died in Bolivia in 1967. Che was born in Rosario and lived in Buenos Aires when he was young, but practically no plazas or museums in the country honor his memory. One exception is this 'museum', and it's not exactly official – in fact, it's *very* unofficial and located in a secondhand antique shop called Bagatela. There's hardly anything to see related to Che, but you'd visit this out-of-the-way spot just to meet Eladio 'Toto' González, an eccentric and kind man committed to making this world a better place. Eladio may tell you stories and show you photos and letters somehow related to the revolutionary's activities and to Cuba in general. He's waiting for the government to donate a space for all his 'Che' paraphernalia. Taxis here from the center are US$3.50, or take the Subte to Primera Junta, the last stop on Línea A.

# Walking Tours

# Walking Tours

Despite the traffic, smoky air and often broken sidewalks, Buenos Aires is definitely a city to be experienced on foot. The city center is compact, there are few hills to puff up, and a relaxing café, bar, restaurant or ice-cream shop is always around the corner. You'll see more of local life if it's in front of your eyes and under your nose rather than behind the glass of an impersonal tour bus zipping through the sights. And if you need to hop to the other side of town, simply jump on a bus or grab a taxi – public transportation is cheap and plentiful. For guided walking tours see p48.

## MICROCENTRO & RETIRO

The Microcentro is the bustling heart of Buenos Aires, a fast-paced center that buzzes along frenetically from dawn to dusk. Many of the capital's most distinguished European-style buildings are here, so look up once in a while and enjoy the view. It might just make you forget which continent you're on.

Start at the leafy **Plaza San Martín 1** (p63), designed by French landscape architect Carlos Thays; notice the statue of a proud José de San Martín astride his horse on the western tip of the plaza. From here, take Arenales past **Palacio San Martín 2** (p64). Turn right when you reach Esmeralda and follow it 2½ blocks to Suipacha and the **Museo Municipal de Arte Hispanoamericano Isaac Fernández Blanco 3** (p65). After browsing through the gorgeous displays, head back down Suipacha to Av Santa Fe and turn left. You'll pass the **Secretaría de Turismo de la Nación 4** (p195), which offers excellent information on the city and Argentina.

Follow Av Santa Fe around to the Círculo Militar (1909), a striking building that now houses the **Museo de Armas 5** (p64). If you like guns, swords and cannons, you'll definitely like this place. Then, head to the start of pedestrian Florida and walk south; it's a welcome break from BA's incessant traffic, but you'll be dodging thousands of pedestrians instead. After two blocks you'll come to the elegant **Galerías Pacífico 6** (p52), one of the capital's most beautiful malls. Even if you don't like to shop, you should take a peek inside at the ceiling

*The tower of the Cabildo (p55), left, Plaza de Mayo*

murals; there's often free (donation) tango just outside. Now go back up to Córdoba and turn left, heading west and crossing the impressive Av 9 de Julio (which porteños boast is the widest street in the world). It's certainly daunting, and crossing it in one go is almost impossible without running. Soon you'll come to Teatro Nacional Cervantes (p65), a beautiful theater containing the small and modest **Museo Nacional del Teatro 7** (p65), while right across the street is the notable **Templo de la Congregación Israelita 8** (p57). Walk south a couple of blocks to the **Teatro Colón 9** (p59), one of BA's most impressive buildings; tours here are excellent.

From the Colón, head south another couple of blocks and turn left at Av Corrientes. You'll soon cross Av 9 de Julio again, but under the shadow of the BA's famous **Obelisco 10** (p57). Just after you cross, turn left at Pellegrini and then right at pedestrian Lavalle, where you'll amble along until the junction at Florida. If you need a break, stop at **Richmond 11** (p119) – a café with classic old-world atmosphere. After your *café con leche* (white coffee), go to Av Corrientes and turn left; detour down San Martín a half-block to investigate the **Museo Mitre 12** (p52) and **Museo de la Policía Federal 13** (p52).

## Walk Facts

**Start** Plaza San Martín
**End** Plaza de Mayo
**Distance** 5km
**Duration** 4 hours

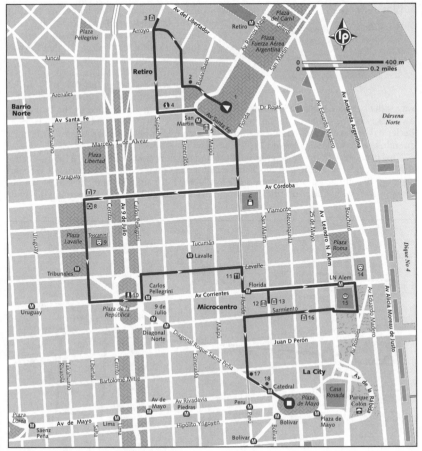

Continue on Av Corrientes to the monstrous **Luna Park 14** (p123) – one of BA's largest stadiums – and then circle around BA's main post office, the noteworthy **Correo Central 15** (p52). Go back west via Av Sarmiento to the **Museo Histórico Dr Arturo Jáuretche 16** (p52); stop inside if you like money (and who doesn't?). Once you hit Florida again, make your way south to Diagonal Roque Sáenz Peña, where you'll see the Spanish Renaissance **Banco de Boston 17** (cnr Florida & Bartolomé Mitre), built in 1924. Stroll past **Edificio Menéndez-Behety 18** (Diagonal Roque Sáenz Peña 543), built in 1926 and the one-time headquarters of a Patagonian wool empire, and stop at Plaza de Mayo, where the following walk begins.

## PLAZA DE MAYO TO CONGRESO

**Plaza de Mayo 1** (p53) is full of history; this is the main location where throngs of citizens gather to air their grievances – and there have certainly been many in Argentine history. Every Thursday at 3:30pm the Madres de la Plaza de Mayo still march around the plaza, as they have for years, to protest Dirty War atrocities. At other times, couples stroll while tourists come to take photos of the plaza's numerous attractions, and colorful vendors sell flags and patriotic pins. Note the Pirámide de Mayo in the center of the plaza; it's a small obelisk marking the first anniversary of BA's independence from Spain. The **Casa Rosada 2** (p53) is the plaza's main attraction; visit its modest museum in the basement. Next up is the **Catedral Metropolitana 3** (p54), the city's most important cathedral. Finally check out the **Museo del Cabildo 4** (p55), but don't expect overly impressive exhibits.

**Walk Facts**

**Start** Plaza de Mayo
**End** Plaza del Congreso
**Distance** 2km
**Duration** 2½ hours

From Plaza de Mayo, head south via Defensa to **Museo de la Ciudad 5** (p55), which traces part of the city's history. Across the way is the baroque **Basílica de San Francisco 6** (Alsina 430), which was opened by the Franciscan order in 1754 and is one of the capital's oldest churches. Inside, a large tapestry by Horacio Butler has replaced a fire-damaged altarpiece. A couple of blocks down is another historic church, the **Basílica de Santo Domingo 7** (p53).

Now head west along Av Belgrano to Perú and north to **Manzana de las Luces 8** (p54), Buenos Aires' old center of learning. A block and a half further on is Av de Mayo; turn left and start walking. If you need a break, there's **Café Tortoni 9** (p118), arguably the city's most famous historic café; step inside and find out why. After a drink and a snack, keep going on Av de

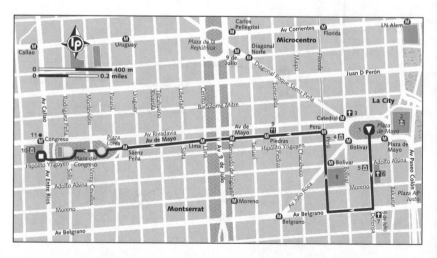

*Faena Hotel & Universe (p156), Puerto Madero*

Mayo, holding your breath while you cross Av 9 de Julio. You'll see your destination before you reach it: Plaza del Congreso and its green-topped **Palacio del Congreso 10** (p58). Just off the plaza, you'll notice the rococo **Confitería del Molino 11**, a closed *confitería* (snack shop) that presently molders in BA's air. It was designed by Italian architect Francisco Gianotti and originally opened its doors in 1916 as a bakery, café and salon where artists and politicians would meet, but closed in 1997 for financial reasons.

# PUERTO MADERO

Amble around Buenos Aires' youngest barrio, Puerto Madero, with its brick warehouses converted into some of the city's trendiest lofts, offices, hotels and restaurants. Reminiscent of London's docklands (indeed this area's original blueprints drew on London's Millwall and Royal Albert

## Walk Facts

**Start** Tourist kiosk at Dique 4
**End** Reserva Ecológica Costanera Sur
**Distance** 4km
**Duration** 3 hours

Docks for inspiration), this affluent barrio is still a work in progress, with newly built five-star hotels dropping millions of US dollars into the mix. Cobbled promenades make walking a pleasure for pedestrians, and there are plenty of good restaurants and cafés in which to rest. It's worth some exploration, and most of the time there won't be a vehicle in sight.

Begin by visiting the **tourist office 1** (p195) at Dique 4. The folks here can tell you about the area and give you a map covering the Reserva Ecológica Costanera Sur, where you'll be wandering later on. Also ask them about the Museo Fortabat, a museum housing Argentine socialite Amalia Fortabat's art collection – it might have finally opened its doors by the time you arrive. Then head down the cobbled pedestrian mall, glancing up once in a while to check out the lofts – which sport expensive water views – above. Across the way, you'll see more buildings, including some of the city's most elite hotels.

After crossing your first street (Av Güemes), you're at Dique 3. Up ahead is the attention-grabbing **Puente de la Mujer 2** (p55), a suspension bridge designed by Spaniard Santiago Calatrava and mostly built in Spain; it was shipped to Buenos Aires and assembled here. Pass the bridge and stop at the **Museo Fragata Sarmiento 3** (p55) – you can't miss it, as it's aboard the only ship you'll see. Walk the plank, pay your ticket and explore all the fascinating holds of this vessel.

Next up, backtrack a few steps and cross over the Puente de la Mujer; note the small dedication plaque at the other end. Keep marching south, crossing Calle Villaflor to reach the sparkling **Faena Hotel & Universe 4** (p156), a super expensive hotel designed by the world-famous architect Philippe Starke. If you're thirsty, stop and have a coffee at the outdoor café. Then head just a little way down to Calle R Vera Peñaloza and turn left. You'll saunter a few hundred meters to the **Reserva Ecológica Costanera Sur 5** (p56), a marshy ecological reserve

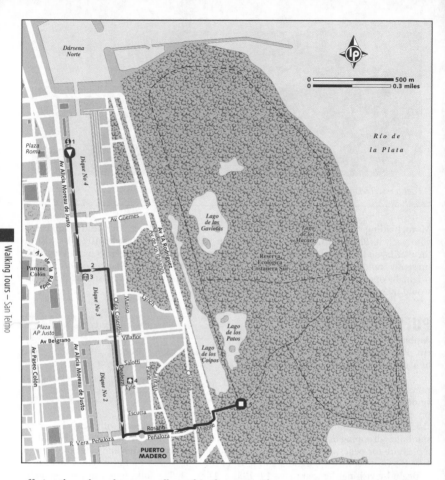

offering the only real nature walks within the center. If you come on a weekend or holiday, there will be bike rentals (p138) on the street near the entrance.

Wander around inside the reserve and keep an eye out for the myriad bird life and, if you're lucky, reptile or mammal life (binoculars would come in handy right about now). Further in at the eastern shoreline of the reserve you can get a close-up view of the Río de la Plata's muddy waters.

There's only one official entrance to the reserve, so you'll have to loop back to the entrance and retrace your steps to where you started in Puerto Madero. And if it's dinnertime, you'll have plenty of choices for a meal with a view (see p90).

## SAN TELMO

San Telmo is a lovely neighborhood of cobbled streets, colonial mansions and tango. It's a wonderful place to amble around, so feel free to stray from the guidelines of this walk which is best done on Sunday, when San Telmo's antiques market is in full swing.

### Walk Facts

**Start** Parque Lezama
**End** Casa Mínima
**Distance** 1.25km
**Duration** 2 hours

*Paintings on display at the Feria de San Telmo (p151)*

Start at Parque Lezama, at the southern edge of San Telmo – bus No 29 from the center gets you within a block. Take a glance around the extensive **Museo Histórico Nacional 1** (p61), located right in the park. Afterwards, stroll through the park, noting the old men playing chess at the cement tables; on a warm weekend afternoon this park fills with youthful activity. Across Av Brasil you'll notice the blue spires of the **Iglesia Ortodoxa Rusa 2** (p60), an attractive Russian Orthodox church.

Walk north up Defensa. If it's a Sunday, this street will be lined with stores and booths selling handicrafts and antiques, especially as you near Plaza Dorrego. But before you get there, hard-core film buffs and modern art junkies can stop at the **Museo del Cine Pablo Ducros Hicken 3** (p61) or the **Museo de Arte Moderno 4** (p61); if you're not a fan, they're not worth it. Just across Av San Juan, however, is the interesting old mansion **Pasaje de la Defensa 5** (p60).

A half-block from the plaza is the **Museo Penitenciario 6** (p61), and right next door the **Iglesia Nuestra Señora de Belén 7** (p60). After checking them out, get back on to Defensa. This street is the main antiques row in the city, so you'll be window-shopping (or more) all up its length; while you may not find many real bargains, there's always something interesting to discover.

Back on Defensa you'll soon reach the heart of the barrio, Plaza Dorrego, where the capital's most well-known market, the **Feria de San Telmo 8** (p151), takes place. It's quite a scene, and even if you don't like to shop, you shouldn't miss it. At Carlos Calvo turn left and find the entrance to the **Mercado San Telmo 9** (p60), an old covered market selling more antiques and some produce.

Keep walking up Defensa, and turn right at Pasaje San Lorenzo to see **Casa Mínima 11** (Defensa 380), a decaying white stucco-and-brick example of the narrow-lot style known as *casa chorizo* (sausage house). Barely 2m wide, the lot was reportedly an emancipation gift from slave owners to their former bondsmen. Finally, if you're hungry for a *parrillada* make sure your last stop is at the lively **Desnivel 10** (p93). The cheap and luscious meat plates here will add back on whatever calories you expended on this walk.

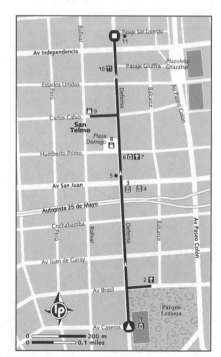

# RECOLETA

Recoleta is the Rolls Royce of Buenos Aires. It's where the rich live in luxury apartments and mansions while spending their free time shopping in expensive boutiques such as Cartier and Armani.

It's where the privileged proudly walk their purebred dogs and have their hair dyed an even bluer hue. It's where the elite sip at elegant cafés in their best Sunday threads – even on Thursdays. And it's also where they're all finally put to rest.

**Walk Facts**

**Start** Cementerio de la Recoleta
**End** Alvear Palace Hotel
**Distance** 3km
**Duration** 3 hours

Start your walk at the entrance to **Cementerio de la Recoleta 1** (p67). You could easily spend hours in here carefully examining the hundreds of elaborate sarcophagi. When you're ready for the living again, come back out of the heavenly gates and turn right; cross the street at the corner and turn right again. You'll be walking by the shopping mall **Village Recoleta 2**; step in for a peek if you'd like – just make sure you have your credit card fully charged. If not, keep going straight, then turn left at Azcuénaga and walk a block. At the intersection you'll see the **Facultad de Ingeniería 3** (p66), an engineering school and a wonderfully Gothic statement. Follow Av Las Heras a couple of blocks, then turn right at Av Pueyrredón. Go three

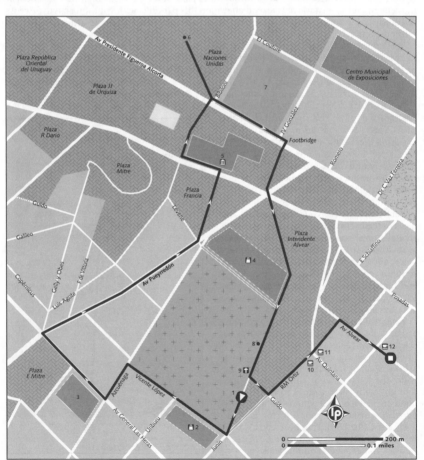

blocks up and you'll see the home-oriented mall **Buenos Aires Design 4** (p147) on your right; it's worth a look if you like furniture and home décor. Now cut across Plaza Francia and head to the **Museo Nacional de Bellas Artes 5** (p68), a noteworthy museum containing both national and international classical art. After you've had an eyeful of impressionist masters, walk around the museum to the right, cutting across the grassy field to Av Presidente Figueroa Alcorta. Be very careful crossing the street to Plaza Naciones Unidas, where you'll see the giant metal flower sculpture **Floralis Genérica 6** (p66); at night the petals curl and close like a real flower. After snapping a few photos, head back down Alcorta – passing by the mammoth **Facultad de Derecho 7** (law school) along the way. Cross the footbridge and make your way back to Plaza Intendente Alvear; if it's a weekend you'll have a whole crafts market to explore. After you tire of the hippies and mimes at the market, stop by the **Centro Cultural Recoleta 8** (p68) and glance inside the pretty **Iglesia de Nuestra Señora del Pilar 9** (p66) next door.

Now that you're tired, amble down restaurant-filled RM Ortiz and make an entrance at either **La Biela 10** (p120) or **Café de la Paix 11** (p120), where you can sit outside on their sunny terraces. If you're looking for something even more elegant, however, go another couple of blocks to the sumptuous **Alvear Palace Hotel 12** (p164), where plush seats, fine service and a hot afternoon tea awaits.

# PALERMO

Palermo's Parque 3 de Febrero, with its gardens and nearby museums and zoo, is a highlight of this walk; in the barrio's peaceful green spaces (and aristocracy's old stomping grounds) you can glimpse how the city's residents let their hair down when they manage some free time. It's best on weekends

## Walk Facts

**Start** Av del Libertador
**End** Plaza Serrano
**Distance** 5km, depending on stops
**Duration** 4 hours or more, depending on stops

when the lakeside ring road is cut off to vehicular traffic and there are bicycle rentals for those feeling lazy. There's also significantly more bustle on sunny weekends, with families and sports fanatics making use of the open grassy lawns for picnics or impromptu *fútbol* (soccer) games.

Have a taxi drop you at the intersection of Av del Libertador and Av de la Infanta Isabel. Stroll up into the park, stopping at the **bike rentals 1** (p138) if you feel like pedaling. Further along, those interested in modern art can peek into the **Museo de Artes Plásticas Eduardo Sívori 2** (p70), a spacious gallery with contemporary art and relaxing café. Head across the road and cross the bridge to the **rosedal 3** (rose garden), where you can stop to sniff the pretty blooms, then continue along the lakeside road. Parents with kids might want to pause at the nearby **planetario 4** (p71), though shows don't start till the evening.

Head along Av Berro for about 500m to the **Jardín Japonés 5** (Japanese garden; p70), a meticulously maintained garden with koi ponds, pretty bridges and a tea shop. After exploring this little paradise you have a choice; if you like to shop, walk two blocks down Av Presidente Figuero Alcorta to **Paseo Alcorta 6** (p150), a large modern shopping mall with bright shops and a good children's play area. If you're more interested in museums, go a block past Paseo Alcorta to

*Detail, Museo de Arte Latinoamericano de Buenos Aires (p70), Palermo*

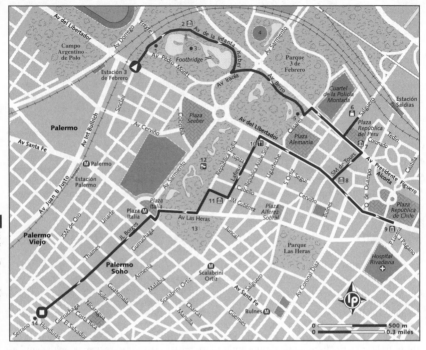

the **Museo de Arte Latinoamericano de Buenos Aires 7** (Malba; p70), which is a relatively new museum showcasing some of the best art in Latin America. Other museums in the area include the **Museo de Motivos Argentinos José Hernández 8** (p72) and the **Museo Nacional de Arte Decorativo 9** (p73).

Back on Av del Libertador, stop in at **Un Altra Volta 10** (p94) for a luscious ice-cream cone or refreshing drink; pastries and snacks are also on offer. After relaxing a bit, go around the corner and walk down Lafinur to the **Museo Evita 11** (p72), where you can check out the collected memorabilia on Argentina's most famous female personality. Outside, turn left on JM Gutiérrez to República India and follow it down to Av Las Heras, then walk the long block to Plaza Italia and the entrance of the **Jardín Zoológico 12** (zoo; p70). If you still have some energy, buy a ticket and stroll inside. If you have less energy you can check out the **Jardín Botánico Carlos Thays 13**, just across the street; this garden stocks various species of trees and plants, but it's also where porteños abandon their unwanted cats – you'll see dozens of felines here.

Those ready for a strong drink can cross Av Santa Fe into Palermo Viejo, where many bars can be found – especially around **Plaza Serrano 14** (p117).

# Eating

# Eating

The quality of ingredients in this richly agricultural country is excellent and the food is usually well prepared, so you're likely to have a good meal no matter where you end up. In fact, you'll eat so well in Buenos Aires that the only way you'll be able to keep the weight off during your visit is by power walking from lunch to dinner.

While variety of cuisine is limited in many areas, this certainly isn't the case in Palermo Viejo (a sub-neighborhood of Palermo). Here, dozens of surprisingly good, upscale restaurants serving international cuisine have popped up in the past few years.

## Opening Hours

Restaurants are generally open daily from noon to 3:30pm for lunch and 8pm to midnight or 1am for dinner; some restaurants stay open till 3am for dinner on weekends (we note specific hours in reviews only if a restaurant has widely different opening times from these). Few places are open early in the morning since Argentines don't eat much breakfast. Cafés (see p118) are an exception and are often open from morning to night without a break, with many offering the whole enchilada: breakfast, lunch, afternoon tea, dinner and late-night snack. Buenos Aires' café culture has been alive and kicking since the 19th century, and there are many atmospheric cafés in which to relive the city's rich past.

## How Much?

Since the devaluation of the peso, Buenos Aires has become a wonderfully affordable place to eat out. You can find delightful pasta lunch specials in good restaurants for as little as US$3, and steak dinners with salad, wine and tip whittle your wallet for only US$10. Some places advertise themselves as *tenedor libre,* which means 'all-you-can-eat'.

*Chef, Un Altra Volta (p94), Palermo*

## Booking Tables

Reservations are usually unnecessary, except for weekend dinners at popular restaurants (exceptions are noted in the reviews).

## Tipping

You should tip about 10% of the total bill; keep in mind that tips can't be added to credit-card purchases. Many of the fancier restaurants add a US$1 per person *cubierto* (cover charge), which covers the use of utensils and bread.

# MICROCENTRO & PLAZA DE MAYO

The Microcentro isn't particularly well known for its great cuisine, as it tends to be much more lunch oriented and clears out after the businessfolk are done with work. (Who wants to stick around the workplace for dinner?) There are still plenty of decent restaurants, however, even if they're sometimes aimed more towards tourists than locals.

**BROCCOLINO** Map pp222-4 *Italian*
☎ 4322-7754; Esmeralda 776; mains US$3-7;
☺ lunch & dinner

Pick from over 25 varieties of toppers for your rigatoni, *fusilli* or spaghetti. If you can't decide, try the delicious vegetarian ravioli with Sicilian sauce (spicy red peppers, tomato and garlic). Portions are famously large, service is quick and efficient and there are daily specials. Plenty of appetizers, meats and desserts (think apple strudel, *tiramisu* and cheesecake) make decisions and diets even harder. Very popular with both locals and tourists alike.

**GRANIX**
Map pp222-4 *Vegetarian All-You-Can-Eat*
☎ 4343-4020; 1st fl, Av Florida 165; all-you-can-eat US$4; ☺ lunch Mon-Fri

This is one of the best vegetarian places in Buenos Aires, and the most popular. It's modern, clean, spacious and open only for lunch. Choices are all good, from the attractive salad bar to hot entrées, and you can be sure none of Argentina's meat culture has landed here. The menu changes daily, and the cost of takeout is a bit less than eating on the premises.

**LA ESTANCIA** Map pp222-4 *Parrilla*
☎ 4326-0330; Av Lavalle 941; mains US$3-13;
☺ lunch & dinner daily

Tourists gawk and take photos of meat roasting on the grill – the smell filling the air is enough of an appetizer. This steakhouse has been serving up barbecued goods since 1962, though the fun murals probably haven't been around that long. Substantial salads, along with many wines, are also served in this large restaurant. On weekends there are tango and folk shows.

Eating – Microcentro & Plaza de Mayo

### Top Five Microcentro, Puerto Madero & Congreso

- **Broccolino** (left) More Italian staples than you can shake a breadstick at
- **La Caballeriza** (p91) A good meaty choice in upscale Puerto Madero
- **Chiquilín** (p92) Lively atmosphere, great service and sizzling steaks
- **Granix** (left) Take a break from the meat at this vegetarian wonderland
- **Laurak Bat** (p92) An oldie and goodie, but you gotta like Basque food

**LA HUERTA**
Map pp222-4 *Vegetarian All-You-Can-Eat*
☎ 4327-2682; Av Lavalle 895; all-you-can-eat US$3;
☺ lunch daily

Here's another of the Microcentro's noncarnivore paradises, attracting health-conscious businessfolk at midday. It offers up a buffet full of vegetarian pasta, pizza, empanadas, omelettes, tarts, *locro* (a traditional corn and meat stew) and *milanesas de soja* (breaded soybean 'steak'), along with plenty of salad ingredients and healthy juices. The atmosphere is efficient, Spartan and clean; it's on the 2nd floor, so head on upstairs.

**LA SORTIJA** Map pp222-4 *Parrilla*
☎ 4328-0824; Av Lavalle 663; mains US$2-5;
☺ lunch & dinner

Don't want to spend a wad and want your food fast and in a bright, modern sit-down environment with a little local flavor? Here's a steal of a place, where you can fill up on a chunk of grilled meat, salad and drink for US$3.50 all told. The *vacío* (a chewy but tasty flank cut) is only US$2 per half-portion, and a *choripán* (sausage sandwich) goes for just US$0.50. It's very popular so go after the lunch rush.

### REY CASTRO Map pp222-4 *Cuban*
☎ 4342-9998; Perú 342; mains US$4-6.50;
☽ lunch & dinner

Rustic arches surround the spacious, smoky atmosphere, and Castro's music plays while trendy diners sample Cuban dishes such as *ropa vieja* (a shredded meat stew). On weekdays happy hour runs from 6pm to 9pm, and on weekends there's live music, dancing and a raucous drag show. Authentic Cuban cigars are for sale, and even Americans can buy them legally.

### SABOT Map pp222-4 *Argentine*
☎ 4313-6587; 25 de Mayo 756; mains US$4-7;
☽ lunch Mon-Fri

Reflecting what Buenos Aires' food is all about is this porteño eatery that draws everyone from CEOs and bank managers to secretaries and porters. The capital's best roasted goat and pepper steak are on the menu, but vegetarians have some options also. Your best bets might just be the daily specials, chalked up on blackboards. Service is efficient, prices are moderate and customers are like members of a club. Reservations are a must after 1:30pm.

# PUERTO MADERO

You'll find restaurant after restaurant in this tastefully renovated waterfront area, which is popular for business power lunches on weekdays and with tourists for dinner. Almost all have views of the attractive nearby dikes, and many sport outdoor covered terraces; these tables are first to fill up in warm weather. Keep in mind that the majority of the restaurants are elegant and sophisticated, and consequently more expensive than in other parts of Buenos Aires (though still quite affordable from a Western standpoint).

### BICE Map pp222-4 *Italian*
☎ 4315-6216; Alicia Moreau de Justo 192; mains US$7-16; ☽ lunch & dinner

The pasta is outrageously good here – try the black fettuccini with shrimp or the spinach and ricotta ravioli with four-cheese sauce. Risotto, meats and fish like trout, salmon and tuna will also tickle your taste buds, with fine service orchestrating it all. Desserts include gelato, crepes and mousse with pears. Get a table out back near the water.

### CABAÑA LAS LILAS Map pp222-4 *Parrilla*
☎ 4313-1336; Alicia Moreau de Justo 516; mains US$9-19; ☽ lunch & dinner

The rustically refined decor and furniture set the mood for fine beef, wine and service, but as famous as this place is – some consider it the best *parrilla* in Buenos Aires – it's tuned to the tourist dollar and consequently way overpriced. Frankly, we've had better meat elsewhere but it's hard to beat the reputation of the 800g, 3in-thick, baby-beef steak. Reserve or else.

*Diners at Chiquilín (p92), Congreso*

# Where's the Beef? *Dereck Foster*

In the beginning there were none. Then the first Spanish settlers arrived with a few members of the Andaluz breed, and soon the lush, huge Pampas were being rapidly populated with wild, rough cattle that, for the next three centuries provided settlers and the indigenous population with abundant beef. These wild herds, roaming freely over the flat, unfenced Pampas, ushered in the gaucho, almost as wild and untamed as the cattle he controlled.

In 1823, when the first fences around Buenos Aires went up, the first pedigree bull was imported from England, a shorthorn considered the father of today's modern Argentine herd. In 1862 the first Hereford bulls were imported from England, followed shortly after by Aberdeen Angus stock. Argentina's herds are today based on Hereford, Aberdeen Angus and shorthorn (Durham) herds, with a great deal of minor breeds in support. These herds, even in today's technological world, are almost totally free-range, roaming the natural grasses and alfalfa fields until being sent to market. This is the main reason behind the high quality of Argentine beef, combined with the habit of hanging (ageing) the carcasses for a shorter period than in the USA or Europe.

Local cuts are also different from traditional US and European cuts, and the cut influences how the meat is cooked. (Argentines, lamentably, tend to overcook their excellent beef. Obtaining a rare or even juicy cut is not always easy.) Note that beef cuts and names are not uniform throughout Argentina, as many areas use local names and cuts. This can cause some surprises when menus are translated into English (as many are).

Beef is prepared in many ways, but none so widely or as picturesquely as on a *parrilla* (grill or barbecue) or a *spiedo* (spit). Oven roasting is a distant second choice. Lesser cuts are either stewed or boiled, as in a *puchero* (like a Spanish *cocido* or French pot-au-feu). Ground beef has become a major medium ever since McDonalds and Burger King set up shop and imposed the burger on the younger generation.

Finding a *parrilla* in Argentina is as easy as falling out of bed, and other alternatives, such as the *choripán* (basically a sausage sandwich, but also beef-filled in many cases), are available in the open air and unlikely places. In fact, about the only place where beef of some sort is hard to find is in Patagonia, where the famous grass-fed lamb is king. In the Andean areas and the central hills of Córdoba, kid (young goat) offers an alternative, but beef, in spite of its high cost for the average Argentine, still reigns supreme.

The most popular and best cuts off a grill are *bife de chorizo* (rump steak), *tira de asado* (short ribs), *vacío* (flank steak), *colita de cuadril* (tail of rump, triangle), and *lomo* (tenderloin). Also served right off the grill but more often served cold is *matambre* (flank and skirt steak), rolled up with a vegetable and boiled-egg filling. If visiting a butcher shop you might see a sign offering *ros bif*. Do not be led astray. *Ros bif* is a cheap boiled or stewed meat.

A properly loaded *parrilla* will contain other 'meats' as well, such as *chinchulines* (lower intestine), *chorizo* (a thick sausage with low-fat content), *salchicha* (a long, thin cousin of the chorizo), *mollejas* (sweetbreads) and *ubre* (udder), along with kidneys, liver, chicken and more. This is called a *parrillada mixta* (mixed grill), and should not be missed.

## LA CABALLERIZA Map pp222-4      *Parrilla*
☎ 4514-4444; Alicia Moreau de Justo 580; mains US$5-9; ⏰ lunch & dinner

This popular restaurant is designed like a renovated barn – a very *fancy* barn. It works though, and as you nibble your juicy *bife de chorizo* (rump steak) you can imagine hearing some neeeiighs. An extensive menu also sports salad, side dishes and desserts. Good prices and better food keep the back patio packed with businessfolk at lunch, so consider making reservations.

## RODIZIO Map pp222-4      *Parrilla*
☎ 4334-3638; Alicia Moreau de Justo 838; lunch US$11, dinner US$13; ⏰ lunch & dinner

Rodizio is a restaurant where you pay one price for all the Brazilian *churrasquería* (barbecued steak) you can wolf down. Slabs of meat head straight to your table, where a knife-wielding waiter sheers off slices for your visual and eating pleasure. A cold appetizer buffet, along with one dessert and a coffee, are included in the price. Kids under 12 pay US$4 to US$6.

## TGI FRIDAYS Map pp222-4      *American*
☎ 4342-7816; Alicia Moreau de Justo 1010; mains US$5-8; ⏰ breakfast, lunch & dinner

Best if you're in town with finicky American kids. True to the familiar chain, there's old-time decor, colorfully dressed wait staff and plenty of cheeseburgers and chicken wings for the little ones. Or try the Southwest enchiladas, fajitas and *quesadillas*, and add a chocolate sundae, mud pie or strawberry shortcake to bring on an afternoon siesta. Color photos and value lunches on the menu make ordering easy. There's another branch at the Alto Palermo shopping center at Coronel Díaz and Arenales.

# CONGRESO & AVENIDA CORRIENTES

The Congreso area is mostly a conglomeration of cheap *parrillas* and fast food, with the occasional Chinese, Korean or Peruvian restaurant thrown in. However, this area also contains Buenos Aires' Little Spain neighborhood (in the blocks around Avs de Mayo and Salta) and here you'll find a few good Spanish and Basque eateries.

### BIWON Map pp226-7 *Korean*
☎ 4372-1146; Junín 548; mains US$4-8;
🕑 lunch & dinner

Most likely the best Korean food in BA. Go for the *bulgogi* (grill the meat yourself at the table), *bibimbap* (rice bowl with meat, veggies, egg and hot sauce – mix it all up) or *kim chee chigue* (kimchi soup with pork – for adventurous, spice-loving tongues only!). Your Korean favorites are all here, including those little dishes of pickled salty morsels automatically brought to your table for you to nibble – delicious! The English on the menu really helps.

### CERVANTES II Map pp226-7 *Parrilla*
☎ 4372-5227; Juan D Perón 1883; mains US$2-5;
🕑 lunch & dinner

Here's another wonderfully affordable and local *parrilla* that simply bustles with the lunchtime crowd. Act like a local and order the *agua de sifón* (soda water) to go along with your *bife de chorizo*, or savor some inexpensive *ravioles con tuco* (ravioli with sauce). Short orders like *milanesas* (breaded steaks), omelettes and fish dishes are also available. Large portions and efficient service keep the crowds coming and going.

### CHIQUILÍN Map pp226-7 *Parrilla*
☎ 4373-5163; Av Sarmiento 1599; mains US$3.50-8;
🕑 lunch & dinner

Come by around midnight on a Saturday night and you'll notice that this traditional *parrilla* – two full floors of it – is packed with happy diners. Chiquilín has been faithfully serving its delicious meats for over 50 years, and the experience shows. Dressed up wait staff are efficient, and the hanging hams and wine bottles add a congenial atmosphere. Specials like paella on Monday and *puchero* (a meat-and-vegetable stew) on Wednesday add welcome detours to the regular menu.

### EL HISPANO Map pp226-7 *Spanish*
☎ 4382-7534; Salta 20; mains US$3.50-11;
🕑 lunch & dinner

When you tire of *parrilla* and want something exotic, visit this Spanish eatery. Order the rabbit stew, octopus *cazuela* (stew), frogs a la Provençal, snails a la Andaluza…or just paella. This classic and atmospheric restaurant has been around for a while and also cooks a range of seafood dishes, including grilled trout, mussels, oysters and fried calamari. Spanish desserts such as *natilla* (custard) and *arroz con leche* (rice pudding) round off your special meal.

### LAURAK BAT Map pp226-7 *Basque*
☎ 4381-0682; Belgrano 1144; mains US$5-7;
🕑 lunch & dinner

Popular with homesick Basques, this modest yet traditional restaurant is set around an atrium showcasing an old Guernica tree brought from the home country. Seafood specialities include *abadejo al pil pil*, *merluza en salsa verde* (both fish dishes), *cazuela de kokotxas* (fish-cheek stew) and mussels a la Provençal. For dessert there's *leche frito* and *tarta vasca*.

### PIPPO Map pp226-7 *Parrilla*
☎ 4375-5887; Paraná 356; mains US$1.50-4;
🕑 lunch & dinner

Dishing up large servings of *parrilla* and pasta for small prices, Pippo is still going strong after 66 years and no wonder – it's a wonderfully casual place with your basic Argentine fare. Service is fast and efficient, the tablecloths are paper and there's a nonsmoking section in back – all good if you bring the kids. Interestingly enough, there's another **Pippo** ( ☎ 4375-2709; Montevideo 341) on the other side of the same block.

### PIZZERÍA GÜERRÍN Map pp226-7 *Pizza*
☎ 4371-8141; Av Corrientes 1368; slices US$0.50;
🕑 7am-2am

After watching a movie on Corrientes it's late, you're hungry and have only a few pesos left – what do you do? Well you can come here, point at a prebaked slice behind the glass counter and eat standing up, for really cheap. To be more civilized, however, sit down and order fresh – this way you'll get a greater variety of toppings for your pizza, and it'll still only cost you US$2. Empanadas and plenty of desserts are also available.

# SAN TELMO & CONSTITUCIÓN

Surrounding Plaza Dorrego are several café-restaurants that will serve you outdoors in the pleasant sunshine – except, of course, when vendors jam the plaza for the Sunday flea market. In general, San Telmo offers some of the best high-quality, low-priced dining in the city, especially for *parrillas*. Pricier and more innovative restaurants are moving in, however, with some nightlife to go along with them.

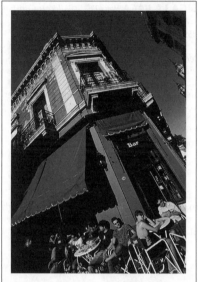

*Bar Plaza Dorrego (below), San Telmo*

### ABRIL Map p225 *International*
☎ 4342-8000; Balcarce 722; lunch US$3-4, dinner US$7; ☽ lunch & dinner
This is probably San Telmo's best bistro, offering an excellent three-course prix-fixe dinner that changes daily. Choices from the limited menu may include beef, chicken, pasta and fish entrées, but rest easy that they'll all arrive very well prepared and beautifully presented. Abril's small, intimate dining room is softly illuminated by candlelight, and the neighborhood's tango atmosphere adds to the romance – it's a good place to bring your date.

### BAR PLAZA DORREGO Map p225 *Café*
☎ 4361-0141; Defensa 1098; mains US$3-8; ☽ 8am-2am Sun-Thu, 8am-6am Fri & Sat
You really can't beat the atmosphere at this old joint; sip your *café cortado* (coffee with milk) or *submarino* (hot milk with chocolate) by the sunny picture window and watch the world pass by. Meanwhile, traditionally suited waiters,

piped-in tango music, antique bottles and scribbled graffiti on walls and counters might take you back in time – at least until your hamburger lands on the table. (More typically Argentine fare is also available.) When it's not too busy they'll set out tables on the sidewalk – another experience in itself.

### DESNIVEL Map p225 *Parrilla*
☎ 4300-9081; Defensa 855; mains US$1.50-3; ☽ lunch & dinner Tue-Sun, dinner Mon
This famous local joint is packed at lunch like a rock concert, serving up the traditional chorizo (sausage) sandwich and a super tasty *bife de lomo* (tenderloin steak). Add salad and a double espresso, and you can walk away happy and buzzing for US$5. The sizzling grill that greets you out front might be torturous while you wait for a table to open up – this place is very popular, and ridiculously crowded on Sundays.

### LA FARMACIA Map p225 *International*
☎ 4300-6151; Bolívar 898; mains US$4-6; ☽ lunch & dinner
La Farmacia is quite possibly the hippest artsy restaurant in town, and gay-friendly to boot. Head up to the 2nd floor for an intimate table or casual sofa lounging, or to the slightly slanted rooftop patio for some fresh air. It's a creative space serving innovative tidbits like lamb ratatouille, salmon ravioli and spinach *ñoquis* (gnocchi). Apple crepes and lemon pie are for dessert, and there's a tiny store for some après-dinner shopping.

### PAPPA DEUS Map p225 *Italian*
☎ 4361-2110; Bethlem 423; mains US$3-8; ☽ 9am-2am
Come by on a weekday, and a strategic spot on the plaza – right under a shady umbrella – will double the enjoyment of your pumpkin- and spinach-filled black ravioli. Other innovative dishes, all thoughtfully presented, include lamb with roasted peppers and a crisp prosciutto salad. For the non-adventurous there are pizza and *parrilla* selections on the menu. Try the *tiramisu* – it isn't bad at all.

## PARRILLA 1880 Map p225 *Parrilla*

☎ 4307-2746; Defensa 1665; mains US$2-5; ☽ lunch & dinner Tue-Sun

For a good, solid *parrilla* experience make your way down south to this popular joint, right across from Parque Lezama. The atmosphere is thick with history and locals enjoying all the juicy cuts of meat coming out from the open grill in front – try the *ojo de bife* (rib eye) or *pechito de cerdo* (pork ribs). Plenty of other dishes, like pasta and salads, are also available – just remember to make reservations on the weekends, even for lunch.

## PRIDE CAFÉ Map p225 *Café*

☎ 4300-6435; Balcarce 869; mains US$1.50-3; ☽ 10am-10pm Sun-Fri

This cute little modern corner café is set out in black and white, with changing art on the walls. Gay men swamp the place on Sundays during San Telmo's antiques fair, and good music complements the homemade pastries and 'queer coffee.' Salads, sandwiches and sushi nights add interest, though you might also tuck yourself away, martini in hand, to peruse the foreign mags or watch DVDs on the small screen behind the counter.

## SIGA LA VACA Map p225 *All-You-Can-Eat*

☎ 4315-6801; Alicia Moreau de Justo 1714; lunch US$6-9, dinner US$8-9; ☽ lunch & dinner

Only the truly hungry should set foot in this *tenedor libre parrilla*, where mountains of food are available for consumption. Work your way from the appetizer/salad bar to the grill, where the good stuff hangs out. The secret is, when your tummy says 'no more', don't take that as an answer – this way, you'll only need to eat once that day. Prices vary depending on the meal and day.

# LA BOCA

You won't have trouble finding a colorful joint in which to grab a bite here in La Boca – there are quite a few on the four touristy streets to which you should stick like glue – though they're all somewhat similar and far from the cutting edge of international cuisine. Veer off the beaten path, looking like a lost rich tourist, and you run the risk of meeting the local bullies who want your lunch money.

## Licking Your Way Through BA

Because of Argentina's Italian heritage, Argentine *helado* is comparable to the best ice cream anywhere in the world. Amble into an *heladería* (ice-cream shop), order up a cone (you usually pay first) and the creamy concoction will be artistically swept up into a mountainous peak and handed over with a small plastic spoon stuck in the side. Important: *granizado* means with chocolate flakes.

Chains like Freddo (located throughout the city) have some great stuff, but the best Argentine ice cream might very well come from smaller places that make their own batches; look for the words *elaboración propia* or *elaboración artesanal*. All types of *heladerías*, however, offer their customers dozens of tempting flavors, from the conventional vanilla and *dulce de leche* variations to exotic fruits and other unexpected mixtures. During winter, when Argentines eat less ice cream, the best *heladerías* often close. During the hot Buenos Aires summer, though, you'll find yourself among many sweet-toothed porteños standing in line waiting to dig in to these delicious treats.

Here are some of the tastiest *heladerías* in town:

- **Freddo** (Map pp230-1 ☎ 0800-3337-3336; cnr Ayacucho & Quintana, Recoleta) for other branches, check www.freddo.com.ar
- **Munchi's** (Map pp228-9 ☎ 0800-555-5050, cnr MT de Alvear & Av Florida, Retiro) for other branches, check www.munchis.com.ar
- **Persicco** (Map pp232-3 ☎ 0810-333-7377, cnr Salguero & Cabello, Palermo)
- **Vía Flaminia** (Map pp222-4 ☎ 4342-7737, Av Florida 121, Microcentro)
- **Un Altra Volta** (Map pp232-3 ☎ 4805-1818, Av del Libertador 3060, Palermo)
- **Heladería Cadore** (Map pp226-7; ☎ 4374-3688, Av Corrientes 1695, Congreso)

*Customers at Persicco (left)*

### EL OBRERO Map pp220-1 *Parrilla*
☎ 4362-9912; Caffarena 64; mains US$3-7; ☽ lunch & dinner Mon-Sat

If there was ever a restaurant you'd go to for ambiance and history, this would be the one. The family here has been running this place for 70 years. On display are unfinished bottles of wine, along with plenty of photos – testament to famous diners that include Bono, Robert Duvall and various Argentine celebrities. The food isn't spectacular, but the atmosphere makes it taste so much better. Take a taxi here and back.

# RETIRO

As in the Microcentro, Retiro's restaurants tend to pack up with businesspeople during the lunch hour; you'll find midday specials at almost every place competing for this market. Most cafés and bars also serve meals and can be more atmospheric and interesting places to eat than traditional restaurants. Many places do takeout – which can sometimes be cheaper than dining in – and then all you have to do is find yourself a nice grassy spot or shady bench in nearby Plaza San Martín where you can enjoy your impromptu picnic.

### EL CUARTITO Map pp228-9 *Pizza*
☎ 4816-1758; Talcahuano 937; pizza slices US$0.50-0.70; ☽ 10am-2am

In a hurry? Think fast, order and pay for your piece of pie, then munch at the counters standing up. Not only is it cheaper and faster this way, but you can chat up the chap next to you and enjoy the old sports posters without turning around. You can't get more local, and while it's mostly full of businessmen and male waiters the gals are equally welcome.

### EMPIRE BAR Map pp228-9 *Thai*
☎ 4312-5706; Tres Sargentos 427; mains US$5-12; ☽ lunch & dinner Mon-Fri, dinner Sat

This popular spot is filled with both tourists and locals for its *almost* authentic Thai cuisine – it seems Argentines couldn't handle the real thing. Kevin Rodriguez, once from New Jersey, now serves up crispy wrapped prawns, *paneng* chicken in red curry or *tom ka gai* for lunch; for dessert, try the banana fritters or mango (if it's in season) with sweet rice. Surroundings are modern and snazzy, as is the music.

### FILO Map p225 *International*
☎ 4311-0312; San Martín 975; mains US$4-8; ☽ noon-2am

It's hard to figure what's best at this trendy place, especially when you look at the dizzying menu. At least your choice is likely to be excellent; 20 varieties of pizza and 15 kinds of salads (try the smoked salmon) are all highly regarded. Other choices include *panini*, pasta and meats, along with a whirlwind of desserts. The highly artistic atmosphere is also wonderfully creative – don't forget to check out the art gallery downstairs.

### GRAN BAR DANZÓN
Map pp228-9 *International*
☎ 4811-1108; Libertad 1161; mains US$4-8; ☽ dinner

It's hard to be hipper than this ultimate lounge-bar-restaurant. A very cool-looking conservation system makes it possible to order many wines by the glass, or you can browse the extensive wine list for bottles. The menu is graced with dishes along the lines of duck *confit* with *taleggio* cheese, risotto with king crab, and portabello, pear and arugula salad. There's also some excellent sushi. This place attracts the young and fashionable like a model shoot, so dress well and come early if you want a table.

### LA CHACRA Map pp228-9 *Parrilla*
☎ 4322-1409; Córdoba 941; mains US$4-10; ☽ noon-2am

Resist the urge to ride on the stuffed cow in the entryway and ogle the *asado* roasting in the window instead. Inside, old-world waiters serve succulent grilled meats – including seven kinds of *lomo* – while deer and boar heads high on the walls watch patrons munch on their bovine cousins. Plenty of salads and side dishes round out the menu.

### LA ESQUINA DE LAS FLORES
Map pp228-9 *Vegetarian*
☎ 4813-3630; Córdoba 1587; mains US$1.50-3; ☽ 8:30am-8:30pm Mon-Fri, 8:30am-3pm Sat

One of BA's most enduring vegetarian alternatives, this modern restaurant also has a small health-food store on the ground floor (buy soy flour, whole-wheat breads and organic *mate*). There's a tiny fast-food section, but if you prefer to sit down, go upstairs and choose from the imaginative menu, which changes daily. They've even got a dish for macrobiotics.

## Top Five Retiro & Recoleta

- **Cumaná** (opposite) Always packed for its Northern Argentine specialties
- **Filo** (p95) Great food, artsy atmosphere and a menu that covers it all
- **Gran Bar Danzón** (p95) BA's trendiest crowd-watching eatery and winery
- **Lotos** (below) Cheap, healthy vegetarian grub and a health-food store to boot
- **Munich Recoleta** (opposite) Old-world atmosphere in Recoleta's restaurant row

**LE SUD** Map pp228-9  *French Mediterranean*
☎ 4131-0130; Arroyo 841; mains US$12-20;
🕑 breakfast, lunch & dinner

For a taste of Europe, dress up in your best threads, slip on your gourmet tie and head on over to Le Sud, one of BA's top restaurants and elegantly ensconced in the posh Sofitel Hotel. Award-winning chef Thierry Pszonda (below) whips out simple yet authentic French fusion cuisine sprinkled with fresh herbs, spices and oils straight from the Mediterranean. Order the stewed rabbit or lemon ravioli and you'll be in Provence before it's time for dessert.

**LOTOS** Map pp228-9  *Vegetarian*
☎ 4814-4552; Córdoba 1577; mains US$1-2;
🕑 11:30am-6pm Mon-Fri, 11:30am-4pm Sat

Right next door to La Esquina de las Flores is this equally renowned vegetarian spot. It's cafeteria-style, so just point at what looks good. Choices include delicious healthy soups, extensive salad ingredients and filling entrées. In the basement is a good **health-food store** ( 🕑 8:30am-8pm Mon-Fri, 8:30am-4pm Sat) where dry noodles, fresh-baked breads, organic tea, whole grains, herbal remedies and fresh tofu await your inspection.

**MUMBAI** Map pp228-9  *Indian*
☎ 4315-0075; Paraguay 436; mains US$4-7.50;
🕑 lunch & dinner Mon-Fri, dinner Sat

Indian-run and fairly authentic is this new restaurant serving the business district. Good dishes include the *chicken tikka masala* (tandoori-cooked in a curry sauce) and *gosht saag* (lamb served with spinach). Biryani rice dishes are also tasty and a bit lighter, and vegetarians have their own section of the menu. There's a nonsmoking section and the atmosphere is smart and softly imbued with soothing music.

**NUCHA** Map pp228-9  *Café*
☎ 4813-9507; Paraná 1343; coffee & snacks US$2-3;
🕑 8am-9pm Mon-Thu, 9am-2am Fri & Sat, 9am-9pm Sun

Modern, trendy and very popular are good terms to describe this little café right across from Plaza Vicente López on the edge of Retiro. There *must* be something in the tempting pastry counter – cheesecake, *medialunas* (croissants) or lightly layered afternoon cake – to go with your imported tea, iced coffee with ice cream or *mate*. The upscale crowds, from little old ladies to slick young hipsters, flood in for afternoon tea and *sandwichitos de miga* (thin, crustless sandwiches). Breakfast is also served. There's another branch in Palermo ( ☎ 4802-1615; Salguero 2587).

**YATASTO** Map pp228-9  *Northern Argentine*
☎ 4315-3772; Suipacha 1015; mains US$2-5;
🕑 lunch & dinner

Don't be put off by the bars in the windows – this is a congenial place, and absolutely packed with businesspeople during weekday lunchtimes. Spicy northern Argentine cuisine such as empanadas, tamales and filling *locro* is served in the slightly claustrophobic interior. Try the *manzana asada* (grilled apple) for your sweet tooth.

## Chef Thierry Pszonda  *Dereck Foster*

Nobody disputes that Thierry Pszonda, the executive chef of the intimate and elegant Le Sud in the Sofitel Hotel, holds rank as one of the top chefs in Buenos Aires. A mere 34 years old, his résumé is already packed with awards and recognitions both from within Argentina and abroad. The latest feather in his cap has been his membership into the Maîtres Cuisiniers de France.

After training in France under the tutelage of Jean Crotet and Michel Bering (Michelin two stars), and Jacques Lameloise (Michelin three stars), Pszonda ran the kitchens of such restaurants as Le Biblo, Au Bec Fin and La Bourgogne before taking over at Le Sud.

Pszonda styles himself a naturalist in the kitchen, and herbs and spices are given free rein in his creations. He also keeps in close contact with his suppliers, guaranteeing quality and continuity in his ingredients.

# RECOLETA & BARRIO NORTE

Upscale Recoleta, as you would imagine, has its share of expensive eateries – though they aren't necessarily the best in town. We list some good-value choices below. There are two blocks' worth of cafés, bars and restaurants on RM Ortiz in front of the cemetery ('Restaurant Row' as it's called), but many are aimed towards tourists and tend to be unexceptional. They're great for outside eating and people watching, however, as most have pleasant terraces out front.

### ARTE SANO Map pp230-1      *Vegetarian*
☎ 4963-1513; Mansilla 2740; mains US$1.50-3.50;
🕑 8am-10pm Mon-Fri, 9am-8pm Sat
This small, bright and pleasant health-food eatery cooks up excellent dishes, such as *budín tricolor* (chard, carrot and squash tart), *milanesa de soja* and whole-wheat pizza. Desserts are good for the body, like the yogurt with granola or fruit salad. The small attached store sells things like brown rice, powdered ginger and baked goods. Also on offer are yoga classes and natural-food workshops.

### CUMANÁ Map pp230-1     *Northern Argentine*
☎ 4813-9507; Rodriguez Peña 1149; mains US$2-5;
🕑 lunch & dinner
If you've never tried *cazuela*, your time is up – and this is definitely the place to have some. Cumaná specializes in these deliciously homey, stick-to-your-ribs pot stews, which are filled and baked with squash, corn, eggplant, potatoes and/or meats, among other tidbits. Also popular are the pizzas, empanadas, pastas and *calzones*. But come early 'cause the prices here are ridiculously low and the masses all want a part of the action; this place always hops, and empty tables are scarce.

### EL SANJUANINO
Map pp230-1     *Northern Argentine*
☎ 4805-2683; Posadas 1515; mains US$2.50-5.50;
🕑 lunch & dinner
This friendly little place probably has the cheapest food in Recoleta. Sit at one of the eight tables and order spicy empanadas, tamales or *locro*. The brick curved ceiling adds to the local atmosphere, but you can be like most

folks and take your food to go – Recoleta's lovely parks are just a couple of blocks away.

### GRANT'S Map pp230-1     *All-You-Can-Eat*
☎ 4823-5894; Junín 1155; lunch US$3-6, dinner US$4.50-6; 🕑 lunch & dinner
This *tenedor libre* is run by efficient Chinese folks, just like most others in town. Grant's is one of the best, however – the buffet tables overflow with a fantastic assortment of foods too numerous to mention. There will be plenty of *parrilla* and dessert selections, don't worry. You'll be rolling out of this joint no matter what, so try to choose carefully and eat slowly – you get more in that way. The all-you-can-eat price depends on the meal and on the day of the week. Be aware that drinks are mandatory and cost extra. There's another **Grant's** ( ☎ 4801-9099; General Las Heras 1925) near Ayacucho.

### MUNICH RECOLETA
Map pp230-1     *International*
☎ 4804-3981; RM Ortiz 1871; mains US$5-8;
🕑 lunch & dinner
This traditional old place hasn't changed much since Borges was a regular; even the waiters seem to be the same. The food is consistently good; try the omelettes, brochettes, grilled salmon or vegetable soup (this last one especially good in winter). Service is outstanding – one reason you might find more porteños than tourists eating here, unlike at the other flashier, restaurants in this row. Finish off your meal with the tasty *flan casera* (homemade flan) and even the animal heads on the wall will seem to smile with you.

# PALERMO

Palermo is ground zero for innovative cuisine in Buenos Aires. Hundreds of restaurants, many of them serving wonderfully creative and very good food, have popped up here in the past few years. All are waiting to tingle your taste buds, and most won't disappoint – competition keeps quality high, and new restaurants are opening up all the time. Saturation will eventually weed out the weak, but in the meantime enjoy the huge variety at your wallet's fingertips – it's a great time to be eating in Buenos Aires, especially in this area.

Another neighborhood in Palermo with exceptional restaurants is Las Cañitas (p69).

## Top Five Palermo

- **Olsen** (p109) Scandinavian designs, super-cool food and Sunday brunch
- **Bar Uriarte** (p107) Surprisingly great food and hip atmosphere
- **Central** (p108) An ultramodern eatery serving some of Palermo's tastiest entrées
- **Sudestada** (p110) Really stunning Southeast Asian food and a must-try
- **Río Alba** (right) One of BA's best steakhouses, with more substance than chic

### ANASTASIA Map pp232-3      *Parrilla*
☎ 4802-8640; cnr Bulnes & Cabello; mains US$3-7;
☖ lunch & dinner

Reservations are a good idea – this popular *parrilla* fills up early. The *pastas caseras* (home-made pastas) are mighty fine – try the *ñoquis* – but most folks come here for the succulent grilled meats, roasted to perfection. Brick walls and a dim atmosphere exude richness and sophistication, attracting businesspeople and an older, well-dressed clientele. *Mate* is on the menu to help wash down those tasty ribs.

### BELLA ITALIA Map pp232-3      *Italian*
☎ 4802-4253; República Árabe Siria 3285; mains US$5-7; ☖ dinner Mon-Sat

Some of Buenos Aires' best Italian food is cooked up at this fancy little place. Try the delicate *tagliatelle* (a thin ribbon pasta served here with bacon), the lemon ravioli with salmon and arugula or the braised rabbit. The *tiramisu* seems a bit too creamy to be authentic, but offerings such as dessert wines and grappa help offset this flaw. Bella Italia also has a café just up the street on the next block, which serves similar but lighter fare.

### KANSAS Map pp232-3      *American*
☎ 4776-4100; Av del Libertador 4625; mains US$3-8;
☖ lunch & dinner

This large, contemporary restaurant is way too popular for its own good, but the American-style burgers are very much a novelty and keep drawing the crowds. Another temptation is the Houston barbecued ribs and delicious pastas, but those watching their waists can order the crisp salads instead (portions are huge). Comfortable booths in the dim, elegant dining room are a nice touch, and you can peek at Palermo's racetrack out back. Come early or wait – they don't take reservations.

### KATMANDU Map pp232-3      *Indian*
☎ 4963-3250; Córdoba 3547; mains US$4-6.50;
☖ dinner Mon-Sat

For an authentic taste of India, hike up to Katmandu (bus No 106 goes up Córdoba from the city center), which serves some wonderfully tasty and authentic food. The tandoori *gosht* is delicious lamb marinated in milk and saffron, while the coconut fish curry is marinated in yogurt, ginger and cardamom. Samosas are also served, and the garlic *naan* (a thick flat bread) is especially satisfying.

### MYKONOS Map pp232-3      *Greek*
☎ 4779-9000; Olleros 1752; mains US$4.50-10;
☖ dinner

This Greek restaurant at the edge of Belgrano is a peaceful place…at least until they start breaking plates during their nightly traditional dance show. Beautiful murals could transport you to the Mediterranean, as might the fairly good *tzatziki* (a cucumber and yogurt sauce), *spanakopita* (spinach pastry), *musaka* (eggplant with spicy meat) and of course the Greek salads. Other treats include octopus or salmon dishes, and there's *baklava* for dessert. And don't forget – the jig starts at 9:30pm.

### RÍO ALBA Map pp232-3      *Parrilla*
☎ 4773-5748; Cerviño 4499; mains US$4-10;
☖ lunch & dinner

This well-regarded *parrilla* serves some of the tastiest grilled meat in town. Try the house specialty, the *ojo de bife* (rib eye). This is steak at its best, and at US$5 the half-portion is more than enough for most. All dishes are excellent, however, including the salmon and pork. Atmosphere is modest, but they're concentrating on food, not decor, and you'll thank them for it. With luck, you'll get a waiter who remembers your party of 12's order without having to write a single thing down.

## PALERMO VIEJO

You may hear the terms 'Palermo Soho' (north of the railroad tracks) and 'Palermo Hollywood' (south of the tracks) used to describe the sub-neighborhoods of Palermo Viejo, itself a subsection of Palermo. The majority of Buenos Aires' fashionable ethnic restaurants are found in these areas, with many of them scattered near lively Plaza Serrano.

*(Continued on page 107)*

**1** Tango show at Confitería Ideal (p118), Microcentro **2** Street scene in Barrio Norte (p66) **3** The Madres de la Plaza de Mayo (p53) **4** Showtime at Café Tortoni (p118)

1 Statue of General Belgrano silhouetted against the Casa Rosada (p53), Microcentro
2 Galerías Pacífico (p144) shopping centre, Microcentro
3 A local paseaperros (dog walker), Palermo (p66) 4 Antiques display (p145) on Defensa, San Telmo

1 *Feeding the llamas at Jardín Zoólogico (p70), Palermo*
2 *Mast of the floating Museo Fragata Sarmiento (p56), Puerto Madero* 3 *Palacio de las Aguas Corrientes (p57), Congreso*
4 *Museo Municipal de Arte Hispanoamericano Isaac Fernández Blanco (p65), Retiro*

1 Char-grilling beef at the Feria de Mataderos (p151) 2 Delightful choices at Vía Flaminia (p94), Microcentro 3 Barbecued chorizos, Feria de Mataderos (p151) 4 La Peña del Colorado, Palermo (p124)

**1** Quaffing mate *(p14)* **2** Freddo *(p94) ice-cream shop, Recoleta* **3** Buffet at Alvear Palace Hotel *(p164), Recoleta* **4** Wine display, Club del Vino *(p124), Palermo Viejo*

*1 Brightly painted houses in La Boca (p62)* *2 Floralis Genérica sculpture (p66), Recoleta* *3 Mercado de Abasto (p75), Once* *4 Palacio del Congreso (p57), Congreso*

**1** *Centro Cultural Torquato Tasso (p129), San Telmo* **2** *Gran Bar Danzón (p95), Retiro* **3** *Folk music at La Peña del Colorado (p124), Palermo* **4** *Petit Paris Café (p120), Retiro*

*1* Iguazú Falls (p169), Paraná, Brazil *2* Plaza Independencia (p172), Montevideo, Uruguay *3* Beachfront, Punta del Este (p180) *4* Lighthouse on the ruins of the Convento de San Francisco (p176), Colonia

*(Continued from page 98)*

## AL ANDALUS

Map pp232-3        *Spanish Moorish*
☎ 4832-9286; Godoy Cruz 1823; mains US$4-6;
☽ dinner Tue-Sat

Chef Ricardo Araujo has traveled extensively to bring you a changing menu of classic Mediterranean dishes. Choices are limited but to the point – try the risotto with goat cheese, white fish with tomato vinaigrette or *konya* (lamb ball) with yogurt and pilaf. Complex sauces and exotic spices tie dishes together well, while the desserts are delicious works of art. Al Andalus isn't as snazzy as other nearby restaurants, but it's been around longer than most and is a good choice for a tasty, peaceful night out.

## ARTEMESIA Map pp232-3    *Semivegetarian*

☎ 4863-4242; José Antonio Cabrera 3877; mains
US$4-6; ☽ lunch Tue-Sat, dinner

Focusing on mostly vegetarian healthy fare is this artsy eatery. Homemade bread arrives first, followed by your choice of a carrot-cilantro dip, bruschetta or perhaps a quinoa salad. Main dishes include broccoli ravioli, squash tart, veggie stir-fry and salmon in Thai coconut sauce. The food is well prepared and flavorful, and best of all you feel good about eating it. Wash it down with their sweet ginger lemonade.

## BAR 6 Map pp232-3      *International*

☎ 4833-6807; Armenia 1676; mains US$5-8.50;
☽ breakfast, lunch & dinner Mon-Sat

The long bar, velvet sofas, curved wood ceiling and reggae music might temporarily distract you from the short menu and chalkboard specials, but don't let them. The grilled salmon is excellent and the pastas quite fine, though some think the veggie stir-fry could do with a dash more inspiration. This place lives on its reputation though, and other dishes of better esteem might include the grilled lamb, Mediterranean linguine and white fish with citrus, ginger and corn.

## BAR URIARTE Map pp232-3    *International*

☎ 4834-6004; Uriarte 1572; mains US$6-8;
☽ lunch & dinner

Serving some of Palermo Viejo's best food and wine is this ultratrendy and mighty good-looking eatery. While the noise levels might be too loud for a romantic night out, the food more than makes up for it – sample the rabbit ravioli, risotto with creamed corn, marinated zucchini with ricotta or lamb carpaccio. And while the entrées might not fill you to the brim, the luscious desserts certainly will – the chocolate mousse with raspberries is simply unforgettable.

## BIO Map pp232-3    *Organic Health Food*

☎ 4774-3880; Humboldt 2199; mains US$4-5;
☽ 9am-midnight Tue-Sun, 9am-noon Mon

The supremely health-conscious should make a beeline to this casual corner joint, which specializes in organic fare. Soy burgers, tofu with steamed veggies and whole-wheat pastas will feed your soul, along with mushroom salads and the Mediterranean couscous with dried tomatoes. Daily specials cost US$3.50 and include a drink, but probably not the organic wine. Fresh juices are also available.

*Eating – Palermo*

---

## Pass the Beef....Errr, Make That the Tofu

Argentine cuisine is internationally famous for its succulent grilled meats, but this doesn't mean vegetarians – or even vegans – are completely out of luck.

Most restaurants, including *parrillas*, serve a few items acceptable to most vegetarians, such as green salads, omelettes, mashed potatoes, pizza and pasta dishes (just make sure they're not topped with a meat sauce). Remember that *carne* is beef. *Pollo* (chicken), *cerdo* (pork) and the like are considered in a different category, though they are sometimes referred to as *carne blanca* (white meat). *Pescado* (fish) and *mariscos* (seafood) are sometimes available. *Sin carne* means 'without meat,' and the words *soy vegetariano/a* (for male/female speaker) meaning 'I'm a vegetarian' will come in handy when explaining to an Argentine why in the world you don't eat their delicious steaks.

Also – luckily for nonmeat eaters – vegetarian restaurants have become more common in Buenos Aires over the past two decades. The ones reviewed in this chapter are **Artemesia**, **Granix**, **La Huerta**, **La Esquina de las Flores** and **Lotos**, but there are others. The latter two have small but good health-food places, or you can try **Dietética Viamonte** (Map 222-4; ☎ 4322-4364; Viamonte 859; ☽ 8:30am-7:30pm Mon-Fri, 8am-1pm Sat), which probably has the most extensive selection of vegetarian and health foods in the city center, including bulk grains, cereals, dried fruit, bakery goods and organic lotions.

Best of luck to all vegetarians visiting BA, and may the Argentine beef gods forgive you.

*Entrance to Filo (p95)*

### CLUNY Map pp232-3 *International*
☎ 4831-7176; El Salvador 4618; mains US$6-8;
🕑 lunch & dinner

You can't get much more attractive, hip or elegant than Cluny, which features an interior patio, flattering lighting, comfy white sofas and simply gorgeous ambiance. The food's top-notch too, with a good selection of steaks, salmon and pastas – don't miss the black ravioli stuffed with lamb. A short but well chosen wine list will complete your exceptional experience here.

### DASHI Map pp232-3 *Japanese*
☎ 4776-3500; Fitzroy 1613; mains US$6-11;
🕑 lunch & dinner

Some of the sweetest sushi in town is rolled up at sleek and minimalist Dashi, though it tends to be heavy on the salmon (as in all of Buenos Aires). The boat platters are still bedazzling, however, especially after lovely appetizers like gyoza, miso soup and yakitori skewers. Other Japanese delicacies include tempura, teriyaki and *teppan* (table grills). It's all first-rate, so enjoy.

### DOMINGA Map pp232-3 *International*
☎ 4771-4443; Honduras 5618; mains US$5-8;
🕑 lunch & dinner Mon-Sat

Dominga is easily one of the best restaurants in Palermo Viejo for contemporary cuisine. The salmon teriyaki comes perfectly cooked (or most importantly, not overdone) and is wonderfully presented on a bed of steamed vegetables, while the chicken in green curry is well spiced and the seafood risotto with lemon might just knock your socks off. Interestingly enough, there's also a large selection of respectable sushi and sashimi, while the minimalist patio adds visual inspiration.

### FREUD & FAHLER
Map pp232-3 *International*
☎ 4833-2153; Gurruchaga 1750; mains US$5.50-8;
🕑 dinner

From the eclectic ambiance to the illustrated menu, this artsy restaurant gives diners a personal touch. It also ensures they'll have much to discuss, even when not gazing at the large painting of Sigmund Freud looming in the back. While presentation is beautiful, portions will leave you wanting more – though this means you'll have space for the *flan mixto*. Don't forget to shake hands with the loquacious chef on the way out the door.

### CENTRAL Map pp232-3 *International*
☎ 4776-7374; Costa Rica 5644; mains US$6-8;
🕑 lunch & dinner

The minimalist decor and cool young things perched on their high stools (or lounging prettily on the low sofas) are right out of a fashion magazine, but Central is much more than that. The thoughtful and creative menu, which changes with the seasons but remains always excellent, ranges from trout with Mediterranean vegetables to baked squash tarts and tender grilled steaks. Tasty appetizers and luscious desserts deliver the goods equally well, though the dim candlelight makes it hard to see past your fork.

### CHUECA Map pp232-3 *International*
☎ 4963-3430; Soler 3283; mains US$6-7;
🕑 dinner Wed-Sat

Located in a discreet purple building tucked away on a sleepy Palermo Viejo street, Chueca – named for the gay district in Madrid – offers an excellent dining experience in a hyperstylish but very comfortable atmosphere. The menu is small but compensates by being excellent: try the tasty chicken with mango sauce. Midnight drag shows liven things up until closing, when the mostly gay clientele start thinking about hitting the clubs.

## GREEN BAMBOO

Map pp232-3            *Vietnamese*
☎ 4775-7050; Costa Rica 5802; mains US$6.50-11;
☾ dinner

There's no beef noodle soup in this hip and lounge-like Vietnamese restaurant, so instead order the excellent stir-frys and flavorful mixed bowls. Just a dozen entrées grace the menu, which rotates every six months but always includes meat, chicken and seafood dishes, along with a few vegetarian options. Exotic spices are well used, but ask for extra spicy if you like some tingle. There are plenty of appetizers and mixed drinks, and the desserts look awesome (we were on a diet that night, but the next table was not).

## KRISHNA Map pp232-3     *Indian/Vegetarian*
☎ 4833-4618; Malabia 1833; mains US$2.50-3.50;
☾ lunch & dinner Wed-Sun, lunch Tue

Colorful thematic decor and low tables offer a special experience with a slice of hippiness. This tiny and casual vegetarian spot is popular for its thalis, soy burgers, *koftas* (balls of ground vegetables) and cheese/chutney crepes. Drinks are equally exotic – sample the ginger lemonade, mango lassi or carrot/beet/orange-juice combo. For dessert there's apple pancakes. Food may not be completely authentic, but for BA it's certainly quite passable.

## LOMO Map pp232-3       *Modern Parrilla*
☎ 4833-3200; Costa Rica 4661; mains US$5-8;
☾ lunch & dinner Tue-Thu, dinner Mon

The bamboo walls and corrugated-steel roof work well here, and combined with the stony terrace up top make for a very trendy meal out. Choose the lamb chops with herbs, seafood risotto or *lomo aguaribay*, which comes peppered and on a bed of steamed vegetables. More exotic selections include *jabalí* (wild braised pork), Patagonian trout and salmon and shrimp ravioli. While portions aren't large, flavors are finely tuned and presentation is beautiful. For dessert order the apple pear crumble and avoid the too-sweet filo pastry.

## MARK'S DELI & COFFEEHOUSE

Map pp232-3             *Deli Café*
☎ 4832-6244; El Salvador 4701; mains US$2.50-3;
☾ 8:30am-9:30pm Mon-Sat, 10:30am-9pm Sun

If you're missing your pastrami on wheat, check out what's on offer at this casual deli. Sandwiches, salads and soup are fresh, tasty and well-prepared, though authenticity is off – the sandwich bread is a little pasty and the caesar salad isn't made with romaine. However, super-cool patio seating and sunny sidewalk tables keep the place buzzing, as do the iced coffee and double mochas. The clean, modern interior and good music don't hurt its hipness either.

## OLSEN Map pp232-3     *Northern European*
☎ 4776-7677; Gorriti 5870; mains US$5.50-11;
☾ lunch & dinner Tue-Sat, 10:30am-8pm Sun

Olsen is famous for its Sunday brunch, but chef Germán Martitegui cooks up other meals with equal aplomb. Arrive for dinner and you might order lamb ravioli with blackcurrant compote, venison with roasted quince or grilled tuna in yogurt dressing. Lunches are prix fixe, generously sized and excellent as well. The ambiance – complete with peaceful garden out front – is stunningly Scandinavian, and you'll enjoy it even more after downing a shot of vodka, assiduously kept at exactly 18° below zero.

## RAVE Map pp232-3       *International*
☎ 4833-7832; Gorriti 5092; mains US$4-7; ☾ dinner
Attractive both inside and out, this dimly lit restaurant offers up mostly pasta, meats and fancy salads – not especially exciting in innovative Palermo Viejo, except the food's pretty good. Try the shrimp, spinach and ricotta ravioli or go for the daily special. For dessert, the Rave Copón is a large parfait of chocolate mousse and cream. If you're lucky, a magician will come around the tables and do tricks. Another quirk is an actual bed you can eat on (very romantic). This place is popular with a gay clientele, perhaps because of the good-looking male wait staff.

## RISTORANTE O

Map pp232-3     *Mediterranean/Argentine*
☎ 4833-6991; Thames 1626; mains US$5.50-7;
☾ lunch Sat & Sun, dinner

This tranquil little bistro would be excellent for a romantic date, with its minimalist decor, soothing music and white tablecloths. Look out past the patio to the kitchen, from where your rich seafood risotto or delicate baby-leaf salad might emerge. The Mediterranean-Argentine menu changes with the seasons, but is sure to remain excellent and good value.

## SARKIS Map pp232-3     *Middle Eastern*
☎ 4772-4911; Thames 1101; mains US$2-5;
☾ lunch & dinner

Here's a popular and bustling Middle Eastern restaurant featuring a family-style experience with a midwestern decor. Sarkis has an extensive menu heavy on the meat, but if you're a carnivore you'll enjoy it – try the excellent *kafta al fierrit* (grilled sausage with onions) and top it off with baklava for dessert. The noise and flurry of activity may not be ideal for a romantic evening, but for great food, an enormous list of wines and convivial atmosphere you shouldn't miss this place.

### SUDESTADA

Map pp232-3           *Southeast Asian*
☎ 4776-3777; Guatemala 5602; mains US$5-8.50; ⏲ lunch & dinner Mon-Sat

Fusion is the name of the game here, and the players are Thailand, Vietnam, Malaysia and Singapore. Sudestada's well-earned reputation comes from its spicy curries, tender stir-frys and delicious noodle and vegetarian dishes. The grilled rabbit is fantastic, but if ordering spicy keep in mind *it's really spicy* – most Argentines can't handle the heat here. Desserts are huge, and alcoholic drinks come with exotic Asian flavor – or sip an equally intoxicating Thai iced tea.

### XALAPA   Map pp232-3         *Mexican*
☎ 4833-6102; El Salvador 4800; mains US$2-4; ⏲ dinner

Featuring cuisine and ambiance bordering on the authentic, this is one of the few places that diverges from the Argentine tendency toward mild and offers truly spicy food. The *enchiladas poblanas* are a delicious alternative for those needing a piquant night out; for those unaccustomed to the heat there are chili warnings on the menu. Frozen margaritas and a large selection of Mexican beers offer alcoholic relief.

# LAS CAÑITAS

The following are in the small but popular Las Cañitas neighborhood of Palermo, which is roughly bounded by Avs Luis María Campos, Ortega y Gasset and Dorrego. Most eateries are within three blocks on Av Báez, and traffic really jams up here on the weekends. There's plenty of good choices beyond those listed below, so don't be afraid to try a different place filled with happy-looking diners.

### EH! SANTINO

Map pp232-3          *Italian/Argentine*
☎ 4779-9060; Av Báez 194; mains US$4-9; lunch & dinner Mon-Sat, lunch Sunday

This trendy spot is best known for its tasty Italian food, such as the mushroom risotto or black *sorrentinos* (large round ravioli). The *pollo santino* (chicken fried with scallions) is very popular, and the salads are good. A large variety of mixed drinks and desserts are international crowd-pleasers, as is the large-screen TV showing sports and music videos.

### EL PORTUGUÉS   Map pp232-3   *Parrilla*
☎ 4771-8699; Av Báez 499; mains US$4-10; ⏲ lunch & dinner

This is a good, solid neighborhood *parrilla*; it's modern and casual, so don't expect the snazziness of other nearby Las Cañitas restaurants. Do expect the many hanging braids of garlic to keep vampires away. Portions are huge; the half *bife de chorizo* runs less than US$6 and can easily feed two carnivores. If you like chicken you'll have over a dozen choices. And try the crispy *mollejas* (don't ask), grilled especially well here. Lunch specials are cheap at US$3 and include side dish, dessert and drink.

Diners at Bar 6 (p107)

## LAS CHOLAS

Map pp232-3          *Northern Argentine*
☎ 4899-0094; Arce 306; mains US$2.50-4;
🕑 lunch & dinner

Las Cholas found the golden rule of many successful restaurants: quality food, trendy design and bargain prices. This corner eatery attracts the young and hip and feeds them traditional Argentine and Latino food like *locro*, empanadas, tamales, *puchero* and *cazuelas* (meat and veggie stews). You can also try *mate*. Come early 'cause it fills by 9pm – and they don't take telephone reservations.

## MORELIA Map pp232-3        *Pizza*

☎ 4772-0329; Av Báez 260; mains US$4-9; dinner

Come for the pizza, because it's simply excellent here. Choose from 24 kinds – the Napolitana (with tomatoes and garlic) is wonderfully simple, though the Montecattini (prosciutto and arugula) beats most pies too. Ask for it *a la parrilla* and it'll arrive thin and crisp. For dessert, the *frambuesas* (raspberries) with ice cream are a piece of heaven and better than the chocolate mousse. Ambiance is romantically dark; so much so you might have trouble reading the menu, but not your date's satisfied smile.

## NOVECENTO

Map pp232-3          *International*
☎ 4778-1900; Av Báez 199; mains US$4-9; lunch & dinner

Breakfast is served on weekday mornings – a rarity here in Buenos Aires – but it's rather skimpy (just a few croissant sandwiches on the menu). Dinners are elegant, however. Start with the fried calamari and then go for the penne with wild mushrooms or farfalle with salmon pasta. The fine atmosphere is accented with pristine white tablecloths, soft music and romantic candlelight. There's a good selection of dessert wines and after-dinner liqueurs as well.

## SOUL CAFÉ Map pp232-3      *International*

☎ 4778-3115; Av Báez 246; mains US$3.50-8;
🕑 dinner Tue-Sun

This self-proclaimed 'boogie restaurant' is just that, with '60s posters on the tables and soul music on the speakers – all in a red-tinted atmosphere. Creative dishes include lots of sushi, wok-fried creations, 'funk salad' and *langostinos paranoicos* (shrimp with garlic and white wine). Plenty of alcoholic beverages liven things up, as will the James Brownie (which comes with ice cream and chocolate sauce – yum).

# BELGRANO

Generally speaking, Belgrano tends to feed its locals more traditional Argentine fare than innovative cuisine, and this neighborhood is so far north that not many tourists venture here for food. There are a few notable restaurants to try if you happen to be around, however. And if you like Chinese food, there are a fair number of authentic restaurants in Buenos Aires' tiny Chinatown worth checking out.

## BUDDHA BAR          *Asian Fusion*

☎ 4706-2382; Arribeños 2288; mains US$3-8.50;
🕑 dinner Wed-Sun

Tearing up Belgrano's Chinatown scene is this elegant newcomer, offering creative new Japanese, Thai and Vietnamese fusions. Order the Thai beef salad, teriyaki fish, duck with citrus and mushrooms or the 'lotus' veggie stir-fry. The dining area is a slick red lounge with moody music, and for extra quirkiness there's an attached Asian art gallery and orchid room.

## CONFITERÍA ZURICH      *Café*

☎ 4784-9808; Echeverría 2200; mains US$2-5;
🕑 breakfast, lunch & dinner

Suited-up waiters offer professional service, while the classic atmosphere here puts life in perspective by seeming to say 'enjoy drinking coffee or afternoon tea a bit more!'. If you're peckish there are salads and sandwiches, or just nibble on some dainty croissants while you watch the world go by at the plaza across the way. Things are especially exciting when the weekend *feria* is in full swing.

## GARBIS         *Middle Eastern*

☎ 4789-9300; Monroe 1799; mains US$2.50-7.50;
🕑 lunch & dinner

Steaming for shish kebab? Fretting for falafels? Perhaps you've been dreaming of dolmas. These and other Middle Eastern delicacies are made here, along with Greek dishes such as moussaka and heaps of others. Buffet meals, served every day except Sunday, are the best value if you're hungry; they include the cold appetizer and dessert tables and one main entrée that you order fresh (drinks cost extra). There's another **branch** (☎ 4511-6600; Scalabrini Ortiz 305) in Palermo .

## SUCRE
*International*

☎ 4782-9082; Sucre 676; mains US$5-12; ⓨ lunch & dinner

One of Buenos Aires' most sophisticated dining experiences can be found at this elegant Belgrano restaurant. Sucre's ambiance sports that ultramodern look of high ceilings, wood floors, exposed pipes, metal ramparts and gleaming open kitchen. The excellent, finely presented cuisine comes from a creative international menu that changes every two months, and the 22-page wine list covers all the best that Argentina's wineries have to offer. Check out the central bunker: a temperature-controlled, bomb-proof bodega. Delicate desserts and good coffee end things quite nicely.

## TODOS CONTENTOS
*Chinese*

☎ 4780-3437; Arribeños 2177; mains US$3-5; ⓨ lunch & dinner Tue-Sun, dinner Mon

Its popularity says it all: this is one of city's best Chinese restaurants. In the heart of BA's Chinatown – which is about four blocks long – this eatery offers a comfortable environment and good, cheap entrées like *chow fun*, egg-drop soup and wok-fried beef or chicken dishes. Vegetarians should be happy with the veggie and tofu selections. On weekdays for lunch there are cheap daily menu combos.

# Drinking

# Drinking

Buenos Aires has some great drinking holes, from classic Irish pubs to sports-screen wonders to gay magnets to hip modern lounges. At most of them you'll find a good range of beers, both domestic and imported, as well as tasty wines, hard liquor and a sometimes dizzying array of cocktails. Some bars are oriented toward travelers and expats, who tend to be bigger drinkers (and freer spenders); you won't often see Argentines rip-roaring drunk. Opening hours are long, with happy hours occasionally stretching to midnight on weekends and many bars not closing until early morning, or until the last tipsy customer stumbles out the door.

## BARS

For one of the most happening scenes in town, head to Plaza Serrano (in Palermo Viejo) at 2am on a Friday or Saturday night, where hordes of youths hang out on the benches and drink beer – mostly in a controlled manner. Those who can afford it settle in at one of the many trendy bars surrounding the plaza.

## MICROCENTRO & PLAZA DE MAYO

The Microcentro has a good variety of bars and pubs, many of which cater to the business crowds at lunch and after the final work bell rings. After the business types have finished blowing off steam you'll find the crowd turns to tourists and the well-coiffed.

### BAR SEDDON Map pp222-4

☎ 4342-3700; Defensa 695; ☽ 6pm-4am Tue-Fri, 9pm-6am Sat, 5pm-2am Sun

Antique train mirrors decorate this popular and historical San Telmo nightspot, and the live entertainment covers all. Jazz, blues, rock, tango, Cuban and even funk bands play almost every night of the week. Come by midnight on a Saturday or you may not find a seat in the house.

### Top Five Bars

- **Gibraltar** (right) Good food, good vibes and good time
- **Gran Bar Danzón** (p95) Pretty bar with tasty wine
- **Janio** (p117) Great hangout in Palermo Viejo
- **Milión** (opposite) Fancy ex-mansion with good cocktails
- **Mundo Bizarro** (p117) Cozy lounge with good tunes and funky lighting

### LE CIGALE Map pp222-4

☎ 4312-8275; 25 de Mayo 722; ☽ 6pm-late Mon-Fri, 8pm-late Sat & Sun

A moody atmosphere of electronica and smoky air characterizes this sultry watering hole. It's packed with black-clad youth and grungy foreigners on weekends, when there's often live music. The fairy lights really shine on Tuesday's 'French' nights. Cocktails cost US$3–4 and include mai-tais, sex on the beach and mojitos.

## SAN TELMO

There are some eclectic yet casual drinking holes in San Telmo that are worthy of a long sit-down. Considering how popular the neighborhood is with travelers, many bars are often full of foreigners.

### FIN DEL MUNDO Map p225

☎ 15-5314-4729; cnr Defensa & Chile; ☽ 6pm-late Mon-Sat, 3pm-late Sun

During the week this funky little cornerside bar is a quiet, friendly affair, but on weekends things really hot up and the action literally spills out onto the sidewalk. Rotating art exhibitions keep the walls interesting.

### GIBRALTAR Map p225

☎ 4362-5310; Peru 895; ☽ 6pm-4am Mon-Thu, 6pm-6am Fri & Sat, 12:30pm-4am Sun

This is one of BA's best expat bars. Good comfortable spaces and decent attempts at foreign

## Speed & Vodka

Sleepless nights aren't just for insomniacs anymore. In a culture that begins clubbing at two in the morning and doesn't stop until well past dawn, an upbeat beverage is crucial for powering through those sleepless nights. Enter 'Speed and Vodka,' a heady mix of that famous clear alcohol that's mixed together with an energy drink such as Red Bull (think a handful of sugars, a sprinkling of vitamins and a strong dose of caffeine). It's so popular with the young crowd that it's scary, and the warning label for diabetics and pregnant women doesn't help. Careful downing these things – as the Argentine equation goes, vodka plus speed equals drunk.

cuisine (try the generous Vietnamese, Indian or American dishes) make for a generally happy vibe, and the bar's a good spot for those alone to hang out. Homesick Brits can watch English football, play darts and eat roast on Sunday, while pool tables out the back occasionally host competitions.

### TROTAMUNDOS Map pp222-4

☎ 4343-8342; Defensa 683; ⏰ 11am-2am Tue-Wed, 11am-6am Thu-Sat, closed Sun & Mon

Red lights, jazzy music, interesting art on the walls and furniture made from recycled wood are what define this small and sultry restaurant-bar-lounge, as does the fact it's partly owned by Alfredo Casero, a well-known Argentine actor and singer. There's a no-cover disco downstairs on Friday and Saturday nights, and live tango, jam sessions or old films shown on Sundays.

# RETIRO

There aren't a boatload of bars in upscale Retiro, but if you do find one try to dress up and look good – everyone else will, and they'll be checking you out.

### DADÁ Map pp228-9

☎ 4314-4787; San Martín 941; ⏰ noon-2:30am Mon-Thu, noon-4:30am Fri & Sat, closed Sun

The intimate, creative and very cool atmosphere sets this downtown bistro-bar apart, as does the moody art on the walls and ceilings. Tasty potions are mixed behind the funky tiled countertop, which stylishly holds patrons' concoctions. Jazz tunes turn to bossa nova as night falls, when fresh tourists looking for fun replace worn businessmen heading home.

### DRUID IN Map pp228-9

☎ 4312-3688; Reconquista 1040; ⏰ noon-late Mon-Fri, 8pm-late Sat

Just half a block from the popular Kilkenny and sporting a more intimate ambience is this modest Irish pub. There's live Scottish bagpipes

on Thursdays, Celtic music on Fridays and jazz on Saturdays. A wide range of aged whiskeys, imported liquor, blended cocktails and more than 30 beers temper the pizza, sandwiches and British food that are served.

### EL VERDE Map pp228-9

☎ 4315-3693; Reconquista 878; ⏰ 8pm-4am Mon-Fri, 8pm-5am Sat & Sun

What sets this downtown pub apart is its orientation – toward a hip *older* scene. You may not find anyone under 50 here, but that doesn't mean everyone's sporting a cane. Live music and dancing gets the old blood going, and this place can really rock – it gets as loud and smoky as any of its younger counterparts. Deer heads on the walls add quirkiness.

### GRAN BAR DANZÓN Map pp228-9

☎ 4811-1108; Libertad 1161; ⏰ 7pm-3am

An excellent, sexy wine bar; see p95.

### KILKENNY Map pp228-9

☎ 4312-7291; MT de Alvear 399; ⏰ 5:30pm-6am Mon-Fri, 8pm-6am Sat & Sun

Buenos Aires' most popular Irish bar has become, well, just too damn popular. Weekends are a crush, and hefty doormen keep the non-drinking riffraff out – there's actually a minimum consumption quota for busy nights. Thumping music makes it hard to chat up your date, but the dark woodsy atmosphere is congenial enough and harbors deep booths, tall counters and a wraparound bar. Come early on weekdays if you want a decent seat.

### MILIÓN Map pp228-9

☎ 4815-9925; Paraná 1048; ⏰ 6pm-2am Sun-Wed, 6pm-3am Thu, 8pm-4am Fri & Sat

This richly elegant, dimly lit and very sexy bar takes up three floors of a renovated old mansion. The garden out back is a pleasant leafy paradise, but up the grand marble staircase is the solid tiled balcony, which holds the best seats in the house. There are elegant tapas to

Drinking – Bars

## Argentine Wine *Dereck Foster*

Argentina is the fifth-largest producer of wine in the world, and happily much of it is world class. Argentine wines cover an incredibly wide spectrum, with more than 50 grape varietals in cultivation. Two in particular are considered representative of the country. The white Torrontes is a very fruity and dry wine whose grapes thrive in the Andean foothills, while the Malbec is a close cousin to Cabernet Sauvignon and has an intense, almost black color. Malbec is considered to be Argentina's 'national' wine, and has won many prestigious awards at wine competitions around the globe; it reaches its zenith in the high vineyards of the Andes.

Wine is sold by the bottle or by the glass in restaurants, but it is still not customary to bring one's own bottle. Luckily, restaurants are increasingly adding bilingual sommeliers to help the wine-curious visitor. And fancy wine bars are becoming increasingly common in Buenos Aires, where you can sample different varieties of wine while nibbling on tasty snacks.

Many wine shops will offer to ship your wine if you are buying a case (six bottles) or more, though you'll pay an arm and a leg for this convenient service. Also, check with your airline's regulations: you may be required to carry on your (limited) bottled purchases, rather than checking them in your luggage.

Drinking – Bars

accompany the wide range of cocktails; try the special slushy mojito, mint julep or Long Island iced tea. Downstairs a small restaurant serves international dishes as electronic music plays in the background and art films are projected onto the high ceilings.

### TEMPLE BAR Map pp228-9
☎ 4326-5744; MT de Alvear 945; ☿ 11am-3am Mon-Thu, 11am-5am Fri, 6pm-5am Sat, closed Sun

This Irish pub in Retiro fills with thirsty businessmen after the working day is done. A big-screen TV, darts and billiards help them blow off steam, as do the Quilmes, Guinness and Heineken on tap. Music runs to rock, jazz and blues, with occasional cover bands entertaining. The food menu's pretty extensive, and the full booze list keeps everyone buzzing.

## RECOLETA

Exclusive Recoleta offers a small mix of expat hangouts and spiffy watering holes. As with Retiro, it won't hurt to act like the locals and look good. If you're looking for the gay scene, the intersection of Avs Santa Fe and Pueyrredón offers some action.

### BULLER BREWING COMPANY
Map pp230-1
☎ 4808-9061; RM Ortiz 1827; ☿ noon-late

Yes, a microbrewery in Buenos Aires and Recoleta no less. Seven beers are brewed on the premises, including wheat, stout, brown ale and India pale ale – and they're pretty good, especially the Oktoberfest. Buller is a popular place, often full of foreigners, with live rock on weekends. Plenty of snacks and pizza are served.

### DEEP BLUE Map pp230-1
☎ 4827-4415; Ayacucho 1240; ☿ 11am-4am Mon-Fri, 8pm-4am Sat & Sun

As the name implies, there's plenty of blue around, including the pool-table surfaces (though upstairs they're orange). Corrugated metal ceilings and a rowdy DJ contribute to the feisty atmosphere, where drinks reach the US$5 mark and smoky air pervades the neon sheen. Tex-Mex and burgers satisfy the hungry, while happy hour runs till midnight on Saturdays – the only night the basement disco is open.

### SHAMROCK Map pp230-1
☎ 4812-3584; Rodríguez Peña 1220; ☿ 6pm-4am

Rockin' during the 'longest' happy hour in town, which runs from 6pm to midnight daily, this contemporary Irish joint in Barrio Norte is decked out in dark wood and has become a classic meeting place for the expat drinking community. DJs rule from Thursdays to Saturdays, when the Basement Club disco (good sound system) opens up at 1am. Live rock groups jam it up on Sunday nights.

### THE SPOT Map pp230-1
☎ 4811-8955; Ayacucho 1261; ☿ 8pm-late Mon-Fri, 10pm-late Sat, closed Sun

Friendly English-speaking bartenders mix good cocktails at this intimate and modern Recoleta saloon. The music's a bit loud for the space and there doesn't seem to be quite enough tables, but that leaves plenty of room for the stray dart. Ladies get two-for-one drinks on Thursdays, while DJs serve up high-tech, pop and '80s tunes on Fridays and Saturdays.

# PALERMO

You'll find one of Buenos Aires' hippest drinking scenes in and around Palermo, especially near Plaza Serrano in Palermo Viejo. Las Cañitas, another sub-neighborhood of Palermo, has a lively three blocks of nonstop restaurants, bars and discos, and is also worth a drop-by. Palermo is also where you'll find a few gay and lesbian bars, mostly to the south near Av Córdoba.

## ACABAR Map pp232-3
☎ 4772-0845; Honduras 5733; ☾ 8pm-2am Mon-Sun, 8pm-5am Fri & Sat

This unusual place is actually a restaurant until around 1am, at which time folks come to drink and play games – well, not *that* sort necessarily, but the board and puzzle kind. Large groups of young people in denim and sneakers make for a casual feel, and the countless mazelike spaces are decked out in artsy and colorful décor. Sip your Tom Collins or mango daiquiri, but don't expect peace among the weekend mayhem, when reservations for the restaurant are a must.

## BACH BAR Map pp232-3
Cabrera 4390; ☾ 10pm-late Tue-Sun

This small bar is most popular with lesbians, but plenty of guys make it here too. The live drag shows on weekends are downright raucous, and make the crowd laugh and be happy. Sultry dancing among the tables is not unheard of, even in these tight spaces. There's no admission charge, but a minimum consumption of US$1, which shouldn't be a problem for most foreigners.

## BOICOT Map pp232-3
☎ 4861-7492; Bulnes 1250; ☾ 10pm-3am Fri & Sat

This is a lesbian bar, so guys, unless you're wearing a really convincing corset the bouncer won't let you in the door. The modestly large space inside is comfortably hip, with flashing colored lights and booths covered in romantic drapes. Three pool tables in the back are for the toughies while the livelier patrons dance to rock and *cumbia* (Colombian dance music) among the tables.

## EL CARNAL Map pp220-1
☎ 4772-7582; Niceto Vega 5511; ☾ 9pm-6am Thu-Sun, 9pm-3am Mon-Wed

Weekends are great here, and Thursday nights are also very tight, when El Carnal serves as precursor to Club 69's drag show across the way. The reggae rocks and you can smell the herbs burning. On warm nights the rooftop terrace, with its bamboo cubbies and billowy curtains, can't be beat for a chill out.

## FINIS TERRA Map pp232-3
☎ 4831-0335; Honduras 5190; ☾ 9:30am-2am Mon-Thu, 9:30am-6am Fri & Sat, noon-2am Sun

This intriguing lounge, located in Palermo Viejo, offers an unusual nighttime experience. Thursdays and Fridays feature an Argentine version of storyteller Garrison Keillor delicately maneuvering through the minutiae of life, while Saturdays have an erotic storytelling headliner. If you're hungry, steak and pizza grace the menu – along with an enormous drink list. Shows usually start at 9:30pm, but call ahead to confirm.

## JANIO Map pp232-3
☎ 4833-6540; Malabia 1805; ☾ 8am-4am

This is one of the busiest restaurant-bars in Palermo Viejo, and a prime place to see and be seen. By day you can lounge at a sidewalk table and take in the sunshine, while at night the airy rooftop terrace is an excellent choice. Pink Floyd and a burgundy color scheme hang in the air, while frozen margaritas or cool whiskey shots appease the trendy masses.

## MUNDO BIZARRO Map pp232-3
☎ 4773-1967; Guatemala 4802; ☾ 8pm-3am Sun-Wed, 8pm-4am Thu, 8pm-5am Fri & Sat

Red lights, black counters and a definite lounge feel give this Palermo Viejo bar a very young, very trendy touch. Come early to grab a comfy booth; smoke and noise levels increase as the night wears on. On Mondays there's sushi, on Tuesdays and Wednesdays it's two-for-one, and on Sundays there's cheap burgers and beer. Rockabilly, hip-hop and rock music are standard offerings.

## SITGES Map pp232-3
☎ 4861-3763; Av Córdoba 4119; ☾ 10:30pm-late Wed-Sun

Dangerously stuffed on a Saturday night this gay and lesbian 'pre-disco' bar plays loud, beat-laden music for the amorous crowd. On Wednesdays and Thursdays there's a drag show, and on Sundays there's karaoke. Come early on weekends for the aphrodisiac sushi dinner. Entry is a minimum consumption of US$2.

### UNICO Map pp232-3

☎ 4775-6693; Honduras 5604; ☽ 9am-4am Sun-Thu, 9am-6am Fri & Sat

If you like your bars loud and crowded, you'll love this Palermo Viejo corner magnet. It's not overly large, so on weekends people tend spill out the door onto the sidewalk tables. For an extra shot of energy try the *café Vienés* – hot coffee graced with a dollop of ice cream. Plenty of tapas, sandwiches and salads, along with the ultracool music, could make it a long night.

### VAN KONING Map pp232-3

☎ 4772-9909; Báez 325; ☽ 8pm-late Tue-Sun

About half the patrons at this intimate Las Cañitas pub are foreigners; the first Wednesday of the month is Dutch night, and the third

is Belgian night (drinks are two-for-one). Great rustic spaces make it feel like the inside of a boat; after all, it's a 17th-century style seafaring theme complete with dark wood beams, flickering candles and blocky furniture. The bars on two floors serve 40 brews, with Heineken, Guinness and Quilmes on draft.

### VOODOO LOUNGE Map pp232-3

☎ 4772-2453; Báez 340; ☽ 8pm-late Tue-Sun

This small club is very popular with the under 25s, and certainly packs them in on weekends when there are sometimes live rappers on stage. There's an upstairs schmooze lounge and the whole scene is hip and fashionable without being pretentious. Unfortunately there is an admission charge; it's US$2.50 for women and US$4 men (includes one drink though).

# CAFÉS

Cafés are an integral part of porteño life, and you shouldn't miss popping into one of these beloved hangouts to sip dainty cups of coffee and nibble biscuits with the locals. There are plenty of cafés in the city, so while you're walking around seeing the sights you're bound to run across one and find an excuse for a break. Some cafés are wonderfully atmospheric and guaranteed to take you back in time.

For a background on these enduring legacies of the Argentine social history see the boxed text, opposite.

## MICROCENTRO & PLAZA DE MAYO

The Microcentro has some of the oldest cafés in town. They're wonderfully atmospheric and superconvenient for a coffee break while you're checking out the center.

### CAFÉ TORTONI Map pp222-4

☎ 4342-4328; www.cafetortoni.com.ar; Av de Mayo 829; ☽ 8am-3am Mon-Sat, 8am-2am Sun

The classic Tortoni is arguably Buenos Aires' most well-known and traditional café; established in 1858, it claims to be the oldest in Argentina. Both locals and tourists mix here, taking in the grand old surroundings while sipping coffee, nibbling snacks or playing pool in the back. Service can be a bit jaded, as with any touristy destination. Good tango shows are offered nightly, with jazz on weekends.

### CONFITERÍA IDEAL Map pp222-4

☎ 4601-8234; Suipacha 384; ☽ 8am-10pm Mon-Fri, 9:30am-9:30pm Sat & Sun

This classic café, now 88 years old and counting, is best known for its almost-daily tango

classes and *milongas* (dances) on the upper floor. It now seems a bit dim, stodgy and impersonal, but remains a Buenos Aires experience. Stay on the ground level for coffees and pastries while you listen to the music and dancers above.

*Kilkenny (p115) Irish bar*

## Buenos Aires' Cafés

Thanks to its European heritage, Buenos Aires has a serious café culture. Porteños will spend hours dawdling over a single *café cortado* (coffee with milk) and a couple of *medialunas* (croissants), discussing the economy, politics, recent loves lost or the nuances of that latest soccer play. Indeed, everything from business transactions to marriage proposals to revolutions has originated at the local corner café. It's hard to imagine Argentina functioning without this beloved traditional institution.

Some of the capital's cafés have been around for over a hundred years, and many still retain much of their original furniture, architectural details and atmosphere. They've always been the haunts of Argentina's politicians, anarchists, intellectuals and old literary greats. **London City** (below) boasts that Julio Cortázar wrote his masterpiece *The Prizes* at one of its tables, while the **Richmond** (below) says Jorge Luis Borges drank hot chocolate there. The most famous of them all, however, is the **Tortoni** (opposite), which was founded in 1858 and claims to be the oldest café in the country. Today it attracts as many tourists as it does locals, and despite the less-than-perfect service is still worth a sit-down for its old-time aura.

Most cafés have adapted to modern times by serving alcohol as well as coffee, and offer a surprisingly wide range of food and snacks; you can order a steak as easily as a cup of coffee. A few even double as bookstores, or host live music, tango shows, poetry readings, films and other cultural events. So although they can transport you back in time, they'll still offer services keeping you in the present.

Cafés have long hours and are usually open from early morning to late night, making them easy places to visit. And visit you should; sipping coffee and languidly hanging out at one of these atmospheric cafés, perhaps on some lazy afternoon, is part of the Buenos Aires experience. At the very least, they're great for a late tea or a welcome break from all that walking you'll be doing.

### FLORIDA GARDEN Map pp228-9
☎ 4312-7902; Florida 899; ☾ 6:30am-midnight Mon-Fri, 7am-10pm Sat, 8am-10pm Sun

Always attracting a crowd, this upscale two-level café is popular with politicians, journalists and other influential sorts. Modern touches, such as the glass walls and copper-covered columns, hardly betray its 40 years, but there's certainly history – Jorge Luis Borges and Pérez Célis both used to hang out here before the era of skinny lattes. The people-watching is excellent, both inside and out.

### LA PUERTO RICO Map pp222-4
☎ 4331-2215; Adolfo Alsina 416; ☾ 7am-8pm Mon-Fri, 7am-4pm Sat

The Tortoni's rival (going strong since 1887) is less atmospheric and less touristy but equally historic. A block south of Plaza de Mayo, it still serves great coffee and pastries, the latter baked on the premises. Old photos on the walls hint at a rich past and the Spanish movies that have been filmed here. On Saturday nights there's a tango dinner-show (reservations a must).

### LONDON CITY Map pp222-4
☎ 4343-0328; Av de Mayo 599; ☾ 7am-10pm Mon-Sat

After you've shopped your way down Florida, this swank and classy café offers a good rest for those tired feet. It's been serving java addicts for over 50 years, and claims to have been the spot where Julio Cortázar wrote his first novel. Your hardest work here, however, will most likely be choosing which luscious pastry to consume with your freshly brewed coffee, before continuing to buzz your way up the avenues.

### RICHMOND Map pp222-4
☎ 4322-1341; Florida 468; ☾ 8am-10pm Mon-Sat

If you're looking for a billiards game or chess match, head to the basement at this very traditional café that's been serving the city since 1917. Or just sink yourself into a leather chair and admire the Dutch chandeliers and English-style surroundings while sipping your hot chocolate – just like Jorge Luis Borges did. He probably didn't have the 16 choices for coffee, however. For those who value clean air, there's also a nonsmoking section out the back.

## CONGRESO & AVENIDA CORRIENTES

There are a few pleasant cafés in these neighborhoods, especially around the artsy theatre district on Av Corrientes.

### EL GATO NEGRO Map pp226-7

☎ 4374-1730; Av Corrientes 1669; ⏱ 9:30am-midnight Mon-Thu, 9:30am-1:30am Fri & Sat, 3pm-midnight Sun

Tea-lined wooden cabinets and a spicy aroma welcome you to this pleasant little sipping paradise. Enjoy imported cups of coffee or tea along with breakfast and dainty *sandwiches de miga* (thin crustless sandwiches, traditionally eaten at tea time). Tea is sold by the pound, and exotic herbs and spices are also on offer.

# RETIRO

The relatively small neighborhood of Retiro has a few places in which to satisfy that java bean addiction.

### PETIT PARIS CAFÉ Map pp228-9

☎ 4312-5885; Av Santa Fe 774; ⏱ 7am-10pm Mon-Sun

This well-situated and elegant café is a great stop for your daily java jolt. Large picture windows do much to help you enjoy views of Plaza San Martín, while the busy street traffic offers a good sense of this bustling city. The PP is a popular place with businessmen and little old ladies.

# RECOLETA

Across from the Recoleta cemetery you'll find a couple of the city's most popular coffee joints – they're pretty much a must-stop break after your wanders through the ancient sarcophagi.

### CAFÉ DE LA PAIX Map pp230-1

☎ 4804-6820; Av Quintana 595; ⏱ 7:30am-2am Mon-Thu, 7:30am-4am Fri, 7:30am-5am Sat, 7:30am-2am Sun

Across the way from Recoleta's famous cemetery is this modern yet traditional café. It sports a patio for warm days, with super views of Recoleta's park greenery and the church Nuestra Señora del Pilar. The menu is full of basic lunch fare such as sandwiches, salads and pizzas, so order up; you'll be styling with the best.

### CLÁSICA Y MODERNA Map pp230-1

☎ 4812-8707; www.clasicaymoderna.com; Av Callao 892; ⏱ 8am-2am Mon-Sat, 5pm-2am Sun

Serving up coffee since 1938, this cozy, intimate bookstore-café continues to ooze history and atmosphere from its brick walls. It is also nicely lit, offers plenty of reading material and serves upscale meals. There are regular live performances of folk music, jazz, blues and tango; Mercedes Sosa, Susana Rinaldi and Liza Minnelli have all chirped here.

### LA BIELA Map pp230-1

☎ 4804-0449; Av Quintana 600; ⏱ 7am-3am Mon-Thu, 7am-4am Fri & Sat, 8am-3am Sun

Before or after dining (and on Sunday mornings in particular) the older porteño elite while away the hours here, high on caffeine. It's a classic Recoleta landmark, and the pleasant front terrace is certainly a temptation on a sunny afternoon – especially when the weekend *feria* (street market) is in full swing. Try the pricey 'special coffees' – some are laced with alcohol.

# Entertainment

# Entertainment

Buenos Aires is like a runaway Mack truck when it comes to delivering the goods on entertainment. Want to take in a show? Choose from the dozens of theater companies putting out first-rate productions, be it singing, dancing, acting or all three. Movies are a way of life here in the capital, and you'll find both independent films at classic old theaters and the most recent blockbusters at modern cineplexes. After enjoying your US$10 steak dinner (with wine, of course), you can sit at a bar or café until two in the morning, then head off to the clubs – they'll *just* be getting started. And since devaluation, all of these options are available at absolute bargain prices.

Entertainment in Buenos Aires? We're talking a royal flush here, my friend. And we haven't even mentioned tango – think about watching a show, taking a class or dancing in a *milonga* (tango hall). Head to the local stadium for the most passionate game of *fútbol* (soccer) you've ever seen. And, when was the last time you were a spectator at an exotic polo game? Even gamblers can scratch their itch: there's a high-stakes boat at the southern end of Puerto Madero, and a large casino in the riverside suburb of Tigre. (Plus the pony races, of course.) Buenos Aires is absolutely brimming with things you should try, and almost anyone can find something to do every day of the week and at practically every hour of the day.

To help you get started, most newspapers have entertainment supplements published on Friday; the *Buenos Aires Herald*'s 'Get Out' is in English and particularly handy. Free publications in Spanish include *Llegás* and *Ciudad Abierta*, which cover art, theater, workshops, cinema, music and current events. More traveler-oriented is the free bimonthly booklet *Buenos Aires Day & Night*, which has listings in English and Spanish. Most of these publications are available at tourist offices or hotels.

The Internet holds countless websites that detail BA's current activities. Try www.whatsupbuenosaires.com for information in English; www.adondevamos.com and www.buenosaliens.com are both in Spanish.

## Tickets & Reservations

*Carteleras* (discount ticket offices) along Av Corrientes sell a limited number of heavily discounted tickets for many entertainment events such as movies, live theater and tango shows, with savings of up to 50%. Buy tickets as far in advance as possible, but if you want to see a show or movie on short notice – especially at midweek – you can also phone or drop by to check what's available.

**Cartelera Baires** (Map pp226-7; ☎ 4372-5058; www.entradascondescuento.com; Av Corrientes 1382; ✆ 10am-10pm Mon-Thu, 10am-11pm Fri, 10am-midnight Sat, 2-10pm Sun) In Cine Lorange.

**Cartelera Espectáculos** (Map pp222-4; ☎ 4322-1559; www.123info.com.ar in Spanish; Lavalle 742; ✆ noon-10pm Mon-Fri, noon-11pm Sat, noon-9pm Sun) Right in the middle of the movie district.

**Cartelera Vea Más** (Map pp226-7; ☎ 4370-5319; ✆ 10am-10pm) In the Paseo La Plaza complex, local 2.

*Carlos Gardel (p26) poster, Palermo*

## Luna Park

If unique large-scale spectacles such as the Beijing Circus, the New York Ballet, the Philadelphia Philharmonic, Julio Iglesias or Tom Jones come to town, the dressing rooms of **Luna Park** (Map pp222-4; ☎ 4324-1010; www.luna park.com.ar in Spanish; cnr Bouchard & Av Corrientes) are probably their destination. Bordered by the thoroughfares of Lavalle, Bouchard, Av Corrientes and Madero, Luna Park was originally a boxing stadium built on the old grounds of the Pacific Railway. Finished in 1931, the venue gradually became the mecca of choice for public events needing large spaces. When Carlos Gardel died in a plane crash in 1935, his wake was held here for the thousands of grieving fans. In 1944, a relatively unknown actress named Eva Duarte first met general Juan Perón here during a benefit for the victims of an earthquake in San Juan Province. And on November 7, 1989, Diego Maradona was married here before 11,000 fans.

But Luna Park never forgot its roots; throughout its history, 25 boxing titles have been decided within its walls. Many other sports, including volleyball, basketball and tennis, are also occasionally highlighted at this stadium, and productions such as fashion shows, ice-skating spectacles and mass religious baptisms have found their way here as well. With a capacity of 15,000 (Argentina's largest enclosed stadium) Luna Park can easily handle these crowds, which also come to see recent big-time performers such as Liza Minnelli, Luciano Pavarotti, Norah Jones, Ricky Martin, David Byrne and Chrissie Hynde.

# LIVE MUSIC

Many cultural centers offer live music, including the **ND/Ateneo** (Map pp228-9; ☎ 4328-2888; www.ndateneo.com.ar in Spanish; Paraguay 918), which offers a wide variety of concerts from bossa nova to jazz to instrumental.

## ROCK & BLUES

Buenos Aires boasts a thriving rock music scene. The following are smaller venues that showcase mostly local groups; when international stars come to town they tend to play soccer stadiums, such as River Plate, which holds 65,000. Blues isn't as popular as rock, but still has its own loyal following.

### BLUES SPECIAL CLUB Map pp220-1
☎ 4854-2338; Almirante Brown 102; ⊙ Wed-Sun
Fridays are good for jam sessions, while on Saturdays at midnight the shows really start rockin'. This is a good-sized, semi-artsy venue, and blues folk such as Dave Meyers, Phil Guy, Eddie King and Aaron Burton have all added to the dark and smoky atmosphere. There are plans to bring jazz, tango, salsa and rock, as well as country gigs, to the club in the future.

### CEMENTO Map pp226-7
☎ 4304-6228; Estados Unidos 1234; ⊙ Thu-Sat, sometimes Sun
This hole-in-the-wall is mighty unimpressive on the outside, but the cavernous space inside has played host to such well-known Argentine rock groups as Babasonicos, Los Gardelitos and Attaque 77. After 20 years this classic still caters mostly to *rock nacional*, though the

occasional punk and heavy metal gig manages to weasel in. Unless there's a big-ticket name on the roster, the night wears on with several smaller groups trying to make a point.

### EL SAMOVAR DE RASPUTÍN Map pp220-1
☎ 4302-3190; Del Valle Iberlucea 1251; ⊙ Fri & Sat
Check out the photos of Napo, the hippyish owner, with Keith Richards, Eric Clapton and Pavarotti. Blues biggies Taj Mahal and James Cotton have also played at this very eccentric La Boca joint, though Argentine bands entertain most of the time. On weekend afternoons you can sit outside and enjoy a cheap local *asado* (barbecue). Bus No 29 gets you here from the city center.

### LA TRASTIENDA Map pp222-4
☎ 4342-7650; www.latrastienda.com in Spanish; Balcarce 460; ⊙ shows Fri & Sat
This restaurant-theater-CD store manages to multitask even further by also offering Wednesday night salsa classes. The large theater in the back seats over 350, and showcases all sorts of live groups from rock to Latin pop to tango, as well as dance and theater. Tickets cost around US$5 to US$12, but for international groups such as the Wailers (who played here in 2004) the charge might be more. If the website doesn't work, call for the current schedule.

### MITOS ARGENTINOS Map p225

☎ 4362-7810; www.mitosargentinos.com.ar in Spanish; Humberto Primo 489; ☙ Tue-Sun

This cozy old brick house in San Telmo has hosted rock, blues and tango groups for over 10 years. Rock music plays nightly during the week, while tango rules on Sundays (free shows are offered from noon to 6pm, and classes from 6pm to 8pm). Dinner is served Tuesday to Sunday, but lunch is only on weekends.

## JAZZ

Jazz is on the move in Buenos Aires, and you may see more and more bars, cafés and other venues invite jazz artists to entertain their crowds. **Café Tortoni** (p118) has jazz on Fridays at 9pm and Saturdays at 11pm, while **Clásica y Moderna** (p120) occasionally hosts jazz groups.

### CLUB DEL VINO Map pp232-3

☎ 4833-0048; JA Cabrera 4737; ☙ Fri-Sun

This elegant spot, reminiscent of a small winery, is prettily lit up with fairy lights from the outside. Inside there's a good restaurant, a pleasant fountain courtyard, an intimate theater and a tiny so-called 'wine museum.' Live jazz (along with tango, folk, blues and even flamenco) plays here for US$5 to US$10. The schedule changes weekly, so give the club a buzz.

### NOTORIOUS Map pp230-1

☎ 4815-8473; www.notorious.com.ar in Spanish; Av Callao 966; ☙ nightly

This pretty slick joint is one of Buenos Aires' premier jazz venues. Up front you can sit at modern glass tables and listen to CDs before you buy them. Out the back, the café (overlooking a verdant garden) hosts live jazz shows every night at either 9pm or 10pm. Admission ranges from US$3.50 to US$5. There's another branch on **Av Corrientes** (Map pp226–7; ☎ 4371-0370; Av Corrientes 1743) in the Foro Gandhi bookstore. Log on to the website for schedules.

### THELONIOUS BAR Map pp232-3

☎ 4829-1562; Salguero 1884; ☙ Fri & Sat

Ensconced on the 2nd floor of an old mansion is this intimate, dimly lit, artsy jazz bar with high brick ceilings and a good sound system. An interesting menu and good range of cocktails keep the hunger at bay. Thelonious is traditionally known for its great jazz lineups, but these days you can hit a wailing DJ night instead. Call ahead to figure out what's going on.

## FOLK

*Música folklórica* definitely has its place in Buenos Aires. There are several *peñas* (traditional music clubs) in the city, but many other venues occasionally host folk performances. A couple include **Club del Vino** (left) and **Clásica y Moderna** (p120). The **Centro Cultural San Martín** (p189) often has folk offerings.

### GUAYANA Map pp226-7

☎ 4381-4350; Lima 27; ☙ daily; shows Fri & Sat

For great local working-class flavor, check out this nondescript *confitería* (snack shop) near Av 9 de Julio. It's not fancy at all, just a local spot offering cheap food and surprisingly good music. It does, however, claim to be the oldest *peña* in Buenos Aires! Live tango and folk tunes play from 12:30am to 5am on Friday and Saturday nights. The entertainment's free; just remember to order something (minimum consumption a measly US$1).

### LA PEÑA DEL COLORADO Map pp232-3

☎ 4822-1038, www.lapeniadelcolorado.com.ar in Spanish; Güemes 3657; ☙ closed Mon

Itching to pick up a guitar and strum along with singing porteños in rustic brick-and-stucco spaces reeking of local flavor and cigarette smoke? La Peña will provide the guitar, or bring your own; large groups compete here nightly. Almost-nightly folk shows and guitar classes are pluses, as is the food. Try northern specialties such as *locro* (a corn and meat stew), *chipá* (chewy cheese balls) and *humitas de Chala* (like tamales) – the spicy empanadas are excellent.

## CLASSICAL MUSIC & OPERA

### LA SCALA DE SAN TELMO Map p225

☎ 4362-1187; www.lascala.org.ar in Spanish; Pasaje Guiffra 371

This San Telmo venue puts on classical groups, piano, tango, musical comedies and other musical-related shows and workshops.

### TEATRO AVENIDA Map pp226-7

☎ 4381-0662; www.balirica.org.ar in Spanish; Av de Mayo 1222

This 1906 venue highlights Argentine productions, mostly opera, classical and flamenco.

### TEATRO COLISEO Map pp228-9

☎ 4816-6115; MT del Alvear 1125

Classical music, ballet, opera and jazz entertain at this theater most of the year.

### TEATRO COLÓN Map pp226-7

☎ 4378-7344; Libertad 621

Buenos Aires' premier venue for the arts, Teatro Colón has hosted some very prominent figures such as Enrico Caruso, Plácido Domingo, Luciano Pavarotti and Arturo Toscanini. The Orquesta Filarmónica de Buenos Aires often features guest conductors from throughout Latin America. Ballet and opera can be as cheap as US$1 to US$2 for standing room only, though tickets usually start at US$3.50 to US$9 and run up to US$75. Occasional free concerts are given; scan the website for current events.

### TEATRO GENERAL SAN MARTÍN

Map pp226-7

☎ 0800-333-5254; www.teatrosanmartin.com.ar in Spanish; Av Corrientes 1530

Along with art galleries, ballet, photography, cinema and theater, this large complex hosts classical ensembles.

# CLUBS

Buenos Aires' *boliches* (discos) are the throbbing heart of its world-famous nightlife. Spaces range from small plain venues to grandiose buildings with elegant lines and minimalist décor. All have bouncers at the door keeping the masses in order; those lucky locals who know them personally get a kiss on the cheek and easy entry. Your foreign accent may (or may not) speed things along as well.

Keep in mind that very few clubs open before midnight or 1am, and it's not cool to arrive before 2am or even 3am. If you don't want to crash before your time, take a nap after dinner; you may easily be up until 7am. And remember to dress as stylishly as you can, as you'll have lots of fashion competition – especially if you're a woman.

Admission prices can range from US$3 to US$7 depending on the day, the show and your sex (women generally get in cheaper). Price of admission sometimes includes a drink, and can occasionally top US$10 if a famous international DJ is spinning. Some clubs offer dinners and shows before the dancing starts.

Porteños are fickle and lean toward the newer and better, so some clubs often take a new name, and the change sometimes includes a slight remodel. This is especially true for gay clubs; at least most remain at the same address. Check out the website www.brandongayday .com.ar (in Spanish) for current raves; there are many such last-minute parties happening in BA at any one time, so ask around.

### AMERIKA Map pp232-3

☎ 4865-4416; Gascón 1040; 🕑 Fri-Sun

This huge club attracts all types, but Fridays are especially popular with gays (check out the dark room), while Saturdays have a good mixed crowd and tend to be packed. The music's techno, dance, '90s and Latin, and despite the *canilla libre* (all-you-can-drink; except on Sunday), it's not completely insane – although the floors do get sticky. Video screens and occasional shows keep things interesting.

### ANGEL'S Map pp226-7

Viamonte 2168; 🕑 Thu-Sat

Angel's is very popular with transvestites – many in skimpy outfits, high-heeled boots and platinum wigs. It's a hot, humid and claustrophobic scene, which explains the shirtless guys and tropical feel. *Marcha* (Brazilian-style) music plays upstairs, and a male-stripper show riles the crowd on Saturday nights. Stay near the exit door if you're concerned about escaping potential fires.

### ASIA DE CUBA Map pp220-1

☎ 4894-1328; Dealessi 750, Puerto Madero Este; 🕑 nightly

Try not to let the pair of women in tiny leather outfits dancing on stage distract you from the delightfully eclectic mix of music, ranging from old hits to disco to Latin house. While

## Top Five Clubs

- **Asia de Cuba** (above) Bring a thin dress and a thick wallet, 'cause style has a price.
- **Glam** (p126) Meet the pretty boys in pretty spaces at one of BA's best gay clubs.
- **Club Niceto** (p126) Dance with obnoxious trannies at the killer one-size-satisfies-all drag show put on by Club 69.
- **Opera Bay** (p127) Fairytale building, gorgeous location and plenty of bars to keep you hydrated.
- **Mint** (p127) Great DJs spin for the local youth and international crowd; check out the patio!

*Jazz at Notorious (p124), Recoleta*

admission is one of the steepest in Buenos Aires (US$8, including one drink), the music and the even mix of tourists and Argentines make it worth checking out – this is one of BA's best clubs and perfectly sized. Avoid the cover charge by grabbing dinner there beforehand.

### AZÚCAR Map pp232-3
☎ 4865-3103; Av Corrientes 3330; ⏰ nightly

The cha-cha-cha moves, neon lights and humid atmosphere might briefly take you to a more tropical locale than BA – but then a line dance brings you back. It's a fairly tame joint, however, with plenty of cheap salsa, tango and even American rock classes available in the early evenings. It's not central, but is very accessible by Subte (Estación Gardel) and diagonally across from the gorgeous Abasto mall.

### CLUB NICETO Map pp220-1
☎ 4779-9396; Niceto Vega 5510; ⏰ Thu-Sat

The most popular drag shows in town happen here on Thursday nights, when theater company Club 69 takes over. Fifteen actors jump on stage at about 3am, riling up the crowd with wonderfully skimpy outfits and fun theatrical antics, then join in to dance the night away. It's a wild ride that shouldn't be missed. Fridays through Sundays see different shows, music, DJs and bands.

### COCOLICHE Map pp220-1
☎ 4331-6413; Rivadavia 878; ⏰ Fri & Sat

One of the newest clubs in BA is this electronic-music paradise, based in a modest yet slightly glamorous old mansion. Strut in and be welcomed by a long bar and tasty good cocktails. But it's the downstairs basement that holds

the main attractions, which include cutting-edge bands and some of the best DJs in town. When you need a break, head to the 2nd-floor chill-out room, but make sure to grab a drink (and perhaps a date) first.

### CONTRAMANO Map pp230-1
Rodríguez Peña 1082; ⏰ Wed-Sun

Still packing them in after 20 years is this Recoleta venue. It's for more mature gay clientele; women aren't allowed in, and why would they want to? It's mostly a bunch of older men checking each other out. Fridays are best here, though drag and stripper shows, along with a raffle, run on Sundays. Our prediction: they'll be playing bingo within a year.

### EL LIVING Map pp228-9
☎ 4811-4730; MT del Alvear 1540; ⏰ Thu-Sat

At 10 years old, this small and classic disco is ancient but going strong. Fridays are the best nights, and if you come earlier you can have dinner. A room with a bar runs music videos and is strewn with spotlights, low tables and chain-smokers, while the main dance hall is strobed for epileptic effect and lined with cushy sofas for the wallflowers. Music runs the '80s rock to English beat gamut.

### GLAM Map pp230-1
☎ 4963-2521; JA Cabrera 3046; ⏰ Thu-Sat

Housed on three floors in an old mansion with tall brick hallways, this mazelike gay club really rocks out. The guys are very good-looking and are here to dance and get to know each other better – there are no shows to distract, just casual lounges, pretty bars and free condoms at the door. Thursdays and Saturdays are the biggest nights here.

### LA SALSERA Map pp232-3
☎ 4864-1733; Yatay 961; ☾ Fri-Sun

Despite its slightly odd location, La Salsera is one of the best spots for salsa and merengue in BA. This place rocks and offers a great scene; just about everyone seems to be dancing and having fun. Upstairs it's much darker and more sedate, and the place to go after you've developed a thirst from all that moving around; there's also a chill-out garden. Salsa classes are available earlier on.

### MALUCO BELEZA Map pp226-7
☎ 4372-1737; Sarmiento 1728; ☾ Wed, Thu-Sun

Located in an old mansion is this popular Brazilian *boliche*. It's a really packed place, with crowds swaying to samba music and live bands on Saturdays. Lithe professional dancers hop on stage and further stir the excitement, but if you like it more sedate head upstairs where it's darker and more laid-back (but still loud). Dinner/shows are available on Wednesdays and Saturdays.

### MINT Map pp232-3
☎ 4771-5870; Av Costanera R Obligado & Sarmiento ☾ Wed-Sat

Mint is one of the cooler clubs in BA, where folks concentrate on having a good time on the dance floor rather than looking like a movie star off it. A good group of local youth and tourists populate the large spaces, and guest DJs offer an entertaining mix of US and Latin hits that keep the crowds riled up. A kick-ass riverside patio is best for kicking back and smooching with your date. Wednesdays are 'after office' so it opens early.

### MUNDO LATINO Map pp222-4
☎ 4371-0802; Esmeralda 565; ☾ closed Sun

There are no fancy shows here but folks really open up anyway, singing along to their favorite tunes while putting it on. Music includes pop, samba, *cumbia,* or anything with Latin beats that fits in. Saturdays are *canilla libre,* which really brings in the fun-seekers – or those here to watch. Just a couple of doors away is Sudaca, another popular salsa spot.

### MUSEUM Map pp222-4
☎ 4543-3894; Perú 535; ☾ Wed & Sat

This distinctly chic disco features a Wednesday night 'after-office' party where fun-loving porteños cast aside their cubicles, throw down two-for-one drinks and dance their way over the midweek hump. Saturday nights feature rotating shows and renderings of Latin music and American chart-toppers from the '80s and '90s, so you'll definitely want to check out this beating pulse in the heart of San Telmo.

### OPERA BAY Map pp222-4
☎ 4315-8666; Grierson 225; ☾ Wed-Sat

So it looks like a flattened Sydney Opera House – it's still got a dramatic setting, with a back deck and pool that look over pretty Puerto Madero at night. This huge club makes staying together with friends difficult, but the multiple bars make getting a drink easy. The four rooms play different music, from early Beatles to Argentine dance. Wednesday nights see 'after-office' parties that go from 7pm to 2am; men outnumber women 3-1 on these nights and are especially aggressive after a hard day's work.

### PACHÁ Map pp232-3
☎ 4788-4280; near cnr Costanera Norte & La Pampa; ☾ Fri & Sat

Bring a picture ID; the heavy bouncers check for those under 21. Famous guest DJs from countries such as Israel and Germany spin tunes for the spruced-up and snobby clientele attracted to this 'temple of electronic music' and its good sound system. Saturday nights are nicknamed 'Clubland' and are especially popular with gays, but not exclusively so. It's lost some of its luster (as all clubs do after time) but still holds a spot near the top. Take bus No 45 from the city center.

### PALACIO BA Map pp222-4
☎ 4331-3231; Adolfo Alsina 940; ☾ Fri & Sat

Fridays are known for the *canilla libre,* while on Sundays the venue changes to the 'Big One' – both nights are popular with cute and slightly snobby gays. (Saturdays see a straighter crowd that likes electronica.) All nights are blessed with three floors of open balconies, chandeliers and thick drapes – a palace indeed. Colored lights and thick disco beats let you know you're not in Kansas anymore.

### PARADA OBLIGADA Map pp232-3
☎ 4899-2240; Charcas 4338; ☾ Thu-Sat

OK, this is another gay bar-disco. But if you're a bit pudgy and balding, this is *your* place. Most of the guys here fit this description, but they're also having a blast. Downstairs is a mod bar area for intimate chitchat and ice-blue drinks, while upstairs things really get down and dirty – especially when the stripper show at 1:30am gets going. Find the dark room if you really need some excitement.

## PODESTÁ Map pp232-3

☎ 4832-2276; Armenia 1740; ☺ Thu-Sat

This dark two-level club is full of loud thumping beats and denim-clad local youth. On Thursdays there are live rock bands upstairs, while the rest of the time electronic, house and '80s music is pumped out by invited DJs. It's free before midnight, but don't come early; this place really gets going after 3:30am.

## SEARCH Map pp230-1

☎ 4824-0932; Azcuénaga 1007; ☺ nightly

This small and dark basement club fills to the brim on Saturday nights, when there's a good stripper and drag queen show. It's a mix of gays and straights, with older folks on weekdays and younger ones on weekends. Don't expect a fancy disco here, just a little bit of casual fun.

## TEQUILA Map pp232-3

☎ 4781-6555; cnr Costanera Norte & La Pampa; ☺ Wed-Sun

You'll have a somewhat decent shot at getting into this place...if you happen to be an invited model or celebrity. Known as one of the most exclusive clubs in Buenos Aires, Tequila brings in a noticeably attractive and hip clientele, so come very well dressed. The pleasant terrace and relatively intimate dance floor provide a comfortable and unique atmosphere, and the cocktail service is quite exceptional. Your best bet is to try to arrive early for dinner or drinks; if you can somehow manage to get in the door after 1:30am, the admission is US$10.

## UNNA Map pp228-9

Suipacha 927; ☺ Sat night

Too bad no guys are allowed here – a metal detector at the door keeps guns and penises out. Downstairs, the small, womblike basement is full of hot young lesbians who are either dancing to the beats, smooching in a dark corner or ogling their next date. The music here ranges from pop to electronica to salsa to *cumbia*, and the occasional show and free beer manages to entertain the girls well enough (again, sorry guys).

## Buenos Aires – Happier & Gayer

There is a live and kicking gay scene in BA, and it's become even livelier since December 2002, when Argentina became Latin America's first country to accept civil unions between same-sex couples. Gays and lesbians here now have the same rights as heterosexuals when it comes to legal and social benefits. Tolerance is good news for everyone, and Buenos Aires is benefiting by having outstripped Rio as South America's number one gay destination. Perhaps this will also widen the scope of BA's November Marcha del Orgullo Gay (gay pride parade; www.marchadelorgullo.org.ar in Spanish), as it's pretty limited for now – at least compared to other international cities like San Francisco or Sydney.

Unless you know where to look, however, you won't see much of BA's gay culture. Most clubs are located around Barrio Norte and Palermo, but the porteño need for new and exciting places keeps encouraging many to change their names (though not necessarily location) from time to time. Look up current sweetheart spots in free booklets such as *La Otra Guía, Queer X* and *Latino* available at gay bars, cafés and discos. Free gay maps have also become widely available, even at tourist offices. And heftier gay magazines such as *NX* and *Imperio* can be bought at newsstands.

The main nighttime cruising area is around Avs Santa Fe and Pueyrredón, where the gay community goes for discount admission coupons that get handed out on street corners (some also available in gay establishments). If you need to load yourself up on caffeine for the night to come, settle in at **El Olmo** (Map pp230–1; ☎ 4821-5828), right at the intersection; it's a spot traditionally patronized by older gays, but everyone is welcome. Other gay nightspots are listed under the bars (p114) and clubs (p125) sections of this book. And remember: go to bars after midnight, don't arrive in clubs before 2am, and be ready to party hard till the early morning light.

For daylight romps, head to San Telmo's Sunday antiques fair and take a break at **Pride Café** (p94), which is fabulously gay-friendly. Or head east to Puerto Madero for a walk at the lovely **Reserva Ecológica Costanera Sur** (p56), another notable cruisey spot.

For general gay information, there's **Lugar Gay** (p161) in San Telmo. It's a B&B, but acts as a gay cultural center and can clue you in on the current scenes. Other resources include **Grupo Nexo** ( ☎ 4375-0359; www.nexo.org in Spanish; Av Callao 339, 5th fl) and **Comunidad Homosexual Argentina** (CHA; ☎ 4361-6382; www.cha.org.ar in Spanish; Tomás Liberti 1080). For travel details there's the gay-oriented agency **Pride Travel** (Map pp228–9; ☎ 5218-6556; www.pride-travel.com; Paraguay 523, 2E). The website www.friendlyapartments.com.ar specializes in renting apartments to gay visitors, and if you want to check activities online try www.thegayguide.com.ar – it's aimed at foreigners and offers city tours. In November 2004 there was even a gay and lesbian cinefest (www.diversafilms.com.ar). Gay pride has arrived in Buenos Aires, and it's definitely here to stay.

# DANCE

## TANGO

Tango's popularity continues to boom, both at the amateur and professional levels and among all ages and classes. Offerings for tango shows are everywhere in Buenos Aires, but many of these are more expensive, tourist-oriented spectacles that don't come close to what many consider 'authentic' tango – they can still be very entertaining and awe-inspiring, though. Most of these sensationalized shows include various tango couples, an orchestra, folkloric dancers and singers. All come with a dinner option, which of course raises the price. Most require advance reservations, and some include pick-up from your hotel.

More modest shows cost far less – no more than around US$8. Some are free but require you to eat at their restaurant. If you don't mind eating there anyway this is a great deal. For free (or donation) tango, head to San Telmo on a Sunday afternoon. Dancers do their thing right in the middle of Plaza Dorrego, though you have to stake out a spot to snag a good view. Another sure bet is weekends on El Caminito in La Boca; it's not quite as crowded here as in San Telmo. If you don't want to head so far south, however, see what's happening on Florida in front of Galerías Pacíficos – there are often dancers entertaining a crowd there, too (the mall itself has free tango shows at 8pm from Friday to Sunday). All of these buskers are quite good, so remember to toss some change into their hats.

Two of the best sources on local tango trends are the free booklets *el tangauta* and *BA Tango*, both of which are chock-full of ads for shows, classes and *milongas* (dance halls). They're often available at tango venues or tourist offices.

The following listings offer different types of tango shows; for classes and *milongas* see p130. The website www.tangodata.com.ar has information on the city's *milongas*, classes and shows.

### BAR SUR Map p225

☎ 4362-6086; www.bar-sur.com.ar; Estados Unidos 299; show US$30

For intimate tango this is your place – there are only a dozen tables in the dim atmosphere. The dancers do a good job of not knocking over your drink with their high leg kicks.

### CAFÉ HOMERO Map pp232-3

☎ 4775-6763; JA Cabrera 4946; show US$3.50-8.50

This cozy local *tanguería* (tango venue) in Palermo Viejo offers intimate tango shows, folkloric music and boleros. It has great local flavor; good seats and tapas are available.

### CAFÉ TORTONI Map pp222-4

☎ 4342-4328; www.cafetortoni.com.ar in Spanish; Av de Mayo 829; shows US$6

Excellent shows are put on twice nightly at this most classic of Buenos Aires cafés, starting at 8pm Monday, 9pm Tuesday to Thursday and 8:30pm Friday to Sunday. A second showing is available about two hours later on those same nights.

### CAMINITO TANGO SHOW

☎ 4301-1520; Del Valle Iberlucea 1151

The show's free, and you only get it with your inexpensive lunch (the very limited dishes run

US$2 to US$3.50). The dinner show is only on Friday nights, when you should reserve ahead.

### CENTRO CULTURAL TORQUATO TASSO Map p225

☎ 4307-6506; Defensa 1575; shows US$3.50-7

This colorful, spacious venue offers cheap but good tango shows featuring well-known artists. Sometimes dinner/show combinations are available. Rock and folk music also plays.

### CHIQUILÍN TANGO Map pp226-7

☎ 4373-5163; www.chiquilin-tango.com.ar; Montevideo 310; show US$15, show & dinner US$30

Brand spanking new when we visited, this place has yet to become established. It looks great, however, and if the show's quality is anything like the traditional restaurant's food this place should take off. Hopefully the prices will remain low.

### EL BALCÓN Map p225

☎ 4362-2354; Humberto Primo 461, 1st fl

Grab a balcony spot on a Sunday afternoon and watch both the tango show *and* the antiques fair on Plaza Dorrego at the same time. The show's free, but your meal is not – order something. Tango shows run Fridays to Sundays only.

# Milongas & Dance Lessons

Tango classes are available just about everywhere, from youth hostels to dance academies to cultural centers (p188) to the *milongas* (dance halls); even some cafés offer them. With so many foreigners flooding Buenos Aires to learn the dance, many instructors can now teach in English. Private teachers are also ubiquitous; there are so many good ones that it's best to ask someone you trust for a recommendation. Or check free tango publications such as *el tangauta* and *BA Tango*, which are full of offerings. *Milongas* and group classes are very affordable and usually cost only US$2 to US$3 per session.

For general information, contact the **Academia Nacional del Tango** (Map pp222–4; ☎ 4345-6967; www.anacdel tango.org.ar in Spanish; Av de Mayo 833; ⌚ 10am-8pm Mon-Fri), above the **Café Tortoni** (p118), which also offers classes. Also check the bilingual www.tangodata.com.ar for general information; there are countless other tango websites.

Other types of dance are also available in Buenos Aires. **El Camarín de las Musas** (Map pp232–3; ☎ 4862-0655; www.elcamarindelasmusas.com.ar in Spanish; Mario Bravo 960) offers many kinds of dance, including modern, jazz, African and Greek. **Danzario**, reviewed below, is another good choice, as are **Centro Cultural Ricardo Rojas** (p189) and **Centro Cultural Konex** (p188). Some gyms, such as **Megatlon** (p139), and Latin clubs such as **La Salsera** (p127) offer salsa classes, as does Danzario, La Viruta and Confitería Ideal (all listed below).

**Centro Cultural Torquato Tasso** (Map p225; ☎ 4307-6506; Defensa 1575) Daily classes in Spanish are offered at this large warehouse-like venue across from Parque Lezama in San Telmo. It's a well-known, lively and artsy place that also puts on good weekend shows with famous musicians. *Milongas* (with shows) happen on Sundays at 10pm.

**Confitería Ideal** (Map pp222–4; ☎ 5265-8069; www.confiteriaideal.unlugar.com in Spanish; Suipacha 384) The mother of all tango halls, with many tango classes offered every day except Sunday, and *milongas* on Monday, Wednesday though Friday (when live orchestras play) and Sunday. The atmosphere is classic and the history rich. BA tango at its most traditional.

**Danzario** (Map pp232–3; ☎ 4863-8401; Guardia Vieja 3559) Among the dances offered at this dance academy are African, Arabian, folk, jazz, flamenco, salsa and, of course, tango. The only classes given in English are salsa and tango, however. Prices vary widely, running from US$2 and up.

**El Beso** (Map pp226–7; ☎ 4953-2794; Riobamba 416) Another traditional and popular place that attracts about 2000 people every week for its good *milongas* (Tuesday, Saturday and Sunday nights) and daily classes. The space upstairs has a good feel, and there's a convenient bar as you enter.

**Gricel** (Map pp232–3; ☎ 4957-7157; www.clubgricel.com in Spanish; La Rioja 1180) This old classic (far from the center – take a taxi) offers tango classes nightly; the *milongas* on Fridays have more modern music and are for younger folks, while those on Saturday and Sunday attract an older crowd and an occasional live orchestra.

**La Catedral** (Map pp220–1; ☎ 15-5325-1630; Sarmiento 4006) If tango can be trendy and hip, this is where you'll find it. The rough 'n' tumble warehouse space almost adds an element of danger, especially when the trapeze artists start swinging for the Friday show. A hazy air and funky art on the walls make this more of a party; there are plenty of wallflowers, tourists and socialites. Tango is casual; wearing jeans is OK. The best *milonga* is Tuesday.

**La Viruta/La Estrella** (Map pp232–3; ☎ 4774-6357; www.lavirutatango.com; Armenia 1366) Still going strong after 10 years, this venue is located in Palermo Viejo at the large and modern building of the Asociación Cultural Armenia. *Milongas* take place Wednesday and Friday through Sunday, while classes in Spanish are given Wednesday through Sunday. Salsa, folk and 'rock' classes are also available.

**Niño Bien** ( ☎ 4147-8687; Humberto Primo 1462) Takes place on Thursdays at the Central Regional Leonesa, attracting a large variety of aficionados – some consider it the best *milonga* in town. It has a great atmosphere, large ballroom and good dance floor, but it still gets very, very crowded (come early). It's far from the center – take a taxi.

**Salon Canning** (Map pp232–3; ☎ 4832-6753; Scalabrini Ortiz 1331) A great dance floor and some of BA's finest dancers (no wallflowers here) grace this traditional venue. Well-known tango company Parakultural (www.parakul tural.com.ar in Spanish) often stages good events here involving live music, tango DJs, singers and dancers. *Milongas* and classes in Spanish every day.

**Sin Rumbo** ( ☎ 4571-9577; Tamborini 6157) One of the oldest tango joints in BA, Sin Rumbo is considered the pinnacle of *milongas*. It's a place for older professional *tanguistas* (tango dancers); not many tourists get here. *Milongas* take place Monday, Wednesday, Friday and Saturday nights. Robert Duvall apparently makes occasional appearances. It's far from the center; take a taxi.

### EL CHINO Map pp220-1

☎ 4911-0215; Beazley 3566; ⏱ 1:30pm Fri & Sat

You'll find an authentic, almost 'underground' tango hall in this converted warehouse. Shows come free with the affordable *asado* dinner. Take bus No 188 from Plaza Italia or Plaza Miserere (Once), or bus No 46 from Plaza Constitución.

### EL QUERANDÍ Map pp222-4

☎ 4345-1770; www.querandi.com.ar in Spanish; Perú 302; show US$35, dinner & show US$49

This large corner venue, also a fancy restaurant, offers traditional tango on a high stage; dark wood details add elegant atmosphere.

### EL VIEJO ALMACÉN Map p225

☎ 4307-7388; www.viejoalmacen.com; cnr Balcarce & Independencia; show US$35, show & dinner US$50

This long-running (since 1969) and highly re-garded tango show features exceptional pro-fessional singers, dancers and musicians. Note that the restaurant is across the street from the theater.

### ESQUINA CARLOS GARDEL Map pp232-3

☎ 4867-6363; www.esquinacarlosgardel.com.ar; Carlos Gardel 3200; show US$40, show & dinner US$60

One of the newest and priciest shows in town. Perhaps the fact that Gardel sang at this old cabaret adds to the novelty. It's been refur-bished since then, of course, and seats 450. The balcony costs double.

### LA VENTANA Map pp222-4

☎ 4331-0127; www.la-ventana.com.ar; Balcarce 431; show US$35, dinner & show US$50

Along with tango dances, there are folk shows and altiplano music here. The beautiful venue is brick-lined, atmospheric and large, so try to get a table closer to the stage.

### SEÑOR TANGO Map pp220-1

☎ 4303-0231; www.senortango.com.ar in Spanish; Vietes 1655; show US$34, show & dinner US$54

Señor Tango is the closest you'll get to Las Vegas in Buenos Aires. Some might think it the best show in town, and it's certainly the most outrageous (live horses are involved). Dish out the bucks and you can be the judge.

## FLAMENCO

For more information on flamenco ven-ues and classes check *Contratiempo*, a free monthly newsletter available at some tourist offices, cultural centers and the Spanish em-bassy. **Club del Vino** (p124) occasionally hosts flamenco shows.

### ÁVILA BAR Map pp226-7

☎ 4383-6974; Av de Mayo 1384; ⏱ Wed-Sat

Offering flamenco for years now is this cozy little Spanish restaurant. Compared to other venues the dinner/shows here aren't a bargain – on Wednesdays and Thursdays they run US$17, and Fridays and Saturdays they're US$20 – but

Entertainment – Dance

*Dancers at Chiquilín Tango (p129)*

mains can include rabbit, paella and seafood stews, with dessert and drinks thrown in. Show-time's around 11pm and reservations are a must on weekends.

### CANTARES Map pp226-7

☎ 4381-6965; www.cantarestablao.com.ar in Spanish; Rivadavia 1180; ☽ Wed-Sun

In the heart of BA's Little Spain neighborhood is this new flamenco venue, located in the old Taberna Español, which once hosted the Spanish poet Federico García Lorca. It's a small space but the dances are authentic and the tapas tasty. On Wednesdays, Thursdays and Sundays you can opt for the show only (US$5), but Fridays and Saturdays the only option includes dinner (US$10). Reservations are highly recommended.

### TIEMPO DE GITANOS Map pp232-3

☎ 4776-6143; www.tiempodegitanos.com.ar; El Salvador 5575; ☽ Wed-Sun

This Palermo Hollywood venue offers flamenco shows in an intimate restaurant setting. Nibble on tapas and sip from the extensive wine list while tapping (or clapping) along to the beat. Dinner/shows start at 9pm or 10pm and cost US$12 to US$17; reserve in advance.

# THEATER

Av Corrientes, between Avs 9 de Julio and Callao, has traditionally been the capital's center for theater, but there are now dozens of venues throughout the city. During the peak winter season upwards of a hundred different scheduled events may take place, though you can find a good variety of shows any time during the year. The *Buenos Aires Herald* and other local newspapers are a good source for listings of major theater productions; some deserving theater companies, however, receive relatively little attention from the mainstream media. Seek them out if you're looking for something different. Tickets are generally affordable, but check *carteleras* (discount ticket offices; p122) for bargain seats.

The following venues, both large and small, offer productions such as theater, opera, dance, music and art exhibits. Contact them for current events and opening times.

### EL CAMARÍN DE LAS MUSAS

Map pp232-3

☎ 4862-0655; www.elcamarindelasmusas.com.ar in Spanish; Mario Bravo 960

Three relatively small theaters seat 60, 70 and 100 at this trendy three-year-old venue that offers contemporary dance, plays and theatrical workshops. There's a good café in front.

### TEATRO AVENIDA Map pp226-7

☎ 4381-0662; www.balirica.org.ar in Spanish; Av de Mayo 1222

This theater dates from 1906 and shows just Argentine productions, mostly opera with occasional flamenco.

### TEATRO COLÓN Map pp226-7

☎ 4378-7344; Libertad 621

Teatro Colón is Buenos Aires' premier venue for the arts (p125), including theater; everyone who's anyone has played, acted, sung or danced here.

### TEATRO DE LA RIBERA

☎ 4302-9024; www.teatrosanmartin.com.ar; Pedro de Mendoza 1821

This small, colorful theater, funded by famous Argentine painter Benito Quinquela Martín, was built in 1971 and holds almost 650.

### TEATRO DEL PUEBLO Map pp222-4

☎ 4326-3606; www.teatrodelpueblo.org.ar in Spanish; Diagonal Roque Saénz Peña 943

A smaller venue with two halls in the basement, this theater shows modern, independent productions.

### TEATRO EL VITRAL Map pp226-7

☎ 4371-0948; Rodríguez Peña 344

This intimate theater, with three halls seating from 36 to 165 people, shows a range of comedy, drama, music and theater productions.

### TEATRO GENERAL SAN MARTÍN

Map pp226-7

☎ 0800-333-5254; www.teatrosanmartin.com.ar; Av Corrientes 1530

This major venue has several auditoriums (the largest seats over 1000) and showcases international cinema, theater, dance and music, covering both conventional and more unusual events. It also has art galleries and often hosts impressive photography exhibitions.

*Teatro Nacional Cervantes (below)*

### TEATRO GRAN REX Map pp226-7
☎ 4322-8000; Av Corrientes 857
A huge theater seating 3,500, this place hosts a myriad of musical productions, including Cindi Lauper (no foolin').

### TEATRO LA PLAZA Map pp226-7
☎ 6320-5300; Av Corrientes 1660
This theater runs both classic and contemporary productions, including tango, theater and comedy.

### TEATRO NACIONAL CERVANTES
Map pp228-9
☎ 4816-4224; www.teatrocervantes.gov.ar in Spanish; Libertad 815
Opened in 1921 this theater is architecturally gorgeous but faded, with three halls, a grand lobby and red velvet chairs. It presents theater, comedy, musicals and dance at affordable prices.

### TEATRO OPERA Map pp222-4
☎ 4814-3056; Av Corrientes 860
A classic theater, and open to all artists; from piano recitals to rock concerts to tango to ballet.

### TEATRO PRESIDENTE ALVEAR
Map pp226-7
☎ 4374-6076; www.teatrosanmartin.com.ar; Av Corrientes 1659
Inaugurated in 1942 and named after an Argentine president whose wife sang opera, this theater holds over 700 and shows many musical productions, including tango.

# CINEMAS

Buenos Aires is full of cinemas, whether they be historical neon classics or slick modern multiscreens. The traditional cinema districts are along pedestrian Lavalle (west of Florida) and on Avs Corrientes and Santa Fe (all easy walking distance from downtown). Newer cinemas, however, aren't necessarily located in any one particular area – many are in shopping malls spread throughout the city. Not surprisingly, most newer places show international blockbusters, while quirkier underground flicks have to seek out less conventional venues.

Ticket prices are cheap at US$3 to US$4, and most cinemas offer half-price discounts for matinees, midweek shows or first screenings of the day. There is usually a *trasnoche* (midnight or later showing) scheduled for Friday and Saturday nights.

Check the *Buenos Aires Herald* for original titles of English-language films. The entertainment sections of all the major newspapers will have movie listings as well, but be aware that Spanish translations of English-language film titles often don't translate directly. Except for children's films and cartoon features, which are dubbed, foreign films almost always appear in their original language with Spanish subtitles.

## Mega-Movie Theaters

If you're looking for something a little bit more mainstream, the following big cinemas show more blockbuster-style productions:

**Abasto-Hoyts Cinema** ( ☎ 4319-2999; Av Corrientes 3247)

**Cine Gaumont 1, 2, 3** (Map pp226–7; ☎ 4371-3050; Rivadavia 1635)

**Cine Lorca 1 & 2** (Map pp226–7; ☎ 4371-5017; Av Corrientes 1428)

**Cine Metro 1, 2, 3** (Map pp226–7; ☎ 4382-4219; Cerrito 570)

**Cinemark Puerto Madero** (Map p225; ☎ 4315-3008; www.cinemark.com.ar in Spanish; AM de Justo 1960)

**Galerías Pacífico 1 & 2** (Map pp222–4; ☎ 4319-5357; Florida 753)

**Patio Bullrich 1-6** (Map pp228–9; ☎ 4814-7447; Av del Libertador 750)

**Village Recoleta** (Map pp230–1; ☎ 4800-0000, www.villagecines.com in Spanish; cnr Junín & López)

**Cine Cosmos** (Map pp226–7; ☎ 4953-5405; www.cinecosmos.com in Spanish; Av Corrientes 2046) and **Sala Leopoldo Lugones** (Map pp226–7; ☎ 4374-8611; Av Corrientes 1530) often show retrospectives, documentaries, foreign film cycles and art-house movies, along with more commercial flicks. Some cultural centers (p188) have their own small cinemas, while places such as **Alianza Francesa** (p189) and **British Arts Centre** (p189) showcase movies in their respective languages.

# Sports, Health & Fitness

# Sports, Health & Fitness

Most porteños make an effort to look good, and many partake in a variety of different outdoor sports as part of that effort. Biking, tennis and *fútbol* (soccer) are all popular sporting activities in Buenos Aires, both for health and fun. And when the weather's just right, the city's green spaces fill with recreation-minded walkers and joggers.

When the weather sucks, many turn to the city's numerous indoor health clubs. A healthy and good-looking body is highly desired in stylish BA, and many train faithfully for those perfect biceps. Other less traditional indoor physical activities, such as yoga and Pilates, are becoming more mainstream.

## WATCHING SPORTS

### SOCCER

Argentina claims some of the best soccer in the world. The national team won the World Cup in both 1978 and 1986, and they walked away with gold at the 2004 summer Olympics.

Argentines are avid fans of the sport, and on game day (and there are many) you'll see TVs everywhere tuned to the soccer channel. Cheers erupt when goals are scored, and after a big win, cars sporting team flags go honking by (especially around the Obelisco). Soccer is a national obsession, and witnessing this passion at a live game is part of the Buenos Aires experience.

Tickets for *entradas populares* (bleachers) and *plateas* (fixed seats) cost anywhere from US$3.50 to US$15, but they can skyrocket if a team is doing well. Especially popular games, such as the *súper clásico* between River and Boca, command higher rates. As a traveler and tourist, you should always buy a seat in the *platea*; the *popular* section is a real experience, but can get far too rowdy with ceaseless standing, singing, drinking, jumping, pot smoking, and even occasional fighting. It's also where the *barra brava* (the Argentine equivalent of hooligans) sits.

Tickets are available at stadiums, or try www.ticketek.com.ar (in Spanish), which sells tickets to certain games. Some companies make it easy for you by providing ticket, transportation and guide to a match. **Tangol** (Map pp228–9; ☎ 4312-7276; www.tangol .com; Florida 971, local 59) is a recommended company that charges from US$35 for this privilege.

Don't carry anything to a game that makes you stand out as a tourist. Keep pricey cameras hidden (or leave them at home), avoid wearing jewelry and don't carry more money than you'll need that day. Games are usually safe, but passion can heighten emotions and sometimes things get carried away. For more information on Argentine *fútbol* see www.futbolargentino.com.ar (in Spanish) and www.afa.org.ar.

The following are some of the clubs based in Buenos Aires:

**Argentinos Juniors** (Map pp220-1; ☎ 4551-6887; Punta Arenas 1271)

**Boca Juniors** ( ☎ 4362-2260; www.bocajuniors.com.ar; Brandsen 805)

**Club Atlético Vélez Sársfield** (Map pp220-1; ☎ 4641-5663; www.velezsarsfield.com in Spanish; Juan B Justo 9200)

**Club Deportivo Español** (Map pp220-1; ☎ 4612-8111; www.almargen.com.ar/cde in Spanish; Santiago de Compostela 3801)

**Club Ferrocarril Oeste** (Map pp220-1; ☎ 4431-8282; www.ferroweb.com.ar in Spanish; Avellaneda 1240)

**Club Huracán** (Map pp220-1; ☎ 4942-1965; www .clubhuracan.com in Spanish; Av Presidente Figueroa Alcorta 2570)

**River Plate** (Map pp220–1; ☎ 4788-1200; www .cariverplate.com.ar in Spanish; Av Presidente Figueroa Alcorta 7597)

**San Lorenzo de Almagro** (Map pp220–1; ☎ 4918-8192; www.sanlorenzo.com.ar in Spanish; Varela 2680)

### BASKETBALL

The basketball scene in Buenos Aires has been picking up significantly since 2002, when Argentina played in the World Basketball Championship in Indianapolis. They only won silver, but made history by beating the US Dream Team in international competition. Then, with a similar roster, they defeated the US squad again (along with Italy in the finals) to win gold in the 2004 summer Olympics – their first basketball medal ever. No team had beaten the Americans in the Olympics since 1992, when pro basketballers were allowed to play. Argentina's best players are Emanuel 'Manu' Ginobili, Juan 'Pepe' Sánchez and Ruben Wolkowyski, all of whom have played for or currently play in the NBA.

Today BA has three major squads, with the most popular being Boca Juniors. You can watch them play in La Boca at **Estadio Luis Conde** (La Bombonerita; ☎ 4309-4748; www .bocajuniors.com.ar; Arzobispo Espinoza 600); tickets are cheap at US$3.50 or less. BA's other basketball teams are Obras Sanitarias and Ferrocarril Oeste.

## HORSE RACING

For a little betting excitement visit Palermo's **Hipódromo Argentino** (Map pp232–3; ☎ 4778-2800; www.palermo.com.ar in Spanish; cnr Av del Libertador & Dorrego). The grand building, designed by French architect Fauré Dujarric, dates from 1908 and holds up to 100,000 spectators.

The track is usually open Mondays and weekends, but race times vary so call ahead for exact times. The most important races take place in November (here) and December (at San Isidro's famous grass racetrack). Admission into the grounds is US$3 or less.

## POLO

Given Argentina's history of horses and the past century's British influence, polo is a high-profile sport – if not exactly for the masses. Residual gaucho tradition makes Argentine polo rougher and more competitive than in Europe.

Polo matches take place in Buenos Aires from September to mid-November, culminating in the annual Campeonato Argentino Abierto (Argentine Open Polo Championship), which is held in Palermo. For current information, contact the **Asociación Argentina de Polo** (Map pp222–4; ☎ 5411-4777; www .aapolo.com in Spanish; Hipólito Yrigoyen 636), which keeps a schedule of polo-related activities throughout the country.

Just across from the Hipódromo Argentino, the **Campo Argentino de Polo** (Map pp232–3; cnr Av del Libertador & Dorrego) is the site of the most important events, but the northern suburb of Pilar has the highest density of polo clubs.

If you've got the bucks and have the inclination to take a few polo lessons, contact **La Martina** (☎ 02226-430777; www.lamartinapolo.com; US$300 per day). It's a plush polo-oriented *estancia* in Vicente Casares, about a 45-minute drive from BA.

---

## Of Heroes & Fallen Angels

Diego Armando Maradona, or 'Santo Diego' to his fans, stands alongside or even above Eva Perón as a populist hero of Argentina. Born into stifling poverty as the fifth of eight children, Maradona would emerge as the precocious star of *fútbol* (soccer), famously playing for the Boca Juniors and eventually leading Argentina to World Cup glory. His story was one of struggle, talent and plenty of luck.

After the Falklands War left Argentina utterly humiliated by the British, Maradona managed to give his nation a little revenge. He scored two very different goals in the 1986 World Cup quarter finals against Britain, managing to surreptitiously punch the ball in for the first (thus showing off Argentina's *viveza criolla*, or sly cheating) and dribbling past the entire British defense on the second (considered by some the greatest goal in history). When asked about using his hand for the first goal, Maradona claimed it was '*La Mano de Dios*' ('The Hand of God') that helped him. Some of Argentina's honor had now been restored, and she would then go on to win the World Cup that year. Maradona continued his career in Naples, Italy, signing unprecedented contracts for millions and bringing his SSC Napoli *fútbol* team unfathomed greatness.

However, Maradona's future in *fútbol* would ultimately be marred by massive cocaine abuse, weight gain, and an eventual ban in 1991 from *fútbol* for using performance-enhancing drugs. Today his every move is recorded by the media and keenly watched by all of Argentina; when pressure becomes too much he flees to Cuba and to his close friend and fellow icon Fidel Castro. And while rumors still fly high and wide about Cuba being his holiday drug pad, he will always remain 'Santo Diego,' an endeared hero to Argentina and fallen angel who very much symbolizes the country in which he was born.

## PATO

Of gaucho origins, the polo-like game of *pato* (literally 'duck') takes its name from the original game ball – a dead duck encased in a leather bag. The unfortunate fowl has since been replaced by a ball with leather handles, and players no longer face serious injury in what was once a very violent sport.

For information on *pato* matches and tournaments, which usually take place outside the city, contact the **Federación Argentina de Pato** (Map pp222–4; ☎ 4331-0222; www.fedpato .com.ar in Spanish; Av Belgrano 530, 5th fl), in Montserrat. Tournaments are usually in October or November and take place in Palermo's polo grounds.

# OUTDOOR ACTIVITIES

Buenos Aires is a big concrete city, so you'll have to seek out the outdoor spots in which to work out. Extensive greenery in Recoleta and Palermo provides good areas for recreation, especially on weekends when certain areas are closed to cars. You can also head to the Reserva Ecológica Costanera Sur, an ecological paradise just east of Puerto Madero that might just make you forget you're in a big city; it's excellent for walks, runs and leisurely bike rides.

An interesting sports complex for those seeking outdoor activities is **Perú Beach** ( ☎ 4793-5986; www.peru-beach.com.ar in Spanish; Elcano 794). Short soccer pitches, a covered roller rink, a freestanding climbing wall, skateboard ramps and watersports such as windsurfing and kayaking bring the youth in. Sometimes it seems more of a happy social scene than anything else, which makes it great for families. A grassy lawn, an outdoor café and even a DJ booth (but no actual beach) means that the joint is packed on a warm sunny weekend. It's located in Acassuso, a suburb way north of Buenos Aires' center, just across from the Tren de la Costa's Barrancas station.

## CYCLING

The capital has some pleasant green spaces to spin your wheels. Bike paths run along some roads in Parque 3 de Febrero, where **bicycle rentals** (Map pp232–3; ☎ 4776-6348; per hr US$2; 11am-sunset Mon-Fri, 8am-8pm Sat & Sun) are available in good weather. Look for them on Av de la Infanta Isabel near Av Libertador. Four-wheeled pedal carts can also be rented here. Weekends are especially nice, since the lake ring road is closed to motor vehicles.

For more serious cycling head to Palermo's **Nuevo Circuito KDT** (Map pp232–3), where **Sprint Haupt** ( ☎ 4807-6141; Salguero 3450; per hr US$1-2; 9am-7pm Wed, Fri-Sun, 9am-8:30pm Tue & Thu) rents bicycles for use inside the banked velodrome. Park entry is US$0.75.

The **Reserva Ecológica Costanera Sur** (Map pp220–1; sunrise-sunset), on the eastern side of Puerto Madero along the coast, is green and tranquil and has some flat dirt roads that are great to bike on. Cheap **bike rentals** (per hr US$1.50; daily summer) are available during daylight hours on weekends, just outside the entrance.

If you want to head out of the center, take the Tren de la Costa to the Barrancas station, where there's **bike rentals** ( ☎ 4793-0265; per hr US$3) and you can coast the smooth pedestrian path back to the previous stations and/or up to the San Isidro station. It's a pleasant loop that runs along the coast at times.

For those who need a more structured program, several companies offer bike tours. Try **Urban Biking** ( ☎ 4855-5103; www.urban biking.com; Vera 1401), which offers three to 3½-hour city tours (US$24), along with night tours (US$20) and longer trips to Tigre (US$34) and La Plata (US$50). There's also **Bike Tours** (Map pp228–9; ☎ 4311-5199; www .biketours.com.ar; Florida 868 14H), which has similar trips for US$25 to US$30; it also rents bikes for US$15 per 24 hours.

## SWIMMING

Some upscale hotels have swimming pools that are open to nonguests, including the **Crowne Plaza Panamericano** (p155; from US$27 per day) and the **Hilton** (p156; weekday/weekend US$22/30). A few of the larger gyms have indoor pools (see opposite). Otherwise try Palermo's **Club de Amigos** (Map pp232–3; ☎ 4801-1213; www.puntacarrasco.com.ar in Spanish; Figueroa Alcorta 3885), which has a covered pool open December to February;

Punta Carrasco (Map pp232–3; ☎ 4807-1010, cnr Av Costanera Norte & Sarmiento) has an outdoor pool open December to March. Both charge US$5 to US$7 for daily splashes.

## GOLF

BA's most convenient course is the 18-hole Campo Municipal de Golf (Map pp232–3; ☎ 4772-7261; Tornquist 1426; ☽ sunrise-sunset Tue-Sun). Greens fees are weekdays/weekends US$20/30 – reserve in advance. Practice your long shots at the Asociación Argentina de Golf's driving range (Map pp232–3; ☎ 4804-8649; Av Costanera 1835; 50 balls US$2; ☽ from 8am) and Costa Salguero Driving Range (Map pp232–3; ☎ 4805-4732, Avs Costanera & Salguero; 50 balls US$2; ☽ from 8am).

## TENNIS

There are both cement and clay tennis courts at Punta Carrasco (left). Facilities are good and they're open from 8am to midnight daily. Rates (depending on the court and day) are US$4 to US$8 per hour. You can buy balls here, and racquets are occasionally available to rent, but don't count on it.

Nearby is Parque General Manuel Belgrano (Map pp232–3; ☎ 4807-7879; Salguero 3450), with eight clay courts; they're open from 8am to 10pm weekdays, till 8pm weekends. Rates are US$3 to US$5 per hour; floodlights at night cost an extra US$1.

You'll need your own equipment; call ahead to reserve.

# FITNESS, HEALTH & LIFESTYLE

Buenos Aires has a good range of indoor health clubs, many with modern equipment and such luxuries as indoor pools and spas. The yoga and Pilates movements are gaining hold, with most health clubs and even some cultural centers offering classes. Spa services are excellent and available in the more upscale parts of town.

## DAY SPAS

Some of the best day spas in town are at the five-star hotels, such as the Castelar Hotel & Spa (p159), Four Seasons Buenos Aires (p162) and Crowne Plaza Panamericano (p155).

### AQUA VITA SPA Map pp230-1

☎ 4812-5989; www.aquavitamedicalspa.com in Spanish; Arenales 1965

A small, futuristically lit spa in Recoleta, Aqua Vita's services include facials, sauna, hydromassage, crystal and stone massage and exfoliation. Rates vary wide for the many services, but start at US$37.

### EVIAN SPA Map pp232-3

☎ 4807-4688; www.aguaclubspa.com in Spanish; Cerviño 3626

Services at this Palermo spa include Thai massage, reflexology sessions and skin treatments. Day rates start at US$55; reservations are a must.

## HEALTH CLUBS

### LE PARC Map pp222-4

☎ 4311-9191; www.leparc.com in Spanish; San Martín 645

Good modern machines are centered around an open floor plan connected by catwalks and topped with a glassy ceiling. There's a small indoor pool, terrace, trendy café, sports shop and sauna; many classes are available. Day rates are US$7, but indoor soccer and squash are extra.

### MEGATLON Map pp222-4

☎ 4322-7884; www.megatlon.com in Spanish; Reconquista 335

The king of BA's gyms has about a dozen branches throughout the city. The Reconquista branch is conveniently located right at the center. Expect most or all gym services, including weights, aerobic machines, a sports and supplements shop, a wide variety of classes and athletic courts for basketball, volleyball and soccer. Some branches have an indoor pool, and many have weight areas open 24 hours. Day rates start at US$5.

### SPORT CLUB CECCHINA Map pp226-7

☎ 5199-1212; www.sportclub.com.ar in Spanish; Bartolomé Mitre 1625

Great for muscle-popping weights and modern aerobic machines; exercising areas are spacious, and there's also a large indoor swimming pool and café. Sport Club has over 10 locations in BA; day rates are US$7.

## Top Five Buenos Aires Workouts

- The gym – Where the beautiful people go to see and be seen in spandex and Lycra; plenty of mirrors feed the ego. Gyms are good for swimmers, and the larger ones have sports courts and spas.
- Jogging in Palermo's parks – You might see more walkers, strollers and bikers, but this is one of the best places to run in the city; on weekends the lake ring road is off-limits to vehicles.
- Biking in the Reserva Ecológica Costanera Sur – Another great spot to run or bike, with long gravel trails and scenic views. Get ready to dodge families and couples on weekends, though.
- Shopping – Don't laugh; some of those malls have kilometers of walking potential, and that doesn't even count the arm stretches when you're trying to get that tight skimpy blouse over your head.
- Sex – With all that energy spent on looking good and kissing in the park, let's assume porteños are getting their share – and often.

# YOGA & PILATES

Most gyms offer yoga and Pilates classes, as does **El Camarín de las Musas** (p130) and the **Arte Sano** (p97) restaurant in Recoleta. Also check cultural centers such as **Centro Cultural Konex** (p188) which offers Swasthya yoga classes. Classes are usually in Spanish, though the language barrier shouldn't be too much of a problem with yoga.

### CENTRO GREYG Map pp232-3
☎ 4832-3559; centrogreyg@hotmail.com; JL Borges 2295
This Palermo Viejo studio has Hatha and Sai yoga classes three times weekly for US$3.50 per class; your first session is free.

### PARA BIEN PILATES Map pp228-9
☎ 4315-1077; parabien@hotmail.com; San Martín 1009, 1A; 🕑 8am-7pm Mon-Fri
It's a very small place but right downtown; four 50-minute classes with machines cost US$25.

### TAMARA DI TELLA PILATES Map pp232-3
☎ 4833-0603; www.cuerpodiet.com in Spanish; cnr Aráoz & Juncal; 🕑 8am-9pm Mon-Fri, 9am-2pm Sat
This well-known 'Pilates Queen' has over a dozen branches throughout the city. Facilities are modern and costs per four sessions are US$25.

### VIDA NATURAL Map pp232-3
☎ 4826-1695; www.yogacentro.com.ar in Spanish; Charcas 2852; 🕑 8:30am-12:30pm & 2-8:30pm Mon-Fri, 8:30am-12:30pm Sat
Vida Natural is in Palermo and offers Ashtanga, Hatha and Iyengar yoga. Four sessions per month cost US$19; per class it's US$5. Therapeutic massage and chakra balancing are also available.

# CLIMBING WALLS

### BOULDER Map pp232-3
☎ 4802-4113; Arce 730; 🕑 3-11pm Mon-Fri, 3-9pm Sat & Sun
Boulder, in Las Cañitas, Palermo, is the only decent indoor climbing wall in the city. It's not huge, but has a good wall (with bare cement floor) and tiny, padded bouldering cave. They'll set up a rope if you don't lead climb; belays are included in the US$3 day-use fee. They rent harnesses, and shoe use is free (though they don't stock all sizes).

# MARTIAL ARTS

### YMCA Map pp222-4
☎ 4311-4785; www.ymca.org.ar in Spanish; Reconquista 439
Those looking to karate their way through Buenos Aires can check out the YMCA, where weekly two-hour classes go for US$13 per month.

### KURATA DOJO Map pp232-3
☎ 4774-4409; www.kuratadojo.org.ar in Spanish; Oro 2254
In Palermo Viejo, this good Aikido school offers classes that cost US$3, or US$20 per month (includes three classes per week).

# PIERCING & TATTOOS

The best place to look like a fashionable trendsetting punkster is **Galería Bond** (p148), on Santa Fe 1670. It's full of tattoo parlors, piercing studios and cutting-edge skateboarder clothing, and a is great place to hang out – if grunge is your thing. Hours are 10am to 9pm Monday to Saturday.

# Shopping

# Shopping

Despite a major drop in the purchasing power of the Argentine peso over the last few years, Buenos Aires' citizens continue to shop as if there's no tomorrow. Just a peek into the nearest mall on a weekend will make you wonder how people who seem to be making so little can spend so much. As the saying goes, 'An Argentine will make one peso and spend two.' And that's not the only reason porteños love to shop; it's not only an act of hedonistic consumerism, but yet another social pursuit requiring you to look good while you're doing it. After all, you never know who's checking you out (or who you're going to run into).

Shopping is also a family event, with many malls catering to children by offering special play areas and video arcades. Paseo Alcorta (p150) in Palermo has an especially large kids' playground on the 3rd floor, while Mercado de Abasto (p152) in Once sports an excellent children's museum (really an amusement center). Almost all modern malls also have multiscreen cinemas, stroller rentals and large food courts complete with fast-food outlets and ice-cream parlors. Some even offer health clubs, beauty shops and Internet cafés. With these types of services, families (and tourists) can easily spend all day shopping and playing at the mall.

There are plenty of areas to shop outside the malls as well. Florida is a must for any tourist, even if you don't like to buy stuff; it's a multipurpose pedestrian strip that buzzes with shoppers, tourists, performers and commuters. As a large avenue, Av Santa Fe is a bit less pedestrian friendly, but equally prominent as the city's main service and shopping artery. San Telmo is *the* place for antiques, while Av Corrientes, between Avs 9 de Julio and Callao, has many of BA's bookstores (most books are in Spanish, however). Av Pueyrredón near Once train station is the place for cheap (though not the highest quality) clothing, and the largest concentration of jewelry shops is on Libertad south of Av Corrientes. Palermo Viejo has become a great neighborhood to browse in, with dozens of designers setting up shop alongside trendy houseware stores and kitschy boutiques (not to mention excellent restaurants). For more on fashion, see p16.

Finally, let's not forget the weekend street fairs (p151). On a sunny weekend afternoon they're a wonderful place to be, and you'll have many to experience.

All have crafts or antiques stalls to browse through, and many also offer street performers and tango shows.

## Top Five Shopping Strips

- Av Santa Fe between Aráoz and Libertad (Map pp232–3) – Almost 30 blocks of shops selling everything. Continues in Belgrano as Av Cabildo, with an even higher concentration of stores, movie theaters and fast-food outlets. Put on your walking shoes.
- Calle Florida (Map pp228–9) – A pedestrian shopper's paradise. Souvenir stores, newsstands, leather shops, clothing boutiques and plenty of services for both locals and tourists. Along with its little sister, Lavalle (also pedestrian), it's the walking lifeblood of Buenos Aires' downtown.
- Av Alvear (Map pp228–9) – The Cadillac of shopping streets, ritzy Alvear has more upscale boutiques than you can shake your overcharged credit card at. International designers Luis Vuitton, Giorgio Armani, Nina Ricci, Bang & Olufsen, Hermès and Cartier share real estate with fancy art galleries and rich mansions.
- Calle Defensa (Map p225) – San Telmo's antiques row is a magnet for tourists and collectors, especially on Sunday when the barrio's antiques market is in full swing. Don't come expecting rock-bottom bargains; international demand and an adjustment to devaluation have kept prices high, especially for the best pieces.
- Av Pueyrredón between Av Corrientes and Rivadavia (Map pp232–3) – In the barrio of Once, Pueyrredón is packed solid with clothes, shoes, accessories, appliances, luggage and household bargains. Street merchants hawk watches and electronic gizmos; this zone bustles like a bee on steroids. Goods are the cheapest in town, but quality is lower.

## Opening Hours

Store hours generally run from 9am or 10am to 8pm or 9pm weekdays, with many open for at least a few hours on Saturday. Most stores close on Sunday. Almost all shopping malls are open from 10am to 9pm daily, with a few closing at 10pm.

## Consumer Taxes

Taxes are included in quoted or marked prices: what you see is what you pay. Some places, however, might add a *recargo* (surcharge) to credit card purchases – ask before you buy.

If you buy more than US$70 in merchandise from a store that displays a 'Tax Free Shopping' sign you're entitled to a tax refund. Just ask the merchant to make out an invoice for you (you'll need ID); upon leaving the country show the paperwork to a customs official, who'll stamp it and tell you where to obtain your refund.

## Bargaining

As in other Western countries, bargaining is not acceptable in most stores. At street markets you can try negotiating for better prices; just keep in mind you may be talking to the artists themselves (who are trying to make a living here). San Telmo's antiques fair is an exception; prices here will definitely be inflated for tourists, and you need to know how to bargain.

# MICROCENTRO & PLAZA DE MAYO

### BUENOS AIRES SPORTS

Map pp222-4 *Sports*
☎ 4326-4980; Viam onte 766; ☻ 9:30am-8pm Mon-Fri, 9:30am-2pm Sat

This large, modern store carries plenty of outdoor clothing, plus sports equipment such as bicycles, backpacks, tennis racquets, climbing equipment and footwear (each store may carry different items). Several of its branches are in shopping centers such as **Unicenter** (p152) and **Paseo Alcorta** (p150).

### EL ATENEO Map pp222-4 *Books & Music*
☎ 4325-6801; Florida 340 & 629; ☻ 9am-10pm Mon-Thu, 9am-midnight Fri & Sat, noon-10pm Sun

Buenos Aires' landmark bookseller stocks a limited number of books in English and also has a decent selection of music CDs. There are several branches within the city, including a gorgeous branch in the Gran Splendid, an old renovated cinema in **Barrio Norte** (Map pp230–1; Av Santa Fe 1860).

### EL COLECCIONISTA Map pp222-4 *Music*
☎ 4322-0359; www.elcoleccionis tacd.com.ar in Spanish; Esmeralda 562; ☻ 10:30am-8:30pm Mon-Fri

This small place has an eclectic selection of jazz, blues, salsa, Celtic and symphonic rock. They'll buy used musical instruments, so trade in that guitar you're tired of lugging around. Staff are knowledgeable.

### FLABELLA Map pp222-4 *Tango Shoes*
☎ 4322-6036; www.flabella.com; Suipacha 263; ☻ 10am-11:30pm Mon-Sat

Glittery, gleaming, gorgeous men's and women's tango heels (all handmade) are sold at this small boutique. For more selection try nearby **Candela Tango** ( ☎ 4326-5377; www.sui pacha256tango.com.ar), just a few stores up at Suipacha 256.

*El Ateneo (left) bookstore*

## GALERÍAS PACÍFICO

Map pp222-4 *Shopping Mall*

☎ 5555-5110; www.galeriaspacifico.com.ar in Spanish; Florida & Av Córdoba; ⏲ 10am-9pm Mon-Sat, noon-9pm Sun

Centrally located right on pedestrian Florida is this gorgeous mall which is always full of shoppers looking for the most stylish fashions or sitting pretty at the downstairs food court. The murals covering the ceiling were painted by famous artists; for more information on this building see p52. There are free tango shows at 8pm Friday to Sunday, and a free folkloric show at 8pm on Thursday.

## LIBRERÍA ALBERTO CASARES

Map pp222-4 *Books*

☎ 4322-6198; www.acasares.servisur.com in Spanish; Suipacha 521; ⏲ 10am-8pm Mon-Fri, 10am-2pm Sat

This bookstore has been specializing in antique books for collectors and bibliophiles since 1975. It also carries old maps, manuscripts and historical documents; they'll search for a particular item and ship it internationally.

## MONTAGNE

Map pp222-4 *Camping & Outdoors Equipment*

☎ 4312-9041; www.montagneoutdoors.com.ar in Spanish; Florida 719; ⏲ 10am-8:30pm Mon-Sat, noon-8pm Sun

This shop sells outdoor clothing that is stylish, good quality and made in Argentina. Choose from a small selection of tents, backpacks and camping gear upstairs. There are several other Montagne branches, including one in **Barrio Norte** (Map pp230–1; Av Santa Fe 1780).

## MUSIMUNDO Map pp222-4 *Music*

☎ 4322-9298; www.musimundo.com in Spanish; Florida 267; ⏲ 9:30am-9:30pm Mon-Sat, 11am-9pm Sun

With over 50 branches throughout the city, this is BA's largest music retailer. Listening stations make selecting the hippest CDs a snap. Other branches can be found in the **Microcentro** (Map pp222–4; Lavalle 925), as well as in **Barrio Norte** (Map pp230–1; Av Santa Fe 1844), **Congreso** (Map pp226–7; Av Corrientes 1753) and many of the central shopping centers.

## TONEL PRIVADO Map pp222-4 *Wine*

☎ 4328-0953; www.tonelprivado.com in Spanish; Suipacha 299; ⏲ 9am-8pm Mon-Fri

One of almost 10 branches of this popular wine store; carries a large selection of Argentine wines and imported liqueurs, and offers wine-tasting classes. Look for other stores at the following shopping malls: **Galerías Pacífico** (left), **Paseo Alcorta** (p150) and **Patio Bullrich** (p147).

# CONGRESO & AVENIDA CORRIENTES

## AQUILANTI Map pp226-7 *Books*

☎ 4952-4546; aquilanti@sinectis.com.ar; Rincón 79; ⏲ 11am-7pm Mon-Fri

Looking for antique books on Argentina, Latin America, Spain, history, politics or literature? Search for it here, or email them – they'll search for you and ship internationally.

## FREE BLUES Map pp226-7 *Music*

☎ 4057-4751; Rodríguez Peña 438; ⏲ 10:30am-8pm Mon-Thu, 10.30am-9pm Fri

Buy, sell or trade your used CDs and LPs here. It's a small, friendly store with a good selection of blues, rock, pop, jazz, country, tango and rockabilly.

## WILDLIFE

Map pp226-7 *Camping & Outdoors Equipment*

☎ 4381-1040; wildlifesports@hotmail.com; Hipólito Yrigoyen 1133; ⏲ 10am-8pm Mon-Fri, 10am-1pm Sat

If you're looking for all manner of outdoor and camping equipment in a somewhat funky environment, this is it. Crampons, knives, tents, backpacks, climbing ropes, foul-weather clothing and military gear can be found at this somewhat musty-smelling place.

## ZIVAL'S Map pp226-7 *Music*

☎ 5128-7500; www.tangostore.com; Av Callao 395; ⏲ 9:30am-10pm Mon-Sat

This is one of the better music stores in town, especially when it comes to tango, jazz and classical music. Listening stations and a big sale rack are pluses, and they'll ship CDs, VHS tapes, books and sheet music abroad too (check the website).

# SAN TELMO

## GABRIEL DEL CAMPO Map p225 *Antiques*

☎ 4361-2061; gabrieldelcampo@hotmail.com; Defensa 990; ⏲ 10am-7pm

You'll find wonderfully unique things at this exceptional shop, from Asian tapestries to shelves made from rowboat hulls to Eiffel Tower sculptures to carousel animals to old doors. Religious objects and lighthouse models also take up space here.

### GALERÍA CECIL Map p225 *Antiques*
Defensa 845; 🕘 9am-8pm
Walk past the café in front and wander around the tiny antique stalls in the back; there are cameras, lacework, silverware, toys, glassware and ceramic vases. Across the street is Paseo de 900, which is a bit grungier but more fun.

### HERNANI Map p225 *Antiques*
☎ 4362-4437; Defensa 1047; 🕘 11:30am-6:30pm
An old family business for generations, this very upscale antique store sells only top-drawer pieces. Grand old furniture, huge mirrors, giant urns, shiny chandeliers, rich tapestries and reproductions of famous statuary give this place a museum-like feel. Prices are in the thousands of (US) dollars.

### IMHOTEP Map p225 *Antiques*
☎ 4862-9298; Defensa 916; 🕘 11am-6pm Sun-Fri
Come find amazing old knickknacks at this eccentric shop. Small oddities such as Indian statuettes, ceramic skulls, Chinese snuff boxes, precious stone figurines and gargoyles make up some of the bizarre collectibles here. The boar's head is a nice touch as well.

### JUAN C PALLAROLS Map p225 *Silverwork*
☎ 4361-7360; www.pallarols.com.ar in Spanish; Defensa 1039; 🕘 10am-7pm Mon-Fri
The Pallarols family has been creating some of the world's best custom-made silverwork since the 1750s. Traditional skills have been passed down through generations and continue today with Juan's son Adrián; the family's 200-year-old tools are still being used to create the unique pieces displayed at this shop.

### L'AGO Map p225 *Boutique*
☎ 4362-4702; Defensa 970; 🕘 10am-8pm
L'ago is something rare in San Telmo – a store that doesn't sell antiques. Study the creative window displays at this hip boutique, then walk in to check out papier-mâché boxes, metal insect figures, desktop sculptures, innovative lamps, darling toys and other fun objects.

### SILVIA PETTROCIA Map p225 *Antiques*
☎ 4362-0156; spantiques@velocom.com.ar; Defensa 1002; 🕘 10:30am-7:30pm
Some of San Telmo's most gorgeous antiques can be found at this store, which is chock-

full of Italian statuary, old furniture, giant urns, fancy light fixtures and grand picture frames – great fodder for your Riviera mansion.

# RETIRO
## CAMPING CENTER
Map pp228-9 *Camping & Outdoors Equipment*
☎ 4314-0305; www.camping-center.com.ar in Spanish; Esmeralda 945; 🕘 10am-8pm Mon-Fri, 10am-5pm Sat
High-quality camping and mountaineering equipment, rock-climbing gear and general backpacking products (including brand-name clothing from the US) are available at this modern store.

## CASA LÓPEZ
Map pp228-9 *Leather Goods*
☎ 4311-3044; www.casalopez.com.ar; MT de Alvear 640/658; 🕘 9am-8pm Mon-Fri, 9:30am-7pm Sat, 10am-6pm Sun
Bring your limousine: some of BA's finest quality leather jackets, luggage, bags and accessories live here. Service is overly attentive; there are two shops almost next to each other here, and other branches at **Galerías Pacífico** (opposite) and **Patio Bullrich** (p147).

## EL FENIX Map pp228-9 *Wine*
☎ 4811-0363; Av Santa Fe 1199; 🕘 8am-8pm Mon-Sat
This large corner store offers a wide selection of fine Argentine wines, imported liquors (such as whiskey), deli items and even Havana cigars. They'll deliver to anywhere in Buenos Aires.

## GALERÍA 5TA AVENIDA
Map pp228-9 *Shopping Mall*
Av Santa Fe 1270; 🕘 11am-8pm Mon-Sat
Those looking for secondhand clothing (some with vintage overtones) need to make an obligatory stop at this modest shopping mall. Used funky wearables are sold here at several

shops, and prices are pretty affordable for even the grungiest backpacker.

## GALERÍA AGUILAR

Map pp228-9　　　　　　　　　　*Art Gallery*
☎ 4393-1852; www.galeriamuseoaguilar.com; Suipacha 1176; 🕙 8am-9pm

Wall-to-wall, floor-to-ceiling abstract, geometric, landscape and portrait paintings fill this gallery-museum, which claims to stock 1500 paintings. There are black-and-white etchings by Antonio Berni, along with works by Argentine artists Xul Solar, Benito Quinquela Martín and Emilio Pettoruti.

## GALERÍA FREDERICO KLEMM

Map pp228-9　　　　　　　　　　*Art Gallery*
☎ 4312-3334; www.fundacionfjklemm.org in Spanish; MT de Alvear 626; 🕙 11am-8pm Mon-Fri

Honoring the self-proclaimed 'Andy Warhol' of Argentina is this bright basement gallery. The permanent and changing displays highlight modern art sculptures, contemporary (and sometimes bizarre) installations and such things as interesting but hard to understand digital paintings.

*Laura Driz (p149) boutique, Palermo*

## GALERÍA RUBBERS

Map pp228-9　　　　　　　　　　*Art Gallery*
☎ 4816-1864; www.rubbers.com.ar in Spanish; Av Alvear 1595; 🕙 11am-8pm Mon-Fri, 11am-1:30pm Sat

This contemporary and very upscale art gallery, on the edge of Recoleta and Retiro, exhibits only established Argentine painters and sculptors. There's a beautiful branch in **Barrio Norte** (Map pp230–1; Av Santa Fe 1860), on the 3rd floor of the Gran Splendid El Ateneo bookstore.

## GALERÍA RUTH BENZACAR

Map pp228-9　　　　　　　　　　*Art Gallery*
☎ 4313-8480; www.ruthbenzacar.com in Spanish; downstairs at Florida 1000; 🕙 11:30am-8pm Mon-Fri

Right at the head of pedestrian Florida is this clean and contemporary basement art gallery. Some of the finest and most creative Argentine modern artists have been showcased here since 1965. International artists such as Leo Castelli, Soledad Lorenzo and Christopher Grimes have also been highlighted.

## JOYERÍA CONTEMPORÁNEO

Map pp228-9　　　　　　　　　　*Jewelry*
☎ 4312-7522; www.vivianacarriquiry.com.ar, www.paulalevyjoyas.com.ar in Spanish; Florida 971, Suite 46; 🕙 11am-8pm Mon-Fri, 11am-4pm Sat

Paula Levy and Viviana Carriquiry create stunning silver jewelry in this small store on the 2nd floor at the back of the same shopping mall that houses Tangol (p195). Pieces sport simple, modern and delicate geometric designs that sometimes mimic vertebrae; occasional copper, bronze or glass accents add interest.

**KEL** Map pp228-9　　　　　　　　　*Books*
☎ 4814-3788; www.kelediciones.com in Spanish; MT de Alvear 1369; 🕙 9am-7pm Mon-Fri, 9:30am-1:30pm Sat

It's mostly books in English that you'll find lining the shelves in this bookstore. There are books on literature, travel, cooking, philosophy, art, history and religion, along with novels and dictionaries.

## KELLY'S REGIONALES

Map pp228-9　　　　　　　*Crafts & Souvenirs*
☎ 4311-5712, Paraguay 431; 🕙 9:30am-7:30pm Mon-Fri, 9:30am-4pm Sat

If you're looking for that perfect cowhide to throw over your sofa or a cutting-edge Mapuche poncho to wear with your miniskirt you'll probably find it here. There are fine animal masks from Salta and gaucho paraphernalia such as *mate* gourds, along with cheap souvenir knickknacks.

## LA MARTINA

Map pp228-9                          *Polo Equipment*
☎ 4576-7999; www.lamartina.com; Paraguay 661;
🕑 10am-8pm Mon-Fri, 10am-2pm Sat
You'll need to look stylish on polo fields, so bring your bank account and pick up the finest quality leather riding boots, pith helmets, polo mallets and saddles; colorful polo shirts are even stocked here.

### LIBRERÍA ABC Map pp228-9          *Books*
☎ 4314-8106; www.libreriasabc.com.ar; Av Córdoba 685; 🕑 9am-8pm Mon-Fri, 10am-1:30pm Sat
This large bookstore, which carries half its stock in English or German, is the likeliest place in town to find current Lonely Planet guides. There's a good selection of novels, literature, travel books and maps; it also sells used books.

### LIONEL FRENKEL

Map pp228-9                       *Crafts & Souvenirs*
☎ 4312-9806; San Martín 1085; 🕑 9am-7:30pm Mon-Fri, 9:30am-6pm Sat
Shop here for leather jackets, handbags, jewelry, precious stone figurines and gaucho gear. For tackier souvenirs head to the basement; service personnel are overly attentive.

### MARÍA VÁZQUEZ

Map pp228-9                       *Designer Boutique*
☎ 4815-6333; www.mvzmariavazquez.com.ar in Spanish; Libertad 1632; 🕑 10am-9pm Mon-Fri, 10am-6pm Sat
One of the better-known Argentine designers, MVZ creates lingerie-like cocktail dresses in thin silks, lacy cotton and smooth satin. Details such as beads, sequins and glitter add a catchy sheen to her sexy productions, which also include signature jeans. Celebrities such as Shakira, Xuxa and Naomi Campbell have claimed her threads. MVZ has other branches in shopping malls around town.

### PATIO BULLRICH

Map pp228-9                          *Shopping Mall*
☎ 4814-7412; www.altopalermo.com.ar in Spanish; Av del Libertador 750; 🕑 10am-9pm
Buenos Aires' most exclusive shopping center once hosted livestock auctions, but these days

it tends toward sales of Persian rugs, double-breasted tweed suits and Dior's latest designs. Three floors hold fine boutiques such as Lacoste, Lacroix and Versace, along with fancy coffee shops, a cinema complex and a food court.

### WELCOME MARROQUINERÍA

Map pp228-9                          *Leather Goods*
☎ 4312-8911; www.welcome-leather.com.ar; MT de Alvear 500; 🕑 10am-2pm & 3-7:30pm Mon-Fri, 10am-1:30pm Sat
Going strong since 1930, this upscale leather shop offers pricey luggage, briefcases, handbags, accessories and a small selection of both men's and women's shoes.

### WINERY Map pp228-9                *Wine*
☎ 4311-6607; www.winery.com.ar in Spanish; Leandro N Alem 880; 🕑 9am-11pm Mon-Sat
This is an attractive chain store that offers a large selection of Argentine wines. It offers tasting of 35 different wines by the glass at this location; sample five for US$3 to US$8.50. The café and wineshop are upstairs, the modern lounge-restaurant downstairs. There's a smaller branch with just a café in the **Microcentro** (Map pp222–4; Av Corrientes 302).

# RECOLETA & BARRIO NORTE
## BUENOS AIRES DESIGN

Map pp230-1                          *Shopping Mall*
☎ 5777-6000; www.designrecoleta.com.ar in Spanish; Av Pueyrredón 2501; 🕑 10am-9pm Mon-Sat, noon-9pm Sun
The newest, trendiest and finest home furnishings are all under one roof here. This is the ideal place to look for that perfect oriental rug, snazziest light fixture and most exotic decor. Furniture and housewares, bath design, appliances…the list goes on.

### CAT BALLOU

Map pp230-1                       *Designer Boutique*
☎ 4811-9792; Av Alvear 1702; 🕑 11am-8pm Mon-Fri, 10:30am-2pm Sat
Alicia Goñi designs the delicate clothing, while Florencia Pieres creates much of the jewelry and decorations at this cool corner boutique. Fabrics are silky, frilly, satiny, velvety and wispy – just the sort of things that feel good on your skin. Designs are gorgeous, original, limited in number and very romantic.

## GABRIELA CAPUCCI

Map pp228-9                              *Boutique*

☎ 4815-3636; Av Alvear 1477; ⊙ 10:30am-8pm Mon-Sat

This is a fun retro store, unlike many on this street. Bright patchwork dresses, creative handbags, wispy scarves, vintage tops, velvet pillows and eclectic accessories fill this small space. Crocheted flowers, glittery sequins, huge beads and fake pink orchids decorate camouflage, satin and animal prints. Colors are bright, and the costume jewelry is wild.

## GALERÍA BOND

Map pp230-1                          *Shopping Mall*

Av Santa Fe 1670; ⊙ 10am-9pm Mon-Fri

For the slickest tattoos and piercings in town, you can't beat this grungy shopping center. Buenos Aires' skateboarder-wanna-bes, along with their punk rock counterparts, also come here to shop for the latest styles in youthful fashion. Hello Kitty and heavy metal actually end up mixing quite well.

## GUIDO MOCASINES Map pp230-1    *Shoes*

☎ 4813-4095; www.guidomocasines.com.ar in Spanish; Rodríguez Peña 1290; ⊙ 9:30am-8pm Mon-Fri

Men come here for sleek, smooth leathers to place on their feet; expect fine service, upscale prices and some of the best quality in BA. There are a few conservatively styled women's shoes as well. There's another branch, also in **Recoleta** (Map pp230–1; Quintana 333).

## LIBRERÍAS TURÍSTICAS

Map pp230-1                                  *Books*

☎ 4963-2866; www.libreriaturistica.com.ar in Spanish; Paraguay 2457; ⊙ 9am-7pm Mon-Fri, 10am-1pm Sat

This Barrio Norte bookshop carries many guidebooks and maps of Buenos Aires, Argentina and the world. It has books in six languages, though the majority are in Spanish.

## LÓPEZ TAIBO

Map pp230-1      *Men's Shoes & Leather Goods*

☎ 4804-8585; www.lopeztaibo.com; Av Alvear 1902; ⊙ 10am-8pm Mon-Fri, 10am-6pm Sat

Absolutely the best leather goods can be found at this Recoleta boutique, offering excellence and tradition since 1897. The good-looking, black-clad staff offers attentive service to the well-dressed businessman or traveler searching for shoes, belt, jacket or briefcase.

## PERUGIA BOTTIER

Map pp230-1                        *Women's Shoes*

☎ 4804-6340; perugia@sion.com; Av Alvear 1866; ⊙ 10am-9pm Mon-Fri, 10am-2pm Sat

This is one of Buenos Aires' finest women's shoe stores and has been going strong for 40 years. The European-inspired designs are made from Argentine and Italian leather and change seasonally. Custom-made orders take eight days, cost from US$140 to US$300 and can be shipped abroad.

## ROSSI Y CARUSSO

Map pp230-1                          *Leather Goods*

☎ 4811-1965; www.rossicaruso.com; Av Santa Fe 1601; ⊙ 9:30am-8pm Mon-Fri, 10am-7pm Sat

A stuffed horse will entertain your spouse while you check out the best leathers in town. Choose from fancy boots, belts, bags, saddles, gaucho knives and silver *mates*. It's expensive and the service is professional; don't come dressed scruffy. There are two other branches, one in **Barrio Norte** (Map pp230–1; Av Santa Fe 1377) and the other in **Galerías Pacífico** (p144).

# PALERMO

## ALTO PALERMO

Map pp232-3                           *Shopping Mall*

☎ 5777-8000; www.altopalermo.com.ar in Spanish; Av Coronel Díaz 2098; ⊙ 10am-10pm

Smack on bustling Av Santa Fe, this popular, shiny mall offers dozens of clothing shops, bookstores, jewelry boutiques, and electronics and houseware stores. Look for Swatch, Adidas, Hilfiger and Levis. Services include a health club, food court and cinema complex.

## ARTE ÉTNICO ARGENTINO

Map pp232-3                                *Textiles*

☎ 4832-0516; www.arteetnicoargentino.com; El Salvador 4600; ⊙ 11am-7pm Mon-Fri, 10am-1pm Sat

Bright and beautiful woven *mantas* (blankets) are the main attraction here. The most detailed ones are the most expensive; all are made from wool and natural dyes and can also be used as light rugs. The nearby warehouse stocks rustic furniture, but you'll need to call for a private showing.

## ATÍPICA Map pp232-3                    *Crafts*

☎ 4833-3344; El Salvador 4510; ⊙ 2-8pm Mon-Fri, 11am-8pm Sat

This tiny shop, on the edge of Palermo Viejo, stocks crafts from local artists, along with

## Clothing Sizes

**Measurements approximate only, try before you buy**

**Women's Clothing**

| | | | | | | |
|---|---|---|---|---|---|---|
| Aus/UK | 8 | 10 | 12 | 14 | 16 | 18 |
| Europe | 36 | 38 | 40 | 42 | 44 | 46 |
| Japan | 5 | 7 | 9 | 11 | 13 | 15 |
| USA | 6 | 8 | 10 | 12 | 14 | 16 |

**Women's Shoes**

| | | | | | | |
|---|---|---|---|---|---|---|
| Aus/USA | 5 | 6 | 7 | 8 | 9 | 10 |
| Europe | 35 | 36 | 37 | 38 | 39 | 40 |
| France only | 35 | 36 | 38 | 39 | 40 | 42 |
| Japan | 22 | 23 | 24 | 25 | 26 | 27 |
| UK | 3½ | 4½ | 5½ | 6½ | 7½ | 8½ |

**Men's Clothing**

| | | | | | | |
|---|---|---|---|---|---|---|
| Aus | 92 | 96 | 100 | 104 | 108 | 112 |
| Europe | 46 | 48 | 50 | 52 | 54 | 56 |
| Japan | S | | M | M | | L |
| UK/USA | 35 | 36 | 37 | 38 | 39 | 40 |

**Men's Shirts (Collar Sizes)**

| | | | | | | |
|---|---|---|---|---|---|---|
| Aus/Japan | 38 | 39 | 40 | 41 | 42 | 43 |
| Europe | 38 | 39 | 40 | 41 | 42 | 43 |
| UK/USA | 15 | 15½ | 16 | 16½ | 17 | 17½ |

**Men's Shoes**

| | | | | | | |
|---|---|---|---|---|---|---|
| Aus/UK | 7 | 8 | 9 | 10 | 11 | 12 |
| Europe | 41 | 42 | 43 | 44½ | 46 | 47 |
| Japan | 26 | 27 | 27½ | 28 | 29 | 30 |
| USA | 7½ | 8½ | 9½ | 10½ | 11½ | 12½ |

crafts from northern artists who use indigenous techniques for their works. All are unique pieces and include picture frames, wall hangings, ceramics, glass, textiles, jewelry and even furniture. Quality is high and prices fair.

### CALMA CHICA Map pp232-3    *Housewares*
☎ 4831-1818; Honduras 4925; ⏰ 10am-8pm Mon-Sat, 2-8pm Sun

The very creative and well-designed household items here would be best in a hip dorm room, but anyone can find something to love. Unusual chairs, pillows, lighting fixtures and cowhide rugs highlight CC's broad range of stock.

### EL CID Map pp232-3    *Men's Clothing*
☎ 4832-3339; www.el-cid.com.ar in Spanish; Gurrachaga 1732; ⏰ 1-8:30pm Mon, 10am-8:30pm Tue-Sat, 4-8pm Sun

Some of the classiest men's threads can be found at this Palermo Viejo boutique. Shop for Nestor Goldberg's designer shirts, pants, jackets, accessories and jeans. There's another branch located in **Retiro** (Map pp228–9; Reconquista 949).

### FERIA DE PULGAS Map pp220-1    *Antiques*
Cnr Álvarez Thomas & Dorrego; ⏰ 10am-8pm

This dusty and dim covered flea market sells antiques – precious things such as ancient wooden beds, glass soda bottles, ceramic vases, paintings, clocks, chandeliers and even old cars. It's a pile-up, so you'll have to sift through to find your treasure. Look for Claudio Giannini's funky stall; he's a prolific artist who sells his creative paintings for under US$35.

### HERMANOS ESTEBECORENA
Map pp232-3    *Men's Clothes*
☎ 4772-2145; www.hermanosestebecorena.com in Spanish; El Salvador 5960; ⏰ 11am-1pm & 1:30-9pm Mon-Fri, 11am-9pm Sat

Attractive and functional men's clothing is the specialty here. The Estebecorena brothers apply their wide creative skills toward well-constructed leather shirts, shoes and even underwear. More traditional duds are also available, from solid coats to dressy suits to casual wear.

### LA MERCERÍA
Map pp232-3    *Accessories & Crafts*
☎ 4831-8558; Armenia 1609; ⏰ 9am-8pm Mon-Thu, 9:30am-8:30pm Fri & Sat, 1-8pm Sun

Bright and colorful accessories such as scarves, hats, jewelry, pillows and lots of handbags line the shelves at this luscious place. Fabrics and materials offering a wonderful tactile experience include lace, knits, wool yarns, beads and buttons, many of which you can buy – this boutique doubles as a crafts store.

### LAURA DRIZ
Map pp232-3    *Designer Boutique*
☎ 4834-6576; Honduras 4778; ⏰ 11am-8pm Mon-Sat

At six years old, this is one of the 'oldies' in Palermo Viejo. LD uses slinky, clingy fabrics such as satin and silk for her nightwear, while sportswear ranges from 'colonial' to 'art nouveau.' Nordic sweaters pepper her fall lineup.

### LAURA O
Map pp232-3    *Furniture & Housewares*
☎ 4832-8778; www.laurao.com; Uriarte 1554; ⏰ 10am-8pm Mon-Sat

Gorgeous creamy couches and beds – most in white, beige and browns, fill much of this large modern warehouse space. You'll want to dive right in, they look so comfortable. Tables are crafted of solid, rustic wood, and a few housewares such as glasses, linens and velvet pillows add welcome texture to the ambience.

## MARIANA DAPPIANO

Map pp232-3       *Designer Boutique*
☎ 4833-4731; www.marianadappiano.com in Spanish; Honduras 4932; ⊙ 10:30am-8pm Mon-Sat

Designing for eight years makes Mariana Dappiano one of the first on the Palermo block. Her mega-creative, pattern-dominated fashions range from thin denim tops to sultry clingy wraps with uneven hemlines. A few unusual shoes and handbags fill out the simple store.

## MISHKA Map pp232-3       *Shoes*
☎ 4833-6566; El Salvador 4673; ⊙ 11am-8pm Mon-Sat

Well-regarded designer Chelo Cantón was an architect in a previous incarnation, but now – with Pia Petrossi's help – manages to somehow create glittery, mostly low-heeled shoes with a creative and conservative vibe. Boots are also on the plank but don't seem as cool.

## NADINE ZLOTOGORA

Map pp232-3       *Designer Boutique*
☎ 4831-4203; www.nadinez.com; El Salvador 4683; ⊙ 11am-8pm Mon-Sat

Nadine Z's gorgeous dresses and tops combine feminine styles with kick-ass fabrics, creating fantastically romantic wearables. Thick yet flowing base textiles, often in floral prints, are layered with lacy tulle and silky edging and are a feast for the eyes as well as the skin.

## OBJETO Map pp232-3       *Designer Boutique*
☎ 4834-6866; Gurruchaga 1649; ⊙ 11am-8pm Mon-Sat

Rodrigo Abarquero and Debora Di Stilio have displayed some of the wackiest, most outrageously fun clothes in this tiny boutique. Wear them to parties and everyone will ask 'where did you *get* that?' Dresses hang with crazy accoutrements such as leather and plastic cut-outs, doll eyes and Japanese animé themes. Creativity and unconventionality dominate; these aren't your regular street duds.

## ODA Map pp232-3       *Boutique*
☎ 4831-7403; Costa Rica 4670; ⊙ 11am-8pm Mon-Sat

Over a dozen crafts artists are represented at this simple boutique. Offerings include unusual costume jewelry, knit hats, creative wood toys, painted trays, glass ashtrays and small metal sculptures. All are handmade creations and would make good original gifts.

## PASEO ALCORTA

Map pp232-3       *Shopping Mall*
☎ 5777-6500; www.altopalermo.com.ar in Spanish; Salguero 3172; ⊙ 10am-10pm

One of the largest and most upscale malls in the city. All the popular Argentine women's clothing shops are represented, as are international boutiques such as YSL, Lacroix and Dior. Other stores sell leather goods, kid's clothes, men's designs, sportswear and accessories. There's a large food court, cinema complex and children's play area.

## RAPSODIA Map pp232-3       *Designer Boutique*
☎ 4833-5814; www.rapsodia.com.ar; El Salvador 4757; ⊙ 11am-8pm Mon-Sat

A must for fashionable female travelers is this trendy boutique carrying a large selection of wearable fashions. Old and new are blended with exotic twists into creative feminine styles that will please most shoppers. It's fancy and cool, and will make you feel great walking amongst the most stylish porteñas.

*Mercado de Abasto (p152)*

# Street Markets

**Feria Artesanal** (Map pp230-1; Plaza Intendente Alvear; 10am-7pm) Located in Recoleta, this is probably BA's most popular street fair, with hundreds of booths selling leather accessories, jewelry, hats, handmade crafts, kitschy souvenirs and dozens of other creative goods. Hippies gather, bakers circulate their pastries and mimes perform (or just stand very still). It's much bigger on weekends.

**Feria Artesanal** (cnr Caminito & Mendoza; 10am-6pm Thu-Sun) Tango themes dominate the goods at this small and lively crafts fair, giving La Boca even more color than usual. Tango dancers and buskers compete for your attention, and along Caminito itself are many drawings, paintings and pictures to buy.

**Feria de Antigüedades** ( ☎ 4743-8371; www.delanticuario.com; Estación Las Barrancas; 9:30am-8pm Sat, Sun & holidays) This cute antiques market, in the northern suburb of Acassuso, has goods cheaper than the San Telmo fair but it's smaller and less crowded. Dig through old housewares, silverwork, records, books, small collectibles, lighting fixtures and antique hardware. The best way here is on the Tren de la Costa, which begins in Olivos at Estación Maipú; get to this train station from downtown via buses Nos 59, 60 and 152.

**Feria de Mataderos** (Map pp220-1; ☎ 4687-5602; www.feriademataderos.com.ar in Spanish; cnr Avs Lisandro de la Torre & de los Corrales; 11am-9pm Sun & holidays Apr-Nov, 6pm-midnight Sat Dec-Mar) In the southwestern barrio of Mataderos is this excellent folk market. Merchants offer handmade crafts, cheap *parrilladas* (mixed grills) and tasty sweets. Folksingers, costumed dancers and gauchos on horseback entertain, and there's a **gaucho museum** ( ☎ 4687-1949; Av de los Corrales 6436; admission US$0.35; 12-6:30pm Sun Mar-Dec) nearby. From downtown, take bus Nos 155 (also marked 180) or 126; the market is about an hour's ride away, but worth it.

**Feria de San Telmo** (Map p225; Plaza Dorrego; 10am-5pm Sun, occasionally Sat afternoon) Tourists and locals alike flock to this wonderful *feria* – you'll find antique seltzer bottles, jewelry, gaucho items, artwork, vintage clothing, collectibles and just about everything else. Tango shows, buskers and mimes entertain while sidewalk cafés provide welcome breaks. Prices aren't rock-bottom, but you can find some unique stuff. Walk along Defensa four blocks to Parque Lezama, where a crafts and flea market takes place at the same time.

**Feria Plaza Belgrano** (Map pp220-1; Plaza Belgrano, cnr Juramento & Cuba; 10am-8pm Sat, Sun & holidays) Belgrano hosts a pleasant neighborhood market that's great on a sunny weekend. You'll find high-quality imaginative crafts, as well as some kitschy junk. The performers and tarot readers draw a crowd, too.

**Feria Plaza Serrano** (Map pp232-3; Plaza Serrano; noon-7pm Sat & Sun) Costume jewelry, hand-knit tops, funky clothes, hippie bags, creative slumped glass and leather accessories fill the crafts booths at this popular fair on fashionable Plaza Serrano in Palermo Viejo. It's not large but the nearby designer boutiques and trendy bars can easily fill the rest of your lazy afternoon.

**RETRO** Map pp232-3          *Designer Boutique*
☎ 4831-4141; Malabia 1583; 11am-8pm Mon-Sat
Seven designers stock this trendy store, all offering a different theme. One is Kukla, who does casual street clothes and jeans in colorful and very wearable styles. Another is Lupe Posse, with elegant evening dresses, racy tops and feminine suits in blacks and neutrals. All are worth a peep.

**SALSIPUEDES**
Map pp232-3          *Designer Boutique*
☎ 4831-8467; Honduras 4814; 10:30am-9pm Mon-Fri, 10:30-8pm Sat
This tiny store doesn't carry huge lineups, but what it does have can really pack the girls in. Some of the hippest, most youthful styles around live here in informal creative knits and fine fabrics; colors and patterns are bold and lots of fun to try on.

**SPOON** Map pp232-3          *Housewares*
☎ 4831-3786; www.spoon.com.ar in Spanish; Honduras 4876; 11am-8pm Mon-Sat
Quirky but ultramodern household items here use many different materials. Browse through the store and check out the creative lighting, simple leather sofas, unusual dishware, colorful glass bowls, metal platters, wood and leather boxes, and bright picture frames.

**VARANASI** Map pp232-3          *Designer Boutique*
☎ 4833-5147; www.varanasi-online.com; El Salvador 4761; 11am-8pm Mon-Sat
Victor and Mario were originally architects before turning to design, and now they've been creating fashions for 20 years. Here they've created lines spanning from urban wear to party dresses – you'll stand out for sure in their frilly, embroidered and layered inventions. It's fun stuff and definitely wearable on city streets.

# OUTSIDE THE CENTER
## MERCADO DE ABASTO
Map pp232-3 *Shopping Mall*
☎ 4959-3400; www.altopalermo.com.ar in Spanish; cnr Av Corrientes & Anchorena; ◷ 10am-10pm
One of the most beautiful malls in Buenos Aires, this remodeled old market holds more than 200 shops, a large cinema, a covered plaza, a kosher McDonald's and a good children's museum. It's in Once, Carlos Gardel's old neighborhood. See also p75.

## UNICENTER
*Shopping Mall*
☎ 4733-1166; www.unicenter.com.ar in Spanish; cnr Paraná & Panamericana; ◷ 10am-10pm
With around 300 shops, Unicenter claims to be the biggest shopping center in South America. The complex houses 14 movie screens, a bowling alley, a small amusement park and parking for 6,500 cars. It's located in the northern suburb of Martínez; **Manuel Tienda León** (☎ 4314-3636) runs buses here from Buenos Aires' downtown area.

# Sleeping

# Sleeping

Buenos Aires' tourist boom, which began in 2002 after the peso plummeted, has exploded the accommodations front. Over 100 youth hostels have opened in the last few years and more are mushrooming all the time. Budget and midrange hotels are common, and many are upgrading their facilities. A good range of five-star hotels (think Hilton, Sheraton, Four Seasons) exists already, and more are being built – especially around the Puerto Madero area. You shouldn't have trouble finding the type of place you're looking for, but make a reservation if traveling during any holidays or the busier months such as July, August and November. During the scorching summer months of December and January many porteños (BA residents) head to the beach on vacation, but this is when foreign tourists stop by on their way to Patagonia or Iguazú Falls. Snagging a room ahead of time isn't a bad idea.

Prices are generally a bargain for anyone traveling with hard currency. Hostel beds cost about US$6 to US$8. Two people can get a good budget room with bathroom for US$15 to US$25 at a cheap hotel, while for US$30 to US$75 you can add amenities such as minifridge, in-room safe, king-size beds and free toiletries. Anything around US$100 is four-star luxury, and if you pay more than US$150 you're getting into the five-star category and should expect fine, fine service and the best amenities.

Listings in this chapter are by neighborhood and are in alphabetical order; cheap sleeps are noted at the end of each section.

Many places will help you with transportation to and from the airport if you reserve ahead of time. If you're driving, note that while many midrange to high-end places have a garage or access to parking, many charge extra for this service. Breakfast is included almost everywhere, even at hostels; exceptions are noted in the reviews.

## Longer-Term Rentals

The guesthouses listed at the end of this section are generally oriented more toward weekly or monthly accommodations, but you have many other choices as well. Any accommodations listed in this guide will significantly discount a long-term stay. See if you can manage to negotiate a deal in advance.

You can also check out the *Buenos Aires Herald* (www.buenosairesherald.com/clas sifieds) or *La Nación* (http://clasificados .lanacion.com.ar/Indexinmuebles.asp in Spanish) for apartment rentals.

### Apartments Online

Many new website services have also developed to meet this outside demand for apartments; these also tend to be expensive. You can see pictures of rental properties, along with a price and a list of facilities. Usually the photos match what you will get, but keep in mind that a location on a noisy street isn't such a good deal. Some of these websites are listed following.

www.adelsur.com

www.apartmentsba.com

www.argentinago.com

www.argentinahomes.com

www.bytargentina.com

www.friendlyapartments.com/apart.htm

www.midtownba.com.ar

www.roomargentina.com

www.stayinbuenosaires.com.ar

Traditionally you need to get yourself an Argentine guarantor to cover your rent in case of delinquency, but so many long-term foreigners are now pouring into Buenos Aires that a plethora of rental agencies are popping up to help them find apartments without this requirement. Expect to pay a much higher monthly rate for this service, however; locals usually commit to at least one or two years when obtaining a lease, and pay less. The websites listed on this page are a great place to start your research.

## Things to Know about Accommodations in BA

Many of the prices we quote in this guidebook, particularly for the four- or five-star hotels, are rack or high-season rates (but not the very highest peak rates). We figure it's more pleasant when you arrive and find prices lower than you expected, rather than higher. But you don't always have to pay the official posted rate, whether it's in a guidebook or at the hotel itself.

Your best bet for getting a cheaper price is to book in advance. You can do this via most hotels' websites (look for the word *promociones*, or specials). Calling ahead and talking to a salesperson with the power to negotiate prices can also be fruitful, especially if you plan on staying more than a few days. And note that most hotels at these higher echelons add a 21% value-added tax, known as the Impuesto de Valor Agregado (IVA), to your final tally; if you don't want a surprise, ask if this tax is included in the prices you're quoted.

Another thing to be aware of is some hotels' two-tier pricing structure. Foreigners from 'richer' Western countries are sometimes charged a much higher rate than Argentines. Again, this is especially true with five-star hotels such as the Hilton, Sheraton and Four Seasons. Most of the hotels we've included in this book do not follow this two-tier pricing structure (though almost all museums, along with certain companies such as Aerolíneas Argentinas force foreigners to pay for premium tickets). Most two- or three-star hotels, on the other hand, often charge the same whether you book in advance or just show up, and they usually – but not always – charge everyone (no matter what their origin) the same price.

### LA CASA DE HILDA
Map pp230-1                                      *Guesthouse*
☎ 4826-1031; lacasadehilda@yahoo.com.ar;
Arenales 2634; monthly s US$200-434, d US$267-500,
tr US$300-534

Here's a homey guesthouse in upscale Recoleta. The three-bed dorm and three private rooms share bathrooms; the two apartments have private bathrooms and kitchenettes (the one on the 3rd floor, which sleeps two, is most private). Services include laundry, daily maid and kitchen use, but meals (including breakfast) aren't part of the deal. A resident cat prowls the grounds.

### LA CASA DE MARINA
Map pp222-4                                      *Guesthouse*
☎ 4343-9229; www.lacasademarina.s5.com;
Balcarce 621, 3rd fl, apt 6; monthly s US$134-200,
d US$234

Just four modest rooms, some of them tiny, are available here at this very small San Telmo guesthouse; all of the rooms share bathrooms and a kitchen. Friendly Marina knows the area's history and also speaks English, Portuguese and some French, along with Spanish. There's a worn living room but no TV; meals are not provided.

# MICROCENTRO & PLAZA DE MAYO

Buenos Aires' Microcentro area, along with being very central, has the best range and largest quantity of accommodations in the city. Toward the north you'll be closer to the busy pedestrian streets of Florida and Lavalle, as well as the neighborhoods of Retiro and Recoleta (and their upscale stores). The Plaza de Mayo area, however, contains more historical government buildings and the bustling banking district, and is within walking distance to San Telmo. Nights tend to be a bit calmer here, as most businesspeople who work here flee the center after the day is done.

### CLARIDGE HOTEL Map pp222-4        *Hotel*
☎ 4314-7700; www.claridge.com.ar; Tucumán 535;
d US$127

Rooms here aren't huge, but they're comfortable, classically decorated and fairly quiet (thank the double-paned glass). Bigger suites come with Jacuzzis for soaking your tired feet after strolling up and down Florida, just a stone's throw away – or you can splash into the heated outdoor pool. Gym, sauna and excellent spa services are available.

### CROWNE PLAZA PANAMERICANO
Map pp222-4                                      *Hotel*
☎ 4348-5000; www.buenosaires.crowneplaza.com;
Carlos Pellegrini 551; d US$188

You won't be staying at this five-star for the rooms or services; it's the 23rd-floor pool you're after. The atrium is bright, there's a small bar for poolside drinks, and the terrace views down Av 9 de Julio are simply awesome. Spa services and a gorgeous lobby full of businesspeople and fancy tourists complete the picture.

*Rooftop pool, Crowne Plaza Panamericano (p155)*

### FAENA HOTEL & UNIVERSE

Map pp222-4     *Hotel*

☎ 4021-5555; www.faenaexperience.com; Marth Salotti 445; s/d from US$375

The newest of BA's shiny five-star gems, this Philippe Starke–designed beauty is so much more than a place to stay. The French designer's cutting-edge style has produced the city's first large-scale boutique hotel, along with futuristic private condos and a plethora of services such as a Turkish bath, spa, beauty salon, cabaret lounge, business center, lovely pool and even a gourmet market, not to mention restaurants and a café. Views are exceptional, as are the prices.

### GRAN HOTEL ARGENTINO

Map pp222-4     *Hotel*

☎ 4334-4001; www.hotel-argentino.com.ar; Carlos Pellegrini 37; s/d from US$24/34

This modest semi–art nouveau hotel, situated on busy Pellegrini, isn't quite the three-star establishment it claims to be. It still has good, tasteful rooms, however, and stylish (if small) halls and lobby. Get an inside room for quiet nights, and a more expensive room if you want a remote control.

### GRAN HOTEL HISPANO

Map pp222-4     *Hotel*

☎ 4345-2020; www.hhispano.com.ar; Av de Mayo 861; s/d US$27/33

Don't be put off by the tiny lobby; upstairs, the patio, atrium and halls are spacious and pleasant. Rooms are cute, squeaky clean and come with fridges – look at a few as they vary in size. The hordes claim rooms here quickly, so reserve in advance.

### GRAND KING HOTEL

Map pp222-4     *Hotel*

☎ 4393-4012; www.grandking.com.ar; Lavalle 560; s/d from US$57

As you enter you'll notice the strange ramp system in the lobby, but it seems to work as a practical design element. At this hotel you're basically paying for the location on pedestrian Lavalle, which makes your stay a relatively quiet one. Rooms are small and comfortable enough for most, but hardly luxurious – though they are stocked with minibars. If you want something bigger try one of the junior suites (US$93).

### HILTON Map pp222-4     *Hotel*

☎ 4891-0000; www.hilton.com; Macacha Güemes 351; s/d US$200/260

For those seeking the best in town. From the snazzy lobby to the luxurious rooms (of which there are more than 400), the Hilton offers all the amenities you'd expect in this price range: top-notch service, great views from the back and a killer outdoor pool. It's located in Madero Este, just east of the Microcentro.

### HOTEL AVENIDA Map pp222-4     *Hotel*

☎ 4331-4341; www.advance.com.ar/usuarios /havenida; Av de Mayo 623; s/d US$17/24

Just 34 rooms (some with balcony) greet you at this quiet, friendly place. There's a pleasant breakfast area and the location is great – right near Plaza de Mayo. Remember to bring cash as your credit card will do you no good here.

### HOTEL CARSSON Map pp222-4     *Hotel*

☎ 4131-3800; www.hotelcarsson.com.ar; Viamonte 650; s/d US$45/49

The upscale Carsson is centrally located. Inside rooms are quiet but face a boring lightwell, while outside ones are bright but noisy; the more expensive rooms have larger bathrooms but are otherwise the same. Triples are the best, with pleasant inner-garden views. All rooms come with a minibar and security box.

## HOTEL FACÓN GRANDE

Map pp222-4          *Hotel*

☎ 4312-6360; www.hotelfacongrande.com in Spanish; Reconquista 645; s/d US$34/44

The pleasant gaucho-themed lobby is amusing, as are the dressed-up staff. Rooms aren't quite up to gaucho standard, but they're comfortable enough at these prices – and the minibar and plenty of free toiletries make up for something. Guests receive a welcome drink, and there's a small playroom for the kids.

## HOTEL FROSSARD Map pp222-4     *Hotel*

☎ 4322-1811; www.hotelfrossard.com.ar; Tucumán 686; s/d US$20/27

Here's a little gem in the Microcentro – an intimate hotel with 18 high-ceilinged rooms in a charming older building. Doubles are small and cozy, but triples have more breathing room. The location is excellent; pedestrian streets Florida and Lavalle are just a block away.

## HOTEL GOYA Map pp222-4       *Hotel*

☎ 4322-9311; www.goyahotel.com.ar; Suipacha 748; s/d from US$19/27

This intimate, friendly, spotless, central, quiet and comfortable hotel is an excellent deal. 'Classic' rooms have open showers, while the 'superior' rooms are more luxurious and have bigger bathrooms. But go for the gold – the US$47 presidential suite comes with a sofa and Jacuzzi.

## HOTEL LA FAYETTE Map pp222-4    *Hotel*

☎ /fax 4393-9081; www.lafayettehotel.com.ar; Reconquista 546; s/d US$66/70

The bathrooms are small, but the 83 spotless rooms are large, comfortable and come with desks. Double-paned windows guarantee peace and quiet, while the lobby is pleasantly upscale. The range of amenities include a minibar and there are hairdryers in the bathrooms. You'll be close to pedestrian streets Florida and Lavalle.

## HOTEL NOGARÓ Map pp222-4      *Hotel*

☎ 4331-0091; www.hotelnogaro.com; Av Julio Roca 562; d US$88

Elegant and sophisticated earth-tone designs make this four-star hotel a good upscale choice in the Plaza de Mayo area. Bathrooms are small, but the atmospherically lit rooms are modern, clean and comfortable, and come with hardwood floors. Ask for a tub with jets – it shouldn't cost much more.

## HOWARD JOHNSON DA VINCI

Map pp222-4          *Hotel*

☎ 4326-6607; www.davincihotel.com.ar; Tucumán 857; s/d US$51/57

This is another branch of the popular American chain, well situated near the pedestrian streets of Florida and Lavalle. The 48 rooms are clean and modern, and come with king-size beds. Facilities include pool, gym and sauna.

## NH CITY HOTEL

Map pp222-4          *Hotel*

☎ 4121-6464; www.nh-hotels.com; Bolívar 160; d US$142

The NH chain's signature style is hip and distinctive minimalism, with muted earth-tone colors, natural accents and rich textiles showcasing their design. Expect classy, tasteful rooms and excellent services – this particular hotel has a beautiful rooftop swimming pool with city views. Their other branch in the Microcentro is the **NH Latino** ( ☎ 4321-6700; Suipacha 309), which is a bit less pricey at US$109, but check for Internet specials for either hotel.

## NH JOUSTEN Map pp222-4       *Hotel*

☎ 4321-6750; www.nh-hotels.com; Av Corrientes 280; d US$129

This very cool hotel chain (there are four NH hotels in BA) does great minimalist things with wood, tile, glass and fabrics. Rooms are gorgeous and simple, but tastefully designed – go for the larger corner ones. Part of the roof has a wonderful terrace with views, and looming above that is the luxurious presidential suite.

## TUCUMÁN PALACE HOTEL

Map pp222-4          *Hotel*

☎ /fax 4311-2298; Tucumán 384; s/d US$17/20

It might be old and past its prime, but you get fairly large, decent and centrally located rooms, some with sofas and – at no extra charge – stained rugs. Bathrooms have both open showers and hairdryers, so try not to get electrocuted. Rooms with balconies are on the 6th floor only. It's popular so book ahead.

# CHEAP SLEEPS

## HOSTEL CLAN Map pp222-4      *Hostel*

☎ 4334-3401; www.hostelclan.com.ar; Adolfo Alsina 912; dm US$6, d US$15

Here's a good party hostel, with built-in Spanish school, free bike rental and guitar playing and singing in the lobby. It's a great friendly place to meet people and have fun, but you'll need to accept a general funkiness and laid-back staff. Dorms are spacious and each of the seven doubles comes with hammock (all rooms share bathrooms). There are pool and table tennis tables in the common room, along with a backpacker 'museum' of stuff travelers have left behind. Many activities are organized.

### HOTEL ALCÁZAR

Map pp222-4             *Hotel*

☎ 4345-0926; Av de Mayo 935; s/d US$12/15

Long popular with budget travelers, these old digs have basic but somewhat charming fan-cooled rooms of all different sizes. Some sport balconies, so you can have it noisy but bright. You should reserve in advance – the location is good and prices even better. Breakfast costs extra.

### HOTEL EL CABILDO Map pp222-4     *Hotel*
☎ 4322-6695; Lavalle 748; s/d US$12/15

Management here hasn't changed in years, and neither have the low prices. Rooms are basic but clean and fairly spacious, and the location right on pedestrian Lavalle simply can't be beat. Call ahead to reserve.

### HOTEL MAIPÚ Map pp222-4       *Hotel*
☎ 4322-5142; Maipú 735; s/d without bathroom US$8/10, with bathroom US$10/12

Head on up the old marble staircase into the gloomy tiled hallway; your senses will tingle at the faded glory of this classic old building in the middle of all the action. The Hotel Maipú is certainly not without its charm, however, and future remodels may well improve things a bit. In the meantime, guests may continue to enjoy the friendly service, high ceilings, saggy beds, peeling paint, convenient location and dirt-cheap prices.

### HOTEL SUIPACHA INN

Map pp222-4             *Hotel*

☎ 4322-0099; www.hotelsuipacha.com.ar; Suipacha 515; s US$19-24, d US$27-34

This relatively small hotel (just 27 rooms) is a good and very popular budget choice, so book ahead if you plan on staying here. The larger 'superior' rooms come with kitchenette and more space, though standard ones are fine for what they are. Double-paned windows and kitchen use are surprising perks in this price category.

### MILHOUSE YOUTH HOSTEL

Map pp222-4             *Hostel*

☎ 4345-9604; www.milhousehostel.com; Hipólito Yrigoyen 959; dm US$6-7, d US$21-23

This 150-bed hostel's location in a beautiful old mansion, along with a plethora of activities, services and party atmosphere, attracts backpackers from all over South America. Dorms and private rooms are well kept, and most surround a pleasant open patio on three floors. Common spaces are boisterous, and there's a pool table and rooftop terrace. Free tango and salsa classes are available.

### PORTAL DEL SUR

Map pp222-4             *Hostel*

☎ 4342-8788; www.portaldelsurba.com.ar; Hipólito Yrigoyen 855; dm US$7-9, s/d US$20/26

One of the best of Buenos Aires' new hostels is in this charming old building, which has been nicely remodeled into beautiful dorms and sumptuous, hotel-quality private rooms. The main central area is a little bit dim despite a glass ceiling, but there are some nice touches such as the old tiled floors and a good kitchen. The highlight here has to be the sunny, wooden rooftop deck – complete with a view – and attached airy common lounge. Some rooms have air-con, and free tango and salsa classes are available.

### V & S YOUTH HOSTEL

Map pp222-4             *Hostel*

☎ 4322-0994; www.hostelclub.com; Viamonte 887; dm US$7, s US$20, d US$22-24

This modern and comfortable hostel (50 beds) has good vibes, a good location and good common spaces. There's a large-screen TV that shows free movies daily, and a pleasant kitchen-dining-lobby area that makes for easy socializing. Dorms are good-sized, clean and carpeted. The double in front is beautiful, but traffic makes it a bit noisy. Free salsa, tango and Spanish classes keep backpackers busy and happy.

---

## Top Five Hotels

- **Crowne Plaza Panamericano** (p155) Best rooftop view
- **Four Seasons Buenos Aires** (p162) Best spa
- **Alvear Palace Hotel** (p164) Best tea
- **Hilton** (p156) Best outdoor pool
- **Faena Hotel & Universe** (p156) Best looking

# CONGRESO & AVENIDA CORRIENTES

This region contains many of the city's theaters and cultural centers. Lively Av Corrientes has many modest shops, services and bookstores along with some of BA's older cinemas. The Plaza de Congreso area is always moving, sometimes with mostly peaceful public demonstrations. It's not quite as packed as the Microcentro and has a less touristy flavor, but still bustles day and night.

## BROADWAY ALL-SUITES
Map pp226-7        *Hotel Suites*
☎ 4378-9300; www.broadway-suites.com.ar; Av Corrientes 1173; s/d from US$100

The fancy lobby – with its colorful high-backed sofas – emulates a hip lounge, and there's wonderful things done with leather, glass, stone, wood and tile. All are integrated into the beautifully modern suites in colors such as beige, grey and white. Decor is simple, and little perks such as CD players, microwaves and safety boxes are welcoming.

## CASTELAR HOTEL & SPA
Map pp226-7        *Hotel*
☎ 4383-5000; www.castelarhotel.com.ar; Av de Mayo 1152; s/d US$55/82

The high-ceilinged lobby is grand, and while the standard rooms are just good enough the superiors are bigger and more luxurious. Federico García Lorca, the Spanish poet and playwright, apparently spent time here once. Spa services, including a Turkish bath, are available. It's a good value for the location and charm.

## COLUMBIA PALACE HOTEL
Map pp226-7        *Hotel*
☎ 4373-1906; www.columbiapalacehotel.com.ar; Av Corrientes 1533; s/d US$23/28

The furniture's a bit outdated and worn, but rooms are fairly clean and solid. Its location is on busy Av Corrientes in the heart of the bustling theater district. If the traffic din wears you down, get an inside room.

## FIAMINGO APART HOTEL
Map pp226-7        *Hotel Suites*
☎ 4374-4400; www.fiamingoapart.com.ar in Spanish; Talcahuano 120; s/d US$27/34

Families should make a beeline to this place; the good suites are very spacious and come with kitchenette (no stove – just microwave and sink). Staff are friendly and windows are double-paned for peace and quiet. It's a great deal for the price, but call first to confirm and reserve.

## HOTEL CHILE
Map pp226-7        *Hotel*
☎ 4383-7877; hotelchile@argentina.com; Av de Mayo 1297; s/d US$14/20

This popular old standby continues to offer an art nouveau facade outside and 70 decent budget rooms inside. Corner rooms have the best balconies and views, but are noisy and have only fans. Inside rooms come with air-con and are darker and more peaceful.

## HOTEL DE LOS DOS CONGRESOS
Map pp226-7        *Hotel*
☎ 4372-0466; www.hoteldoscongresos.com; Av Rivadavia 1777; s/d US$30/34

The modern rooms here are small but clean and beautiful, with relaxing color themes and decor. The lobby and tiled halls are nice too, with a scratch here and there – but for the price and location, this place is a fairly good deal.

## HOTEL IBIS
Map pp226-7        *Hotel*
☎ 5300-5555; www.hotelibis.com; Hipólito Yrigoyen 1592; s/d from US$27

This place is popular, and it's no wonder; prices are low and the location is great, right on Plaza del Congreso. Rooms are neat and practical, and the shiny lobby connects with a comfy dinerlike restaurant. Minuses include showers only (no bathtubs), but snag a room with view to the front and you can soak in the views rather than the tub.

## HOTEL LYON
Map pp226-7        *Hotel Apartments*
☎ 4372-0100; www.hotel-lyon.com.ar in Spanish; Riobamba 251; s/d US$34/57

If you're a traveling family or group, this place is for you. Old apartments were converted to very spacious, simple rooms with entry halls, large bathrooms and separate dining areas with fridges (but no kitchens). Furniture is outdated but slightly charming. Up to five folks can be accommodated in each apartment.

*Artsy decor at Lulu Guesthouse (p165)*

### HOTEL MARBELLA Map pp226-7 *Hotel*
☎ 4383-8566; www.hotelmarbella.com.ar; Av de Mayo 1261; s/d US$17/33

The rooms at this hotel are basic but clean – try to secure one with a larger balcony. More spacious (and more expensive) rooms are also available, and there's a posh modern bar-restaurant where breakfast is served. From here it's an easy tramp to either Plaza del Congreso or Plaza de Mayo.

### HOTEL MILAN Map pp226-7 *Hotel*
☎ 4373-0736; www.milanhotel.com.ar; Montevideo 337; s/d US$20/24

Here's a pint-sized hotel with tiny stand-up lobby and 50 small, clean and modest rooms. It's nothing to write home about, but prices are good and the location is great – it's right in the heart of the bustling theater district. Lots of people want to stay here so book ahead.

### HOTEL MOLINO Map pp226-7 *Hotel*
☎ 4374-9112; www.molinohotel.com.ar in Spanish; Av Callao 164; s/d US$20/24

Singles are small and have open showers that get everything wet, but rooms in general are neat and come with tasteful decor. The staff is friendly and the lobby sparkles; this is a good choice in Congreso.

### HOTEL PALACE SOLÍS Map pp226-7 *Hotel*
☎ 4371-6266; hotelsolis@secomp.com.ar; Solís 352; s/d US$12/20

It's a little far from the city center and doesn't look like much from the outside, but the dimly lit grand old sitting room inside is impressive. The 51 basic rooms (some are dark) sport outdated furniture, but it's a good place overall and popular for its fair prices.

### NUEVO HOTEL CALLAO
Map pp226-7 *Hotel*
☎ 4374-3861; www.hotelcallao.com.ar; Av Callao 292; s/d US$19/24

The comfortable and modern rooms here are immaculate and spacious, and many have balconies. Two are bigger and rounded, located in the cupola edge of the building. Reserve ahead of time, or come in the morning to try to snag a room.

### NUEVO MUNDIAL HOTEL
Map pp226-7 *Hotel*
☎ 4383-0011; www.hotel-mundial.com.ar in Spanish; Av de Mayo 1298; s US$10-17, d US$16-24

The best rooms at this somewhat scruffy place are Nos 702 and 711 – these come with large balcony and views. Other rooms are either wood-floored or carpeted and can be different sizes (but not different prices). Halls are worn and the lobby is small, but it's cheap and very popular with tourists – call ahead to reserve.

## CHEAP SLEEPS

### BA STOP Map pp226-7 *Hostel*
☎ 4382-7406; www.bastop.com; Av Rivadavia 1194; dm US$6, s/d US$12/18

Here's a pleasant and intimate hostel located in the heart of Little Spain, BA's Spanish district. There are just 32 beds (and three bathrooms for them all!), good common areas, artsy decor, high ceilings and table tennis and pool tables. It's small, congenial and a good place to meet other travelers. There's a piano in the dining room in case you need to practice your scales.

### GRAN HOTEL ORIENTAL
Map pp226-7 *Hotel*
☎ 4951-6427; ghoriental@hotmail.com; Bartolomé Mitre 1840; s/d US$10/13

Downstairs rooms are a bit dark and showers are small, but the simple, high-ceilinged rooms are comfortable enough to make this place a great bargain for peso-pinchers. Just don't

Sleeping – Congreso & Avenida Corrientes

expect many services. The tiled lobby and hallways are narrow but modern and functional.

## HOTEL CAOCA Map pp226-7 *Hotel*
☎ 4383-9950; Bartolomé Mitre 1688; s/d US$10/10
You can't get much cheaper than this Chinese-run hotel. Rooms are pretty decent, and the building has some personality (and lots of Chinese decor). The managers don't speak much English or even Spanish; your Mandarin should come in handy, however. Rooms with shared bathroom cost even less at US$7.

## HOTEL NUEVO REINA
Map pp226-7 *Hotel*
☎ 4381-2496; Av de Mayo 1120; s/d without bathroom US$7/10, with bathroom US$10/14
This once-elegant building still has some charm that's apparent in the grand old halls, high ceilings and original light fixtures. Old rooms are decent and slowly being remodeled, so prices will probably go up soon – after all, the newer, fixed-up rooms are beautiful (US$20/30). Tango classes are given in the airy breakfast room (but not during breakfast).

# SAN TELMO

San Telmo has some of the most atmospheric flavor in Buenos Aires. Buildings are more charming, historical, and less modernized than in the center, and tend to have fewer stories. More and more restaurants and nightspots are popping up here, though it still calms way down when the night curtain drops. Most of your accommodations options here will be in the more modest hostel and guesthouse categories rather than high-class hotels.

## BOQUITAS PINTADAS *Boutique Hotel*
☎ 4381-6064; www.boquitas-pintadas.com.ar in Spanish; Estados Unidos 1399; d US$45-94
With six themed rooms sporting a different decor every two months, this self-proclaimed 'pop' hotel lands in a class by itself. The art is as creative and bizarre as the local artists can imagine it. And luckily it doesn't detract from the small but gorgeous terraces, hot tub or snazzy bar downstairs. The only drawback is its location, which is west of San Telmo, in Constitución. Reserve in advance.

## EL SOL DE SAN TELMO
Map p225 *Guesthouse*
☎ 4300-4394; www.elsoldesantelmo.com; Chacabuco 1181; s/d US$15/30
Here's a fine budget guesthouse in an old and faded but charming house. There are 12 modest rooms with high-ceilings, wood floors and the occasional private bathroom. Guests have use of the kitchen and leafy rooftop patio, along with the salon for tango classes. Staff here can also hook you up with a yoga teacher. Breakfast is extra.

## LUGAR GAY Map p225 *Guesthouse*
☎ 4300-4747; www.lugargay.org; Defensa 1120; s US$25-35, d US$35-50
First: it's for gay men only. Second: there are sunny rooftop terraces for nude sunbathing, so try not to be offended (as if). Only four of the eight hip and elegant rooms have a private bathroom, but most come with stunning

views of the church out back. There's a tango salon and tiny café right on the premises, a hot tub and solarium up top and a kitchenette for all. They also give out information on BA's gay scene, whether you stay here or not.

## MANSION DANDI ROYAL
Map p225 *Boutique Hotel*
☎ 4307-7623; www.hotelmansiondandiroyal.com; Piedras 922; d US$69-140
Upscale tango lovers shouldn't miss this place. An early 1900s family mansion has been lovingly renovated into a luxurious themed hotel complete with tango murals on walls, glass chandeliers, a curved wooden staircase and a myriad of other period details. Rooms are gorgeous; most come with antique furniture, king-size beds, clawfoot tubs and balconies. There's a small rooftop lap pool, sunny patios and a small gym. Tango classes and *milongas* (dances) – the real reason you're staying here – take place in the basement studios or next-door salon.

# CHEAP SLEEPS

## GARDEN HOUSE *Hotel*
☎ 4305-0517; www.gardenhouseba.com.ar; San Juan 1271; dm US$6, d US$18-20
This isn't your typical hostel – it's much more intimate and personal. Anna and Javier, along with their friendly staff, offer six doubles and two dorms (all with shared bathroom) along with some comfortable and welcoming common spaces. It's a bit far from center, but the

good vibes are worth it. Excellent weekly *asados* (barbecues) take place on the terrace, and guests receive one free Spanish class.

### HOTEL CARLY Map p225 *Hotel*
☎ 4361-7710; hotelcarly1@yahoo.com; Humberto Primo 466; s/d US$6/7

Right near Plaza Dorrego is this passable old hotel. It has two small kitchens, a few tiled patios, an ancient atmosphere and simple rooms with high ceilings, dim lights and saggy beds. At these prices you can't ask for much more. Rooms with shared bathroom are available.

### SANDANZAS HOSTEL Map p225 *Hotel*
☎ 4300-7375; www.sandanzas.com.ar; Balcarce 1351; dm US$6-7, d US$17-20

This small 'cultural' hostel has just 26 beds and is enthusiastically run by its five young owners, all artists or social workers. It's a colorful place with good-sized dorms, five doubles (only one with private bathroom) and occasional music concerts in the common area. The location is in a gritty blue-collar neighborhood near Plaza Lezama. Coffee and tea are served all day, and there are free bike rentals.

### VIA VIA HOSTEL Map p225 *Hotel*
☎ 4300-7259; www.viaviacafe.com; Chile 324; dm US$4.50, d US$10

This intimate hostel, in a remodeled 1850s house with modern decor and indoor-ourdoor hallways, offers five private rooms and one six-bed dorm (all share bathrooms). It's not a party place and tends to be tranquil despite the café and all its cultural activities (theater, music, art shows) out front. The location is in a lively area of San Telmo; breakfast is extra.

# RETIRO

Retiro is a great place to be, *if* you can afford it – many of BA's most expensive hotels, along with some of its richest inhabitants, have planted roots here. Close by are leafy Plaza San Martín, the Retiro bus station and many upscale stores and business services. Recoleta and the Microcentro are just a short stroll away.

### ASPEN SUITES
Map pp228-9 *Apartment-Hotel*
☎ 4313-9011; www.aspensuites.com.ar; Esmeralda 933; d US$80-195

It's hardly luxurious, the halls are almost ratty and views out the window vary, but both businesspeople and Brazilian tourists alike come for the modern, spacious rooms (all with kitchenettes). Inside rooms are quieter, and there's even a gym and sauna. Call or email for specials.

### CAESAR PARK HOTEL Map pp228-9 *Hotel*
☎ 800-333-2124; www.caesar-park.com; Posadas 1232; s/d from US$344

Breeze into the marble lobby and be surrounded by classy sophistication and men in suits. This is one of BA's best hotels, and you should expect all the amenities – luxurious rooms, fancy shops in the gleaming lobby and an English-speaking staff that jumps when you even sniffle. But don't pay the exorbitant rack rate – call or check the website for specials.

### DAZZLER HOTEL Map pp228-9 *Hotel*
☎ 4816-5005; www.dazzlerhotel.com; Libertad 902; d US$71

From the lobby you'll take the elevator to your comfortable room, and if you're lucky it'll have a grand view of leafy Plaza Libertad. If not, the restaurant on the 2nd floor has a great peep as well. But not everything is dazzling; the furniture is a bit outdated and even scratched, but at least Fido is welcome – the hotel takes pets.

### FOUR SEASONS BUENOS AIRES
Map pp228-9 *Hotel*
☎ 4321-1200; www.fourseasons.com; Posadas 1086; d US$363

Great service, luxury accommodations and all the amenities that define five-star hotels (such as a white terry-cloth robe hanging in the bathroom) can be found here. Rooms are large and elegant, with overstuffed sofas and desks. There's also a gorgeous spa, a gym, an international restaurant and a business center.

### HOTEL BEL AIR Map pp228-9 *Hotel*
☎ 4816-0016; www.hotelbelair.com.ar in Spanish; Arenales 1462; s/d US$80/85

Your first impression is good: the lobby bar is downright sinuous, and the nearby café has upscale tourists sitting pretty. Fancy art hangs from the lobby walls. Upstairs, rooms are beautifully modern and styled with simple yet functional furniture. Robes in the bathrooms are a nice touch, and working travelers will appreciate the business center and meeting rooms.

### HOTEL CENTRAL CÓRDOBA

Map pp228-9 *Hotel*

☎ 4311-1175; www.hotelcentralcordoba.com.ar; San Martín 1021; s/d US$17/20

The snazzy lobby starts things out right, and the rooms (despite being on the small side) are comfortable, neat and clean. This hotel's Retiro location is spot on – the Kilkenny bar is within easy staggering distance – so book well ahead.

### HOTEL PRESIDENTE Map pp228-9 *Hotel*

☎ 4816-2222; www.hotelpresidente.com.ar in Spanish; Cerrito 850; d US$70-80

The best rooms here are on the upper floors and have grand views of Av 9 de Julio. Otherwise they may not be worth the price of admission, though all are comfortable enough and the location is good. Services include a sauna, a gym, a conference center and an elegant café out front. Larger family rooms are also available.

### HOTEL PRINCIPADO Map pp228-9 *Hotel*

☎ 4313-3022; www.principado.com.ar; Paraguay 481; s/d US$45/50

There's nothing too surprising at this place, other than it having good rooms at great prices in a central location. Most of the typical hotel and room services are available, including a minibar, a hairdryer and – for those here to work – a business center.

### HOWARD JOHNSON PLAZA

Map pp228-9 *Hotel*

☎ 4891-9200; www.hjflorida.com.ar in Spanish; Florida 944; s/d from US$139

Smack at the start of pedestrian Florida is this modern hotel, part of the popular HoJo chain. An elevator takes you from the shopping arcade to the attractive atrium lobby and restaurant. The 77 rooms are large, beautiful and quiet; services include a conference room and access to a gym.

### NH FLORIDA Map pp228-9 *Hotel*

☎ 4321-9850; www.nh-hotels.com; San Martín 839; d US$105-125

The Florida is one of the four NH hotels in BA, sporting a hip, snazzy lobby and whip-smart rooms. Decor is contemporary and ultratasteful, utilizing a pleasing palate of natural colors and minimalist sensibilities. Rooms on the 9th floor and up have balconies and reach the upper end of the price scale.

*Detail, Malabia House (p165)*

### SOFITEL BUENOS AIRES

Map pp228-9 *Hotel*

☎ 4131-0000; www.sofitel.com; Arroyo 841; s/d from US$242-532

Sure, it's overpriced (call ahead or check the website for special prices), but you're in one of the best hotels BA has to offer; expect plush king-size beds, fancy toiletries, thick robes and a well-stocked minibar in your luxurious suite. Outside of it are a stunning lobby, a small indoor pool and one of the most well-regarded restaurants in town, Le Sud (p96). Dish out and enjoy it.

### SUIPACHA Y ARROYO SUITES

Map pp228-9 *Hotel Suites*

☎ 4325-8200; www.syasuites.com; Suipacha 1359; ste US$59-67

This hotel is being remodeled but until it's finished it's an interesting combination of modern hipness and a rough-around-the-edges look. All 78 suites are pleasant, comfortable and spacious, and come with a kitchenette. Perks include a sauna, a business center, an outdoor pool and a paddle-tennis court; security is good, as is the location.

## CHEAP SLEEPS

### RECOLETA HOSTEL Map pp228-9 *Hotel*

☎ 4812-4419; www.trhostel.com.ar; Libertad 1216; dm US$8, s/d from US$17

The best thing about this HI-affiliated hostel is its location in an old mansion in trendy Retiro. Ceilings are high and common spaces adequate, but the sex-segregated dorms come pretty tight. Out of the four doubles only one has private bathroom. There's a pleasant courtyard and large dining area.

# RECOLETA & BARRIO NORTE

Most of the accommodations in Recoleta (Barrio Norte is more of a sub-neighborhood) is expensive, and what cheap hotels there are tend to be full much of the time. Buildings here are grand and beautiful, befitting the city's richest barrio, but if you stay in this area you'll only see how a very small percentage of BA's inhabitants live. Still, Recoleta's fabulous cemetery is nearby, along with some lovely parks, museums and boutiques.

### ALVEAR PALACE HOTEL
Map pp230-1                   *Hotel*
☎ 4808-2100; www.alvearpalace.com; Av Alvear 1891; d US$358

Ask any local to name the classiest place in Buenos Aires, and they'll probably say the Alvear. Old-world sophistication and superior service will help erase the trials of that long 1st-class flight into town, while the bathtub Jacuzzi, Hermès toiletries and Egyptian cotton bedsheets aid your trip into dreamland. Three fine restaurants, an elegant tea room and a heated indoor pool await your presence the next day.

### ART HOTEL Map pp230-1         *Hotel*
☎ 4821-4744; www.arthotel.com.ar; Azcuénaga 1268; d US$65-90

This is a stunningly gorgeous addition to the Recoleta hotel scene. The 36 rooms have been artfully designed as tranquil spaces with materials such as wood, glass, metal and textiles. Touches such as curved doors, canopied beds and dark wood floors add to the charm. A gallery in part of the lobby displays local art, while the nearby breakfast area provides classy nourishment.

### ART SUITES Map pp230-1    *Apartment Suites*
☎ 4821-6800; www.artsuites.com.ar; Azcuénaga 1465; d US$109-165

Fifteen luxurious, very modern and spacious apartment suites are offered here. All have minimalist decor, full kitchens, sunny balconies and slick hip furniture. Windows are double-paned for quiet, security is excellent, staff speak good English and there's a daily maid service. Long-term discounts are available; advance reservations required.

### AYACUCHO PALACE HOTEL
Map pp230-1                   *Hotel*
☎ 4806-1815; www.ayacuchohotel.com.ar; Ayacucho 1408; s/d US$30/40

The 64 clean and fairly modern wood-floored rooms here are comfortable yet nondescript. The lobby is decent enough and there's an acceptable range of services. It's a fair deal for the Recoleta area, and you'll only be a few blocks away from the barrio's famous cemetery and weekend crafts fair.

### HOTEL EL CASTILLO
Map pp230-1                   *Hotel*
☎ 4815-4561; www.hotel-elcastillo.com.ar in Spanish; MT de Alvear 1893; s/d US$20/24

This hotel is a mix of old and new styles, which include a grand stairway and nice, comfortable and spacious wood-floored rooms overlooking the street. Despite not serving breakfast (unlike almost every other hotel in BA) it's very popular, so reserve in advance.

### HOTEL LION D'OR Map pp230-1     *Hotel*
☎ 4803-8992; www.hotel-liondor.com.ar; Pacheco de Melo 2019; s/d without bathroom US$8/9, with bathroom US$15-22

Some rooms at these charming old digs are small, basic, and dark; some are absolutely grand and may include a modest fireplace. All are clean and good value, and while a few are a bit rough around the edges most have been modernized. There's a great old marble staircase, and the elevator is just fabulous.

### JUNCAL PALACE HOTEL
Map pp230-1                   *Hotel*
☎ 4821-2770; www.juncalpalacehotel.com.ar; Juncal 2282; s/d US$14/19

This small hotel comes with some classic old details, and adding to the charm is a cozy and intimate atmosphere. The comfortable rooms come with flowery bedspreads – those out front have small balconies. This is a great deal for Recoleta, so it's often fully booked – be sure to reserve in advance.

### LOI SUITES Map pp230-1     *Hotel Suites*
☎ 5777-8950; www.loisuites.com.ar; Vicente López 1955; d US$130-240

A minimalist lobby with leather chairs, white sofas and dark wood coffee tables welcomes you to this contemporary and stylish hotel. Gorgeous rooms are awash in basic colors and simple designs while exuding high-class comfort. Two restaurants, a business center and a lovely large atrium with pool add to the luxurious atmosphere – you shouldn't have much to complain about.

## MAYFLOWER SUITES

Map pp230-1                                    *Hotel Suites*
☎ 4878-7500; www.mayflowersuites.com.ar; Posadas 1557; d US$97

All the suites are large and come with a desk, conservative decor, microwave, fridge and – for those who need a java jolt first thing in the morning – a coffeemaker. Services include a

sauna, a solarium, a gym, a business center and meeting rooms. Reserve ahead to check for better rates.

## PRINCE HOTEL Map pp230-1          *Hotel*
☎ 4811-8004; www.princehotel.com.ar in Spanish; Arenales 1627; s/d US$25/30

The clean and neat little rooms are good value here; some come with balconies. Blemishes include carpet stains and limited services, but at this price you can't complain too much. Be sure to check out the ancient metal elevator.

# PALERMO

Despite being a bit northwest of the center, Palermo has much to offer the traveler. Not only is it full of extensive parklands – which are great for weekend jaunts and sporting activities – but you can't get more choice in cutting-edge restaurants, designer boutiques and hip dance clubs. Many of these places are located in the extensive subneighborhood of Palermo Viejo, which is further subdivided into Palermo Soho and Palermo Hollywood. If you like trendy entertainment, Palermo is your 'hood.

## CASERÓN PORTEÑO

Map pp232-3                                    *Guesthouse*
☎ 4554-6336; www.caseronporteno.com in Spanish; Ciudad de la Paz 344; s/d US$25/40

Tango lovers flock to this special guesthouse, which offers tango classes and help in reserving tango shows. There's a small dance studio behind the pleasant garden, where classes take place, while the 10 rooms come tastefully simple (the best are upstairs and in the back). Some rooms share bathrooms; kitchen use is available. Cons include a noisy school next door and the location, which is a bit far from the center.

## LA OTRA ORILLA Map pp232-3   *Guesthouse*
☎ 4867-4070; www.otraorilla.com.ar; J Álvarez 1779; s US$20-65, d US$25-70

Just five beautiful rooms – four upstairs – greet you at this small but pleasant guesthouse. Each is different in size, shape and color. The large suite has a great view to the leafy back garden, while two of the rooms share bathrooms. The only flaw is a large dog that barks at strangers. Check the website for seasonal discounts.

## LULU GUESTHOUSE

Map pp232-3                                    *Guesthouse*
☎ 4772-0289; www.luluguesthouse.com; Emilio Zolá 5185; dm US$15, d without bathroom US$20-25, with bathroom US$30

Welcome to eight wonderfully artistic and colorful rooms, spread out in this Palermo Viejo house near BA's transvestite red-light

district (which makes walking around at night an adventure). Decor is comfortably rustic, with each simple room sporting a different size and theme. Cute little patios pop up here and there. The cozy attic dorm (the only room with air-con) sleeps four.

## MALABIA HOUSE

Map pp232-3                                  *Boutique Hotel*
☎ 4832-3345; www.malabiahouse.com.ar; Malabia 1555; s US$65-80, d US$90-115

Fifteen luxurious bedrooms, all stocked with modern furnishings, terry-cloth robes and slippers, line this beautifully renovated old house. Common spaces are gracious, charming and include tiny courtyard gardens. Candles, soft music and a comfortable homey feel add peace and romance, while the service is excellent. There's a 15% discount if paying with cash.

# CHEAP SLEEPS

### CASA JARDÍN Map pp232-3 *Hotel*
☎ 4774-8783; www.casajardinba.com.ar; Charcas 4416; dm US$8.50, s/d US$14/24

This isn't your typical hostel; it's a tranquil little place that only sleeps 13 guests and doubles as a casual art gallery. The ceilings are high, there's a great leafy rooftop patio for hanging out, and charm abounds. Creative types would love it here as Nerina – the owner – occasionally hosts open-door art or music events. Keep an eye out for the resident pet tortoise.

### COMO EN CASA Map pp232-3 *Guesthouse*
☎ 4831-0517; www.bandb.com.ar; Gurruchaga 2155; s US$7-19, d US$10-20

Homey atmosphere abounds at this pleasant guesthouse in Palermo Viejo. Mazelike hallways lead to simple rooms of all sizes; the cheapest are small and have shared bathrooms. A two-bedroom apartment (no kitchen) is available for families or groups. Plenty of common spaces and a nice garden add to this intimate stay.

### EL FIRULETE HOSTEL
Map pp232-3 *Hotel*
☎ 4770-9259; www.el-firulete.com.ar; Güemes 4499; dm US$8, s/d US$22/24

El Firulete is a small and clean hostel, well situated near Plaza Italia. There's a cool rooftop area – complete with pleasant airy kitchen – where weekly *asados* take place, sometimes accompanied by one of the guitar-playing owners. The vibe is mellow, and activities are organized for guests.

### GIRAMONDO
Map pp232-3 *Hotel*
☎ 4772-6740; www.hostelgiramondo.com.ar; Güemes 4802; dm US$8-10, s/d US$20-35

This spacious new hostel opened in late 2004 in a remodeled old house. It's a nice place with high ceilings, some charming details and a superhip bar (with great music) in the basement. Rooms surround an open staircase on three floors, and there's a rooftop patio and bar for *asados*.

# Excursions

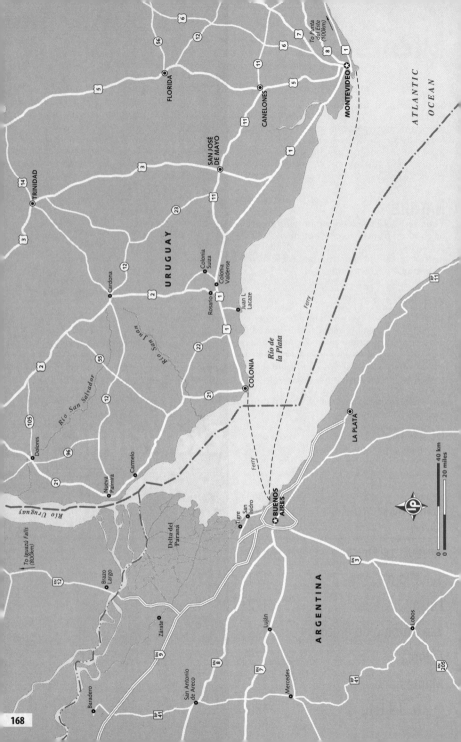

# Excursions

So you've spent days tramping on noisy and busy streets, enjoying all the sights and smells of Buenos Aires. You're ready to get away from the capital and experience something different and more peaceful. Where do you go?

Luckily for you, there are many trips that take you a world away from BA's concrete jungle. Most can be done in a day, but a few are best if you have more time to spare. Laid-back boat trips, peaceful village walks, colonial architecture or sunny beaches are just a boat, train or short plane ride away. For organized tours to some of these places, see Travel Agencies (p195).

## NATURE

Your best bet for a big dose of natural greenery is the **Delta del Paraná** (p170). Only an hour or so away from the center of Buenos Aires, the small city of **Tigre** (p170) provides easy access to the tranquil waterways of the spreading delta. There are no cars or buses here; instead you'll find boat trips that access summer getaway homes, peaceful nature walks and exceptional bird-watching.

## TOWNS & CITIES

**San Isidro** (p171) is just north of BA's center and an upscale suburb offering historical buildings and calm neighborhoods. The devotional center of **Luján** (p172) to the west provides an interesting look into the Catholic heart of Argentina, while Buenos Aires province's gaucho hub is the serene village of **San Antonio de Areco** (p174). **Montevideo** (p177) is Uruguay's capital and lies across the Río de la Plata, but it's easily accessible from downtown BA by ferry; it has a smaller-city feel, a distinct vibe and plenty of crumbling old European architecture worth checking out. Also in Uruguay and equally accessible is **Colonia** (p175), a pleasant little gem with cobbled streets and colonial buildings.

## BEACHES

**Punta del Este** (p180) is the main beach destination for summering Argentines, including the hippest celebrities and hottest fashion models. It fills to the brim January through March, when most porteños flee overheated Buenos Aires.

---

### Visiting Iguazú Falls

Many visitors to Buenos Aires tour the city and then take a side trip to one of the most spectacular sites in South America: Brazil's Iguazú Falls. If you have an extra couple of days it's definitely worth the time and money. Just remember that it's much warmer and more tropical there than in BA, and that in January and February the heat and humidity can be overbearing.

Here are some sample prices for transportation and package deals available:

- One-way bus ticket from BA to Puerto Iguazú: US$35 to US$50, 18 hours
- Round-trip airplane ticket from BA to Puerto Iguazú: US$200, 1½ hours
- Package deal – return airfare, airport transfers and two-nights' stay at a four-star hotel (double occupancy): US$285 per person

During July, on holiday weekends and during *Semana Santa* (Easter week) you should plan way ahead or be prepared to pay premium prices.

Iguazú Falls straddles the Argentine–Brazilian border, and some of the most stunning views are from the Brazilian side, so you shouldn't miss them. As for Brazilian visas, if you are from the US, Canada, Australia or New Zealand, you officially need a visa to enter Brazil. Western Europeans do not. Brazilian visas aren't cheap, and getting one may take some time, especially if you do it in Buenos Aires, so plan ahead.

# TIGRE & THE DELTA

When porteños look for a quick weekend getaway from the cement of Buenos Aires, they make a beeline to the tranquil riverside suburb of Tigre. The city itself is a pleasant enough place, but it's really the Delta del Paraná and its myriad river channels that they're after. Latté-colored waters – rich with iron from the jungle streams flowing from inland Argentina – along with reedy shores are far from any stereotypical paradise, but there are many hidden gems in this marshy region. Boat rides into the delta offer peeks at local stilt houses (raised high to escape storm waters and tides) and colonial mansions, or you can just get off and explore along some peaceful trails. All along the shores are signs of water-related activity, from sailing to kayaking and canoeing to sculling.

Tigre itself is easily walkable and holds some worthy attractions. Be sure to check out the **Puerto de Frutos**, where mostly housewares, wicker baskets, dried flowers and plants are sold along with a modest selection of fruits. Weekends are best, when a large crafts fair adds to the din. To reach the market from the Tren de la Costa's Delta station, walk past the casino back down the tracks and turn left at the stoplight.

The **Museo Naval de la Nación** traces the history of the Argentine navy with an eclectic mix of historical photos, life-sized and model boats and airplanes, artillery displays and pickled sea critters. The **Museo de la Reconquista** was the house where Viceroy Liniers coordinated resistance to the British invasions of the early 19th century; it's small and not terribly interesting. The **Museo Histórico Prefectura Naval Argentina** has small exhibits on the Argentine coast guard's diving and nautical equipment, WWII radios and model boats, among others things.

Right at the Tren de la Costa's Delta station is Tigre's tacky counterpart to Disney World: **Parque de la Costa**. There are roller coasters, games and everything else that makes a theme park enjoyable. Opening hours vary widely throughout the year, so it's a good idea to call beforehand.

The waterways of the delta region offer a glimpse into how locals live along the peaceful canals, with boats as their only transportation. One popular destination is the **Tres Bocas neighborhood**, where you can take residential walks on narrow paths connected by bridges over narrow channels. There are a couple of restaurants overlooking the waters, both great for a lunch stop (see opposite). The nearby houses have descriptive names rather than numbers, and the area even supports a floating medical facility to serve the community's needs. The boat ride to Tres Bocas from Tigre takes just over half an hour; frequent commuter launches leave from Tigre's Estación Fluvial (located next to the tourist office) to various destinations in the delta for US$2.25 to US$3.50 round-trip. These will drop you off or pick you up at any riverside dock – just flag them down as you would a bus. A few companies offer guided tours of the delta region; these all cost US$2 to US$5 and take one to two hours. It's just as easy to take the commuter launches, though, and you'll have much more flexibility.

## Transportation

**Distance from Buenos Aires** 28km
**Direction** Northwest
**Travel time by public transportation** One to 1½ hours
**Bus** No 60 (the one marked Panamericana is faster; US$0.50, 1½ hours)
**Car** Take the Panamericana northwards to ramal (branch) Tigre
**Train** Tigre has two train stations, about 1km apart. From Estación Retiro either take the regular train's Mitre line (US$0.35) all the way to Tigre, or take this same Mitre train line to Estación Mitre, where you transfer to the Tren de la Costa; this very pleasant train ends near Tigre's Puerto de Frutos (US$0.50/1 weekdays/weekends). Bus Nos 59, 152 or 60 – the 60 should be marked Alto, Bajo or Escobar – also go to Estación Maipú. From Estación Maipú you can then board a train to Tigre.

## Sights & Information

**Bonanza Deltaventura** ( ☎ 4798-2254; www.delta ventura.com) Offers marshy adventures that include transportation from your hotel, breakfast, a two-hour hike, a canoe trip and an *asado* (barbecue) for US$45.

**Ente Municipal de Turismo** ( ☎ 4512-4497; www.tigre .gov.ar; ☼ 9am-5pm) Tigre's top-notch tourist office, located behind McDonald's, will help you sort out the confusing delta region. There's a smaller **tourist booth** ( ☎ 4512-4497; ☼ 9am-5pm Fri-Sun) at the train station itself.

Excursions – Tigre & the Delta

**Museo de la Reconquista** ( ☎ 4512-4496; Padre Castañeda 470; admission free; ✆ 10am-6pm Wed-Sun)

**Museo Histórico Prefectura Naval Argentina** ( ☎ 4749-6161; Liniers 1264; admission free; ✆ 10am-noon & 2-6pm Wed-Sun)

**Museo Naval de la Nación** ( ☎ 4749-0608; Paseo Victoria 602; admission US$0.75; ✆ 8:30am-5:30pm Mon-Fri, 10:30am-6:30pm Sat & Sun)

**Parque de la Costa** ( ☎ 4002-6000; www.parquedelacosta .com.ar in Spanish; adult/child US$7/5; ✆ 11am-midnight daily Dec-Feb, 11am-7pm Sat, Sun & holidays Mar-Nov)

**Puerto de Frutos** (Sarmiento 160; ✆ 11am-7pm)

# Eating

Tigre's cuisine is not that stupendous; you'll find mainly traditional Argentine restaurants in town, with the most atmospheric lining Paseo Victoria, a pleasant riverside avenue right next to the Río Luján. Take a nice pre-supper walk, choose an appealing restaurant and sit and watch the boats hum by. Out on the delta, there are a couple of choices in the residential Tres Bocas area (a 35-minute boat ride).

**El Remanso** ( ☎ 4728-0575; mains US$4-6; ✆ lunch & dinner) Just a few minutes' walk from La Riviera, this pleasant eatery offers a similar menu but a less extensive patio area.

**La Riviera** ( ☎ 4728-0177; set meals US$7-8.50; ✆ lunch & dinner) With relaxing sunny patios and river views, it's no wonder this restaurant is so popular. The food is basic but good and includes pasta, meats and fish.

# Sleeping

Reservations are highly recommended on weekends; breakfast is included at most places. The following are in Tigre city.

**Casona La Ruchi** ( ☎ 4749-2499; www.casonalaruchi .com.ar in Spanish; Lavalle 557; s/d US$20/28) This homey, family-run B&B is in an old 1893 mansion. Most of the five romantic bedrooms have balconies; all have shared

bathrooms with original tiled floors. There's a pool and large garden out back.

**Villa Julia** ( ☎ 4749-0242; www.newage-hotels.com; Paseo Victoria 800; s/d US$47/94) The seven rooms are all different at this gorgeous mansion, where original tilework, large balconies and thick robes make for a very special stay. The atmosphere is lovely, and there's a swimming pool and restaurant.

Things are much more peaceful in the delta, just beyond Tigre. Prices listed following are for weekends; weekday stays can be half-off. All of these places provide meals, which may or may not be included in the price – ask ahead for the different packages available. There are many more choices available (including houses to rent); the tourist office has photos, current prices and excellent information.

**Alpenhaus** ( ☎ 4731-4526; www.alpenhaus.com.ar; d from US$97) A 60-minute boat ride from Tigre. This German-themed *hostería* (inn) offers three large and modern alpine-style cabanas (US$140) along with more modest but still pleasant rooms. There's a great pool and grassy lounging areas; the food is inspired by Eastern Europe.

**Atelier** ( ☎ 4731-3532; www.cabaniasatelier.com.ar in Spanish; d from US$60) An 80-minute boat ride from Tigre. The cute stilted cabanas have plenty of amenities, while the grassy grounds (which include a swimming pool) are quite pleasant enough. It's a good place for families, with games available for the kids.

**Hotel l'Marangatú** ( ☎ 4728-0752; www.i-marangatu .com.ar in Spanish; s/d US$25/50) A 50-minute boat ride from Tigre. This good spot is best for sun-worshippers and athletes. On offer are a swimming pool, a volleyball court, a soccer field, water-skiing and kayaking.

**Los Pecanes** ( ☎ 4728-1932; www.hosterialospecanes .com; d from US$40) A 90-minute boat ride from Tigre. You'll feel at home in this friendly, family-run B&B with just three simple but comfortable guestrooms. The homemade meals are healthy, the garden is lovely and there are activities to keep you entertained. English, Spanish and French are spoken.

# SAN ISIDRO

To the north of Buenos Aires is peaceful and residential San Isidro, a charming suburb of cobblestone streets lined with graceful buildings. The historic center is at Plaza Mitre and its beautiful neo-Gothic cathedral.

A stroll through the rambling neighborhood streets behind the cathedral will turn up some luxurious mansions (as well as more-modest houses) and the occasional view over toward the coast. Close by is also the Tren de la Costa's San Isidro station, with a fashionable outdoor shopping mall to explore.

**Quinta Pueyrredón** ( ☎ 4512-3131; Rivera Indarte 48; admission free; 🕑 8am-6pm Tue & Thu, 2-6pm Sat & Sun) is an old colonial mansion set on spacious grounds that open onto wonderful views of the Río de la Plata. The building also houses a historical museum containing period items, including some relating to Argentine icon, General Juan Martín de Pueyrredón, who owned the mansion in the early 1800s. To get there from the cathedral, follow Av Libertador five blocks, turn left on Peña and after two blocks turn right onto Rivera Indarte. Hours vary throughout the year, so call ahead.

Athletes can rent bikes and inline skates from the **Barrancas train station** ( 🕑 US$3 per hr; 🕑 daily in summer, Sat & Sun rest of year) and coast the smooth pedestrian path back toward the previous train stations, crossing over to the coastal side to check out the waterfront. Return to Barrancas station and head north to San Isidro (just one stop beyond Barrancas). There's a small **antiques fair** ( 🕑 9:30am-8pm Sat, Sun & holidays) at this station.

## Transportation

**Distance from Buenos Aires** 15km

**Direction** Northwest

**Travel time** 45 minutes to one hour

**Bus** No 168 drops you on Av del Libertador a couple of blocks from Quinta Pueyrredón

**Car** Take the Panamericana Norte, or go up Av del Libertador all the way from Recoleta

**Train** Take the Mitre train line to Estación Bartolomé Mitre and transfer to the Tren de la Costa, which takes you to Estación Barrancas (US$0.50/1 weekdays/weekends, 15 minutes). Bus Nos 59, 152 or 60 – the 60 should be marked Alto, Bajo or Escobar – also go to the Tren de la Costa, and take 35 minutes.

# LUJÁN

According to legend, in 1630 an ox-drawn wagon containing a small terra-cotta statue of the Virgin Mary suddenly got stuck on the road and would not budge until the image was removed. The wagon was heading to Santiago del Estero, but the devoted owner took this pause as a sign and built a chapel on the site. 'La Virgencita' soon became Argentina's patron saint, and she's since upgraded from the chapel into Luján's striking French Gothic basilica, the **Basílica Nuestra Señora de Luján**.

Luján is essentially a peaceful, religious tourist town, and has a large number of stores and rolling carts selling devotional souvenirs. There's a leafy, elevated riverside area full

*Street stall, Montevideo (p177)*

of restaurants and more shops, and leisurely paddleboat rides are available. One place you shouldn't miss is the gorgeous **Complejo Museográfico Enrique Udaondo.**

This colonial complex (and ex-prison) has exhibitions showcasing the exploits of General José de San Martín and Juan Manuel de Rosas, as well as beautiful *mate* ware, ponchos, silver horse gear, guitars and other gaucho paraphernalia. The pretty patios and gardens are in themselves worth a look.

The nearby **Museo de Transporte** displays a steam locomotive, a hydroplane that was used to cross the Atlantic in 1926 and some fantastic Cinderella-style carriages. The most offbeat exhibits, however, are the stuffed and scruffy remains of Gato and Mancha, the hardy Argentine criollo horses ridden by adventurer AF Tschiffely from Buenos Aires to Washington, DC.

About 7km outside town is the **Fundación Ecológica zoo Luján,** an interesting sort of petting zoo that offers close encounters with Bengal tigers and African lions. There are pony, elephant and train rides for the kids, and an antique tractor collection for pops.

In early October a massive pilgrimage originates in Buenos Aires' barrio of Liniers. Thousands of pilgrims walk the 65km stretch, which takes up to 18 hours; it can be a deeply moving sight.

# Sights & Information

Luján's area code is ☎ 02323.

**Basílica Nuestra Señora de Luján** ( ☎ 420-058; cnr San Martín & 9 de Julio; tours US$0.35; ⏱ tours every 30min 10am-5pm Mon-Fri & 10am-6pm Sat & Sun)

**Complejo Museográfico Enrique Udaondo** ( ☎ 420-245; cnr Lavalle & Padre Salvaire; US$0.65; ⏱ noon-6pm Wed-Fri, 10am-6pm Sat, Sun & holidays) Buy entry tickets for both museums at the corner of Lavalle and Salvaire, on the plaza.

**Fundación Ecológica zoo Luján** ( ☎ 435-738; Acceso Oeste km 58; adult/child under 12 US$4/2; ⏱ 8:30am-sunset) Taxis here cost US$3, or take bus No 57 from Luján.

**Museo de Transporte** ( ☎ 420-245; cnr Lavalle & Padre Salvaire; US$0.35; ⏱ noon-6pm Wed-Fri, 10am-6pm Sat, Sun & holidays)

**Oficina de Turismo** ( ☎ 420-453; San Martín 1, edificio La Cúpula; ⏱ 8am-6pm Mon-Fri, 9am-7pm Sat & Sun) Near the river, down from La Recova restaurant.

**Tourist kiosk** (cnr Lavalle & 9 de Julio; ⏱ 10am-6pm Mon-Fri, 9am-8pm Sat-Sun)

# Eating

The riverfront has many restaurants ready to serve:

**Berlín** ( ☎ 426-767; San Martín 151; mains US$3-5; ⏱ 8am-2am) German specialties here include smoked meats, sausage with sauerkraut and apple strudel. Sunny sidewalk seating is a plus, but the attached ice-cream shop isn't up to scratch.

**La Recova** ( ☎ 422-280; San Martín 1; mains US$2-5; ⏱ 9am-5pm) This lunchtime *parrilla* (restaurant specializing in mixed grills) has some pleasant outdoor seating. On weekends, staff fire up the picture-window grill for a full *asado* (barbecue) experience.

**L'Eau Vive** ( ☎ 421-774; Constitución 2112; mains US$5.50-6.50; ⏱ noon-2:30pm & 8:30-10pm Tue-Sun) Two kilometers from the center you'll find this friendly, nonsmoking French restaurant run by Carmelite nuns from around the world. To get here, taxis cost US$1 or take bus No 501 from the center.

# Sleeping

Rates rise on weekends and holidays, when reservations are in order. All hotels include breakfast.

**Hotel de la Paz** ( ☎ 424-034; hoteldelapaz@hotmail.com; 9 de Julio 1054; s/d US$12/17; Ⓟ ) Well-located and friendly, Hotel de la Paz hints at old-time charm. The homey rooms are small and modest, while bathrooms have open showers.

**Hotel del Virrey** ( ☎ 420-797; San Martín 129; s/d US$13/17; Ⓟ ) The Virrey is a modern hotel right near the basilica, offering 18 decent rooms and a pool.

**Hotel Hoxón** ( ☎ 429-970; www.hotelhoxon.com.ar in Spanish; 9 de Julio 760; s/d US$13/20; Ⓟ ) Rooms at this semi-classy hotel are modern, clean and comfortable. The swimming pool and gym are pluses.

## Transportation

**Distance from Buenos Aires** 65km

**Direction** East

**Travel time** 1½ to two hours

**Bus** Transportes Atlántida (No 57) leaves every 30 minutes from Plaza Italia in Palermo (US$1.50)

**Car** Drive west on RN 7

**Train** Daily departures from Estación Once in Buenos Aires, but change trains in Moreno (US$1)

# SAN ANTONIO DE ARECO

Nestled in the verdant pampas of northern Buenos Aires province, Areco is a peaceful and serene town that dates from the early-18th-century construction of a chapel in honor of San Antonio de Padua. The locals are friendly, and many men around town wear the traditional gaucho beret. It's the kind of place where a hearty *'buenos días'* or *'buenas tardes'* is in order every time you pass someone, and there are more bicycles than cars (with no one locking either). The town is also well known for its silverwork, and many craftspeople have set up shop here.

Areco's compact center and traffic-free streets are very walkable. At the beginning of the 18th century, **Plaza Ruiz de Arellano** was the site of the corrals belonging to the town's founding *estanciero* (ranch owner). In its center, the **Monumento a Vieytes** honors locally born Juan Hipólito Vieytes, a figure in the early independence movement. Around the plaza are several historic buildings, including the **Iglesia Parroquial** (parish church) and the **Casa de los Martínez** (site of the main house of the original Ruiz de Arellano *estancia,* or ranch).

The **Puente Viejo** (old bridge; 1857) across the Río Areco follows the original cart road to northern Argentina. Once a toll crossing, it's now a pedestrian bridge leading to San Antonio's main attraction, the **Museo Gauchesco Ricardo Güiraldes**. This parklike gaucholand features restored or fabricated buildings that include an old flour mill, a re-created tavern and a colonial-style chapel. The main deal is a 20th-century reproduction of an 18th-century *casco* (ranch house), which holds a wooden bed that once belonged to Juan Manuel de Rosas (perhaps the ultimate rural landowner), lots of gorgeous horse gear and various works of gauchesco art. Two rooms are dedicated to Güiraldes himself.

The small **Museo y Taller Draghi** highlights an exceptional collection of silver *facones* (gaucho knives), beautiful horse gear and intricate *mate* paraphernalia. It's mainly the workshop of Juan José Draghi and family, however, and guided tours are given.

Another site worth visiting is the **Centro Cultural Usina Vieja**, an eclectic museum in an old power plant dating from 1901. Check out the funky collection of ancient radios, typewriters, sewing machines and record players. Farm equipment, sculptures, an old-time grocery store and even a small airplane are also on display, as are rotating exhibits of local artists' work.

Areco is the symbolic center of Argentina's vestigial cowboy culture, and on Día de la Tradición (in mid-November) the town puts on the country's biggest gaucho celebration. If you're in the area, don't miss it; attractions include displays of horsemanship, folk dancing, craft exhibitions and guided tours of historic sites.

## Sights & Information

Areco's area code is ☎ 02326.

**Centro Cultural Usina Vieja** (Alsina 660; admission free; ☯ 11am-5pm Tue-Sun) Just half a block from the main plaza.

**Museo Gauchesco Ricardo Güiraldes** ( ☎ 454-780; cnr Güiraldes & Sosa; admission US$0.75; ☯ 11am-5pm Wed-Mon)

**Museo y Taller Draghi** ( ☎ 454-219; Lavalle 387; tourists/locals US$1.75/1; ☯ 10:30am-1pm & 3:30-7:30pm)

**Tourist office** ( ☎ 453-165; Zerboni & Arellano; ☯ 8:30am-10pm Mon-Fri, 8am-8pm Sat & Sun) In a white, stand-alone building in the park.

## Eating

San Antonio de Areco has fewer places to eat than you might expect, but there are some good ones.

**El Almacén** ( ☎ 02325-15-683-233; Bolívar 66; mains US$3-7; ☯ lunch & dinner) Decorated as an early-20th-century general store, this cozy and quaint place cooks mostly basic Argentine dishes. Check out the old gas pump outside.

**La Costa** ( ☎ 452-481; cnr Belgrano & Zerboni; mains US$1.50-4; ☯ lunch & dinner) There's little for vegetarians at this modest *parrilla*, though they can always go for an omelette or salad.

### Transportation

**Distance from Buenos Aires** 113km

**Direction** West

**Travel time** Two hours

**Bus** Frequent buses from Retiro bus station (US$4) drop you five blocks from the center of town

**Car** Take RN8 west to ramal Pilar

## Historic Estancias

Surrounding San Antonio de Areco are a number of *estancias* (ranches) offering overnight accommodations with all meals included. These *estancias* were originally built by rich European immigrants for farming and cattle, but due to financial considerations many have been turned into dude-type ranches with activities that include horseback rides, swimming, *asados* (barbecues), gaucho shows and folk dances. Prices below include all meals, drinks and many of these activities.

One of the oldest is **Estancia La Bamba** ( ☎ 02326-456-392; www.la-bamba.com.ar; s/d from US$70/120), about 15km east of Areco; it dates from 1830, has spa services and once hosted Carlos Gardel (p26). At **Estancia La Cinacina** ( ☎ 02326-452-045; www.lacinacina.com.ar in Spanish; Mitre 9), closest to town, US$13 buys an all-you-can-eat *asado*, entertainment in the form of folk music and dance, and a tour of the *estancia*'s museum. Ring ahead for reservations and schedules.

Unquestionably the most historic of the nearby *estancias* is the Güiraldes family's **Estancia La Porteña** ( ☎ 02326-453-770, in Buenos Aires ☎ 4822-1325; www.estancialaportenia.com.ar; d US$135), which dates from 1850 and has a garden designed by the renowned French architect Charles Thays, who was responsible for BA's major public parks.

**Estancia El Ombú** ( ☎ 02326-92080, in Buenos Aires ☎ 4710-2795; s/d US$111/160) belonged to General Pablo Ricchieri, who first inflicted universal military conscription on the country. Stays here include unlimited drinks and rental bikes.

San Antonio's tourist office can give you more information on accommodations and tours, and in Buenos Aires the **Secretaría de Turismo de la Nación** (Map pp228–9; ☎ 4312-2232; Av Santa Fe 883) can print out a more complete list of estancias around BA.

**Ramos Generales** ( ☎ 456-376; Zapiola 143; mains US$2.50-6; ☻ lunch & dinner) This upscale restaurant offers traditional *parrilladas* and pasta, though a few oddities such as rabbit and *jabalí* (wild boar) are thrown in.

## Sleeping

Prices noted are for weekends, when reservations are advisable and singles unavailable. The following rates include breakfast.

**Hospedaje Balcón Colonial** ( ☎ 456-376; www.balcon colonial.com.ar; Lavalle 536; s/d US$10/17) Three small but clean rooms are on offer at this homey place.

**Hostal de Areco** ( ☎ 456-118; Zapiola 25; d US$17) This place is clustered with two other hotels, which aren't as personable but do have pools. Rooms here are small, but clean and comfortable.

**Hostal Draghi** ( ☎ 454-219; draghi@lq.com.ar; reception at Lavalle 387; d US$22) Just five large, gorgeous rooms (some with kitchenette) are available at this tranquil place. A grassy garden with fountain soothes the spirit, and free bikes are available for guests to use.

**Residencial El Hornero** ( ☎ 452-733; Moreno 250; s/d US$7/12) Here's a little heaven for garden-lovers, with lush greenery surrounded by pleasant patio halls and sitting areas; rooms are casual and modest.

# COLONIA

Charming and quaint are words often used to describe this ideal little getaway from Buenos Aires. On summer weekends, hundreds of Argentines descend upon Colonia (officially Colonia del Sacramento) to escape the searing city heat, walk the tranquil cobblestoned streets and enjoy the spectacular sunsets. And despite the fact that Colonia is located in neighboring Uruguay, frequent ferries make it easy to access from Argentina – even if you only have a day.

Founded in 1680 by the Portuguese Manoel Lobo, Colonia occupied a strategic position almost exactly opposite Buenos Aires, across the Río de la Plata. Its major importance was as a source of smuggled trade items, undercutting Spain's jealously defended mercantile monopoly. British goods made their way from Colonia into Buenos Aires and the interior through surreptitious exchange with the Portuguese in the Paraná delta; for this reason, Spanish forces intermittently besieged Portugal's riverside outpost for decades.

Although the two powers agreed on the cession of Colonia to Spain around 1750, the agreement failed when Jesuit missionaries on the upper Paraná refused to comply with the proposed exchange of territory in their area. Spain finally took control of the city in 1777, when authorities created the viceroyalty of the River Plate. From this time, the city's commercial importance declined as foreign goods proceeded directly to Buenos Aires.

The city's heart – and main tourist attraction – is the **Barrio Histórico**, a historical neighborhood that doubles as a Unesco world cultural heritage site. It's full of colonial architecture and worthwhile sights, starting with the 1745 **Puerta de Campo** (Calle Manuel de Lobos), the restored entrance to the old city. A short distance west is **Plaza Mayor 25 de Mayo**, from which the narrow, roughly cobbled Calle de los Suspiros (Street of Sighs), lined with tile-and-stucco colonial houses, runs south almost to the water. On the south side of this plaza is the **Museo Portugués**, which has good exhibits on the Portuguese period, including Lusitanian and colonial dress.

Off the southwest corner of the Plaza Mayor are the ruins of the 17th-century **Convento de San Francisco**, within which stands the 19th-century **faro** (lighthouse). At the west end of the Plaza Mayor, is the **Museo Municipal** (Calle del Comercio). Diagonally opposite the museum, on the northwest edge of the plaza, is the **Archivo Regional** (Calle de las Misiones de los Tapes 115), which contains a small museum and bookshop.

Head to the west end of Misiones de los Tapes to the dinky **Museo del Azulejo** (tile museum), a 17th-century house with a sampling of colonial tilework (you can sneak peeks through the windows if it's closed). From there, the riverfront Paseo de San Gabriel leads north to **Plazoleta San Martín**. Turn east and you will reach Av General Flores; continue east a block and turn south on Calle Vasconcellos to reach the landmark **Iglesia Matriz** on the shady **Plaza de Armas**, also known as Plaza Manuel Lobo. The church, begun in 1680, is Uruguay's oldest, though it has been completely rebuilt twice. The plaza holds the foundations of a house dating from Portuguese times.

Heading back north to Av General Flores and then beyond it a block further north brings you near the **Museo Español** (San José 164), which has exhibitions of replica colonial pottery, clothing and maps.

At the north end of nearby Calle España is the **Puerto Viejo**, the old port, now a yacht harbor. One block east, the **Teatro Bastión del Carmen** (Calle del Virrey Cevallos & Rivadavia) is a theater and gallery complex that incorporates part of the city's ancient fortifications. The huge chimney is newer, dating from the 1880s.

# Sights & Information

Colonia's area code is ☎ 052. All of the museums in Colonia are open 11am to 5pm daily; one US$0.50 ticket gives you admission to all.

**Main Tourist Office** ( ☎ 26141; General Flores 499; ⏰ 8am-7pm Mon-Fri, 9am-7pm Sat & Sun) Has a hotel reservation office next door (same contact information) that will help travelers find accommodation. There's also a tourist office at the **ferry port** ( ☎ 24897; ⏰ 9am-9pm, but can vary widely) and another near the **Puerta de Campo** ( ☎ 28506; Manuel de Lobos & San Miguel; ⏰ 9am-6pm).

## Transportation

**Distance from Buenos Aires** 60km

**Direction** East

**Travel time** One to two hours by ferry

**Boat** Buquebus (in Buenos Aires ☎ 4316-6500, in Colonia ☎ 22919; www.buquebus.com in Spanish) has fast (US$30 one-way) and slow (US$13 to US$17 one-way) ferries to Colonia. Ferryturismo is part of Buquebus and has identical prices.

# Eating

Colonia has a wide range of good restaurants, most of which close for a few hours in the afternoon.

**El Asador** ( ☎ 31024; Ituzaingó 168; mains US$2.50-6; ⏰ lunch & dinner) This casual *parrilla*, often jammed with locals, serves the usual cuts of meat along with plenty of fish, pastas and *minutas* (short orders).

**El Drugstore** ( ☎ 25241; Vasconcellos 179; mains US$4-10; ⏰ lunch & dinner) Vivid colors and funky modern-art re-productions decorate this creative eatery. Tasty food includes grilled salmon, *ñoquis* (gnocchi) with mussel sauce, abundant salads, fondues and even Japanese *teppanyaki* (meats grilled at your table). There's live music almost nightly.

**Mesón de la Plaza** ( ☎ 24807; Vasconcellos 152; mains US$3.50-7; ⏰ lunch & dinner) Old-time fancy atmosphere makes for an upscale and romantic meal at this eatery on Plaza de Armas. The menu covers mostly meat dishes, but a few fish and pasta mains stand out.

**Pulpería de los Faroles** ( ☎ 30271; Misiones de los Tapes 101; mains US$3-7; ⏰ lunch & dinner) Set in the Barrio Histórico is this upscale spot with brick walls, colorful chairs and cartwheel chandeliers. Food ranges from seafood to pastas and meats, but the menu is limited.

**Viejo Barrio** ( ☎ 25399; Vasconcellos 169; mains US$3-7; ⏰ lunch Thu-Tue, dinner Thu-Mon) Popular for its exceptional homemade pasta dishes is this pleasant restaurant on Plaza de Armas. The menu is small but perfectly formed, and service is good.

## Sleeping

On summer weekends or during Argentine holidays, rates may be higher, and reservations are crucial. If you're stuck, the hotel reservation office next to the main tourist office (see opposite) can help. Most places include breakfast.

**Casa de los Naranjos** ( ☎ 24630; www.colonianet.com /naranjos in Spanish; 18 de Julio 219; s/d US$20/30; **P** ) Just six dark but charming rooms are available at this old colonial posada in the Barrio Histórico. There's a grassy garden with swimming pool, and the US$40 suite is especially nice.

**Hostal Colonial** ( ☎ 30347; hostelling_colonial@hotmail .com; Av General Flores 440; dm US$6, d US$12-16) Good courtyard rooms line this old building; out of five doubles, just two come with private bathroom. Services include kitchen use and free bike rentals, and staff can organize horse rides.

**Hotel Ciudadela** ( ☎ 21183; ciudadel@internet.com.uy; 18 de Julio 315; s/d US$10/20) The clean and comfortable rooms here are a good size and an especially good deal for solo travelers.

**Hotel Rivera** ( ☎ 20807; www.hotelescolonia.com/rivera in Spanish; Rivera 131; s/d US$12/20) Twelve good, modern rooms with some charm are available at this intimate hotel near the bus station and ferry port. There's a small patio in the back.

**La Posada del Gobernador** ( ☎ 22918; posadadelgobern ador@adinet.com.uy; 18 de Julio 205; s/d US$35/45; **P** )

> ### Crossing into Uruguay
>
> Traveling from Buenos Aires into Uruguay is fairly easy and straightforward, but you'll need a valid passport. Nationals of Western Europe, the USA, Canada, Australia and New Zealand will receive a tourist card on entry, valid for 90 days. Other nationals require visas. It's wise to check the current visa situation during your stay, however, as this information can change in the blink of an eye.
>
> Uruguay's unit of currency is the peso, but US dollars and Argentine pesos are widely accepted for tourist services. Uruguay's telephone country code is ☎ 598. The country is one hour ahead of Argentina, but daylight saving may affect time differences.

Its colonial architecture and location in the Barrio Histórico make this hotel an upscale stay, but some cheesy piped-in music detracts a bit. Rooms are good and have their own charm; most open to a patio or balcony. There's a peaceful garden and swimming pool in the back.

**Posada del Río** ( ☎ 23002; www.colonianet.com/delrio in Spanish; Washington Barbot 258; s/d US$12/17) This serene and friendly place, on a tree-lined street close to a pleasant sandy beach, offers 11 small, modest and intimate rooms (ask for one inside around the courtyard).

**Posada Manuel de Lobo** ( ☎ 22463; www.colonianet .com/posadamdelobo; Ituzaingó 160; s/d US$35/45; **P** ) Gorgeous, well-appointed rooms with modern bathrooms, wood floors and old-time charm are available at this well-located spot. Superiors are huge and include a Jacuzzi (US$50 to US$65); there's a pleasant patio as well.

# MONTEVIDEO

Montevideo is probably South America's most laid-back capital. The population is only 1.3 million, but many of these folks are students and young workers, and they give the city a lively buzz. It also has a decidedly European feel, thanks to a large influx of Spanish and Italian immigrants who arrived during the late 19th and early 20th centuries.

Montevideo lies on the east bank of the Río de la Plata. Its key commercial and entertainment area is Av 18 de Julio, but its functional center is **Plaza Independencia**. It's here that you'll find the sombre yet dramatic **Mausoleo de Artigas**, which celebrates the achievements of Uruguay's independence hero. Guards vigilantly watch over Artigas' ash remains without moving a muscle, making you wonder if they scored the most boring job in the world. The underground mausoleum is smack in the middle of the plaza; look for stairs underneath the statue of Artigas on horseback.

Just a block west of the plaza you'll find the **Museo Torres García**, a three-story gallery devoted entirely to Joaquín Torres García (1874–1949). One of Uruguay's most famous artists, García spent much of his career in France, New York and Paris. Works on display show his progression from a fairly conventional landscape painter to a more modern artist influenced by abstract maestros such as Mondrian; also showcased are his unusual portraits of figures such as Columbus, Mozart and Beethoven. Three blocks east of the plaza is the

**Museo del Gaucho y de la Moneda**, located in the Banco de la República. This split-personality museum dedicates its 1st floor to Uruguay's troubled economy and mind-boggling changes of currency over the years. The 2nd floor is a gaucho frenzy; it features all things related to these romantic cowboy figures, from horse gear and ornate *mates* to traditional costumes (both for the gauchos themselves and their horses).

Most of Montevideo's grand 19th-century neoclassical buildings – legacies of the beef boom – have all but crumbled, but vestiges of a colonial past still exist in the **Ciudad Vieja**, the city's picturesque historic center. Many museums are located in this area, including the **Museo de Arte Decorativo**. Back in the 1800s, it seemed the fashion amongst Montevideo's elite was to cram as many baroque knickknacks into one's mansion as possible. This building, once the home of a wealthy merchant, is a testament to this craze, with its large collection of gilded housewares, tapestries, sculptures, ornate pianos and fancy chandeliers. Its opulence is an interesting contrast to the neighborhood's crumbling decay.

Over toward the ferry terminal, at the corner of Castellano and Piedras, is the **Mercado del Puerto**. This wrought-iron superstructure dates from 1868 and shelters a gaggle of reasonably priced *parrillas* and upmarket seafood restaurants. Especially on Saturday afternoons, it's a lively and colorful spot where artists, craftspeople and street musicians hang out. Café Roldós, at the same site since 1886, serves the popular *medio y medio*, a mixture of sparkling and white wines.

East of Montevideo's downtown, the riverfront **Rambla** leads past residential suburbs and sandy **beaches** frequented by *montevideanos* in summer and on weekends – catch bus No 64, which goes from 18 de Julio along the coast road – the beaches get better the further out of town you go.

# Sights & Information

The invaluable **Guía del Ocio**, which lists cultural events, cinemas, theaters and restaurants, comes with the Friday edition of *La República*. Ask at the local tourist office for a copy of *Pimba!*, a free pocket-sized booklet that has more information on bars, clubs and bands. Montevideo's area code is ☎ 02.

**Alianza Francesa** ( ☎ 400-0505; www.alianzafrancesa.edu.uy; Blv Artigas 1229; ✆ 8am-7:30pm) A well-stocked library with books, magazines and CDs. Short-term visitors can avoid membership fees by paying a US$50 refundable deposit.

**Mausoleo de Artigas** (Plaza Independencia; admission free; ✆ 9am-5pm) Tours in Spanish run at 4:30pm; minimum six people.

**Municipal Tourist Office** ( ☎ 903-0649; Palacio Municipal; ✆ 10am-6pm Mon-Fri, 11am-6pm Sat & Sun) Small but well informed. There's a well-equipped **Oficina de Informes** ( ☎ 409-7399; ✆ 9am-9pm) at the bus terminal.

**Museo de Arte Decorativo** (25 de Mayo 376; admission free; ✆ 12:15-6pm Tue-Sat, 2-6pm Sun)

**Museo del Gaucho y de la Moneda** (18 de Julio 998; admission free; ✆ 10am-5pm Mon-Fri)

**Museo Torres García** (Sarandí 683; admission free; 9am-8pm Mon-Fri)

# Eating
## OLD TOWN

Steaks served at *parrillas* inside the **Mercado del Puerto** are so large that they're almost obscene. The best time to visit is on Saturday around lunchtime, when the town market is crammed with locals.

**Confitería La Pasiva** ( ☎ 915-8261; cnr JC Gómez & Peatonal Sarandí; mains US$4-5; ✆ breakfast, lunch & dinner) This hugely popular chain swathes its restaurants with good atmosphere while consistently offering reasonably priced *minutas* and a superb *flan casero* (homemade caramel custard). Other branches are at 18 de Julio 1018 and on the corner of Ejido and 18 de Julio.

**El Palenque** ( ☎ 915-4704; Mercado del Puerto; mains US$7-9; ✆ lunch & dinner) Hugely popular with local businessmen, the Palenque offers a range of seating options – outside on the sunny pedestrian walkway, inside at tables, or at the bar, up close and personal with the *parrilla* rack. The menu covers a huge variety of meats, fish, paella and pastas.

**La Corte** ( ☎ 915-6113; Peatonal Sarandí 586; mains US$3-4; ⏱ lunch daily, dinner Thu-Sat) Here's a hip-looking restaurant that's extremely popular with businessmen, students and everyday *montevideanos*. The extensive menu features meats, seafood and poultry while soft jazz plays; the set lunch is a steal at US$4.

### NEW TOWN

**Arcadia Restaurant** ( ☎ 902-0111; Radisson Hotel, Plaza Independencia; mains US$7-12; ⏱ breakfast, lunch & dinner) The Arcadia sits on the 25th floor of the Radisson, and the views are reason enough to eat here. An added bonus is some of the most imaginative food in town, mixing Uruguayan, Italian and Japanese influences. Cheap sandwiches and burgers are available (US$2 to US$4), but there's a US$2.50 per person cover charge. The *menú del día* (set menu) is a good deal at US$12, as is the US$6 breakfast buffet.

**El Rincón de los Poetas** (cnr Aquiles Lanza & San José; set meals US$3-5; ⏱ lunch & dinner) Classic Uruguayan dishes are on offer at this spot in the Mercado de la Abundancia, which can make for an atmospheric meal with its wrought iron and old-time feel.

**La Vegetariana** ( ☎ 901-6418; Río Negro 1311; mains US$2-3.50; ⏱ lunch & dinner Mon-Sat, lunch Sun) Pay at the front, grab a plate and help yourself from the steam

## Ciudad Vieja Warning

Montevideo is sedate by most standards, but street crime is on the rise. Take the usual precautions, especially in the Ciudad Vieja, which can be dangerous at night. If you want to report a crime, contact the **Tourist Police** ( ☎ 908-9015; Plaza Entrevero).

trays, which include polenta, noodles, ravioli, rice, squash and more. Browse the salad bar too, and then hit the desserts. The veggie food is good at this almost-all-you-can-eat restaurant.

**Restaurante de los Vascos** ( ☎ 902-3519; San José 1168; mains US$2-5; ⏱ lunch & dinner) An excellent selection of Basque and Spanish dishes are on offer here, as is the best paella in town. Red-checked tablecloths and exposed beams add to the atmosphere, while cheap *jarras* (jugs) of red wine are bound to keep you hanging around.

## Sleeping

**Balmoral Plaza Hotel** ( ☎ 902-2393; www.balmoral.com.uy; Plaza Cagancha 1126; s/d US$35/45; Ⓟ ) With excellent views out over Plaza Cagancha, the Balmoral is a good deal in this price range. Rooms are functional, if unexciting, but the hotel also boasts a gym and sauna.

**Hotel Embajador** ( ☎ 902-2457; hotemb@adinet.com.uy; San José 1212; d standard/deluxe US$40/45; Ⓟ ) A comfortable choice that's hugely popular with visiting Argentines, the Embajador's deluxe rooms are a much

*Finger sculpture, Punta del Este (p180)*

Excursions – Montevideo

179

better deal – more spacious and with a bathtub rather than shower stall. Features include a funky lobby fountain and sauna.

**Hotel Lafayette** ( ☎ 902-4646; www.lafayette.com.uy; Soriano 1170; s/d US$28/36; **P** ) The Lafayette's rooms are a good deal, but the location is the real winner. If you can get a room with a view of the river you'll be more than happy. Facilities include gym, sauna, Jacuzzi and babysitting service.

**Hotel London Palace** ( ☎ 902-0024; www.lphotel.com; Río Negro 1278; s/d US$30/35; **P** ) With its antique furniture, hall runners and modern rooms that manage to retain a vestige of style, the London Palace is a step above the rest in this price range.

**Hotel NH Columbia** ( ☎ 916-0001; www.nh-hotels.com; Rambla Gran Bretaña 473; d US$90; **P** ) This minimally decorated hotel (think chrome and abstract art) sits right on the Rambla and the front rooms have great views over the water. Rooms are comfortable and spacious with all the mod cons you'd expect for the price. Rates can almost halve during the off-season and midweek – be sure to ask for discounts.

**Hotel Oxford** ( ☎ 902-0046; www.hoteloxford.com.uy; Paraguay 1286; s/d US$25/35; **P** ) The fancy marble lobby of this semimodern hotel promises big things, and the rooms deliver, more or less – this is a comfortable, reasonable choice. Some rooms have bathtubs, making them a better deal than others, and a babysitting service is available.

**Hotel Palacio** ( ☎ 916-3612; Bartolomé Mitre 1364; d US$14) In the Zona Viva of the old town, this well-renovated classic hotel (think wrought iron and dark woodwork) offers comfortable, if slightly cramped rooms, some with balconies. Cheaper rooms with shared bathrooms are available.

**Hotel Solís** ( ☎ 915-0279; Bartolomé Mitre 1314; s/d with shared bathroom US$7/12, d with private bathroom US$16) A longstanding budget choice on the edge of the old town, the Solís offers ageing but tidy rooms, all with balconies overlooking the street. Rooms with private bathroom also have cable TV, and are one of the better budget deals in town.

**Pensión Nuevo Ideal** ( ☎ 908-2913; Soriano 1073; d with shared/private bathroom US$3.50/7) The lobby of this attractive little hotel is a good indication of what's in store – there's plenty of light, the place is spotless and the decor is tasteful yet restrained. Blasting hot showers are an added bonus.

**Radisson Victoria Plaza** ( ☎ 902-0111; radisson@adinet .com.uy; Plaza Independencia 759; d from US$99; **P** ) The Radisson's tried and tested combination of mod cons and timeless elegance works again at their 25-story hotel overlooking the Plaza Independencia. Facilities include the rooftop Arcadia restaurant (p179), Olympic-sized swimming pool, day spa, gym and jogging track. The hotel also has wireless Internet connection in the lobby and a well-equipped business center.

**Red Hostel** ( ☎ 908-8514; www.redhostel.com; San José 1406; dm US$7, s/d US$15/18) This cool new hostel is located in an old mansion with many of the walls painted in red hues. Dorms are clean and spacious and there's a pleasant rooftop patio. Kitchen access, a fireplace in the common room and breakfast are included.

# PUNTA DEL ESTE

'Punta' – with its many beaches, elegant seaside homes, yacht harbor, high-rise apartment buildings and upscale hotels and restaurants – is one of South America's most glamorous resorts. In January and February the well-heeled hordes of Buenos Aires, many of whom own second houses or apartments here, overrun the hot sands and concrete. Famous celebrities and models come to this Uruguayan hotspot to hang out, do photo shoots and dance the warm sultry nights away, while other beach bunnies sun themselves from sunrise to sunset. Punta's a happening place and super fun to check out during the busy summertime season, but remember that prices during this time skyrocket and rooms can be hard to find.

Punta's center is very walkable – you can casually stroll from one end to the other in less than half an hour. Av Gorlero is just 10 blocks long and the city's main lifeline, offering the biggest concentration of touristy shops, services and casual eateries, while Plaza Artigas holds an artsy crafts fair every evening in summer (but only during the day on weekends in the off-season).

Beaches are the area's main attraction, however. Punta is at the rocky tip of a V-shaped peninsula edged with sandy ribbons. Close to the center and on the Río de la Plata side of the peninsula is Playa Mansa, whose calm sands attract families and low-key beachgoers. Playa Brava is on the east side but less than a five-minute walk away; it has a more active crowd and boasts fierce waves that claim a few lives each year, so be careful when swimming here.

Punta's best beaches, however, are a short bus ride away. Stretching up to the northeast is a run of sand that ends 10km away at **La Barra** and **Bikini beach**, where the rich and good-looking come to party and preen themselves. Disco clubs, restaurants and shops service the trendy crowds, and the people-watching can't be beat. Heading up on the northwest side of the peninsula is another stretch of beaches that ends 15km away at **Punta Ballena**, whose main tourist attraction is **Casapueblo**. This free-form, neo-Mediterranean structure is covered in blindingly white stucco and boasts unforgettable views. It's a luxury hotel, café-bar and art gallery inspired by Uruguayan artist and adventurer Carlos Páez Vilaró, and definitely worth a peep if you're in the area.

## Sights & Information

Punta's area code is ☎ 42.

**Casapueblo** ( ☎ 578041; admission US$3; ☺ 9am-sunset) Buses drop you at a junction 2km away.

**Tourist office** ( ☎ 46519; cnr Rambla Artigas & Calle 31; ☺ 8am-midnight) There are other tourist offices at the **bus station** ( ☎ 494042; ☺ 8am-9pm) and at **Av Gorlero** ( ☎ 441218; Av Gorlero 942; ☺ 9am-10pm).

## Eating

Punta has an eatery for almost any budget, and boasts excellent seafood restaurants. Hours are more limited outside summer, when some places open only on weekends.

**Blue Cheese** ( ☎ 446633; Calle 20 No 717; mains US$7-9.50; ☺ lunch & dinner) Pastas, seafood and meats dominate the menu at this very popular waterside restaurant (be prepared to wait). The salad bar is an added plus (US$3 with purchase of a main) and there's a nice patio out front.

**El Mejillón** ( ☎ 445895; cnr Rambla Artigas & Calle 11; mains US$5.50-13; ☺ breakfast, lunch & dinner) Surrounded by an extensive outdoor patio and water views is this large and modern restaurant. Seven types of *chivito*, the national dish, are available; this is a steak topped with healthy things such as lettuce, bacon, fried egg and potato salad. Lots of seafood, meats and pasta are also on the menu, and the service is attentive.

**El Pobre Marino** ( ☎ 443306; Calle 11 No 694; mains US$5-7.50; ☺ lunch & dinner) The menu is short and uncomplicated, but the seafood is excellent. Order the mussels à la Provençal for starters, then head to the grilled fish with garlic. Paella, polenta, homemade pasta (spinach ravioli) and seafood stew are other choices, while a seafaring theme puts it all in perspective.

**Gure Etxe** ( ☎ 446858; cnr Calle 9 & 12; mains US$4-13; ☺ dinner) Those in search of Basque food need look no further than this modest restaurant. The seafood, meat and omelette dishes are adapted for South American palates so don't expect true authenticity – but at least it's something different.

**Lo de Tere** ( ☎ 440492; cnr Rambla Artigas & Calle 21; mains US$9-20; ☺ lunch & dinner) The surroundings aren't too impressive at this upscale restaurant, but the expressively written menu has international flair while a

Japanese chef adds an exotic touch. Dishes aren't surprising, with a range of chicken, lamb, seafood and beef, but there is mushroom risotto and pasta for the vegetarians.

## Sleeping

Budget accommodation in Punta is limited; reservations are crucial in summer. All prices given are for the summer high season; low-season prices drop by 25% to 50%. Breakfast is included at all hotels.

**El Hostal** ( ☎ 441632; albergues@hostelinguruguay.org; Calle 25 No 544; dm US$10) This small hostel has good four- to six-bed dorms and a small common room up front. There's a side patio for warm-weather days and tiny kitchen for heating water only (no cooking).

**Hotel Azul** ( ☎ 441117; hotelzul@adinet.com.uy; Av Gorlero 540; s/d US$80/90; **P** ) Big, comfortable rooms with non-offensive décor are available at this modern hotel toward the end of the peninsula. Bathrooms are good-sized and halls are carpeted, but don't expect good views.

**Hotel Marbella** ( ☎ 441814; www.hotelmarbella.8m.com; Calle 31 No 615; s/d US$39/55) Close to the bus station is this decent hotel with clean, quiet and good-sized rooms, some with ocean peeks. Fridges are included, and room Nos 105 and 106 have small patios where pets can stay.

**Hotel Remanso** ( ☎ 447412; www.hotelremanso.com.uy in Spanish; cnr Calle 20 & Esq 28; d US$125-140; **P** )

Excursions – Punta del Este

## Transportation

**Distance from Buenos Aires** 360km

**Direction** East

**Travel time** By air 45 minutes, by bus 10 hours

**Airplane** Daily flights with Pluna, LAPA and Aerolíneas (US$150 to US$190); note US$8 departure tax from BA

**Bus** Daily buses from Retiro bus station (US$30); many buses connect with Montevideo (US$5, two hours). Punta's bus station is right near the center.

**Boat** Bus-boat combinations available with Buquebus via Colonia or Montevideo (US$30 to US$60 depending on route and class of boat)

Comfortable modern rooms (superiors come with Jacuzzi) are on offer at this upscale hotel. Facilities include an attractive lobby, a gym, a conference room and a rooftop swimming pool.

**Palace Hotel** ( ☎ 441919; palacepunta@hotmail.com; cnr Gorlero & Esq 11; s/d US$50/75; Ⓟ ) This three-star hotel has acceptable rooms, but is probably best for its colonial-style interior grassy garden – complete with pool. There's an Italian restaurant on the premises, the lobby is pleasant and the hotel accepts pets.

**Residencial 32** ( ☎ 493506; Calle 32 No 640; s/d US$20/35) Twenty-two basic but tidy budget rooms await at this no-nonsense place, which is cheap and right next to the bus station.

**Tanger Hotel** ( ☎ 441333; tangerhotel@hotmail.com; d US$69-103; Ⓟ ) Rooms at this unexceptional spot are homey and small, but the more expensive ones have ocean views. There's a rooftop pool as well as a heated indoor pool, gym and sauna. The astroturfed terrace is a tacky touch. Rates drop a bit in February.

# Directory

# Directory

## TRANSPORTATION
### AIR

Buenos Aires is Argentina's international gateway and easily accessible from North America, Europe and Australasia, as well as other capital cities in South America. Aerolíneas Argentinas, Southern Winds and American Falcon are the main airlines at the moment, but Argentine airlines are in constant flux and come and go frequently.

### Airlines

**Aerolíneas Argentinas** (Map pp222-4; ☎ 0810-222-86527; www.aerolineas.com; Perú 2. Also in **Retiro** (Map pp228-9, Leandro N Alem 1134)

**Air Canada** (Map pp222-4; ☎ 4393-9045; www.aircanada.ca; Córdoba 656)

**Air France** (Map pp228-9; ☎ 4317-4700; www.airfrance.com; 14th fl, Paraguay 610)

**Alitalia** (Map pp228-9; ☎ 4310-9970; www.alitalia.com; Av Santa Fe 887)

**American Airlines** (Map pp228-9; www.aa.com; ☎ 4318-1111; Av Santa Fe 881)

**American Falcon** (Map pp228-9; www.americanfalcon.com.ar; ☎ 0810-222-3252; Av Santa Fe 963)

**Avianca** (Map pp228-9; ☎ 4394-5990; www.avianca.com in Spanish; 4th fl, Carlos Pellegrini 1163)

**British Airways** (Map pp228-9; ☎ 4320-6600; www.britishairways.com; Carlos Pellegrini 1163)

**KLM** (Map pp222-4; ☎ 4326-8422; www.klm.com; 9th fl, Suipacha 268)

**LanChile** (Map pp228-9; ☎ 4378-2222; www.lanchile.com; Cerrito 866)

**Líneas Aéreas del Estado** (LADE; Map p225; ☎ 5129-9001; www.lade.com.ar; Perú 714)

**Lloyd Aéreo Boliviano** (LAB; Map pp222-4; ☎ 4323-1900; www.labairlines.com; Carlos Pellegrini 141)

**Pluna** (Map pp222-4; ☎ 4329-9211; www.pluna.com.uy; Av Florida 1)

**Southern Winds** (Map pp228-9; www.sw.com.ar; ☎ 4515-8600; Av Santa Fe 784)

**Swissair** (Map pp228-9; www.swiss.com; ☎ 4319-0000; 1st fl, Av Santa Fe 846)

**Transportes Aéreos de Mercosur** (TAM; Map pp228-9; ☎ 0810-333-3333; www.tam.com.py in Spanish; Cerrito 1026)

**United Airlines** (Map pp228-9; ☎ 0810-777-8648; www.united.com.ar; 1st fl, Av Eduardo Madero 900)

**Varig** (Map pp222-4; ☎ 4329-9211; www.varig.com.br in Portuguese; 4th fl, Córdoba 972)

### Airports

Almost all international flights arrive at Buenos Aires' **Ezeiza** airport (officially Aeropuerto Internacional Ministro Pistarini), about 35km south of the center. Most domestic flights use **Aeroparque** airport (officially **Aeroparque Jorge Newbery**), a short distance from downtown Buenos Aires. Flight information for both airports, in English and Spanish, is available by calling ☎ 5480-6111 or accessing www.aa2000.com.ar.

The best, most affordable way to and from Ezeiza is taking a shuttle with **Manuel Tienda León** (MTL; Map pp228-9; ☎ 4314-3636; www.tiendaleon.com; in the center cnr Av Eduardo Madero & San Martín). You'll see their stand immediately as you exit customs. Shuttles cost US$7.50 one way, run every half-hour from

---

### Ezeiza Arrival & Departure Tips

When you arrive at Ezeiza and want to change your money, don't go to the first *cambio* (exchange house) you see. For better rates, pass the row of transport booths and veer to the right to find Banco de la Nación's small office; their rates are identical to downtown offices and they're open 24 hours.

Taxis from Ezeiza to the center cost US$15. Taking a taxi from one of the fellows standing in wait can be risky, so play it safe. As you exit customs you'll pass a line of transportation booths; avoid the overpriced taxis here – the city's taxi stand is just behind, and official prices are posted. Taxis from the center *to* Ezeiza, however, are slightly cheaper at US$12. All these prices should include tolls.

There's a **tourist information booth** ( ☎ 4480-0024) just beyond the city's taxi stand.

When you leave Buenos Aires on an international flight you pay a departure tax of US$18 (payable in Argentine pesos or US dollars). If you're heading to Montevideo or Punta del Este this tax will be US$8.

6am to 12:45am and take about 40 minutes. Avoid their taxi service, which is overpriced at US$20; if you want to take a taxi just go around their counter to the nearby freestanding city taxi service, which charges US$15 to the center. MTL also does transfers from Ezeiza to Aeroparque for US$8.

Real shoestringers can take public bus No 86 into town, which costs US$0.50 and can take up to 1½ hours. Catch it outside the Aerolíneas Argentinas terminal, a short walk from the international terminal.

To get from Aeroparque to the center, take public bus Nos 33 or 45 (don't cross the street; take them going south). MTL has shuttles to the center for US$2.75; taxis cost US$3.50.

## BICYCLE

Buenos Aires is not a great city to cycle around. Traffic is dangerous and hardly respectful toward cyclists; the biggest vehicle wins the right of way, and bikes are low on the totem pole. Still, some spots call out for two-wheeled exploration, such as Palermo's parks and the Reserva Ecológica Costanera Sur; on weekends and some weekdays you can rent bikes at these places. You can also join city bike tours, which include bicycle and guide. For more information on all these places see p138.

## BOAT

Buenos Aires has a regular ferry service to and from Colonia and Montevideo, both in Uruguay. Ferries leave from the Buquebus terminal at Avs Antártida Argentina and Córdoba (Map pp228-9). There are many more launches in the busy summer season. For more information, see p175 and p177.

## BUS

Buenos Aires has a huge and complex bus system. If you want to get to know it better you'll have to buy a *Guía T* – it's sold at any newsstand, but try to find the pocket version for US$1. Just look at the grids to find out where you are and where you're going, and find a matching bus number. Most routes (but not all) run 24 hours.

If you're heading out of town you'll probably have to visit BA's modern Retiro bus station (Map pp228-9). It's 400m long, three floors high and has slots for 75 buses. The bottom floor is for cargo shipments and luggage storage, the top for purchasing tickets and the middle for everything else. There's an **information booth** ( ☎ 4310-0700) that provides general bus information and schedules; they'll also help you with the local bus system. Other services include a **tourist office** ( ☎ 4311-0528; ☑ 7:30am-1pm Mon-Sat), on the 2nd floor on the other side of station from bus slot No 34; telephone offices (some with Internet access); restaurants; cafés; and dozens of small stores.

You can buy a ticket to practically anywhere in Argentina and departures are fairly frequent to the most popular destinations. Reservations are not necessary except during peak summer and winter holiday seasons.

## CAR

Anyone considering driving in Buenos Aires should know that most local drivers are reckless, aggressive and even willfully dangerous. They'll ignore speed limits, road signs, road lines and often traffic signals. They'll tailgate you mercilessly and honk even before signals turn green. Buses are a nightmare to reckon with, and parking can be a bitch. Reconsider your need to have a car in this city: public transportation will often get you anywhere faster, cheaper and with much less stress.

If, however, you still want to rent a car, expect to pay around US$35 to US$50 per day (it may be worth trying to make a reservation with one of the major international agencies in your home country, as these can sometimes guarantee stable rates). You'll need to be at least 21 years of age and have a valid driver's license; having an international driver's license wouldn't be a bad idea, though you don't necessarily need one. You'll probably need to present a credit card and your passport, though.

The following agencies are all in Retiro (Map pp228-9):

**Avis** ( ☎ 4326-5542; www.avis.com; Cerrito 1527)

**Hertz** ( ☎ 4816-8001; www.hertz.com.ar; Paraguay 1138)

**New Way** ( ☎ 4515-0331; www.new-wayrentacar.com.ar; MT de Alvear 773)

If you drive in Argentina – especially in your own car – it may be worth joining the Automóvil Club Argentino (ACA), which has many nationwide offices. ACA recognizes members of overseas affiliates, such as the American Automobile Association (AAA), and often grants them similar privileges including discounts on maps, accommodations, camping, tours and other services. ACA membership costs about US$29 per month; for more information contact the **ACA head office** (Map pp232-3; ☎ 4802-6061; www.aca.org.ar in Spanish; Av del Libertador 1850).

## SUBTE (UNDERGROUND)

BA's **Subte** (☎ 4555-1616; www.metrovias.com.ar) opened in 1913 and is the quickest way to get around the city, though it can get mighty hot and crowded during rush hour. At the time of writing it consisted of Líneas (Lines) A, B, C, D and E; a new H line was due to open up in 2005. Four parallel lines run from downtown to the capital's western and northern outskirts, while Línea C runs north–south and connects the two major train stations of Retiro and Constitución.

One-ride magnetic cards for the Subte cost US$0.70. To save time and hassle buy several rides, since queues can get backed up (especially during rush hour).

At some stations platforms are on opposite sides, so make sure of your direction *before* passing through the turnstiles.

Trains operate from 5am to 10pm Monday to Saturday and 8am to 10pm on Sundays, so don't rely on the Subte to get you home after dinner. Service is frequent on weekdays; on weekends you'll wait longer.

The oldest Subte line, Línea A, offers a tarnished reminder of the city's elegant past, with its tiled stations and vintage wood trams. Several stations have impressive murals, most notably those on Línea D, between Catedral and Palermo.

## TAXI & REMISE

Buenos Aires' very numerous (about 40,000) and cheap taxis are conspicuous by their black-and-yellow paint jobs. Meters generally start at US$1.44 day or night so make sure that the meter's set to this amount when you start your ride.

Drivers do not expect a big tip, but it's customary to let them keep small change. Most rides within the center should cost between US$1.75 and US$3.50.

Almost all taxi drivers are honest workers making a living, but there are a few bad apples in the bunch. Try not to give taxi drivers large bills; not only will they usually not have change, but there have been cases where a driver quickly and deftly replaces a larger bill with a smaller one. One solution is to state

how much you are giving them and ask if they have change for it ('¿*Tiene usted cambio de un veinte?*' – Do you have any change for a 20?).

Be wary of receiving counterfeit bills; at night have the driver turn on the light (or *luz*) so you can carefully check your change (look for a watermark on bills). And make sure you get the right change.

If you are obviously a tourist going to or from a touristy spot, it's not a good idea to ask how much the fare is; this makes quoting an upped price tempting, rather than using the meter.

And finally, try to have an idea of where you're going or you might be taking the 'scenic' route (though also be aware there are many one-way streets in BA, and your route to one place may be quite different on the way back). A good way to give the impression that you know where you're going is to give the taxi driver an intersection rather than a specific address.

*Remises* look like regular cars and don't have meters. They cost about the same as street taxis but are considered more secure, since an established company sends them out. Most hotels and restaurants will call *remises* for you.

## TRAIN

Trains serve Buenos Aires' suburbs and nearby provinces; you won't be taking them to get around the center. Here are the most useful train stations (all served by Subte) and their destinations.

### ESTACIÓN RETIRO Map p234
**Belgrano line** (☎ 0800-777-3377) To the northern suburbs
**Mitre line** (☎ 4317-4445) To Tigre, Rosario
**San Martín** (☎ 4959-0800) To the northern suburbs

### ESTACIÓN CONSTITUCIÓN Map p234
**Roca line** (☎ 4304-0028) To the southern suburbs, Rosario, La Plata, Bahía Blanca, Atlantic beach towns

### ESTACIÓN ONCE Map p234
**Sarmiento line** (☎ 0800-333-3822) To the southwestern suburbs, Luján, Santa Rosa

### ESTACIÓN LACROZE Map p234
**Urquiza line** (☎ 0800-777-3377) From the terminus of Subte Línea B to the northwestern suburbs

# PRACTICALITIES

## ACCOMMODATIONS

Accommodations listings in the Sleeping chapter (p154) are ordered by neighborhood, with midrange and top-end places arranged alphabetically, and Cheap Sleeps listed last. In Buenos Aires the average three-star double room with bathroom costs US$50, with seasonal variations (highest in summer, from December to February). Consider that rooms at business-oriented hotels can be more expensive on weekdays than on weekends, and expect the very highest peak rates during holidays like Christmas, New Year's and Easter. Generally we've quoted rack rates for hotels, and these tend to be higher than the specials and discounted rates many hotels will give. Booking online can save you quite a bit, but if you're already there feel free to ask a hotel for its 'best rate.'

For long-term accommodations, including websites that rent out apartments to foreigners, see the Sleeping chapter (p154).

## BUSINESS HOURS

Office business hours run from 8am to 5pm; there can be a little variance, though. Banks close as early as 4pm. Stores and places like travel offices will stay open later, sometimes as late as 9pm.

Restaurants are generally open daily from noon to 3:30pm for lunch and 8pm-midnight or 1am for dinner; they'll stay open later on Fridays and Saturdays. Cafés are an exception and are often open from morning to night without a break. Bars will open in the evenings and stay open all night long. In the center, however, they cater to the business crowd, so most will be open during the day and close relatively early at night.

## CHILDREN

Although it's a megalopolis, Buenos Aires is remarkably child-friendly. Once children are old enough to cross the street safely and find their way back home, porteño parents will send unaccompanied preadolescents on errands or on visits to friends or neighbors. While most visiting parents are not likely to know the city well enough to feel comfortable doing this, they can usually count on their children's safety in public places, though it's always a good idea to keep an eye on them.

This is also a country where people frequently touch each other, so your children may be patted on the head.

Porteños can be helpful on public transportation. Often someone will give up a seat for a parent and child. Baby strollers on the crowded and uneven sidewalks of BA's downtown center are a liability, however; consider a baby carrier instead.

Basic restaurants provide a wide selection of food suitable for children (like vegetables, pasta, meat, chicken and fish), but adult portions can be so large that small children rarely need a separate order. Waiters are accustomed to providing extra plates and cutlery for children, though some places may add a small additional charge.

Poorly maintained public bathrooms lacking counter space are a concern for parents. Always carry toilet paper and wet wipes. While a woman may take a young boy into the ladies' room, it would be taboo for a man to take a girl into the men's room.

Buenos Aires' numerous plazas and public parks, many with playgrounds, are popular gathering spots for families; the most attractive are the wide open spaces of Palermo, including a nearby zoo.

For some suggestions on where to take the little ones, see p71.

## CLIMATE

If they don't know it already, visitors from the northern hemisphere will soon realize that the southern hemisphere's seasons are completely reversed. Summer runs December to February; fall is March to May; winter is June to August; and spring is September to November.

Except for the summer, Buenos Aires' climate is pleasantly humid, with an annual rainfall of 900mm spread evenly throughout the year. The changeable spring, hot summer and mild fall resemble New York City's seasons, but winter temperatures are moderated

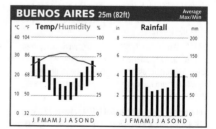

by the South Atlantic and – for a city with a relatively low latitude (34° 37' S) – are more comparable to Los Angeles, Sydney or Cape Town. Frosts are rare – the lowest temperature ever recorded is -5.4°C (22.3°F) – and snow fell only once in the last century, in 1918. It's unlikely to fall again, much less stick, because of the heat generated by the densely built-up city.

# COURSES

Visitors have many opportunities to study almost anything they want in BA, from dance and cooking to languages. Most cultural centers offer classes in Spanish, such as the excellent **Centro Cultural Ricardo Rojas** (see opposite).

Those proficient in Spanish and seeking cooking classes can try **Mausi Sebess** (☎ 4791-4355; www.mausisebess.com; Av Maipú 594), where you can take short classes like Middle Eastern or Thai cooking, and **Gato Dumas** (☎ 4783-3357; www.gatodumas.com.ar; Olazábal 2836; Belgrano), with bigger classes like bar-tending or sushi-making. Mausi may have English-speaking teachers in the future. Both schools offer degrees and are located outside the center in BA's suburbs.

## Language Courses

It's official: Buenos Aires has become a major destination for Spanish-learners. More and more institutes are opening up all the time, so if you are recommended a new place be sure to check it out. The Sunday classified section of the *Buenos Aires Herald* offers several columns of possibilities, including individual tutoring, while the **Instituto Cultural Argentino-Norteamericano** offers Spanish classes (see opposite).

Following are just a few of the options available; all organize social activities and offer homestay programs. Check websites for more information on fees and classes.

**AADE** (Map pp226-7; ☎ 4953-2883; www.espanol.org.ar; Bartolomé Mitre 2062 2nd fl Room 8) Group/private classes US$6/7 per hour; group/private classes of 10 hours per week US$57/$67; group/private classes of 20 hours per week US$107/127.

**BAESP** (Map pp226-7; ☎ 4381-2076; www.baesp.com in Spanish; Av Rivadavia 1559 2C) One-time registration fee US$40. Group/private classes of 10 hours per week US$70/120; group/private classes of 20 hours per week US$100/200.

**Centro de Estudio del Español** (CEDIC; Map pp222-3; ☎ 4315-1156; www.cedic.com.ar, 11th fl, Reconquista

715). Group/private classes US$6/9 per hour. Two- to four-hour daily instruction available.

**Entorno Lingüístico** (Map pp222-3; ☎ 4343-1495; www.entorling.com.ar; Carlos Pellegrini 27, 4E) Group/private classes US$7/9 per hour.

**Instituto de Lengua Española para Extranjeros** (ILEE; Map pp226-7; ☎ 4372-0223; www.argentinailee.com; 3rd fl, Callao 339) One-time US$50 materials fee. Private classes US$16 per hour, group classes US$200 per week.

**Lenguas Vivas** (Map pp228-9; ☎ 4322-3992; Carlos Pellegrini 1515) Monthly Spanish courses of 64 hours for US$135; other languages include German, French, Arabic, Portuguese, Italian, Japanese and Russian.

**Universidad de Buenos Aires** (UBA; Map pp222-4; ☎ 4343-5981; www.idiomas.filo.uba.ar in Spanish; 25 de Mayo 221) Longer-term classes only, for either two months(eight hours per week) or four months (four hours per week). Both cost US$525. In July and August one-month classes available. Italian, German, French, Portuguese and Japanese also taught.

**Vía Hispana** (Map pp228-9; ☎ 4893-2765; www.viahispana.com; Av Córdoba 435, 3B) 20 classes per week US$150; for one/two months price drops to US$540/800. More intensive classes also available. Private classes US$9 per hour.

There are many private tutors in the city, charging in the range of US$7 to US$10 per hour:

**Bruna Monserrat** ( ☎ 4772-3902; brunaespanol@yahoo.com.ar)

**Gisela Giunti** ( ☎ 4371-5122, 15-5626-0162; giseela@yahoo.com)

**Gabriela López** ( ☎ 4361-9843; 15-5455-3176; gabitazz@yahoo.com)

**Jose Serebrenik** ( ☎ 4951-3393; www.joseserebrenik.com.ar)

# CULTURAL CENTERS

Buenos Aires has good cultural centers offering all sorts of art exhibitions, classes and events.

**Centro Cultural Borges** (Map pp222-4; ☎ 4319-5359; www.ccborges.org.ar in Spanish; Viamonte & San Martín; ☯ 10am-9pm Mon-Sat, noon-9pm Sun) One of the best cultural centers in BA, offering inexpensive but high-quality art exhibitions and galleries, cinema, music, lectures, classes and workshops. Tango lessons are also available.

**Centro Cultural de la Cooperación** (Map pp228-9; ☎ 5077-8000; www.cculturalcoop.org.ar in Spanish; Av Corrientes 1543) A relatively new and modern center offering theatre, cinema, music, dance, expositions and workshops. It also boasts a slick café and bookshop.

**Centro Cultural Konex** (Map pp228-9; ☎ 4816-0500; www.centroculturalkonex.org in Spanish; Av Córdoba

1235) Offers innovative theatre and music, with plenty of tango classes in English and Spanish.

**Centro Cultural Recoleta** (Map pp230-1; ☎ 4803-1041; www.centroculturalrecoleta.org in Spanish; Junín 1930) This large cultural center offers many free or inexpensive events, including art exhibitions, a science museum for kids and outdoor film showings on summer evenings. There are cheap tango classes on Tuesdays and Thursdays from 6pm to 8:30pm.

**Centro Cultural Ricardo Rojas** (Map pp226-7; ☎ 4954-5523; www.rojas.uba.ar; Av Corrientes 2038; ☉ 10am-10pm Mon-Sat) This popular and exceptionally good cultural center has a wide range of cheap and excellent classes, including tango, flamenco, percussion, tai chi, *capoeira* (Brazilian dance-fighting), Nietzsche, Hebrew, photography and even intensive mime.

**Centro Cultural San Martín** (Map pp226-7; ☎ 4374-1251; www.ccgsm.gov.ar in Spanish; Sarmiento 1551) One of Buenos Aires' best resources, this large cultural center has free or inexpensive galleries, music, films, lectures, art exhibitions, classes and workshops.

There are also several foreign cultural centers in the Microcentro (Map pp222-4), such as the **Instituto Cultural Argentino-Norteamericano** (☎ 5382-1500; www.icana.org.ar in Spanish; Av Maipú 672) where graduates can take Spanish and other courses; the **Alianza Francesa** (☎ 4322-0068; www.alianzafrancesa.org.ar in French & Spanish; Córdoba 946) which concentrates on French-themed instruction and arts; and the **Instituto Goethe** (☎ 4311-8964; www.goethe.de/hs/bue in German & Spanish; Av Corrientes 319) which offers German-language instruction, a library, lectures, films and even concerts.

The **British Arts Centre** (Map pp228-9; ☎ 4393-6941; www.britishartscentre.org.ar in Spanish; Suipacha 1333; ☉ 3-9pm Tue-Fri, 6-9pm Sat) has well-priced theater, films, music and workshops (among other things) in English and Spanish.

# CUSTOMS

Argentine officials are generally courteous and reasonable toward tourists. If you cross the border frequently and carry a lot of equipment such as cameras or a laptop computer, however, you may find it helpful to have a typed list of the equipment you are carrying (including serial numbers) or a pile of purchase receipts.

Depending on where you have been, officials focus on different things. Travelers southbound from the central Andean countries may be searched for drugs, and those from bordering countries will have fruit and vegetables confiscated.

# DIGITAL RESOURCES

Argentina – and Buenos Aires in particular – has spawned a growing mass of Internet resources.

**www.lonelyplanet.com** One of the best travel sites on the Internet, with bulletin boards, travel news, recent updates, postcards from other travelers and lots more

**www.cdc.gov/travel/temsam.htm** The US Centers for Disease Control's health information site for Argentina and surrounding regions

**www.travel.state.gov** Safety, health and lots more information geared toward US citizens traveling and living abroad

**www.lanic.utexas.edu/la/argentina** A massive list of Argentine websites – if you can't find it here...well, never mind, 'cause you'll find it here

**www.hostels.com/ar.html** Lists many Hostelling International and non-HI affiliated hostels; includes information on how to reserve in advance

**www.buenosairesherald.com** An international view of the country and world, in English

**www.clarin.com.ar** A pretty complete version of Argentina's largest-circulation daily (in Spanish)

**www.lanacion.com.ar** The well-structured home page of one of BA's oldest and most prestigious dailies (in Spanish)

**www.invertir.com/12busin.html** Information slanted toward businesspeople visiting BA, though it has some good stuff for tourists too

**www.turismo.gov.ar** The national Secretaría de Turismo's official website on Argentina

**www.bue.gov.ar** The city's official tourism website on Buenos Aires

# DISCOUNT CARDS

Any traveler of any age can obtain Hostelling International cards for US$14 at the **HI office** (☎ 4511-8712; www.hostels.org.ar/index.php; Room 319, 3rd fl, Av Florida 835). With this card you can obtain US$2 discounts at HI member hostels in Argentina; you can also make hostel reservations here and find out about any other current discounts available to members. Out of the 100-plus hostels in BA, four of them are HI-affiliated; these are the Milhouse, Tango Backpackers, Recoleta and St Nicholas. Nonaffiliation by no means indicates that hostels are inferior.

The International Student Identity Card (ISIC) is available from the travel agency **Asatej** (☎ 4114-7500; www.asatej.net in Spanish; Room 320, 3rd fl, Av Florida 835) for US$11, but you need to have proper student ID to get one. This office is in the same building and same floor as the HI office.

## Disabled Travelers *Ashley Baldwin*

Negotiating Buenos Aires as a disabled traveler is certainly not the easiest of tasks and will require a bit of extra planning. Argentina is, however, years ahead of most Latin American destinations, with a reliable private health-care system if things go wrong and a fair amount of facilities for disabled travelers, and thus it should not be automatically ruled out as a holiday destination.

One of the most obvious hindrances to travelers with disabilities is the city's, narrow, busy and uneven sidewalks. It would not be unusual to spend at least a couple of minutes of your stay easing out of a pothole. The sidewalks are also high, and although disabled ramps do exist, their placement is somewhat sporadic. It's recommended that folks who use wheelchairs explore the city with someone who can assist them, especially when visiting older areas of Buenos Aires such as San Telmo or La Boca.

As far as transportation is concerned, Buenos Aires is much like any other big city. Although buses with disabled access do exist (*piso bajo*, which lowers to provide wheelchair lifts), they are few and far between and access to the city's subway is limited. Disabled travelers are better off sticking to taxis, which usually have the space to accommodate a fold-up wheelchair. Travelers with larger wheelchairs should call a taxi or *remise* (private taxi) in advance to guarantee a car that can accommodate their needs. Travelers with disabilities should also have little problem using the city's train lines. The main station in Retiro runs a frequent service to destinations such as San Isidro and Tigre, and all of the trains on this line are easily accessible.

One of the main problems in Buenos Aires is the lack of wheelchair-accessible bathrooms. Although the city's shopping malls all have at least one, restaurants are not obliged to provide special bathrooms and the main tourist areas, such as Recoleta, San Telmo and La Boca have few accessible facilities.

# ELECTRICITY

Argentina's electric current operates on 220V, 50 cycles. There are two types of electric plugs: either two rounded prongs (as in Europe) or three angled flat prongs (as in Australia and New Zealand). See the excellent website http://kropla.com/electric2.htm for more details. Adapters from one to the other are readily available at any *ferretería* (hardware store), but if you want high quality and selection try **APE** (Map pp226-7; ☎ 4384-8235; Av Sarmiento 1176; ◷ 9am-7:30pm Mon-Fri, 9am-1pm Sat). For a wide range of transformers check out **Alamtec** (Map pp226-7; ☎ 4371-1023; Paraná 220; ◷ 9am-7pm Mon-Fri, 9am-12:30pm Sat).

# EMBASSIES

Some countries have both an embassy and a consulate in Buenos Aires, but only the most central location is listed here.

**Australia** (Map pp232-3; ☎ 4779-3500; Villanueva 1400, Palermo)

**Canada** (Map pp232-3; ☎ 4808-1000; Tagle 2828, Palermo)

**France** (Map pp228-9; ☎ 4312-2409; 4th fl, Av Santa Fe 846, Retiro)

**Germany** (Map pp232-3; ☎ 4778-2500; Villanueva 1055, Palermo)

**Italy** (Map pp228-9; ☎ 4816-6132; MT de Alvear 1125, Retiro)

**Spain** (Map pp230-1; ☎ 4811-0070; Guido 1760, Recoleta)

**UK** (Map pp230-1; ☎ 4808-2000; Dr Luis Agote 2412, Palermo)

**USA** (Map pp232-3; ☎ 5777-4533; Colombia 4300, Palermo)

# EMERGENCY

**police** ☎ 101

**fire** ☎ 100

**ambulance** ☎ 107

**tourist police** ☎ 4346-5748, 0800-999-5000 (Av Corrientes 436, ◷ 24hr) Can provide interpreters

# GAY & LESBIAN TRAVELERS

Argentina is a strongly Catholic country with heavy elements of machismo. In Buenos Aires, however, there is increasing acceptance of homosexuality. For much more information on the gay community see p128.

Argentine men are far more physically demonstrative than their North American and European counterparts, so behaviors such as kissing on the cheek in greeting or a vigorous embrace are considered innocuous even to those who express unease with homosexuals. Lesbians walking hand-in-hand should generally attract little attention, since heterosexual Argentine women frequently do so, but this would be very conspicuous behavior for males. If you are in any doubt, it's better to be discreet.

As everywhere, the gay community has its own slang. Heterosexuals are *paquis* (short for *paquidermos* or pachyderms). Gay men call each other *loca* (crazy girl) or *reina* (queen). Masculine lesbians may be called *bomberos* (firemen) or *camioneros* (truckers).

# HOLIDAYS

Government offices and businesses are closed on the numerous national holidays. If a holiday falls midweek, it's often bumped to the nearest Monday. Your public transportation options are more limited on holidays, when you should reserve tickets far in advance. Hotel booking should also be done ahead of time. See p9 for more on Holidays and Events.

**Año Nuevo** (New Year's Day) January 1

**Jueves y Viernes Santo/Pascua** (Holy Thursday & Good Friday/Easter) March/April

**Día del Trabajador** (Labor Day) May 1

**Revolución de Mayo** (May Revolution) May 25

**Día de las Malvinas** (Malvinas Day) June 10

**Día de la Bandera** (Flag Day) June 20

**Día de la Independencia** (Independence Day) July 9

**Día de San Martín** (date of San Martín's death) August 17

**Día de la Raza** (Columbus Day) October 12

**Día de la Tradición** (day of traditional culture, especially gaucho) November 10

**Día de la Concepción Inmaculada** (Immaculate Conception Day) December 8

**Navidad** (Christmas Day) December 25

# INSURANCE

A travel-insurance policy to cover theft, loss and medical problems is a good idea. Some policies offer a range of lower and higher medical-expense options; the higher ones are chiefly for countries such as the USA, which has extremely high medical costs. There is a wide variety of policies available, so read the small print.

Some policies specifically exclude 'dangerous activities,' which can include scuba diving, motorcycling and even trekking. A locally acquired motorcycle license is not valid under some policies. Check that the policy you're considering covers ambulances or an emergency flight home.

You may prefer a policy that pays doctors or hospitals directly rather than requiring you to pay on the spot and claim later. If you have to claim later, make sure you keep all documentation. Some policies ask you to call back (collect) to a center in your home country, where an immediate assessment of your problem is made.

# INTERNET ACCESS

Buenos Aires is definitely online. Internet cafés and *locutorios* (telephone offices) with Internet access are very common everywhere in the center; you can often find one by just walking two blocks in any direction. Rates are very cheap at about US$0.50 per hour, and connections are quick.

Most four- and five-star hotels have in-room Internet connections for guests traveling with their own computers, and/or 'business centers' with one or more computers and Internet access. Many hostels provide free Internet to guests.

# LAUNDRY

There are many *lavanderías* (laundries) in the city, and they're dirt cheap. Most are closed Sunday. Get your load of travel-filthy threads washed, dried and folded for between US$1.50 and US$2.

# LIBRARIES

The best library for English-speaking travelers is **Biblioteca Lincoln** (Map pp222-4; ☎ 5382-1536; www.bcl.edu.ar in Spanish; Av Maipú 672; 🕒 10am-8pm Mon-Wed, 10am-6pm Thu-Fri), inside the Instituto Cultural Argentino-Norteamericano. You can't check out materials, but you can sit in a quiet, comfortable environment and read the *New York Times* and *Miami Herald*, along with English-language books and magazines. They have a branch in **Belgrano** (☎ 4576-5970) as well. The **Biblioteca Nacional** (Map pp230-1; ☎ 4808-6088; www.bibnal.edu.ar; Agüero 2502; 🕒 9am-9pm Mon-Fri, noon-7pm Sat & Sun) is in a can't-miss, ugly, mushroom-like building and offers books in Spanish along with the occasional literary event and concert.

# MAPS

For those visitors spending some time in Buenos Aires, the best resources are Lumi Transportes' *Capital Federal* and *Capital Federal y Gran*

Buenos Aires, both in compact ring-binder format, with all city streets and bus routes indexed. Argenguide's *Capital Federal/Ciudad de Buenos Aires* is in a foldout format, with a separate index for streets and bus routes. These and many other similar maps are available at newspaper kiosks and bookstores.

The **Automóvil Club Argentino** (ACA; Map pp232-3; ☎ 4802-6061; www.aca.org.ar in Spanish; Av del Libertador 1850) publishes the *Carta Vial de Buenos Aires y Alrededores*, which is useful beyond the city center. The ACA also has fairly good provincial road maps, which are great for motorists planning to journey around Argentina. There are many ACA branches throughout BA and Argentina. Bring your auto-club card from home for map discounts.

## MEDICAL SERVICES

The capital's medical facilities include **Hospital Municipal Juan Fernández** (Map pp232-3; ☎ 4808-2600; Cerviño 3356), and **Hospital Alemán** (Map pp230-1; ☎ 4821-1700; Av Pueyrredón 1640). There's also the **Hospital Británico** (Map p225; ☎ 4304-1081; Perdriel 74) way over in Constitución, but it has a more central branch in **Retiro** (Map pp228-9; ☎ 4812-0040; MT de Alvear 1573) for consultations only; call for an appointment.

## MONEY

Argentina's unit of currency is the peso, which as of April 2005 was almost three to one against the US dollar. Paper money comes in denominations of 2, 5, 10, 20, 50 and 100 pesos. One peso equals 100 centavos; coins come in denominations of 5, 10, 25 and 50 centavos, and 1 peso. The $ sign in front of a price is usually used to signify pesos, so assume this is the case unless otherwise marked.

Don't be dismayed if you receive dirty and hopelessly tattered banknotes; they will still be accepted everywhere. Some banks refuse worn or defaced US dollars, however, so make sure you arrive in Buenos Aires with pristine bills. In a pinch, American Express will probably change your older or written-on bills, and you don't have to be a member.

*Cambios* and banks are common in the city center; banks have longer lines and more limited opening hours but may offer better rates. A good *cambio* to try is **Alhec** (Map pp228-9; ☎ 4316-5000; Paraguay 641; ☼ 10am-4:30pm Mon-Fri).

Counterfeiting, of both local and US bills, has become something of a problem in recent years, and merchants are very careful when accepting large denominations. You should be too; look for a clear watermark or running thread on the largest bills, and be especially careful when receiving change in dark taxis (see p186).

Keep a stash of change with you, both in small bills and coins; when you need those 80 centavos for the bus you'll find *kioscos* (small stores or newspaper stands) won't have enough to give out.

## ATMs

ATMs *(cajeros automáticos)* are everywhere in BA, and having a card is the handiest way to get money. ATMs dispense only Argentine pesos and can be used for cash advances on major credit cards. There's often an English translation option if you don't read Spanish. Cirrus, Plus and Link are the systems most widely used in BA. To avoid a fistful of large-denomination bills, withdraw odd amounts like 290 pesos.

## Credit Cards

Many tourist services, larger stores, hotels and restaurants take credit cards such as Visa and MasterCard, especially for big purchases. Be aware, however, that some businesses add a *recargo* (surcharge) of up to 10% toward credit-card purchases; ask beforehand. Some lower-end hotels and private businesses will not accept credit cards, and tips can't usually be added to credit-card bills at restaurants.

The following local representatives can help you replace lost or stolen cards:

**American Express** (Map pp228-9; ☎ 4312-1661; Arenales 707)

**MasterCard** (Map pp222-4; ☎ 4348-7070; Perú 151)

**Visa** (Map pp226-7; ☎ 4379-3400; basement, Av Corrientes 1437)

## International Transfers

Western Union has many branches in Buenos Aires, including the center at **Av Córdoba** (☎ 0800-800-3030; www.westernunion.com; Av Córdoba 975; ☼ 9am-8pm Mon-Fri).

## Traveler's Checks

Traveler's checks are very impractical in Argentina, but you can have some as backup if you wish; get them in US dollars. Only the fancier hotels and a few banks and *cambios* will change them, and they'll charge a hefty commission. Stores will *not* change them. American Express checks can be cashed without commission at their central office (Map pp228-9; ☎ 4312-1661; Arenales 707) from 10am to 3pm Monday to Friday, though you won't quite get the best rate. Outside BA it's almost impossible to change traveler's checks.

## PHARMACIES

Pharmacies are common in Buenos Aires. The biggest chain is **Farmacity** (www.farmacity.com), with about 60 branches throughout the city; they're modern, bright and well stocked with sundries. They have a prescription counter and are often open 24 hours. It's hard to miss their blue-and-orange color theme.

## PHOTOGRAPHY

A 36-exposure roll of 100 ASA print film will cost you around US$2.50. Slide film ranges from US$4 to US$7 for 36 exposures. Developing for both is widely available.

Many photo stores can transfer images from your digital camera's card to CD. It will cost you US$3 to transfer around 100 photos; you can also get them printed out for US$0.35 per photo. Good stores to try include **Kinefot** (Map pp226-7; ☎ 4374-7445; Talcahuano 244), with two other locations on the same block; **Le Lab** (Map pp222-4; ☎ 4322-2587; Viamonte 624); and **Casa José** (Map pp222-4; ☎ 4394-4204; Av Lavalle 544).

## POST

Correo Argentino (www.correoargentino.com .ar in Spanish), the government postal service, has gotten more reliable over the years. Its main office is **Correo Central** (Map pp222-4; ☎ 4894-9191; Av Sarmiento 151; ⏰ 8am-8pm Mon-Fri, 9am-1pm Sat), which fills an entire city block. Numerous branch post offices are scattered throughout BA.

International letters and postcards to the Americas cost US$1.50, and to Europe and Australia they're US$1.75. Essential overseas mail should be sent *certificado* (registered). For international parcels weighing over 2kg, go to the **Correo Internacional** (Map pp228-9; ☎ 4316-1777; Antártida Argentina; ⏰ 10am-5pm Mon-Fri) near the Retiro bus station. Shipping a 5kg package to North America costs about US$70, to Europe US$85 and to Australia US$105.

You can get mail via poste restante at Correo Central. It costs US$1.50 to retrieve letters, which should be addressed clearly as follows:

Donald SMITH (last name in capitals)
Lista de Correos
Correo Central
Sarmiento 189
(1003) Capital Federal
Argentina

## Private Mail Services

Privately run international and national services are available for valuable mail.

**FedEx** (Map pp222-4; ☎ 0810-333-3339; www .fedex.com) has a central branch at Av Maipú 753 in the Microcentro. Another choice is **DHL International** (Map pp228-9; ☎ 0810-222-2345; www .dhl.com.ar; Córdoba 783). **OCA** (Map pp222-4; ☎ 0810-999-7700; www.oca.com.ar in Spanish; Viamonte 526) makes domestic connections for several international couriers and has many other locations around town.

## SAFETY

Buenos Aires has been getting a bad rap these past few years. A city in hard times makes some people desperate, and you may hear of store robberies or kidnappings – but these activities are generally not aimed at foreigners. Because BA was so safe for many years porteños have gotten a bit shaken up about crime, and it's become a hot conversation topic.

In general, BA is as safe as many other big cities in the world. You can comfortably walk around at all hours of the night in many places, even as a lone woman. You might even see Grandma walking her poodle at midnight. People stay out very late, and there's almost always somebody else walking on any one street at any hour of the night. Some neighborhoods where you should be careful at night, however, are Constitución (around the train station), the eastern border of San Telmo and La Boca (where, outside tourist streets, you should be careful even during the day).

Crime against tourists is almost always of the petty sort, such as pickpockets in crowded markets or buses – things smart travelers can easily guard themselves against. Minor nuisances include lack of respect for pedestrians (do not expect cars or buses to stop or even slow down when you're crossing a street), lax pollution controls and cigarette smoke everywhere.

Remember that using your head is good advice anywhere – don't stagger around drunk, always be aware of your surroundings and always look like you know exactly where you're going, with the attitude that you could kick the ass of anyone who gives you grief. And realize that if you're reasonably careful, odds are the worst thing you experience will be getting short-changed, tripping on loose sidewalk tiles or stepping in the ubiquitous dog pile. Watch your step.

## Police

Local police are not above petty harassment, though this will affect you more if you drive a car. BA's provincial police are the country's single most notoriously corrupt force, though members of the capital's Policía Federal are no angels. So-called safety campaigns often result in motorists receiving citations for minor equipment violations (such as a malfunctioning turn signal) that carry high fines. In most cases, corrupt officers will settle for less expensive *coimas* (bribes), but this requires considerable caution and tact. A discreet hint that you intend to phone your consulate may minimize or eliminate such problems – often the police count on foreigners' ignorance of Argentine law. Another tactic, whether you know Spanish or not, is to pretend you don't understand what an officer is saying.

## TAX & REFUNDS

One of Argentina's primary state revenue-earners is the 21% value-added tax known as the Impuesto de Valor Agregado (IVA). Under limited circumstances, foreign visitors may obtain IVA refunds on purchases of Argentine products upon departing the country. A 'Tax Free' window decal (in English) identifies participants in this program, but always check that the shop is part of the tax-free program before making your purchase.

You can obtain tax refunds on purchases of US$70 or more made at one of these participating stores. To do so, present your passport to the merchant, who will make out an invoice for you. On leaving the country, keep the purchased items separate from the rest of your baggage; a customs official will check them.

With the invoice, you can obtain refunds at Ezeiza, Aeroparque Jorge Newbery, and the Buquebus terminal at Dársena Norte.

## TELEPHONE & FAX

Two companies, Telecom and Telefónica, split the city's telephone services. Competition has sprouted up, however, and cheap international services are now available. Also, inexpensive phone cards can be bought at *kioscos* for as little as US$3.50, allowing you 100 credits' worth of international calls (about 45 minutes to the USA). Making international calls over the Internet using the system net2phone or skype is another cheap option; look for Internet cafés with mics and high-speed connections.

Landlines in BA have eight-digit telephone numbers. When calling a cell phone you'll need to dial 15 before the eight-digit number. If you're calling a BA number from somewhere else in Argentina, you'll need to dial 011 first. When calling BA from *outside* Argentina, first dial your country's international access code, then 54 11 and the eight-digit number. When calling cell phones from outside Argentina, dial your country's international access code, then 54 9 11 and then the eight-digit number, leaving out the 15. Toll-free numbers in BA have a 0800 before a seven-digit number.

The easiest way to make a local or international phone call is to find a *locutorio,* a small telephone office (sometimes marked *telecentro*) with private booths from which you make your calls and then pay at the register. There's a *locutorio* on practically every other block, they cost about the same as street phones, are much quieter, and you won't run out of coins. Street phones require coins or *tarjetas telefónicas* (magnetic phone cards available at many kiosks). You'll only be able to speak for a limited time before you get cut off, so carry enough credit. When making international calls from *locutorios* ask about off-peak discount hours, which generally start at 10pm and on weekends.

It's now possible to use a tri-band GSM world cell phone in BA. Other systems in use are CDMA and TDMA. This is a fast-changing field so check the current situation before you travel; a useful website is www.kropla.com /electric. In BA you can buy cell phones that use SIM chips for about US$65. Cell-phone rentals are available for around US$12 per week, including 50 minutes of local calls; some five-star hotels offer free cell-phone use.

Faxes are cheap and widely available at most *locutorios* and Internet cafés. For emergency telephone numbers see Quick Reference on the inside front cover.

## TIME

Argentina is three hours behind GMT but does not observe daylight saving time. When it's noon in Buenos Aires it's 11am in New York, 8am in San Francisco, 3pm in London and 10pm the next day in Sydney. If your country observes daylight saving time, however, these hours will be different.

Many porteños use the 24-hour clock to differentiate between am and pm.

## TIPPING

In restaurants, it is customary to tip about 10% of the bill, but many Argentines just leave some leftover change. Waiters are generally ill-paid, so if you can afford to eat out, you can afford to tip. Even a small *propina* (tip) will be appreciated, but note that restaurant tips can't be added to a credit-card bill.

Taxi drivers don't expect tips, but it's usual to round up to the nearest peso if the difference isn't much.

## TOILETS

Public toilets in BA are generally decent and often stocked with toilet paper, but soap and towels are rarer. If you're looking for a bathroom while walking around, note that the largest shopping malls (such as Galerías Pacífico) always have public bathrooms available, but in a pinch you can always walk into a McDonald's or large café.

Americans may find bidets a novelty; they are those strange shallow ceramic bowls with knobs and a drain, often accompanying toilets in hotel bathrooms. They are meant for between-shower cleanings of nether regions. Turn knobs slowly, or you may end up spraying yourself or the ceiling.

## TOURIST INFORMATION

The **Secretaría de Turismo de la Nación** (Map pp228-9; ☎ 4312-2232; www.turismo.gov.ar; Av Santa Fe 883; ☿ 9am-5pm weekdays) dispenses information on Buenos Aires and all of Argentina.

The **Comisaría del Turista** (tourist police; ☎ 4346-5748; 0800-999-5000; turista@policiafederal.gov.ar; Av Corrientes 436; ☿ 24hr) can provide interpreters and helps victims of robberies and rip-offs.

There are tourist kiosks situated at **Ezeiza airport** ( ☎ 4480-0224) and **Aeroparque airport** ( ☎ 4773-9805). Both these kiosks are open 8am to 8pm. You can obtain flight information for both airports by calling ☎ 5480-6111.

There are many other tourist kiosks in Buenos Aires. Note that hours may vary throughout the year.

**Microcentro** (Map pp222-4; Av Florida & Diagonal Roque Sáenz Peña; ☿ 9am-6pm Mon-Sat)

**Puerto Madero** (Map pp222-4; Puerto Madero at Dique 4; ☎ 4313-0187; ☿ 11am-6pm Mon-Fri, 11am-7pm Sat)

**Recoleta** (Map pp230-1; ☿ 10:30am-6:30pm Mon-Fri, 10am-7pm Sat-Sun; Av Quintana 596)

**Retiro** (Map pp228-9; Av Florida & MT de Alvear; ☿ 10am-7pm)

**Retiro bus station** (Map pp228-9; ☎ 4311-0528; ☿ 7:30am-1pm Mon-Sat; on 2nd fl on other side of station from bus slot No 34, at suite 83)

**San Telmo** (Map p225; Defensa 1250; ☿ 11am-5pm Mon-Fri, 11am-7pm Sat & Sun)

## TRAVEL AGENCIES

English-speaking staff can assist you at all of the following places:

**Argentinago** (Map pp226-7; ☎ 4372-7268; in USA 786-245-0513; www.argentinago.com; Room 201, 2nd fl, Tucumán 1427) Run by an American; caters to foreign travelers with professional service and offers free services like Internet, fax and even phone calls to North America. Also gives advice on buying property in Buenos Aires.

**Pride Travel** (Map pp228-9; ☎ 5218-6556; www.pride-travel.com; Paraguay 523 2E) Heavily geared toward a gay clientele, but doesn't discriminate against hets. Helps arrange short- or long-term stays in BA, along with city tours and trips around Argentina. Also hands out info on gay BA.

**Say Hueque** (Map pp222-4; ☎ 5199-2517; www.sayhueque.com; 6th fl, Viamonte 749) This friendly, backpacker-oriented agency will not only make the usual air, bus and hotel reservations but also offers city tours and adventure trips around Argentina, especially Patagonia.

**Tangol** (Map pp228-9; ☎ 4312-7276; www.tangol.com; suite 59, Av Florida 971) Here's a traveler-oriented agency offering city tours and shows along with some unusual activities, including helicopter tours and skydiving.

**Tije** (Map pp222-4; ☎ 4326-5665; www.tije.com; 6th fl, San Martín 640) A large discount travel agency with several branches, oriented mostly to local and foreign students and travelers under 35.

**Wow Argentina** (Map pp228-9; ☎ 15-5603-2926; www.wowargentina.com.ar; Av Santa Fe 882 2F) This small, friendly couple-run agency caters to a wealthier clientele and also offers very personal city tours (one or two people, four hours, US$95).

## VISAS

Nationals of the USA, Canada, most Western European countries, Australia and New Zealand do not need visas to visit Argentina, but check current regulations. Most foreigners receive a 90-day visa upon arrival.

To get yourself a 90-day extension, visit the **Dirección Nacional de Migraciones** (Map pp228-9; ☎ 4317-0200; Av Antártida Argentina 1355; ✆ 8:30am to 12:30pm Mon-Fri). Set aside some time and money, as this process can take a while. Strangely enough, overstaying your visa (US$17) is cheaper than paying for an extension (US$35), but probably more stressful.

Another option if you're staying more than three months is to cross into Colonia or Montevideo (both in Uruguay) and return with a new three-month visa; this strategy is most sensible if you are from a country that does not require a visa to enter Uruguay.

## WOMEN TRAVELERS

Buenos Aires is a modern, sophisticated city, and women travelers – even those traveling alone – should not encounter many difficulties. Men do pay more overt attention to women in Latin America, however, and a little open-mindedness might be in order; Argentina's machismo culture is, after all, alive and well.

A few men feel the need to comment on a woman's attractiveness. This often happens when you're walking alone and pass by a man; it will never occur when you're with another man. Comments usually include whistles or *piropos,* which many Argentine males consider the art of complimenting a woman. *Piropos* are often vulgar, although a few can be poetic. Much as you may want to kick them where it counts, the best thing to do is completely ignore the comments. After all, many porteñas enjoy getting these 'compliments,' and most men don't necessarily mean to be insulting; they're just doing what is socially acceptable in Argentina.

On the plus side of machismo, expect men to hold a door open for you and let you enter first, including getting on buses; this gives you a better chance at grabbing an empty seat, so get in there quick.

## WORK

Buenos Aires is *very* short on jobs – many locals are unemployed or underemployed – and foreign travelers shouldn't expect to find any work other than teaching English. Working out of an institute, native English-speakers (certified or not) can earn about US$5 to US$7 per hour. You should take into account slow periods like January and February, when many locals leave town on vacation.

Check the classified section of the *Buenos Aires Herald* for leads, call up the institutes or visit expat bars and start networking.

Most teachers work illegally, heading over to Uruguay every three months for a new visa.

# Language

# Language

It's true – anyone can speak another language. Don't worry if you haven't studied languages before or that you studied a language at school for years and can't remember any of it. It doesn't even matter if you failed English grammar. After all, that's never affected your ability to speak English! And this is the key to picking up a language in another country. You just need to start speaking.

Learn a few key phrases before you go. Write them on pieces of paper and stick them on the fridge, by the bed or even on the computer – anywhere that you'll see them often.

You'll find that locals appreciate travelers trying their language, no matter how muddled you may think you sound. So don't just stand there, say something! If you want to learn more Spanish than we've included here, pick up a copy of Lonely Planet's comprehensive but user-friendly *Latin American Spanish Phrasebook*.

## SOCIAL
### Meeting People
Hi!
¡Hola!
Bye!
¡Chau!
Please.
Por favor.
Thank you (very much).
(Muchas) Gracias.
Yes.
Sí.
No.
No.
Excuse me. (to get past)
Permiso.
Sorry!
¡Perdón!
Pardon? (as in 'what did you say?')
¿Cómo?/¿Qué?
Do you speak English?
¿Hablá inglés?
Does anyone speak English?
¿Hay alguien que hable inglés?
Do you understand? (informal)
¿Me entendés?
Yes, I understand.
Sí, entiendo.
No, I don't understand.
No, no entiendo.

Could you please ...? (polite)
¿Puede ... por favor?
  speak more slowly    hablar más despacio
  repeat that    repetirlo
  write it down    escribirlo

## Going Out
What's there to do in the evenings?
¿Qué se puede hacer a las noches?

What's on ...?
¿Qué pasa ...?
  around here    para acá
  this weekend    este fin de semana
  today    hoy
  tonight    esta noche

Where are the ...?
¿Dónde hay ...?
  places to eat    lugares para comer
  clubs/pubs    boliches/pubs
  gay venues    lugares para gays

Is there a local entertainment guide?
¿Hay una guía de entretenimiento de la zona?

## PRACTICAL
### Question Words
| | |
|---|---|
| Who? (singular/plural) | ¿Quién/Quiénes? |
| Who is it? | ¿Quién es? |
| What? | ¿Qué? |
| Which? (singular/plural) | ¿Cuál/Cuáles? |
| When? | ¿Cuándo? |
| Where? | ¿Dónde? |
| How? | ¿Cómo? |
| How much is it? | ¿Cuánto cuesta? |
| Why? | ¿Por qué? |

## Lunfardo

Below are are some of the spicier *lunfardo* (slang) terms that you may hear on the streets of Buenos Aires.

**boliche** – disco or nightclub
**boludo** – jerk, asshole, idiot; often used in a friendly fashion, but a deep insult to a stranger
**bondi** – bus
**buena onda** – good vibes
**carajo** – asshole, prick, bloody hell
**chabón/chabona** – kid, guy/girl (term of endearment)
**che** – hey
**fiaca** – laziness
**guita** – money
**macanudo** – great, fabulous
**mango** – one peso
**masa** – a great, cool thing
**mina** – woman
**morfar** – eat
**pendejo** – idiot
**piba/pibe** – cool young guy/girl
**piola** – cool, clever
**pucho** – cigarette
**re** – very, as in *re interestante* (very interesting)

### Some Lunfardo Phrases

**¡Ponete las pilas!** – Get on with it! (literally 'Put the batteries in')
**Diez puntos** – OK, cool, fine (literally 'Ten points')
**Me mataste** – I don't know; I have no idea (literally 'You've killed me')
**Le faltan un par de jugadores** – He's not playing with a full deck (literally 'He's a couple of players short of a team')
**Soy Gardel con una guitarra eléctrica** – I'm so stylin' (literally 'I'm Gardel with an electric guitar')
**Che boludo** – the most porteño phrase on earth. Ask a friendly local youth to explain.

## Numbers & Amounts

| | |
|---|---|
| 0 | cero |
| 1 | uno |
| 2 | dos |
| 3 | tres |
| 4 | cuatro |
| 5 | cinco |
| 6 | seis |
| 7 | siete |
| 8 | ocho |
| 9 | nueve |
| 10 | diez |
| 11 | once |
| 12 | doce |
| 13 | trece |
| 14 | catorce |
| 15 | quince |
| 16 | dieciséis |
| 17 | diecisiete |
| 18 | dieciocho |
| 19 | diecinueve |
| 20 | veinte |
| 21 | veintiuno |
| 22 | veintidós |
| 30 | treinta |
| 31 | treinta y uno |
| 32 | treinta y dos |
| 40 | cuarenta |
| 50 | cincuenta |
| 60 | sesenta |
| 70 | setenta |
| 80 | ochenta |
| 90 | noventa |
| 100 | cien |
| 1000 | mil |
| 2000 | dos mil |

## Days

| | |
|---|---|
| Monday | lunes |
| Tuesday | martes |
| Wednesday | miércoles |
| Thursday | jueves |
| Friday | viernes |
| Saturday | sábado |
| Sunday | domingo |

## Banking

Where's the nearest ATM?
¿Dónde está el cajero automático más cercano?
Where's the nearest foreign exchange office?
¿Dónde está la oficina de cambio más cercana?

| I'd like to change ... | Quisiera cambiar ... |
|---|---|
| cash | dinero en efectivo |
| money | dinero |
| a traveler's check | un cheque de viajero |

| Do you accept ... ? | ¿Aceptan ... acá? |
|---|---|
| credit cards | tarjetas de crédito |
| debit cards | tarjetas de débito |
| traveler's checks | cheques de viajero |

## Post

Where's the post office?
¿Dónde está el correo?

I want to send a ...
Quiero enviar ...
| fax | un fax |
| parcel | un paquete |
| postcard | una postal |

I want to buy a/an ...
Quiero comprar un ...
| aerogramme | aerograma |
| envelope | sobre |
| stamp | estampilla |

## Phone & Cell Phones
I want to buy a phonecard.
Quiero comprar una tarjeta telefónica.

I want to make a ...
Quiero hacer una ...
| call (to ...) | llamada (a ...) |
| collect call | llamada con cobro |
| | revertido |

Where can I find a/an ...?
¿Dónde puedo encontrar ...?
I'd like a/an ...
Quiero ...
| adaptor plug | un adaptador |
| charger for my | un cargador para mi |
| cell phone | celular |
| cell phone for | un celular para |
| hire | alquilar |
| prepaid cell | un celular pagado por |
| phone | adelantado |
| SIM card for | una tarjeta SIM para |
| your network | su red |

## Internet
Where's the local Internet café?
¿Dónde hay un cibercafé por acá?

I'd like to ...
Quiero ...
| get online | usar internet |
| check my email | revisar mi correo |
| | electrónico |

## Transportation
What time does the ... leave?
¿A qué hora sale el ...?
| boat | barco |
| bus | colectivo |
| plane | avión |
| train | tren |

What time's the ... (bus)?
¿A qué hora es el ... (colectivo)?

| first | primer |
| last | último |
| next | próximo |

Is this taxi available?
¿Está disponible este taxi?
Please put the meter on.
Por favor, ponga el taxímetro
How much is it to ...?
¿Cuánto cuesta ir a ...?
Please take me (to this address).
Por favor, lléveme (a esta dirección)

## FOOD
| breakfast | desayuno |
| lunch | almuerzo |
| dinner | cena |
| snack | snack |
| to eat | comer |
| to drink | tomar |

Can you recommend a ...?
¿Puede recomendar ...?
| bar | un bar |
| café | un café |
| coffee bar | una cafetería |
| restaurant | un restaurante |

Is the service charge included in the bill?
¿El precio en el menu incluye el servicio de cubierto?

*For more detailed information on food and dining out, see pp88–112.*

## EMERGENCIES
It's an emergency!
¡Es una emergencia!

Call ...!
¡Llame a ...!
| the police | la policía |
| a doctor | un médico |
| an ambulance! | una ambulancia |

Could you help me, please?
¿Me puede ayudar, por favor?
Where's the police station?
¿Dónde está la comisaría?

## HEALTH
Where's the nearest ...?
¿Dónde está ... más cercano?
| dentist | el dentista |

Language

| doctor | el médico |
| hospital | el hospital |

Where's the nearest (night) chemist?
¿Dónde está la farmacia (de turno) más cercana?
I need a doctor (who speaks English).
Necesito un médico (que hable inglés).

## Symptoms
I have (a/an) ...
Tengo …

| diarrhoea | diarrea |
| fever | fiebre |
| headache | dolor de cabeza |
| pain (here) | dolor (acá) |

I'm allergic to ...
Soy alérgica a ... (for a woman)
Soy alérgico a ... (for a man)

| antibiotics | los antibióticos |
| bees | las abejas |
| nuts | las frutas secas |
| peanuts | los maníes |
| penicillin | la penicilina |

## Glossary

**alfajor** – two flat, soft cookies filled with *dulce de leche* and covered in chocolate or meringue
**arbolito** – literally 'little tree'; a street moneychanger
**argentinidad** – rather nebulous concept of Argentine national identity, often associated with extreme nationalistic feelings
**asado** – famous Argentine barbecue, often a family outing in summer
**autopista** – freeway or motorway

**bandoneón** – accordion-like instrument used in tango music
**bárbaro** – local word meaning 'wonderful' or 'great'
**barras bravas** – violent soccer fans; the Argentine equivalent of Britain's football hooligans
**barrio** – neighborhood or borough of the city
**bombilla** – silvery straw with built-in filter, used for drinking *mate*
**boquenses** – inhabitants of La Boca
**bronca** – anger, frustration

**cabezazo** – invitation to dance tango which involves a quick tilt of the head, eye contact and uplifted eyebrows
**cabildo** – colonial town council
**café cortado** – espresso with steamed milk added (macchiato)
**cajero automático** – automatic teller machine (ATM)
**cambio** – see *casa de cambio*
**candombe** – Afro-Uruguayan, percussion-based musical form that enjoys some popularity in Buenos Aires, especially at Carnaval
**canilla libre** – all-you-can-drink
**característica** – telephone area code
**cartelera** – discount ticket agency offering great bargains on tickets to cinemas, tango shows and other performances
**cartoneros** – people who pick through garbage looking for recyclables
**casa de cambio** – foreign-exchange house, often simply called a *cambio*

**castellano** – Spanish (the language)
**caudillo** – 'strongman'; the term was applied to Argentina's iron-fisted rulers of the 19th century
**cebador** – designated *mate* server
**chacarera** – traditional Argentine style of folk music, typically performed on the *bombo* (a small Andean drum) and guitar
**chamamé** – musical form originating in Corrientes province, derived from a blend of Eastern European, indigenous and African styles
**chimichurri** – spicy marinade for meat, usually made of parsley, garlic, spices and olive oil
**chopp** – glass of draft beer
**choripán** – spicy sausage sandwich
**coima** – bribe
**colectivo** – local bus
**confitería** – shop that serves mostly sandwiches and hamburgers
**conventillo** – a tenement that housed immigrants in older neighborhoods of Buenos Aires and Montevideo
**costanera** – seaside, riverside or lakeside road
**cubierto** – in restaurants, the US$1 to US$2 cover charge you pay for utensil use and bread
**criollo** – in the colonial period, an American-born Spaniard; the term now commonly describes any Argentine of European descent; also describes the feral cattle of the Pampas

**desaparecido** – 'disappeared one'; a victim of the 1976–83 Argentine dictatorship
**despelote** – mess, fiasco; often used when describing the current government (see *porquería*)
**dique** – water dike
**dulce de leche** – Argentina's national sweet, found in many desserts and snacks; type of thick, liquid caramel, milky and creamy

**empanada** – meat or vegetable pie; popular Argentine snack
**estancia** – historically speaking, an extensive grazing estate, either for cattle or sheep, under a dominating *estanciero* or manager with a dependent resident labor

force of gauchos; now often destinations for tourists for recreational activities such as riding, tennis and swimming, either for weekend escapes or extended stays

**facturas** – pastries; also a receipt
**feria** – street fair or street market

**gauchesco/a** – relating to the romantic image of the gaucho
**genial** – wonderful, great, fine

**heladería** – ice-cream shop

**ida** – one-way
**ida y vuelta** – round trip
**iglesia** – church
**interno** – telephone extension; often abbreviated 'int'
**IVA** – *impuesto de valor agregado,* or value-added tax; often added to restaurant or hotel bills in Argentina

**kiosco** – small store or newspaper stand

**locro** – corn and meat stew
**locutorio** – private long-distance telephone office that usually offers fax and Internet services as well
**lunfardo** – street slang of Buenos Aires, with origins in immigrant neighborhoods at the turn of the century

**mango** – slang for peso (like the US 'buck' for dollar)
**mate** – shortened form of *yerba mate,* Argentina's popular tea; also refers to the gourd used for drinking *mate*
**milonga** – tango hall; also refers to the dances held at these halls
**milonguero/a** – regular at *milongas*
**minuta** – in a restaurant or *confitería,* a short order such as spaghetti or schniztel
**murga** – Spanish for 'racket' or 'din'; also a *rioplatense* performance style of African and Spanish origins. *La murga porteña* is another term for Buenos Aires' Carnaval festivities.

**nafta** – gasoline or petrol

**paisanos** – country folk
**Pampas** – grassy plains that stretch east of the Andes
**parada** – bus stop
**parrillada, parrilla** – respectively, a mixed grill of steak and other beef cuts and a restaurant specializing in such dishes
**paseaperros** – professional dog walker in Buenos Aires

**pato** – a traditional ball game played on horseback
**peatonal** – pedestrian mall, usually in the downtown area
**peña** – club that hosts informal folk music gatherings
**piqueteros** – picketers (political protestors carrying signs), who often stop traffic while marching in a public place (such as Plaza de Mayo)
**piropo** – sexist remark, ranging in tone from complimentary and relatively innocuous to rude and offensive
**porteño** – inhabitant of Buenos Aires
**porquería** – fiasco, trash, mess; often used when describing the government (see *despelote*)
**propina** – tip (gratuity)
**puchero** – soup combining vegetables and meats, served with rice
**puerto** – port

**recargo** – an additional charge (such as for use of a credit card)
**remise** – a call taxi; they look like regular cars and collect a fixed fare
**rioplatense** – describes anything native to the Río de la Plata region
**ruta** – highway, route

**sainete** – informal dramas focusing on immigrants and their dilemmas
**sandwichitos de miga** – thin crustless sandwiches, traditionally eaten at tea time
**spiedo** – spit; an alternative to the *parrilla*
**Subte** – the Buenos Aires underground railway

**tanguista** – tango dancer
**tarjeta telefónica** – magnetic telephone card
**tenedor libre** – literally 'free fork,' an 'all-you-can-eat' restaurant; less commonly known as *diente libre* ('free tooth')
**trucho** – bogus; widely used by Argentines to describe things that are not what they appear to be

**villa miseria** – shantytown
**viveza criolla** – sly foxiness, a valued quality for some Argentines

**yerba mate** – 'Paraguayan tea' (*Ilex paraguariensis*), which Argentines consume in very large amounts; see also *mate*

# Behind the Scenes

## THE LONELY PLANET STORY

The story begins with a classic travel adventure: Tony and Maureen Wheeler's 1972 journey across Europe and Asia to Australia. There was no useful information about the overland trail then, so Tony and Maureen published the first Lonely Planet guidebook to meet a growing need.

From a kitchen table, Lonely Planet has grown to become the largest independent travel publisher in the world, with offices in Melbourne (Australia), Oakland (USA) and London (UK). Today Lonely Planet guidebooks cover the globe. There is an ever-growing list of books and information in a variety of media. Some things haven't changed. The main aim is still to make it possible for adventurous travelers to get out there — to explore and better understand the world.

At Lonely Planet we believe travelers can make a positive contribution to the countries they visit — if they respect their host communities and spend their money wisely. Every year 5% of company profit is donated to charities around the world.

## THIS BOOK

The 1st and 2nd editions of *Buenos Aires* were written by Wayne Bernhardson. Sandra Bao and Ben Greensfelder wrote the 3rd edition. This 4th edition of *Buenos Aires* was written by Sandra Bao. Ashley Baldwin wrote the 'Fashion' boxed text in the City Life chapter and the 'Disabled Travelers' boxed text in the Directory chapter. Dereck Foster contributed the 'Food' boxed text in the City Life chapter, plus the 'Where's the Beef?', 'Argentine Wine' and 'Chef Thierry Pszonda' boxed texts in the Eating chapter. Josh Hinden wrote the 'Electronica in Buenos Aires' box in the Arts chapter. Thomas Kohnstamm wrote the History chapter. This book was developed and assessed in the Americas office by Jay Cooke, Suki Gear and Alex Hershey. The guide was commissioned in Lonely Planet's Oakland office, and produced by:

**Commissioning Editors** Suki Gear, Jay Cooke and Alex Hershey
**Coordinating Editor** Piers Kelly
**Coordinating Cartographer** Herman So
**Coordinating Layout Designer** Pablo Gastar
**Managing Cartographer** Alison Lyall
**Assisting Editors & Proofreaders** Susie Ashworth, Gabrielle Wilson, Adrienne Costanzo
**Assisting Layout Designer** Michael Ruff
**Cover Designer** Brendan Dempsey
**Project Manager** Glenn van der Knijff
**Language Content Coordinator** Quentin Frayne

**Thanks to** Glenn Beanland, Sally Darmody, Bruce Evans, Ryan Evans, Martin Heng, Kate McDonald and Adriana Mammarella

**Cover photographs** Tango dancers, Dennis Degnan, APL/Corbis (top); La Boca, Joanne McCarthy/Photolibrary (bottom);

Plaque to Evita Perón at the Duarte Family tomb, Recoleta cemetery, Krzysztof Dydynski/Lonely Planet Images (back).
**Internal photographs** by Lonely Planet Images and Krzysztof Dydynski except for the following: p172, p179 Tom Cockrem; p106 (#1) Wade Eakle; p106 (#4) Donald C. & Priscilla Alexander Eastman; p106 (#2, #3) Wayne Walton. All images are the copyright of the photographers unless otherwise indicated. Many of the images in this guide are available for licensing from Lonely Planet Images: www.lonelyplanetimages.com.

## ACKNOWLEDGMENTS

Many thanks to the following for the use of their content: Buenos Aires Subte Map © Metrovías 2004

## THANKS
### SANDRA BAO

Many people helped me on this 4th edition of the *Buenos Aires*, and I thank everyone profusely. My porteño godparents, Elsa and Norberto Mallarini, were always there for me and ready to stuff me with absolutely delicious homemade cooking; Andrew McGregor was a fab roommate and endlessly entertaining — see you at the movies, Wayward Son! Thea Morton was a great help and an even better dinner companion; Jorge Barchi knows more about the working details of BA than anyone I can think of; Roberto Frassinetti and Florencia Rodríguez are super people and outstanding tour guides; Josh Hinden is just a very cool dude; Lucas Markowiecki is in a class by himself. Many thanks also to Sylvia Zapiola, Rachel Loftspring, Carlos Kaplan, Eduardo Tagliani, Marcelo Solís and Romina Hahn for their help and opinions, and to the countless other porteños and expats I met who helped me out in their own way. Thanks to Suki

Gear, for doing all the work back in Oakland. Special gratitude to my supportive parents, David and Fung, and to my brother, Daniel. And especially to my loving husband, Ben Greensfelder, without whose help I could not have finished this book.

# OUR READERS

Many thanks to the travellers who used the last edition and wrote to us with helpful hints, useful advice and interesting anecdotes. Your names follow:

Beatriz Abad, Volkan Akkurt, Martin Allan, Kim Allin, Ralph Alquero, Karl Aragundi, Karl Backhaus, Nick Baulch, Peter Block, William Bradley, Marie Bredstrup, Jenny Brierley, Amanda Bronesky, Richard Brooks, Quentin & Nicky Buckingham, Agi & Shanf Burra, Louise & Kevin Carling, Jenny Chantry, Brandy Chapman, Kay Chitale, Kirsten Claiden-Yardley, Neil Cole, Simona Colombo, Louis Crowe, Patricio Cummins, Erin Daldry, Phil & Ginny Davies, Juan Carlos Dima, Jacqueline Dowling, Roland Ehrat, Patrick Ekerot, Sze Fairman, Nina Fantl, Michael Feder, Andreas Fertin, Christina Fetterhoff, Charlotte Firth, Jennifer Florek, Dominique Friend, Anna Fularz, Cristian Miglioli Gamarra, Fabian Garbolino, Megan Green, Marina Gregor, Wendy Gruber, Oona J Grünebaum, Robert Hall, Imke & Markus Hartig-Jansen, Daryl Hartnett, Eitan Hess, Naida Hindert, Todd Holland, Richard Howitt, Bastiaan Jaarsma, Stephanie Jerosch, Lamar Kerley, Paul K Kim, Justine Kirby, Jo-ann Kolmes, Lars Kuipers, Jerry Lang, Andrea Lee, Howard Lee, Markus Linhart, Alfred Little, Leif Lupp, Ron Machado, Thiago Magalhaes, Linda Massola, Mike McKay, Adam McKissack, Brett Meier-Tomkins, Mariano Mezzatesta, Monica Middleton, Warren Mills, Jesper E Mogensen, Fernando Moser, Kiran Nandra, Clare O'Brien, Carsten Ottesen, Nick Parker, Heather Piepkorn, Julie Pike, Susan Plant, Cameron Plewes, Janice Plewes, Daniel Pokora, Claudia Ponikowski, Annabel Pritchard, Vanessa Quarrie, Ellen Ramseier, Wilhelm Richard, Scott Roberts, Karin Robnik, Tim Rose, Andrew Ruben, Debra Ruben, Dan Ruff, Lawrence Ryz, Al Sandine, Elizabeth Sawyer, Beate Schmahl, Jane Scotti, Meike Seele, Gavin Sexton, Helen & Wolfe Sharp, K Shaw, Robert Shaw, Jennifer Anne Shorr, Vahid Sigari-Majd, Carolina Simon, Anthony Simpson, Diego Singer, Veronika Skvarova, John Stahle, Lisa Starr, Jerri Stephenson, Patrick Stobbs, Louie Strano, David Strother, Ariola Tamay, Daniel Tapia, Jocelyn Taub, Denise Tibbey, Aranea Tigelaar, Natalie Tornatore, Jennifer Uscher, Natalie van Eckendonk, Hiske van Haren, Annelot van Riet, Phillip Wainhouse, Bevan Wait, Herb Watson, Natasha Wolmarans, Darren Wosol, Martin Wunderlich, Georg Schulze Zumkley

**Notes**

# Notes

# Notes

# Notes

# Index

See also separate subindexes for Drinking (p216), Eating (p217), Shopping (p217) and Sleeping (p217).

**000** map pages
**000** photographs

**000** map pages
**000** photographs

## MAP LEGEND
### ROUTES

| | |
|---|---|
| Tollway | One-Way Street |
| Freeway | Mall/Steps |
| Primary Road | Tunnel |
| Secondary Road | Walking Tour |
| Tertiary Road | Walking Tour Detour |
| Lane | Walking Trail |
| Under Construction | Walking Path |
| Track | Pedestrian Overpass |
| Unsealed Road | |

### TRANSPORT

| | |
|---|---|
| Ferry | Bus Route |
| Metro | Rail |
| Monorail | Tram |

### HYDROGRAPHY

| | |
|---|---|
| River, Creek | Canal |
| Intermittent River | Water |

### BOUNDARIES

| | |
|---|---|
| International | Regional, Suburb |
| State, Provincial | Ancient Wall |

### AREA FEATURES

| | |
|---|---|
| Airport | Cemetery, Christian |
| Area of Interest | Forest |
| Beach, Desert | Land |
| Building, Featured | Mall |
| Building, Information | Park |
| Building, Other | Sports |
| Building, Transport | |

### POPULATION

| | |
|---|---|
| ✪ CAPITAL (NATIONAL) | ◉ CAPITAL (STATE) |
| ● Large City | ● Medium City |
| ● Small City | ● Town, Village |

### SYMBOLS

**Sights/Activities**
- Christian
- Jewish
- Monument
- Museum, Gallery
- Other Site
- Swimming Pool
- Zoo, Bird Sanctuary

**Eating**
- Eating

**Drinking**
- Drinking
- Café

**Entertainment**
- Entertainment

**Shopping**
- Shopping

**Sleeping**
- Sleeping

**Transport**
- Airport, Airfield
- Bus Station
- General Transport
- Parking Area

**Information**
- Bank, ATM
- Embassy/Consulate
- Hospital, Medical
- Information
- Post Office, GPO

**Geographic**
- National Park

# Map Section

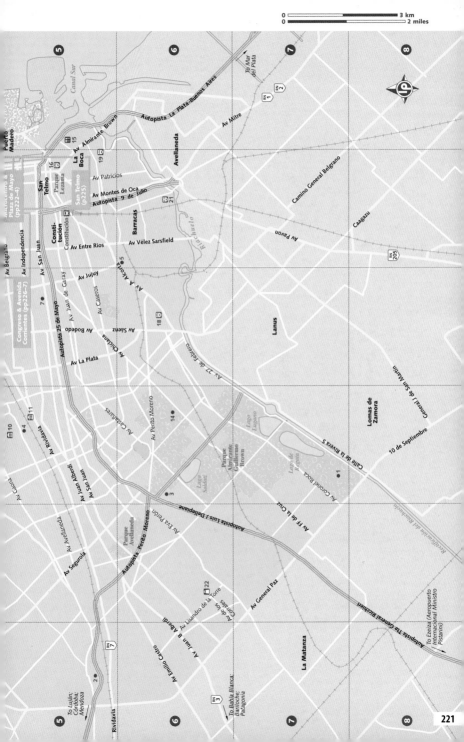

**221**

**223**

# SAN TELMO

0 _____ 400 m
0 _____ 0.2 miles

**A** **B** **C** **D**

To Reserva Ecológica
Costanera Sur
(1km)

**Puerto
Madero**

**San
Telmo**

**Plaza
Dorrego**

To Garden House (500m);
To Niño Bien (700m)

**La Boca**

**Parque
Lezama**

To Hospital
Británico
(1.4km)

**Barracas**

225

# CONGRESO & AVENIDA CORRIENTES

Balvanera

**SUBTE**
Línea A
Línea B
Línea C
Línea D
Línea E

**400 m**
**0.2 miles**

See Microcentro & Plaza de Mayo (pp222–3)

Montserrat

Constitución

Av Independencia

Departamento Central de la Policía Federal Argentina

Monumento a los Dos Congresos

Plaza del Congreso

Palacio del Congreso

Plaza 1 de Mayo

Av de Mayo

Av Entre Ríos

Av Belgrano

Av Rivadavia

Hipólito Yrigoyen

Adolfo Alsina

Moreno

Venezuela

México

Chile

Estados Unidos

Independencia

Lima

Salta

Santiago del Estero

Luis Sáenz Peña

Virrey Cevallos

Solís

Combate de los Pozos

Sarandí

Rincón

Pasco

Pichincha

Bernardo de Irigoyen

Hipólito Yrigoyen

Lima

Edificio MOP

**SUBTE**
- Ⓜ Línea A
- Ⓜ Línea B
- Ⓜ Línea C
- Ⓜ Línea D
- Ⓜ Línea E

Plaza Naciones Unidas

Ⓐ Ⓑ Ⓒ Ⓓ

**❶** Facultad de Derecho

Quiroga

El Couture

JV González

Footbridge

Romero

Dr C Vaz Ferreira

Parque Thays

Autopista Arturo Illia

Calle 10

Calle 5

Padre Mugica

Plaza Intendente Alvear

E Schiáffino

Ayacucho

**❷**

RM Ortiz

Posadas

Quiroga

Av Alvear

Patio Bullrich
54

Vicente López

Guido

Recoleta

Av Quintana

47

59

Av del Libertador

**❸**

Libertad

Cerrito

77

61

Av Callao

Rodríguez Peña

44

98

9

Plaza Pellegrini

Arroyo

70

69

Montevideo

Parera

Juncal

Carlos Pellegrini

Supacha

Esmeralda

Basavilbaso

89

**❹**

24

Plaza Vicente López y Planes

Retiro

68

11

Arenales

18

76

88

46

**Barrio Norte**

62

55

43

75

101
73 74

San Martín

Av Santa Fe

17

45

Talcahuano

Libertad

Cerrito

Av 9 de Julio

80

105 94

84

83
32

Av Santa Fe

**❺**

31

49

MT de Alvear

Uruguay

Paraná

97

37
85

33

25

5

99

82

96

34

14

60

78

79

7

40

58

39

Plaza de Peña

Palacio Pizurno

Plaza Libertad

35

Montevideo

Paraguay

64

90

92

See Congreso & Avenida Corrientes Map (pp226–7)

38

19

**❻**

20
21

3

Av Córdoba

10

104

Plaza Lavalle

See Recoleta & Barrio Norte Map (pp230–1)

0 ▬▬▬▬▬▬▬▬▬ 400 m
0 ▬▬▬▬▬▬▬▬▬ 0.2 miles

| SIGHTS & ACTIVITIES | (pp63–5) | |
|---|---|---|
| Basílica de Santísimo Sacramento. | 1 | E5 |
| Bike Tours | 2 | E6 |
| Centro Cultural Konex | 3 | B6 |
| Centro Naval | 4 | E6 |
| Círculo Militar (or Palacio Paz) | 5 | D5 |
| Edificio Kavanaugh | 6 | E5 |
| Jorge Luis Borges' Last Residence | 7 | D5 |
| Monumento a los Caidos de Malvinas | 8 | E4 |
| Museo de Armas | (see 5) | |
| Museo de la Inmigración | (see 93) | |
| Museo Municipal de Arte Hispanoamericano Isaac Fernández Blanco | 9 | D4 |
| Museo Nacional del Teatro | 10 | C6 |
| Palacio San Martín | 11 | D4 |
| Para Bien Pilates | 12 | E5 |
| Torre de los Ingleses | 13 | E4 |

| EATING | (pp95–6) | |
|---|---|---|
| El Cuartito | 14 | B6 |
| Empire Bar | 15 | E6 |
| Filo | 16 | E5 |
| Freddo | 17 | A5 |
| Gran Bar Danzón | 18 | C5 |
| La Chacra | 19 | C6 |
| La Esquina de las Flores | 20 | A6 |
| Le Sud | (see 69) | |
| Lotos | 21 | A6 |
| Mumbai | 22 | E6 |
| Munchi's | 23 | E5 |
| Nucha | 24 | A4 |
| Yatasto | 25 | D5 |

| DRINKING | (pp115–20) | |
|---|---|---|
| Dadá | 26 | E5 |
| Druid In | 27 | E5 |
| El Verde | 28 | E6 |
| Florida Garden | 29 | E5 |
| Kilkenny | 30 | E5 |
| Milión Bar | 31 | A5 |
| Petit Paris Café | 32 | D5 |
| Temple Bar | 33 | C5 |

| ENTERTAINMENT | (pp122–34) | |
|---|---|---|
| El Living | 34 | A5 |
| ND/Ateneo | 35 | D6 |
| Opera Bay | 36 | G6 |
| Teatro Coliseo | 37 | E5 |
| Teatro Nacional Cervantes | 38 | C6 |
| UNNA | 39 | C5 |

| SHOPPING | (pp145–7) | |
|---|---|---|
| Camping Center | 40 | D5 |
| Casa Lopez | 41 | E5 |
| El Cid | 42 | E5 |
| El Fenix | 43 | C5 |
| Gabriella Capucci | 44 | C3 |
| Galería 5ta Avenida | 45 | B5 |
| Galería Aguilar | 46 | D5 |
| Galería Federico Klemm | (see 41) | |
| Galería Rubbers | 47 | B3 |
| Galería Ruth Benzacar | 48 | E5 |
| Joyeri Contemporáneo | (see 102) | |
| KEL | 49 | B5 |
| Kelly's Regionales | 50 | E5 |
| La Martina | 51 | E5 |
| Librería ABC | 52 | E6 |
| Lionel Frenkel | 53 | E5 |
| Maria Vazquez | 54 | C3 |
| Rossi y Carusso | 55 | B5 |

| Welcome Marroquinería | 56 | E5 |
|---|---|---|
| Winery | 57 | F6 |

| SLEEPING | (pp162–3) | |
|---|---|---|
| Aspen Suites | 58 | D5 |
| Caesar Park Hotel | 59 | C3 |
| Dazzler Hotel | 60 | C6 |
| Four Seasons Buenos Aires | 61 | C3 |
| Hotel Bel Air | 62 | B5 |
| Hotel Central Córdoba | 63 | E5 |
| Hotel Presidente | 64 | C6 |
| Hotel Principado | 65 | E5 |
| Howard Johnson Plaza | 66 | E5 |
| NH Florida | 67 | E6 |
| Recoleta Youth Hostel | 68 | B4 |
| Sofitel Buenos Aires | 69 | D4 |
| Suipacha y Arroyo Suites | 70 | D4 |

| TRANSPORT | (pp184–6) | |
|---|---|---|
| Aerolíneas Argentinas | 71 | E5 |
| Air France | 72 | E6 |
| Alitalia | 73 | D5 |
| American Airlines | 74 | D5 |
| American Falcon | 75 | C5 |
| Austral Líneas Aéreas | (see 71) | |
| Avianca | 76 | E5 |
| Avis | 77 | C3 |
| British Airways | (see 76) | |
| Hertz | 78 | C6 |
| LanChile | 79 | C6 |
| Líneas Aéreas Privadas Argentinas (LAPA) | 80 | C5 |
| Manuel Tienda León (MTL) | 81 | F4 |
| New Way Car Rental | 82 | D5 |
| Southern Winds | 83 | D5 |
| Swissair | 84 | D5 |
| Transportes Aéreos de Mercosur (TAM) | 85 | C5 |
| United Airlines | 86 | F6 |

| INFORMATION | | |
|---|---|---|
| Alhec | 87 | E5 |
| American Express | 88 | D5 |
| Asatej | (see 95) | |
| British Arts Centre | 89 | D4 |
| Buquebus | 90 | D6 |
| Correo Internacional | 91 | F3 |
| DHL | 92 | D6 |
| Dirección Nacional de Migraciones | 93 | F4 |
| French Consulate | 94 | D5 |
| French Consulate | (see 84) | |
| Galería Buenos Aires | 95 | E6 |
| Hospital Británico | 96 | A5 |
| Italian Consulate | 97 | C5 |
| Lenguas Vivas | 98 | C4 |
| Palacio Haedo | 99 | D5 |
| Pride Travel | 100 | E5 |
| Secretaría de Turismo de la Nación | 101 | C5 |
| Swiss Embassy | (see 94) | |
| Tangol | 102 | E5 |
| Tourist Kiosk | (see 48) | |
| Vía Hispana | 103 | E6 |
| Western Union | 104 | C5 |
| Wow Argentina | 105 | D5 |

Gendarmería Nacional

Retiro Bus Station

E de Brasil

Av Ramos Mejía

Plaza Canada

Av Commodore PY

Martín Zuviría

Gilardi

Estación Retiro

Retiro

Plaza del Carril

Plaza Fuerza Aérea Argentina

Av Eduardo Madero

Av Antártida Argentina

Sheraton Buenos Aires

San Martín

Torre Bank Boston

Plaza San Martín

Paolera

Dr Rojas

Reconquista

Edificio Carlos Pellegrini

Torre IBM

San Martín

Florida

Av Leandro N Alem

MT de Alvear

Laminar Plaza

Darsena Norte

Paraguay

Torre Alem Plaza

Tres Sargentos

Torre Catalinas Plaza

25 de Mayo

Av Córdoba

Edificio Alas

Galerías Pacífico

Microcentro

Viamonte

Torre Fortabat

Edificio República

Av Alicia Moreau Justo

Puerto Madero

Olga Cossettini

Dique No 4

See Microcentro & Plaza de Mayo Map (pp222–3)

Buquebus
(Ferries & Hydrofoils to Uruguay)

# RECOLETA & BARRIO NORTE

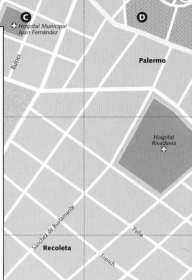

**A**    **B**    **C**    **D**

**SUBTE**

| | | | |
|---|---|---|---|
| M | Línea A | M | Línea D |
| M | Línea B | M | Línea E |
| M | Línea C | | |

Palermo

Hospital Municipal Juan Fernández

Hospital Rivadavia

Bulnes

Sánchez de Bustamante

Peña

Recoleta

French

Juncal

Beruti

Austria

Arenales

Agüero Agüero

Agüero Av Santa Fe

Güemes

Laprida

TM de Anchorena

Hospital Alemán

Charcas

Gallo

50

Hospital de Niños

Mansilla

9

Ecuador

22 Pueyrredón

Av Puerredón

Larrea

Bulnes

Paraguay

Guisé

Av Coronal Díaz

Soler

Billinghurst

Gorriti

11

Paraguay

José Antonio Cabrera

28

37

Plaza Monseñor de Andrea

Av Córdoba

Almagro

Balvanera

0 — 400 m
0 — 0.2 miles

**E**
Plaza
República
de Chile

Táble

José Prasino

**F** Floralis
Generica

Plaza Naciones
Unidas

Av Presidente Figueroa Alcorta

Bibiloni

**G**

**H** ●**1**

Plaza República
Oriental
del Uruguay

Facultad de
Derecho

El Couture

4

Quiroga

Padre Mugica

Plaza JJ
de Urquiza

Av del Libertador

Plaza
R Darío

Av González

Footbridge

Romero

Dr Val Ferreira

Parque
Thays

●**2**

Guido

Plaza
Mitre

Levene

Plaza
Francia

F Schiaffino

10 ●

**2**

Galileo

Celly y Obes

Luis Agote

F de Vittoria

●**54**

Copérnicus

Juan M Gutiérrez

Av Pueyrredón

🅿**23**

**32**

Plaza
Intendente
Alvear

Posadas

52

13

Pacheco de Melo

Plaza
E Mitre

Facultad
de Ingeniería

Cementerio
de La Recoleta

3 ●

5

24
RM Ortiz

19

17

18

51

38

56

14

43

Av Alvear

41

Av Quintana

Plaza
República
del Paraguay

Uriburu

Junín

Village
Recoleta

Guido

33

36

**3**

48

Av General Las Heras

16

Ayacucho

Vicente López

55

Av Callao

Pacheco de Melo

Peña

46

Barrio
Norte

Rodríguez Peña

Montevideo

Parera

Juncal

**4**

49

45

French

44

Plaza Vicente
López y Planes

Azcuénaga

21

26

35

Arenales

●**1**

15

25

53

12

42

Av Santa Fe

Paraná

Uruguay

Talcahuano

**5**

30

José Uriburu

Junín

Ayacucho

Riobamba

34

40

Av Callao

39

27

6 ●

31

Montevideo

MT de Alvear

47

29

Plaza de
Peña

Rodríguez Peña

Pizzurno

Palacio
Pizurno

Retiro

Paraguay

See Congreso & Avenida Corrientes Map (pp226–7)

✚
Hospital
Clínicas José
de San Martín

Plaza de
Houssay

Escuela Naval
Presidente Roque
Saenz Peña

20

Ⓜ
Facultad
de Medicina

Callao

Ⓜ

Av Córdoba

See Retiro Map (pp228–9)

**6**

**231**

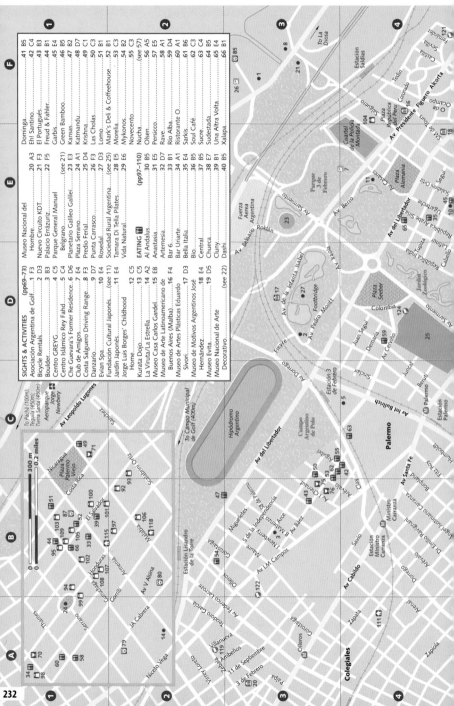

**SIGHTS & ACTIVITIES (pp69-73)**
Asociación Argentina de Golf.....1 F3
Bicycle Rentals.....2 D3
Boulder.....3 B3
Centro GREYG.....4 C5
Centro Islámico Rey Fahd.....5 C4
Che Guevara's Former Residence..6 D6
Club de Amigos.....7 E4
Costa Salguero Driving Range.....8 D7
Danzarin.....9 D7
Evian Spa.....10 E4
Fundación Cultural Japonés.....(see 11)
Jardín Japonés.....11 E4
Jorge Luis Borges' Childhood Home.....12 C5
Kurata Dojo.....13 C5
La Viruta/La Estrella.....14 A2
Museo Casa Carlos Gardel.....15 E8
Museo de Arte Latinoamericano de Buenos Aires (Malba).....16 F4
Museo de Artes Plásticas Eduardo Sívori.....17 D3
Museo de Motivos Argentinos José Hernández.....18 E4
Museo Evita.....19 D5
Museo Nacional de Arte Decorativo.....(see 22)

Museo Nacional del Hombre.....20 A3
Nuevo Circuito KDT.....21 F3
Palacio Errázuriz.....22 F5
Parque General Manuel Belgrano.....(see 21)
Planetario Galileo Galilei.....23 E3
Plaza Serrano.....24 A1
Predio Ferial.....25 D4
Punta Carrasco.....26 D7
Rosedal.....27 D3
Sociedad Rural Argentina.....(see 25)
Tamara Di Tella Pilates.....28 E5
Vida Natural.....29 E6

**EATING (pp97-110)**
Al Andalus.....30 B5
Anastasia.....31 E5
Artemesia.....32 D7
Bar 6.....33 B1
Bar Uriarte.....34 A1
Bella Italia.....35 E4
Bio.....36 B5
Central.....37 B5
Chueca.....38 E7
Cluny.....39 B1
Dashi.....40 B5

Domingo.....41 B5
Eh! Santino.....42 C4
El Portugués.....43 B3
Freud & Fahler.....44 B1
Garbis.....45 B4
Green Bamboo.....46 B5
Kansas.....47 B2
Katmandu.....48 D7
Krishna.....49 C1
Las Cholas.....50 C3
Lomo.....51 B1
Mark's Deli & Coffeehouse.....52 B1
Morelia.....53 C3
Mykonos.....54 B2
Novecento.....55 B2
Nucha.....(see 57)
Olsen.....56 A5
Persicco.....57 E5
Rave.....58 A1
Río Alba.....59 D4
Ristorante O.....60 A1
Sarkis.....61 B6
Soul Café.....62 C3
Sucre.....63 C4
Sudestada.....64 B5
Una Altra Volta.....65 E4
Xalapa.....66 B1

To Pabú (100m);
Tequila (450m);
Tierra Santa (450m);
Aeroparque
Jorge
Newbery

300 m
0.2 miles

To La
Diosa